TRADIVOX

VOLUME V

TRADIVOX

CATHOLIC CATECHISM INDEX

VOLUME V

Andrew Donlevy
Thomas Burke

Edited by
Aaron Seng

SOPHIA INSTITUTE PRESS
MANCHESTER, NEW HAMPSHIRE

Sophia Institute Press
Box 5284, Manchester, NH 03108
1-800-888-9344

www.SophiaInstitute.com

Sophia Institute Press® is a registered trademark of Sophia Institute.

ISBN 978-1-64413-358-3
LCCN 2021942586
First printing

The Manner of Execution at Tyburn.

Dedicated with love and deepest respect
to all the English Martyrs and Confessors.
Orate pro nobis.

CONTENTS

ACKNOWLEDGMENTS

THE publication of this series is due primarily to the generosity of countless volunteers and donors from several countries. Special thanks are owed to Mr. and Mrs. Phil Seng, Mr. and Mrs. Michael Over, Mr. and Mrs. Jim McElwee, Mr. and Mrs. John Brouillette, Mr. and Mrs. Thomas Scheibelhut, as well the visionary priests and faithful of St. Stanislaus Bishop and Martyr parish in South Bend, Indiana, and St. Patrick's Oratory in Green Bay, Wisconsin. May God richly reward their commitment to handing on the Catholic faith.

FOREWORD

T he Catholic faith remains always the same throughout the centuries and millennia until the coming of our Lord at the end of the time, likewise "Jesus Christ is the same yesterday, today and forever" (Heb 13:8). The Catholic faith is "the faith, which was once delivered unto the saints" (Jude 1:3). The Magisterium of the Church teaches us solemnly the same truth in the following words of the First Vatican Council: "The doctrine of the faith which God has revealed, is put forward not as some philosophical discovery capable of being perfected by human intelligence, but as a divine deposit committed to the spouse of Christ to be faithfully protected and infallibly promulgated. Hence, too, that meaning of the sacred dogmas is ever to be maintained, which has once been declared by holy mother Church, and there must never be any abandonment of this sense under the pretext or in the name of a more profound understanding. May understanding, knowledge and wisdom increase as ages and centuries roll along, and greatly and vigorously flourish, in each and all, in the individual and the whole Church: but this only in its own proper kind, that is to say, in the same doctrine, the same sense, and the same understanding (cf. Vincentius Lerinensis, *Commonitorium*, 28)."[1]

An authentically Catholic catechism has the function of learning and teaching the unchanging Catholic faith throughout all generations. The Roman Pontiffs indeed, taught: "There is nothing more effective than catechetical instruction to spread the glory of God and to secure the salvation of souls."[2] Saint Pius X said, that "the great loss of souls is due to ignorance

---

[1] Vatican I, Dogmatic Constitution *Dei Filius de fide catholica*, Ch. 4
[2] Pope Benedict XIV, Apostolic Constitution *Etsi minime*, n. 13

of divine things."[3] Therefore, the traditional catechisms have enduring value in our own day and age, which is marked by an enormous doctrinal confusion, which reigns in the life of the Church in the past six decades, and which reaches its peak in our days.

I welcome and bless the great project of the "Tradivox" in cataloguing and preserving the hundreds of long-lost Catholic catechisms issued with episcopal approval over the last millennium. This project will convincingly show the essentially unchanging nature of the apostolic doctrine across time and space, and so I invite the faithful of the entire world to support this historic effort, as we seek to restore the perennial catechism of the Church. The project of a catechism restoration on behalf of "Tradivox" will surely be of great benefit not only to many confused and disoriented Catholic faithful, but also to all people who are sincerely seeking the ultimate and authentic truth about God and man, which one can find only in the Catholic and apostolic faith, and which is the only religion and faith willed by God and to which God calls all men.

+Athanasius Schneider, O.R.C.,
Titular Bishop of Celerina
Auxiliary Bishop of the Archdiocese of Saint Mary in Astana

---

[3] Cf. Pope St. Pius X, Encyclical *Acerbo nimis*, n. 27

SERIES EDITOR'S
PREFACE

S OME are surprised to find that when a given Catholic is asked to "look
something up in the catechism," he may well respond: "Which one?"
The history of the Catholic Church across the last millennium is in fact
filled with the publication of numerous catechisms, issued in every major
language on earth; and for centuries, these concise "guidebooks" to Catholic doctrine have served countless men and women seeking a clear and
concise presentation of that faith forever entrusted by Jesus Christ to his
one, holy, Catholic, and apostolic Church.

Taken together, the many catechisms issued with episcopal approval
can offer a kind of "window" on to the universal ordinary magisterium—a
glimpse of those truths which have been held and taught in the Church
everywhere, always, and by all. For, as St. Paul reminds us, the tenets of this
Faith do not change from age to age: "Jesus Christ yesterday and today
and the same for ever. Be not led away with various and strange doctrines"
(Heb 13:8-9).

The catechisms included in our *Tradivox Catholic Catechism Index* are
selected for their orthodoxy and historical significance, in the interest
of demonstrating to contemporary readers the remarkable continuity of
Catholic doctrine across time and space. Long regarded as reliable sum-
maries of Church teaching on matters of faith and morals, we are proud
to reproduce these works of centuries past, composed and endorsed by
countless priests, bishops, and popes devoted to "giving voice to tradition."

IN THIS VOLUME

Two catechisms, both by Irish priests of the early 1700s, are included in this volume: *The Catechism, or Christian Doctrine, By Way of Question and Answer*, by Fr. Andrew Donlevy, and *A Catechism Moral and Controversial*, by Fr. Thomas Miles Burke, O.P.

Catholic catechetical instruction received a fresh impulse in the eighteenth century, due to various interventions from Popes Benedict XIII, Clement XIII, and Pius VI. It was in this century that both Donlevy and Burke received their vocation to the priesthood at early ages, but living amid the most oppressive years of the anti-Catholic penal laws, they were obliged to leave their beloved Ireland to receive seminary training abroad. Their priestly lives, like so many others of the period, remain an inspiring and instructive lesson on the truly divine nature of the sacerdotal ministry: for, even at a time when Irish seminarians well understood that they were signing up for a life of poverty, often friendless and dangerous, and not infrequently ending in exile, torture, or death, our Lord was still calling men into his service, and honorable youths like Donlevy and Burke both heard the summons, and answered.

In the Catholic catechetical genre, the second and better-known of the two major Irish textual traditions is traceable to the Butler and Maynooth catechisms, included in Volume IV of this series. The first and more historically complex of the two currents is that of Donlevy's *Christian Doctrine*, recovered below from the original Paris edition of 1742. The young Donlevy would have left his native land in disguise and covert transport, effectively concealing that period of his life from historical study; but it is known that he reached the Irish College at Paris in 1710, where he so distinguished himself for learning and administrative sense that he was appointed prefect in 1728, an office he held there for almost twenty years. The exact date and circumstances of his death in 1746 are unknown, but while serving as prefect, he composed his *Christian Doctrine*. This catechism appears to be an expansion of the more concise work published at nearly the same time, authored by Bishop O'Reilly of the diocese of Derry and later of Armagh (d. 1758); however, the interrelationship of the two is rather difficult to determine, and it is entirely possible that Bishop O'Reilly's catechism was an extracted abridgement of Donlevy's. In either case, the two are markedly similar and together constitute the older of the two main currents of historical catechisms in Ireland.

In his text, Donlevy seeks a simple but more detailed and affective treatment of Catholic doctrine in order to "supplement the Abridgments" and smaller religious tracts of the day. Although writing originally in Irish for the persecuted Catholics of his homeland, he also relented "upon a second thought" and included an English translation, for the benefit of the faithful in other anglophone nations. James Duffy, the well-known Irish Catholic publisher to come a generation later, would meet with great success in republishing Donlevy's *Christian Doctrine* in facing Irish-English pages, which served many years as the normative text in several Irish dioceses. For this reason, we have included the many episcopal approbations as recorded in the identical third edition (Dublin: 1848), and our only noteworthy adjustment to the original text itself has been to change three incongruous subheadings in the "Commandments of the Church" section into correctly corresponding Questions (ns. 235, 237, and 244).

The significance placed upon the supernatural importance of catechesis cannot be overlooked in Donlevy's opening pages, and warrants restating for our own time, unhappily plagued by heedless ignorance (if not open rejection) of immutable divine and natural truths:

> **4. How is it useful and necessary to give attention to the catechism?**
> Because by giving a due attention to it, we learn all that is necessary for salvation; and that without this attention, we shall be ignorant thereof and eternally damned.

Fr. Thomas Miles Burke was one of several Irish Dominicans to go by the same name in the eighteenth and nineteenth centuries, and is often confused with Thomas "de Burgho" Burke, the zealous bishop of Ossory and author of the monumental *Hibernia Dominicana*. Comparatively little is known of Fr. Burke's life, after leaving Ireland to don the religious habit at the Dominican house of Lisbon, which was at that time one of the most prosperous port cities in the world. After ordination, Burke would serve as both professor and master of studies at the Dominican house for several years, composing his *Catechism Moral and Controversial* in days of relative peace and stability, an ocean removed from the troubles of Ireland and lodged in the capital city of a Catholic nation. Little could he have imagined the truly earth-shattering events that would conclude his priestly ministry there.

In the Introduction to his catechism, Burke shows the humble attitude of every catechist worthy of the name, insisting: "In this work I pretend to no other merit than that of a compiler. I am sensible I say nothing but what has been often said before." Indeed, it clearly borrows from the catechism of Bishop Richard Challoner, which had been in use for some twenty years at the time of Burke's writing, as well as several others. The greater length and practical directives of Burke's catechism are attributed to his having composed it for those "who have not had the advantage of the best education" (which audience could include not a few Catholics of our own era), and its inclusion of regular sections on apologetics bears the simple justification that this would have been left out, "if the Catholic Church had no enemies." Written for "such as are already advanced to some knowledge of the Christian doctrine," it remains an excellent reference for high school and collegiate instruction today.

The dramatic conclusion of this priest's earthly life deserves some mention, as it lends both his catechism and personal legacy still greater significance. Having published his text to contemporary acclaim, Burke would serve the next three years in a ministry that was quiet and blameless by all accounts, until All Saints' day, 1755. On the morning of that feast, and while praying the very words of the Roman Canon at Mass, the earth under Fr. Burke's feet began to tremble. The shaking soon became so violent that church bells throughout the city were heard ringing of their own accord, and in fact, they were ringing in steeples as far away as Austria. It was the morning of the Great Lisbon Earthquake, the worst natural disaster in recorded European history.

An earthquake of magnitude 9.0 or higher rent the seabed off the Portugese coast that morning, causing 10 to 16-foot fissures to open even into the center of the city. Those who were able to flee the collapsing buildings ran to the Targus river and coastal docks, only to find the sea itself receding, gathering itself for a tsunami so large that it sent waves as tall as sixty-six feet, far down the North African coast. Deaths were recorded on four separate continents, and in Lisbon, overturned candles and processional lamps for the feast day lent flames to a wind pattern that created a devastating firestorm which lasted for days, asphyxiating those far removed from the blaze itself. In a matter of hours, eighty-five percent of the city lay in utter ruin, with some 30,000–50,000 people dead and more injured. Contemporary chroniclers referred to it simply as "the destruction of Lisbon" or even "the punishment of Lisbon," for none could find any explanation of the timing and nature of the event beyond that of a divine chastisement, and artists often depicted it with avenging angels in the sky. Many learned the truth of Questions 658-59 in Burke's catechism, regarding resignation to the divine will:

> [W]e are not obliged to rejoice at every event that actually happens… [such as] temporal calamities or any other judgment which God executes against [man]; but the good which God proposes by punishments, to wit: either the amendment of sinners, showing of his own justice and glory, etc. is what we are obliged to will; because charity to our neighbor obliges us to will his amendment, and the love of God obliges us to desire his glory.

It is hoped that Fr. Thomas Burke, who went to meet his Lord in the very midst of the holy sacrifice that day, found such favor and mercy before the eternal judge that he is now able to intercede for us, who read his catechism more than two centuries later.

EDITORIAL NOTE

Our *Catholic Catechism Index* series generally retains only the doctrinal content of those catechisms it seeks to reproduce, as well as that front matter most essential to establishing the credibility of each work as an authentic expression of the Church's common doctrine, e.g., any episcopal endorsement, *nihil obstat*, or *imprimatur*. However, it should be noted that especially prior to the eighteenth century, a number of catechisms were so immediately and universally received as reliably orthodox texts (often simply by the reputation of the author or publisher), that they received no such "official" approval; or if they did, it was often years later and in subsequent editions. We therefore include both the original printing date in our Table of Contents, and further edition information in the Preface above.

Our primary goal has been to bring these historical texts back into publication in readable English copy. Due to the wide range of time periods, cultures, and unique author styles represented in this series, we have made a number of editorial adjustments to allow for a less fatiguing read, more rapid cross-reference throughout the series, and greater research potential for the future. While not affecting the original content, these adjustments have included adopting a cleaner typesetting and simpler standard for capitalization and annotation, as well as remedying certain anachronisms in spelling or grammar.

At the same time, in deepest respect for the venerable age and subject matter of these works, we have been at pains to adhere as closely as possible to the original text: retaining archaisms such as "doth" and "hallowed," and avoiding any alterations that might affect the doctrinal content or authorial voice. We have painstakingly restored original artwork wherever possible, and where the rare explanatory note has been deemed necessary, it is not made in the text itself, but only in a marginal note. In some cases, our editorial refusal to "modernize" the content of these classical works may require

Woodcut depicting an early method used in the production of Catholic catechisms, circa 1568.

a higher degree of attention from today's reader, who we trust will be richly rewarded by the effort.

We pray that our work continues to yield highly readable, faithful reproductions of these time-honored monuments to Catholic religious instruction: catechisms once penned, promulgated, and praised by bishops across the globe. May these texts that once served to guide and shape the faith and lives of millions now do so again; and may the scholars and saints once involved in their first publication now intercede for all who take them up anew. *Tolle lege!*

Sincerely in Christ,
Aaron Seng

TRADIVOX
VOLUME V

THE
CATECHISM,
O R
CHRISTIAN DOCTRINE
BY WAY
OF QUESTION AND ANSWER,

Drawn chiefly from the expreſs Word of God, and other pure Sources.

Hear Counſel, and receive Inſtruction, that thou mayeſt be wiſe in thy latter End. *Prov. 19. 20.*

PARIS,

Printed by JAMES GUERIN, at S. Thomas of Aquin's in S. James-ſtreet.

M. D. CC. XLII.
With Approbation, and the King's Licence.

THE

Catechism,

or

Christian Doctrine

BY WAY
OF QUESTION AND ANSWER,

Drawn chiefly from the express Word of God, and other pure Sources.

Hear Counsel, and receive Instruction,
that thou mayest be wise in thy latter End.
Prov. 19. 20.

PARIS,

Printed by JAMES GUERIN, at S. Thomas of Aquin's in S. James-street.

1742
With Approbation, and the King's License.

𝕬pprobations

I do hereby testify to have attentively read and examined the Irish and English catechism, compiled by M. Andrew Donlevy, Director of the Irish Community at Paris, which, in all points, is very conformable to both scripture and tradition, and very useful to all those who are charged with the instruction of the faithful in the kingdom of Ireland, as clearly containing the articles of faith and purity of Christian morality. At Paris, the eighteenth of April, 1741.

Michael O'Gara, A.T. (i.e. Archbishop of Tuam.)

Similar Approbations were given at the same time by—

James Gallagher, B.K. (i.e. Bishop of Kildare),
Patrick Macdonogh, B.K. (i.e. Bishop of Killaloe),
F.B. Kelly, O.S.F. Doctor of Sorbonne,
Patrick Corr, Doctor of Sorbonne, and Provisor of the Irish College,
Mathew Mackenna, Doctor of Sorbonne, and Provisor of the Irish College,
Richard Hennessy, Licentiate of Sorbonne,

And, as to the English part of the work, by—

F.J. Duany, O.E.S.A. Doctor of Sorbonne,
Francis Devereux, Principal of the Irish College.

SECTION I
The Catechism

Chapter 1

The Great Importance of the Catechism, and the Manner of Listening to It with Benefit

1. **What is the catechism?**

   It is a plain and intelligible explanation of the articles of the Christian faith necessary for salvation; and of other points belonging to the service of God.

2. **Is it requisite to make great account of the catechism, and to hearken to it attentively?**

   It is certainly; for it is very good in itself, and likewise both useful and necessary for us.

3. **How is it good in itself?**

   Inasmuch as it is the same doctrine, which Christ and the apostles have taught us.

4. **How is it useful and necessary to give attention to the catechism?**

   Because by giving a due attention to it, we learn all that is necessary for salvation; and that without this attention, we shall be ignorant thereof and eternally damned.[1]

---

[1] Cf. 1 Cor 14:38

5. **What ought to be done, in order to benefit by the catechism?**

There are certain things to be done before, at, and after it.

6. **What is fit to be done before it?**

1) First, it is requisite to come to learn it with a resolution of benefiting by it. 2) To adore and pray to God, when we come to the place where the catechism is to be taught. 3) To behave ourselves quietly and decently.[2]

7. **What else is to be done before it?**

It is proper to pray along with the priest, or catechist.

8. **What prayer do you say?**

I say: "O Lord, through thy great mercy, teach me all that is necessary for knowing thee, for loving thee, and for doing thy holy will."

9. **What is proper to be done while the catechism is taught?**

It is fit we should listen to it with attention, modesty, and respect, just as if our Lord Jesus Christ were speaking to us.[3]

10. **What is fit to be done after the catechism is over?**

It is proper to give thanks to God, and to beg the grace to retain what we heard, and to turn it to our good.[4]

11. **Into how many parts is the catechism divided?**

Into four parts; the first treats of the articles of faith; the second, of the commandments of God and the Church; the third of the sacraments; the fourth, of hope and prayer.[5]

---

[2] Cf. 1 Cor 14:40
[3] Cf. Lk 10:16
[4] Cf. 2 Cor 6:1
[5] Cf. *Catechism of the Council of Trent*, Introductory; Editor's note: The *Catechism of the Council of Trent* is included in Volume VII of the Tradivox series.

LESSON 1

Of the Creation and End of Man

12. Who created you and placed you in the world?
Almighty God.[6]

13. What good has God done you, when he made you?
He gave me, together with a body, a rational, spiritual and immortal soul, capable of possessing himself during all eternity.[7]

14. To what end has God placed you in the world?
In order to know, love and serve him, and thereby merit life everlasting.[8]

15. What must we do to answer that end?
There are four things to be done.

16. What is the first?
It is to believe firmly whatever God has revealed, and the Church teacheth us.[9]

17. What is the second thing?
It is to fulfil the commandments of God and the Church.[10]

18. What is the third?
To receive the sacraments with the necessary preparation.[11]

---

[6] Cf. Gn 1:27; Eph 3:9
[7] Cf. Jn 3:15-16; 1 Jn 3:2; Ws 3
[8] Cf. 1 Thes 4:3
[9] Cf. Mt 18:17; Jn 8:24
[10] Cf. Mt 19:17; Heb 13:17
[11] Cf. Mt 7:6; 28:20; 1 Cor 11:20ff

19. **What is the fourth thing?**

It is to put our hope in God, and to have recourse to him often by prayer.[12]

The Fruit of This Lesson

We should often consider for what end God has placed us in the world; and make use of our body, of our soul, and of every other gift we received, according to the will and intention of our Maker.[13]

LESSON 2

Faith Expounded

20. **What is faith?**

It is a divine virtue, and a heavenly light, whereby we believe all that God has revealed to his Church.

21. **Why is faith called a divine virtue and a heavenly light?**

Because it is God, through his great mercy, that infuses this valuable gift into our souls by which he reveals himself to us.[14]

22. **Is faith necessary for everyone?**

It is; for without faith none can be saved.[15]

23. **Make an act of faith.**

O Lord, I do firmly believe whatever thou hast revealed, and all that thou teachest me by the holy Catholic Church; because thou art most true in thy words.[16]

---

[12] Cf. Os 12:6; Mt 12:21; Eph 6:10-18; Heb 4:16
[13] Cf. 1 Cor 10:31; Col 3
[14] Cf. Jn 6:44; Phil 1:29
[15] Cf. Heb 11:6
[16] Cf. Ps 18:8; 2 Cor 1:18

24. Are we obliged to make an act of faith from time to time?

Everyone that has been baptized is obliged, when he comes to the use of reason and years of discretion, to believe firmly from his heart all that God has revealed to the Church; and to put his faith daily in practice, by living up to the law of God.[17]

25. What else are we obliged to do?

We are undoubtedly obliged to learn, and firmly believe, the principal articles of faith; particularly when we have a mind to receive the sacraments.[18]

26. Where are those principal articles to be found, which we are obliged to learn and believe?

In the Apostles' Creed.

27. Are we obliged to know the Apostles' Creed?

We are obliged not only to know it, but also to know the meaning of the articles it contains.[19]

28. Say the Creed.

I believe in God, the Father Almighty, Maker of heaven and earth; and in Jesus Christ his only Son, our Lord, who was conceived by the Holy Ghost, born of the Virgin Mary, suffered under Pontius Pilate, was crucified, dead and buried, he descended into hell; the third day he rose again from the dead; he ascended into heaven, sitteth at the right hand of God, the Father Almighty; from thence he shall come to judge both the quick and the dead. I believe in the Holy Ghost; the holy Catholic Church; the communion of saints; the remission of sins; the resurrection of the flesh; and the life everlasting. Amen.

[17] Cf. 1 Cor 16:13; Heb 10:38

[18] Cf. Mk 16:16; Heb 10:22; Charles Borromeo, *Acts of the Church of Milan*, Pt. 4, "Instructions for Confessors"

[19] Cf. Mt 13:14-15; Eph 5:17; Charles Borromeo, *Acts of the Church of Milan*, Pt. 4, "Instructions for Confessors"

29. **Why are we obliged to believe all these things?**

Because God, who can neither deceive nor be deceived, has revealed them all.[20]

30. **How do we know for certain that God has revealed them?**

We know it from the holy Catholic Church, which God commanded us to obey, and with which he promised to be to the end of the world; and to teach her all truth.[21]

The Fruit of This Lesson

1) First, to give thanks to God, for the virtue of faith which we received in baptism; to make an act of faith often; to resolve every day, to live and die in the Roman Catholic faith; never to deny our faith, either by word or deed.[22] 2) To endeavor to learn the Christian doctrine; and to teach, or get it taught, the people that are under our care.[23] 3) To love and esteem greatly the Church of God; and likewise to pray for and assist the teachers of the gospel.[24]

LESSON 3

Of God

31. **What is the first thing that every Christian ought to believe?**

That there is only one God.

32. **Who is God?**

God is the Maker of heaven and earth, and sovereign Lord of all things.[25]

---

[20] Cf. 2 Cor 1:18-20
[21] Cf. Mt 18:17; 28:20; Jn 16:13
[22] Cf. Mt 10:33
[23] Cf. 1 Tm 5:8
[24] Cf. 1 Tm 5:17; Heb 13:17
[25] Cf. Gn 1; 1 Tm 6:15

33. Can you expound, any other way, what God is?

Yes; God is an eternal Spirit, infinitely good, infinitely perfect, infinitely powerful; who is in all places, sees all things, and governs all.

34. Why do you say that God is a Spirit?

Because he has neither body nor anything belonging to a body.[26]

35. Why do you say that God is infinitely good and infinitely perfect?

Because he surpasses in goodness all that is good, and that nothing can be as good or as perfect as he is.[27]

36. Why do you say that God is infinitely powerful?

Because he can do whatever he pleases.[28]

37. Why do you say that he is eternal or everlasting?

Because he has neither beginning nor end.[29]

38. Is God everywhere?

Yes: for he is in heaven, and on earth, and in every part of the world.[30]

39. Does God see all things?

Yes: for nothing, nay, not the secret thoughts of man's heart can be hid from him.[31]

40. Why do you say that he governs all things?

Because he takes care of, and looks to everything: he rewards the righteous, and punishes the wicked; and likewise because nothing happens but by his order or permission.[32]

---

[26] Cf. Lk 24:39; Jn 4:24
[27] Cf. Mt 19:17; Jas 1:17; Ps 144:3
[28] Cf. Ps 113:11; Mt 19:26
[29] Cf. Dt 32:40; Ex 15:18; Mi 5:2
[30] Cf. Dt 4:39; Bar 3:25; Ps 138:7; Jer 23:24
[31] Cf. Ps 7:10; Heb 4:13
[32] Cf. 1 Cor 12:6; Acts 17:28; Mt 10:29

41. **What duty are we obliged to pay to God?**

We are obliged to adore his glorious majesty, and to love him above all things.[33]

42. **What else do we owe to our Creator?**

We are obliged to obey him in all things; to be greatly afraid of deserving his wrath; and to suffer patiently what misery and trouble soever he may inflict upon us.[34]

43. **What else do we owe him?**

Never to speak of him but with very great esteem and respect; to consider often that he sees us in every place, and at every moment; and therefore, never to do anything contrary to his will.[35]

LESSON 4

Of the Unity of God, and of the Most Holy Trinity

44. **How many gods are there?**

There is only one God.[36]

45. **How many Persons in God?**

There are three Persons, to wit, the Father, and the Son, and the Holy Ghost.[37]

46. **Is the Father God?**

He is certainly.

---

[33] Cf. Dt 6:13; Mt 4:10; Lk 10:27
[34] Cf. Ex 15:26; Lk 12:4-5; Heb 10:36; 1 Pt 4:1-13
[35] Cf. Gn 18:27; Ps 28:2; 110:9; Gn 17:1; Gal 5:25
[36] Cf. Dt 6:4; 1 Cor 8:4
[37] Cf. Mt 28:19

47. Is the Son God?

He is certainly.[38]

48. Is the Holy Ghost God?

He is certainly.[39]

49. Are they three gods?

No: they are but one God in three Persons; because they have but one only nature, and one divine substance.[40]

50. What do you call these three Persons together?

The most Holy Trinity, or one only God in three distinct Persons.

51. Is the Father more perfect, more wise, or more powerful than the Son, or the Holy Ghost?

He is not; because these three divine Persons are equal in all things; for they are one only God.

52. Is the Father more ancient or elder than the Son or the Holy Ghost?

He is not; because they are all three from eternity.[41]

53. What must be done in order to honor the most Blessed Trinity?

We ought to believe firmly this very obscure truth; to give thanks to God for having given us the knowledge of it; and to adore the God of glory in three Persons, especially morning and evening, and at the beginning of all our prayers.[42]

---

[38] Cf. Jn 1:1
[39] Cf. Acts 5:3-4
[40] Cf. Mt 28:19; 1 Jn 5:7
[41] Cf. Ps 89:2
[42] Cf. Ps 117:9; 62:2; 140:2

54. **What else is to be done?**

We should be diligent in teaching this great truth, or in getting it taught those that are ignorant thereof.[43]

LESSON 5

Of the Incarnation of the Son of God, the Second Person of the Holy Trinity

55. **What do you understand by the incarnation?**

The union of the nature of God and of the nature of man in one divine Person.

56. **Which of the three Persons of the most Holy Trinity took human nature?**

The Son, who is the second Person of the most Holy Trinity.[44]

57. **What doth the taking of human nature mean?**

It means the taking of a body and soul, such as we have.

58. **Where has he taken this body and soul?**

In the womb of the glorious Virgin Mary, his Mother.[45]

59. **How came this to pass?**

By the virtue of the Holy Ghost, the body of Jesus Christ was formed of the very blood of the Blessed Virgin.[46]

60. **Who is Jesus Christ?**

He is the second Person of the most Holy Trinity made man.

---

[43] Cf. Col 3:16
[44] Cf. Jn 1:14
[45] Cf. Mt 1:18
[46] Cf. Mt 1:20; Gal 4:4

61. What signifies the word *Jesus?*

It signifies Savior.[47]

62. Is there not a special honor due to this name?

There is; for it is commanded that at "the name of Jesus every knee shall bow."[48]

63. What signifies the word *Christ?*

It signifies anointed.

64. With what was he anointed?

With all heavenly graces, and with the fullness of the divinity itself.[49]

65. Is Jesus Christ God?

He is certainly.[50]

66. Is he likewise man?

He is both God and man.[51]

67. How many natures in Christ our Savior?

There are two natures, to wit, the divine nature and the human; for he is both God and man.[52]

68. How many persons in Jesus Christ?

There is but one Person, to wit, the Person of the Son of God only.[53]

---

[47] Cf. Mt 1:21
[48] Phil 2:10
[49] Cf. Jn 1:14
[50] Cf. Col 2:9
[51] Cf. Phil 2:6-7
[52] Cf. Rom 9:5
[53] Cf. Council of Ephesus

69. **Where is our Lord Jesus Christ?**

Inasmuch as he is God, he is everywhere; but inasmuch as he is man, he is only in heaven, and in the Blessed Sacrament of the Eucharist.[54]

70. **What obligations do we lie under to our Lord Jesus Christ?**

We are obliged to adore and praise him as our God, and to give him great thanks for becoming man for our sake.

71. **What else are we obliged to do?**

We should humble ourselves for his sake, who, upon our account, humbled his incomprehensible majesty, when he united our poor nature to his own divine Person.[55]

LESSON 6

Of the Redemption of Man

72. **Why was the Son of God made man?**

To redeem and save us.

73. **What means redeeming us?**

It means, to deliver us from sin and everlasting damnation.

74. **Why was mankind thus condemned?**

For the disobedience of our first father Adam, and likewise for the sins we have willfully committed ourselves.[56]

75. **What hath our Lord Jesus Christ done in order to redeem us?**

1) He was born in a stable among brute beasts.[57] 2) He spent thirty-three

---

[54] Cf. Heb 10:12; Mt 26:26
[55] Cf. 2 Cor 8:9
[56] Cf. Gn 3:6; Rom 5:12; Eph 2:3
[57] Cf. Lk 2:7

years in all manner of humiliation and poverty.[58] 3) He died at length on the cross for our sake.[59]

76. **On what day was he born?**
On Christmas day, about midnight.[60]

77. **What has our Savior Jesus Christ done until the age of thirty years?**
He spent his life privately, and almost unknown to the world, in the company of his Blessed Mother.[61]

78. **What has he done from the age of thirty years until the time of his death?**
He taught men the way of salvation, both by word and example; and also wrought a vast many great miracles, to prove and confirm his doctrine.[62]

79. **On what day did he die?**
On Good Friday.

80. **For whom did he die?**
For all mankind, and for each Christian in particular.[63]

81. **Why did he die?**
He died to make satisfaction for our sins;[64] to merit everlasting pleasure and happiness for us;[65] and likewise the graces necessary for obtaining this bliss.[66]

---

[58] Cf. Lk 3:23ff
[59] Cf. Mt 27:50
[60] Cf. Lk 2:8-16
[61] Cf. Lk 2:51
[62] Cf. Lk 4:15ff; 24:19
[63] Cf. 1 Jn 2:2
[64] Cf. Rom 3:23-25
[65] Cf. Jn 10:10
[66] Cf. Rom 7:24-25

82. **What obligations do we owe our Lord Jesus Christ for being our Savior?**
We are obliged to love[67] and thank him for this great benefit;[68] to put our entire hopes in him,[69] and to follow his example.[70]

LESSON 7

Of the Mysteries of Our Lord Jesus Christ

83. **Where was the body of Jesus Christ laid after his death?**
In the sepulchre or grave.[71]

84. **What mean these words of the Creed: *He descended into hell?***
They mean that our Savior's soul went into that part of hell called limbo, to deliver the souls of the just from the captivity they were in.[72]

85. **Did he not rise after his death?**
He rose both glorious and immortal.[73]

86. **When did he rise?**
On the third day after he died; to wit, on Easter Sunday.[74]

87. **Has he ascended into heaven?**
Yes; he ascended by his own proper power.[75]

---

[67] Cf. Rom 8:35
[68] Cf. 1 Tm 1:12
[69] Cf. Mt 1:21
[70] Cf. 1 Pt 2:21
[71] Cf. Mt 27:60
[72] Cf. Eph 4:8-9
[73] Cf. Mt 28:6
[74] Cf. Mt 28
[75] Cf. Acts 1:9-10

88. **When did he ascend into heaven?**

Forty days after his resurrection; to wit, on Ascension day.[76]

89. **Will Christ our Savior come at the end of the world?**

Yes; he shall come visibly to judge every man according to his works.[77]

90. **Shall the judgment of mankind be deferred until the end of the world?**

The general judgment shall be deferred until then.

91. **Is there any other judgment besides the general judgment?**

Yes; there is a particular judgment, which everyone shall undergo at the hour of his death.[78]

LESSON 8

Of the Holy Ghost, the Church, and the Heavenly Treasures Which Are Received in the Church

92. **Who is the Holy Ghost?**

He is the third Person of the most Holy Trinity.[79]

93. **When did the Holy Ghost descend to the Church?**

In ten days after the ascension; to wit, on Whitsunday.[80]

94. **Is the Holy Ghost given now to us?**

He is always given in an invisible manner to such as are rightly disposed to receive him.[81]

---

[76] Cf. Acts 1
[77] Cf. Mt 25:31-32
[78] Cf. Heb 9:27
[79] Cf. Mt 28:19
[80] Cf. Acts 2:1-4
[81] Cf. 2 Cor 13:13

95. **Are we obliged to put our hope in him, and to pray to him as we do to the Father and the Son?**

We are certainly: for these three divine Persons are but one God?[82]

96. **What benefit do we receive from the Holy Ghost?**

He sanctifies and strengthens us; and enlightens and guides the Church, so that she never shall fall into error.[83]

97. **What is the Church?**

It is the congregation of all the faithful under Christ Jesus, their invisible head; and under his vicar on earth, the pope.[84]

98. **Who is the pope?**

He is the visible head of the Church, successor of Saint Peter, and Christ's vicar on earth.

99. **Which is the true Church?**

It is the holy Catholic Roman Church; whose visible head is the pope.[85]

100. **Is it necessary to be in the Church?**

It is, because there is no salvation out of the Church: for there is but one only God, one only faith, and one only baptism.[86]

101. **What means *the communion of saints?***

It means that all the true children of Christ are partakers of the spiritual treasure of the Church.[87]

---

[82] Cf. 1 Jn 5:7
[83] Cf. Jn 14:16, 26
[84] Cf. Mt 16:18; Jn 21:15-17
[85] Cf. Mt 10:2; Jn 21:15ff
[86] Cf. Eph 4:5
[87] Cf. 1 Cor 12:12ff; 2 Cor 1:11

102. **What is the spiritual treasure whereof the members of the Church do partake?**

The sacraments, the Holy Sacrifice of the Mass, the prayers of the Church, and the good works of the righteous.

103. **Is there not some union between the faithful upon earth and the saints in heaven?**

There is: for we pray to them, and they obtain us assistance from God through Jesus Christ.[88]

104. **Does this spiritual treasure of the Church prove beneficial to the souls in purgatory?**

It does: for they receive comfort and succor by the Holy Sacrifice of the Mass, by the prayers and good works of the faithful.[89]

105. **What are the true children of the Church obliged to do?**

It is but just they should give great thanks to God for having made them the children of so great and so good a mother, against whom all her enemies cannot prevail.[90]

106. **What do you understand *by the forgiveness of sins?***

I understand that Jesus Christ gave power to his Church to forgive sins, and effectual means whereby men are sanctified.[91]

---

[88] Cf. Gn 48:16; Zac 1:12ff; Os 12:4; Dn 10:21; 12:1; Jer 15:1; Apoc 8:3-4
[89] Cf. 2 Mc 12:46
[90] Cf. Mt 16:18; 1 Tm 3:15; Gal 4:26; Heb 12:22-23
[91] Cf. Mt 18:18; Jn 20:23

LESSON 9

Of the Resurrection of the Flesh, and of the Life Everlasting

107. **What means *the resurrection of the flesh*?**

It means that all men shall rise with the same bodies which they had in this life.[92]

108. **Shall the wicked as well as the righteous rise again?**

They shall; but the righteous shall have glorious bodies; and those of the wicked shall be ugly and hideous.[93]

109. **What reward will God give the righteous after their death?**

The glory of heaven and life everlasting.[94]

110. **What is *life everlasting*?**

It is to see God face to face, and to love and praise him for all eternity in everlasting pleasure and happiness.[95]

111. **What shall become of the wicked who die in mortal sin?**

They shall be cast into hell, a place where they shall never see God, and shall burn during eternity along with devils.[96]

112. **Whither do those go who die in venial sin only, or who have not made full satisfaction for their sins?**

To purgatory, in order to satisfy the divine justice by the torments they are to suffer there.[97]

---

[92] Cf. Jb 19:26; Jn 5:28-29
[93] Cf. 1 Cor 15:42-51
[94] Cf. Mt 25:34, 46
[95] Cf. Jn 17:3; 1 Jn 3:2; Apoc 19:7
[96] Cf. Mt 25:46
[97] Cf. Mt 5:26; Apoc 21:27

113. What benefit are we to draw from this lesson?

We should think often of the unspeakable reward of the righteous, and of the everlasting torments of the wicked, that thereby we may courageously pursue virtue, and shun vice.[98]

---

[98] Cf. 1 Cor 9:24; Heb 6:11-12

SECTION II
Of the Commandments of God and the Church

Chapter 2

LESSON 1

Of the Commandments of God in General

114. What is the second thing necessary for our salvation?
The fulfilling of the commandments of God and of the Church.[99]

115. Why did God give us his holy commandments?
To the intent they may serve as a rule for our actions, in giving us knowledge of the vices that ought to be shunned, and of the virtues which we ought to embrace.[100]

116. How many commandments has God given us?
Ten.

117. Say them.[101]
1. I am the Lord thy God, who brought thee out of the land of Egypt, and out of the house of bondage; thou shalt not have strange gods before me.

---

[99] Cf. Mt 19:17
[100] Cf. Ps 118:105; Prv 6:23
[101] Cf. Ex 20

2. Thou shalt not take the name of the Lord thy God in vain.

3. Remember to keep holy the sabbath-day.

4. Honor thy father and mother.

5. Thou shalt not kill.

6. Thou shalt not commit adultery.

7. Thou shalt not steal.

8. Thou shalt not bear false witness against thy neighbor.

9. Thou shalt not covet thy neighbor's wife.

10. Thou shalt not covet thy neighbor's goods.

118. **What means do you take for stirring up yourself to fulfil the commandments of God?**

I consider that God is my sovereign Lord, to whom I justly owe obedience; and that his commandments are most lawful, and can easily be fulfilled with the assistance of his grace.[102]

119. **Do you make use of any other means?**

Yes; I think of the great reward which God gives to those who fulfil his commandments; and of the everlasting torments wherewith the transgressors thereof shall be afflicted.[103]

120. **Is it necessary to observe all the commandments?**

Yes; for whosoever transgresseth one only commandment by a mortal sin, deserves eternal damnation.[104]

121. **What is the abridgment or sum of the commandments?**

It is to love God above all things, and our neighbor as ourselves; for this is the accomplishment of the law.[105]

---

[102] Cf. Mt 11:30; 1 Jn 5:3
[103] Cf. Ecclus 1:40
[104] Cf. Jas 2:10
[105] Cf. Mt 22:40; Rom 13:9-10

LESSON 2

First Commandment
I am the Lord thy God, etc.

122. What doth the first commandment oblige us to do?

It obliges us to believe in God, to put our hopes in him, to adore and love him with our whole heart.[106]

123. What is it to adore God?

It is to acknowledge that he is our Maker and sovereign Lord, and to give him all possible honor and praise.[107]

124. Make an act of adoration.

O great God, and Almighty Lord, I adore thee, and do acknowledge thee for my Maker and sovereign Lord.

125. What do you mean by loving God with your whole heart?

I mean, to love him above all things, to be willing rather to suffer death than to offend him.

126. Make an act of the love of God.

O Lord, I love thee with my whole heart, and above all things; because thou art infinitely good, and most amiable, and continually bestowest many favors upon me.

127. Doth this commandment forbid us to honor the saints?

No; because the honor we give them is not the same with that which we give to God; for we honor them only as his friends and faithful servants, and merely upon his account.[108]

---

[106] Cf. Lk 10:27
[107] Cf. 1 Tm 1:17
[108] Cf. Jo 5:14-16; 3 Kgs 18:7; 4 Kgs 2:15; 8:17-22; Apoc 8; 19:10; Rom 13:7-8

128. **Is it lawful to pay any honor or respect to the images of Christ and his saints?**

It is, for the sake of Christ and his saints, of whom they put us in mind; just as we do in regard of the name of Jesus; yet we do not believe that there is any virtue either in the sound of the word, or in the images of Christ and the saints.[109]

129. **But did not God forbid not only to show any honor or respect to images, but also to make "the likeness of any thing either in heaven above, or in earth beneath, or in the waters under the earth"?[110]**

He did indeed expressly forbid the Jews, who were extremely prone to idolatry, even to make any such likeness, lest they should adore and worship them as gods, and thus "have strange gods before (the Lord),"[111] in imitation of the nations round about them, who all adored and served stocks and stones, gods of gold and silver, etc.; but no people do now look on this prohibition of making the likeness of anything as obligatory or binding.

130. **Why so?**

Because there is no danger in this age, that Christians will adore or serve the image or likeness of anything either in heaven or on earth: it is neither stock, nor stone, nor statue of gold or silver, but the excessive love of the world, vanity, too great a tie to our own sentiments, and other disorderly passions, that are the idols or false gods of Christians nowadays.

131. **How do you prove that it is in that sense that God has forbid the Jews to make the likeness of anything either in heaven or on earth?**

It is proved plainly from God's own words, both in the same place, and in several other places of scripture, where he sayeth, "Ye shall not make gods of silver, neither shall ye make unto you gods of gold";[112] which is

---

[109] Cf. Nm 21:8-9; Phil 2:10; Council of Trent, Session 25
[110] Ex 20:4
[111] Ex 20:3
[112] Ex 20:23

the same thing as to say, "Thou shalt not have strange gods before me":[113] Thou shalt not adore nor serve any graven thing either in heaven or on earth: so that it is manifest, that all is but one and the same commandment, explained and set forth at large; and consequently, that no essential part of the commandments is left out in our short catechisms, it being clear to the reason of a child, that if we must have but one only true God, we must not have either image, or likeness, or anything else for our God.[114]

132. What other proof have you for it?

It is, that among the Jews themselves, prone as they were to idolatry, there was, by God's appointment, a religious use of images: for God commanded Moses to make two cherubim or angels of beaten gold, and to place them honorably on the two ends of the mercy-seat which covered the ark: he also commanded him to make a serpent of brass, and set it upon a pole, that everyone that should be bitten by the fiery serpents might look on it and be healed; which Christ declares to be a figure or image of himself exalted on the cross.[115]

Solomon also graved two cherubims of image-work on the walls of the Temple, and covered them with gold; he also wrought cherubims on the veil of the Temple: so that these pictures were always placed before the people whensoever they kneeled and prayed in this holy house.[116]

133. Do not Catholics pray to, and serve images?

No, by no means. We do indeed kneel and pray before them, to keep us from distraction, but not to them, no more than Joshua and the elders of Israel prayed to the ark of the covenant, when they lay prostrate, praying until evening before it; no more than others do pray to the communion-table, when they kneel and pray before it; and as we have the charity to believe upon their word, that they neither pray to, nor adore either the communion-table or the bread and wine they receive kneeling, so should

---

[113] Ex 20:3
[114] Cf. Ex 20:23; 34:15; Lv 19:4; Dt 29:17ff
[115] Cf. Ex 25:17-18; Jn 3:14
[116] Cf. 2 Par 3:7-14

they, it seems, have the like charity for us, seeing the whole Church assembled at Trent, even all of us, men, women, and children, do openly declare and constantly profess, that we neither pray to nor adore images; that we certainly know, they can neither see, nor hear, nor help us; that we firmly believe no confidence ought to be placed in them, nothing ought to be asked of them, and that the honor due to God, ought not, upon any account, to be given to any creature whatsoever, either in heaven or on earth.[117]

134. **What benefit then have we by them?**

They feelingly represent to us the mysteries of our Savior's death and passion, and the sufferings of his saints; they serve as books to the ignorant, and excite us all to follow the example of God's glorious servants.[118]

135. **But since there is neither divinity nor virtue in them, what honor or respect can be shown them?**

The same respect, in proportion, which is given to the name of Jesus; for Christ's holy image is the very same to the eye that his holy name is to the ear.

136. **Give us some other example.**

The same respect with that which is shown to churches and houses of prayer by all those who uncover themselves at their entering therein; the same with that respect which is shown to the Lord's Supper by such as believe it to be but bread and wine, a figure or sign only of Christ's body and blood, and yet receive it kneeling; the same with that respect and honor which God ordered Moses to show to the very ground he stood upon, saying: "Take off thy shoes from off thy feet, for the place whereon thou standest is holy ground."[119]

---

[117] Cf. Council of Trent, Session 25
[118] Cf. Ibid.
[119] Ex 3:5

137. **Does this respect rest in the things to which it is shown?**

No; it is referred straight to Christ and his saints; just as the respect which is usually shown to the throne, and to the king's statue or picture, is, in the judgment of all men, referred to the king himself; and the disrespect shown to the king's image is never supposed to be levelled at either paper, or stock, or stone, but at the king's own person.

138. **Is it not commendable to pay respect to the relics of saints?**

It is, because their bodies were members of Jesus Christ, and the dwelling place of the Holy Ghost, and that likewise they shall one day be glorious in heaven.[120]

139. **For what other reason is respect paid to the relics of saints?**

Because God made use of them to do a great deal of good to those who respect them.[121]

140. **Is it against this commandment to consult fortune-tellers, enchanters or witches, who make a compact with the devil?**

It is undoubtedly; for whatever knowledge they have is from the devil.[122]

141. **In what doth witchcraft or enchantment consist?**

It consists in using of words, or signs, for an end which they have no force or virtue to attain to, either from nature, or God, or the Church.

142. **Do heretics sin against this commandment?**

They do for certain; because they do not sincerely believe what the Roman Catholic Church holds.[123] All those likewise do sin, who either by word or deed show an inclination or bent to heresy by hearing their prayers, or instructions, or otherwise.[124]

[120] Cf. 1 Cor 3:16; 6:15, 19
[121] Cf. 4 Kgs 13:21; Mt 9:20; Acts 5:15; 19:11-12
[122] Cf. Lv 19:31; Dt 18:10-12
[123] Cf. Mt 18:17
[124] Cf. Rom 10:10

143. Is it permitted to read heretical books?

No; it is not allowed either to read or keep them without leave; neither is it permitted to pry into the mysteries of faith, or to doubt of any one article thereof.[125]

144. Does he who is ignorant, through his fault, of the Lord's Prayer, of the Apostles' Creed, of the commandments of God, or those of the Church, sin against this commandment?

He does, without doubt, and so does he who understands them not, through his own neglect.[126]

145. Is it against this commandment to murmur or exclaim against God?

It is certainly: whereas God doth in all things act according to justice; and not only to exclaim against him is a transgression, but it is also against this commandment: 1) First, to have a distrust to God or godly things. 2) To let much time pass without thinking of him, or of the duty we owe him. 3) To hinder others from doing anything that would redound to the honor of God.

146. Doth this commandment forbid to show or have a disrespect for the saints?

It forbids to dishonor not only the saints, but also their relics, their images, or any sacred thing, such as the word of God, the places consecrated to his service, etc.

147. What else does this commandment forbid?

It forbids: 1) First, to despair of salvation, or of the forgiveness of our sins. 2) To presume that God, by his mercy alone, will save us, without any good works. 3) To put our hope in any creature whatsoever more than in God. 4) To commit any sin, or remain in it, through a presumption of God's mercy.[127]

---

[125] Cf. Prv 25:27; Col 1:23
[126] Cf. 1 Cor 14:38; 1 Pt 3:15
[127] Cf. Rom 2:3ff

LESSON 3

Of the Second Commandment
Thou shalt not take the name of the Lord thy God in vain.

148. **What does the second commandment forbid us?**

It forbids us: 1) First, to swear to anything we know, or even doubt to be false. 2) To swear without necessity, although the thing be true and just.[128] 3) To swear what we do not intend to perform; or to neglect fulfilling, when we can, a lawful oath.[129] 4) To swear we shall do what is bad, or not do what is good. 5) To conceal the truth from our lawful superior, when he requires of us to tell it; in which case, we do not only sin, but we are likewise obliged to repair all the damage and harm which happened thereby to our neighbor. 6) To swear by God or the saints' blood, wounds, or limbs. 7) To give to the devil, or curse at any rate, ourselves, our soul or body, our children, our servants, cattle, or anything else whatsoever. 8) To wish either temporal or spiritual harm to ourselves or others. 9) To make a vow without intending to fulfil it; or to make a vow of doing what is evil, or displeasing to God. 10) To break a lawful vow.

149. **From hence, then, it appears that it is an ill custom to be given to swearing?**

It is a very bad custom; wherefore those foolish people sin greatly who matter not whether they have truth or falsehood on their side, or swear to the truth itself without necessity.

150. **What should our speech be, in order to avoid sin?**

Yes, yes; no, no: as our Savior taught and commanded us; for what is more than these, proceedeth from evil.[130]

---

[128] Cf. Mt 5:34-37
[129] Cf. Jer 4:2
[130] Cf. Mt 5:37

LESSON 4

The Third Commandment
Remember thou keep holy the sabbath-day.

151. What is required in this commandment?

We are required to keep and sanctify Sunday, the Lord's day, as God and the Church order us.[131]

152. What works are forbidden on this sacred day?

Servile or laborious bodily works, such as ploughing and harrowing; buying and selling, and such like; but particularly all sort of sin.[132]

153. Are there any other works forbidden besides those that are very toilsome?

Yes: all worldly works whereby we gain any earthly profit, or that withdraw us from the service of God, without real necessity, are likewise forbidden.

154. Is it forbidden to engage others to do any of these works?

Yes; and we are, moreover, obliged to hinder all those under our charge from working.[133]

155. Are those servile or bodily works, which belong to the service of God, a breach of the Lord's day?

No; if they be such as cannot be deferred until another time.

156. Is it forbidden to dress meat, to serve cattle, and the like?

No; it is no breach of the precept to do what regards this day's maintenance, and could not be done the day before it without inconvenience.[134]

---

[131] Cf. Ex 20:8-10; Jer 17:27
[132] Cf. Ex 16:23; Ex 23:12
[133] Cf. Ex 20:10
[134] Cf. Ex 12:16

157. **What are we obliged to do on this day more than on another?**

To pray, and do godly works; such as to hear Mass punctually; to assist at the sermon; to read spiritual books; to say the beads; or do some other good works.

158. **Is it a profanation of the Lord's day to chat, or entertain idle thoughts at divine service, at sermon, or at catechism?**

It is for certain; for God requires that we serve him diligently in spirit and truth.[135]

159. **Does he sanctify the Lord's day, who spends the most part of it in gaming, drinking, divertissements or idleness?**

He does not; for God and the Church instituted holy days, in order that we should give the greater part of the day to God and the salvation of our soul; and a servile useful work is much less displeasing in the sight of God, than excessive divertissements, idleness, and every other bad action.

LESSON 5

Of the Commandments Which Regard Our Neighbor in General; and of the Fourth Commandment in Particular
Honor thy father and mother.

160. **What do these commandments which regard our neighbor treat of?**

Of every duty, and particularly of the love we owe our neighbor.

161. **How are we to love our neighbor?**

As ourselves; that is, to wish our neighbor all the good we wish ourselves; neither to do, nor wish him evil, no more than to ourselves; and to help him in his necessity.[136]

---

[135] Cf. Jn 4:24
[136] Cf. Rom 13:8-10; 15

162. Who is our neighbor?

Everyone, even our enemy.[137]

163. Why are we obliged to love our neighbor?

Because he bears the image of God; and also because God loves him, and commands us to love him as ourselves.[138]

164. What doth the fourth commandment order us to do?

To love and honor our parents and superiors, whether ecclesiastical or civil; to be obedient to them both in word and deed; to assist them in all their necessities, whether spiritual or corporal; and to do all cheerfully and gladly.[139]

165. In what are we obliged to obey them?

In everything that is not contrary to the commandments of God or the Church: for if their commands should be against either, it would not be at all permitted to obey them.[140]

166. What are the obligations of the father and mother in regard of their children?

To nourish, educate and instruct them; to give them a calling or livelihood according to their ability; chiefly, to bring them up in the fear and love of God, and to give them good example.[141]

167. Doth this commandment regard the duty which man and wife owe each other?

Yes, without doubt.

---

[137] Cf. Mt 5:44
[138] Cf. Mk 12:31
[139] Cf. Col 3:20; Rom 13; Heb 13:17; 1 Tm 5:4
[140] Cf. Acts 5:29
[141] Cf. 2 Cor 12:14; Eph 6:4

168. **How is the husband to behave himself in regard of his wife?**

As Christ behaves himself in regard of the Church, that is, lovingly and carefully: for the wife is a member of the husband, as we are all members of Christ.[142]

169. **How is the wife to behave herself towards her husband?**

She ought to be very affectionate and submissive to him, as the Church is to Jesus Christ.[143]

170. **Does this commandment put any obligation on the married couple in regard of those under their charge?**

It obliges them to govern all those that are under their command according to the will of God; and it requires of all those that are under their authority to be heartily submissive and obedient to them in everything that is not plainly contrary to the will of God, or to their own welfare.[144]

171. **What follows from what we have said here?**

It follows clearly: 1) First, that such children as disobey, abuse, or despise their parents, either in thought, word, or deed, do sin grievously; and, for certain, are commonly unfortunate in this life, and eternally miserable in the next. 2) They also sin grievously, who abuse or despise their lawful masters or superiors, whether ecclesiastical or civil. 3) Those parents and superiors sin greatly, who rule not their children and family in the fear and love of God; or treat their children, or inferiors, outrageously, or with exceeding contempt.[145] 4) Man and wife sin greatly, if they provoke and scold each other, or entertain anger and hatred.[146]

---

[142] Cf. Gn 2:23-24; Mk 10:8; Eph 5:25, 28, 30-31
[143] Cf. Eph 5:22-24
[144] Cf. Eph 6:5-9; Col 3:22-23; 4:1
[145] Cf. Eph 6:4; Col 3:21
[146] Cf. Gal 5:15

LESSON 6

The Fifth Commandment
Thou shalt not kill.

172. **What is required in the fifth commandment?**

Not to murder any one; not to covet or wish the death of any person; not to beat any man; not to give or receive a challenge; not to refuse to ask forgiveness of him whom you have affronted; nor to refuse to pardon him who either dishonored, abused, or slandered you.[147]

173. **Why are we obliged to forgive those that abuse or defame us?**

Because our Savior Jesus Christ commands it; and that he himself practiced the same which he orders us to do.[148]

174. **Do not Catholics hold that it is lawful for them to murder heretics?**

Not at all; on the contrary, we know that we are obliged to help them in their necessity, and to wish them all the good we wish ourselves, even when they would oppress and persecute us; for they are always our neighbor.[149]

Moreover, as the Church prays for their conversion, and the conversion of all those who are astray; so ought we, after the example of all the saints, and of our Savior himself, to have great compassion of them, and to pray heartily to God, that he may mercifully enlighten and bring them all to the knowledge of the truth, in order that we all may make one fold under one shepherd.[150]

175. **What else is required in this commandment?**

1) First, to bear neither hatred nor grudge to anyone. 2) To sow no discord nor strife amongst any persons whatsoever. 3) Neither to rejoice at the death of any one, nor grieve for his being alive. 4) Neither to abuse nor

---

[147] Cf. Mt 5:39; Col 3:15; 1 Thes 5:15; 1 Pt 3:9
[148] Cf. Mt 5:44; 18:22, 35; 1 Pt 2:21-23
[149] Cf. Mt 5:44
[150] Cf. Lk 23:34; 1 Tm 2; Mass-Book on Good Friday

defame any one either in his presence or absence. 5) Not to kill the soul of any neighbor, by provoking him to mortal sin. 6) To permit no one to commit a mortal sin, while you can easily hinder it; especially if he be under your command. 7) Not to assist, nor protect, nor harbor incendiaries, murderers, or other malefactors. In short, neither to do, nor wish any evil to another in thought, word, or deed.[151]

176. **What good doth this commandment oblige us to?**

It obliges us to be meek and charitable to all; to render good for evil; and to pray for our persecutors, as Christ commanded us.[152]

LESSON 7

The Sixth and Ninth Commandments
Thou shalt not commit adultery. Thou shalt
not covet thy neighbor's wife.

177. **What do the sixth and ninth commandments forbid us?**

They forbid a man to have any carnal communication with any other woman than his own wife; and a woman with any other man than her own husband; and even to covet or desire any such sinful commerce.[153]

178. **Are immodest looks or unchaste kisses a breach of this commandment?**

They are, as also unchaste touches of ourselves or others, willful pollution, lewd discourses, filthy songs, reading of love-books, and every other impudent or shameless action.[154]

---

151 Cf. Lk 6:27–28, 31ff; 1 Thes 5:15; Rom 1:32
152 Cf. Rom 12:14; 1 Pt 3:8-9; Mt 5:44
153 Cf. Mt 5:28; 1 Cor 7:4
154 Cf. Col 3:5; 1 Thes 4:4

179. **Are unchaste thoughts, without any design of coming to action, a breach of this commandment?**

Yes, if entertained with delight and pleasure.[155]

180. **Is it a more grievous offence to sin with a person in sacred orders, or with a religious man or woman, than with another?**

Yes, it is much more grievous and more abominable; it is likewise a greater offence to sin with a kinsman or kinswoman, or with a married man or woman, than with others.

181. **What is required of man and wife in these commandments?**

Fidelity and compliance in regard to one another, as they promised at their marriage.

182. **How is this abominable sin of the flesh to be avoided?**

The best means for avoiding it is to beware of bad company, and the occasion of sin; to shun intemperance, choice meat and drink, and especially idleness; to subdue the lust and inclinations of the flesh by fasting and praying; to confess often, and communicate with much devotion.[156]

LESSON 8

Of the Seventh and Tenth Commandments
Thou shalt not steal. Thou shalt not covet thy neighbor's goods.

183. **What is forbidden in these two commandments?**

We are forbidden to take, receive, retain, or even desire, either privately or openly, anything belonging to our neighbor, without his consent.

---

[155] Cf. Mt 23:26; Mk 7:21-22; 2 Cor 7:1
[156] Cf. Ecclus 33:29; Gal 5:24; Eph 5:18

184. **How else are these commandments broken?**

They are broken: 1) First, by everyone who is unwilling to pay his debts, or his servant's wages, when it is in his power.[157] 2) By him who retains lost goods, without making an inquiry or search after the owner.[158] 3) By him who cheats in bargaining; deceives by false weights or measures; by playing with set cards; by making signs to his partner; by cogged or false dice; or through the ignorance of the gamester.[159] 4) By him who hinders another by drifts or foul practices, of anything he could lawfully come by.[160] 5) By him who buys or receives anything, which could not be well supposed to belong to the person that presents it.[161] 6) By the negligent servant and journeyman, who spends the time idly, or doth not take care of the things that are entrusted to him. 7) By children, who steal anything from their parents, to spend it foolishly. 8) By parents, when they spend extravagantly the things which they are obliged to spare for their children. 9) And lastly, by him who gives assistance, counsel, or consent, to the committing of any of the aforesaid sins, although the intended evil should never ensue.

185. **Is usury a breach of these commandments?**

Without doubt it is.

186. **What is usury?**

It is a loan of money, corn, butter, meal, and such like, given principally in view of requiring or receiving some hire, or worldly profit in virtue thereof.

187. **How shall a person know that it is not chiefly in view of some worldly advantage he gives a loan?**

If he demands nothing, and be disposed or ready to lend, although he should receive no worldly profit thereby, it is certain, that worldly interest is not his principal view.

---

[157] Cf. Rom 13:8; Jas 5:4
[158] Cf. Ex 23:4; Dt 22
[159] Cf. Prv 11:1; 1 Thes 4:6
[160] Cf. 1 Thes 4:6
[161] Cf. Eph 5:11

188. **Is it not permitted in this case, to follow the law and custom of the country wherein we live?**

No, if they be contrary to the law of God; for neither king nor country upon earth has power to give us leave to transgress the commandments of God.[162]

189. **Has God commanded us not to give a loan to our neighbor, principally in view of getting some earthly profit thereby?**

He has certainly, in many places of scripture, especially in the gospel; and it is therefore, the holy fathers, popes, councils, and the generality of divines, do condemn both usury and usurers.[163]

190. **Is it forbidden us to receive or demand any interest upon any account whatsoever?**

It is not forbidden us either to receive or sue for an equal value of the profit which we certainly lose, or for reparation of the damage we suffered by giving a loan, and that according to the decision of a wise person, provided we signified this loss or damage to the person we gave the loan to before he received it, and that it was not in our power to avoid said loss.

191. **For what end ought we to give a loan?**

To show charity, friendship, or kindness towards our neighbor; for he is an usurer, that has any other principal view, or that demands anything, save only, as we said above, in case of damage and loss of gain, which often happens among merchants.[164]

---

[162] Cf. Acts 4:19

[163] Cf. Ps 14:5.; Ez 18:8, 13, 17; Lk 6:35; Cyprian, *Treatise 12*, Bk. 3, Ch. 48; Gregory of Nyssa, *Homily 4 on Ecclesiastes*; Chrysostom, *Homily 5 on Matthew*, n. 9; Ambrose, *Book on Tobias*, Ch. 4-6, 13-15; Jerome, *Commentary on Ch. 18 of Ezechiel*; Augustine, *Exposition on Psalm 36*, n. 5; *Summa Theologiae*, II-II, q. 78, a. 1, c.; Fifth Lateran Council, Session 10; Alexander III, *On the Third Lateran Council*, "Super eo de usur."; Urban III, Epistle *Consuluit nos*; Sixtus V, Bull *Detestabilis*; Alex. VII, Decret. 10 Martii, 1666; Innocent XI, Decret. 2 Martii, 1679; Third Lateran Council, Can. 25; Second Council of Lyons, Const. 26-27; Council of Vienne, Dec. 29; First Synod of Milan under Charles Borromeo

[164] Cf. Decret. Innocent XI, 2 Martii, 1679

192. **Is there not usury sometimes committed in bargains and contracts?**

Yes, and often too; for it is usury to sell anything dearer than it is actually worth, upon the sole account of giving credit or time for the payment of the price thereof.

193. **How shall one know that his bargain or contract is not sinful?**

Let him ask advice of a pious and knowing man; and consider, that it doth not avail him to gain the whole world, and lose his own soul.[165]

194. **Doth the person sin who pays the interest of a loan?**

No, if he was under a necessity of borrowing; but if he was not, he sinned for tempting his neighbor, by furnishing him an occasion of sinning.

195. **What are the obligations of usurers, and of such as break the seventh commandment?**

They are obliged not only to do penance for the sin they have committed, but also to restore whatsoever they got unjustly, and to repair exactly what hurt and damage soever they have done their neighbor in his reputation or in his goods.[166]

196. **What if they should not make restitution of their neighbor's goods?**

Their children, or heirs, are obliged to do it, in proportion of what they gain by the injustice of their parents and relations.

197. **What if it should not be in our power to give full satisfaction to our neighbor?**

Let us make restitution according to our ability, and resolve to give full satisfaction as soon as it shall be in our power.[167]

198. **To whom ought this satisfaction to be made?**

To the person that suffered the hurt or damage, or to his heirs; if his heirs

---

[165] Cf. Mt 16:26
[166] Cf. Rom 13:7
[167] Cf. 2 Cor 8:12

are not to be found, let the person liable to restitution, consult his spiritual superior.

LESSON 9

The Eighth Commandment
Thou shalt not bear false witness.

199. What is forbidden in this commandment?

To do any injustice to our neighbor, by witnessing what is false, in matter of judgment or law, or in any matter of debate, which tends to his prejudice.

200. Who breaks this commandment in matter of judgment or strife?

He that falsely accuseth another; he that affirms what he knows to be false; he that defends an unjust cause, or that declares not the truth, when he is required to discover it.[168]

201. Who else sins in judgment?

The judges or arbitrators who judge partially, or acquit the guilty and condemn the innocent.

202. How is this commandment broken otherwise than in judgment or in strife?

By revealing without necessity the secret failings of another;[169] by reviling, by slandering, by detracting, or by cursing him;[170] likewise by breaking our promise without a lawful cause; by opening another man's letters,[171] or by thinking ill of him, construing his words or actions in the worst sense, when they could bear a good meaning.[172]

---

[168] Cf. Prv 21:28
[169] Cf. Prv 11:13
[170] Cf. Prv 12:12; Jn 8:44
[171] Cf. Col 3:9
[172] Cf. Mt 7:1

203. **Is lying a breach of this commandment?**

It is certainly.

204. **What is a lie?**

It is to say or signify anything contrary to the knowledge of our conscience, with a design of deceiving another.

205. **Can a lie be lawfully told for a good end?**

It cannot; for it is a sin to tell a lie, let the motive be what it will; because it is contrary to the truth, contrary to God; for the truth is God, and God is the truth.[173]

206. **But, if by words only, I deceive another, in order to do him service, can it possibly be a sin?**

It is not lawful to do evil things, that good may come of them; but every lie is an evil, because it is against the truth.[174]

207. **What is detraction?**

Every discourse, even one only word, or the very carnage that lessens the reputation or esteem of our neighbor.

208. **Is detraction a grievous sin?**

Yes, the Holy Ghost affirms, that a detractor or back biter is no better than a serpent that bites in the dark.[175]

209. **Do they sin who listen to detractors?**

Without doubt, if they willfully and gladly listen to them.[176]

210. **How is a person to behave himself in the company of detractors?**

He ought to hinder the detraction as much as he can, by silencing those

---

[173] Cf. Jn 8:44; 14:16
[174] Cf. Rom 3:8
[175] Cf. Eccles 10:11
[176] Cf. Eph 5:11

who run down their neighbor, if he has a superiority or power over them, by waving the discourse decently; by showing his dislike by his silence and countenance; or lastly, to quit entirely the backbiting company.

211. **Is it permitted on any account to speak ill of another?**

It is lawful, and even sometimes necessary to speak of our neighbor's failing: 1) First, if the sin be certain and public, it can be spoken of, provided it be not with an evil intention, but for some good end, and through some necessity. 2) It can, and ought to be revealed discreetly and decently to the person that can correct the sinner, or hinder him from sinning. 3) It is also permitted and necessary to put a person on his guard against the evil or hurt which hath been designed, and is preparing against him; but let the informer beware of a desire of revenge, of a view of interest, and every other evil intention.

212. **Is flattery a breach of this commandment?**

It is certainly.

213. **What is flattery?**

It is false or excessive praise.

214. **Why do you say that flattery is a sin?**

Because it is commonly contrary to truth, and is apt to nourish and maintain the pride, vainglory, and other failings of the person excessively praised.[177]

---

[177] Cf. Prv 29:5; Eccles 7:6

Chapter 3

LESSON 10

Of the Commandments of the Church

215. **Are we, moreover, obliged to keep the commandments of the Church, together with the commandments of God?**

We are; because God commands us, under pain of damnation, to obey our holy mother, the Church: for our Savior enjoins us to look on every man who heareth not the Church, "as a heathen and a publican."[178]

216. **Is it not enough for us, in order to obtain eternal life, to keep the commandments of God?**

It is certainly; but we are not fully obedient to God, unless we obey the Church: for, according to the word of God, whosoever despiseth the Church, despiseth God himself.[179]

217. **Why did the Church give us commandments?**

In order to fulfil the commandments of God with greater readiness, and more ease.

218. **Say the commandments of the Church.**

1. To keep certain appointed days holy.
2. To observe the commanded days of fast.
3. To eat no flesh meat on Fridays, Saturdays, or other days of abstinence.
4. To confess at least once a year.
5. To receive the Blessed Sacrament of the Eucharist at Easter, or thereabouts.

---

[178] Mt 18:17
[179] Cf. Lk 10:16

6. Not to marry with solemnity, from the beginning of Advent until Epiphany, nor from the beginning of Lent until after Low Sunday.

219. What doth the Church order us in the first commandment?

We have already spoken of what the Church requires in this commandment, when we explained the third commandment of God: for it doth not appear that the Church makes any distinction between the sanctifying of Sunday and of other holy days.

220. What are we commanded in the second precept, to wit, *To observe the commanded days of fast?*

We are commanded to abstain from certain meats, and to eat but one meal in the four-and-twenty hours, during Lent, and on the Ember days and vigils.

221. What meats are we obliged to abstain from?

From eggs and the flesh of the birds of the air, and of the beasts of the earth: unless the spiritual superiors give leave to eat eggs, etc.

222. Is it lawful to abstain thus from certain meats rather than others?

Yes; for, if it be at all lawful to fast and mortify the flesh, with the vices and lusts thereof, which surely no Christian will dare deny, whereas it is so frequently and clearly mentioned in scripture, it must be very lawful and laudable to abstain from such meats as nourish it most, and its disorderly passions.[180]

223. Doth not the apostle Saint Paul say, that the distinction of meats is the doctrine of devils?[181]

Yes; and so do we call it a doctrine of devils, in the sense of the Manichees and other heretics, who taught that certain meats were created by the devil, and consequently bad in themselves. But the meats we abstain from we

---

[180] Cf. 1 Kgs 31:13; 1 Par 10:12; Ps 108:24; Mt 17:20; Acts 13:2-3; 2 Cor 11:27
[181] Cf. 1 Tm 4:1-5

know to be from God, and good in themselves; we eat them with thanksgiving the day before and the day after the fast; we take them to be the most substantial and nourishing food; for which reason alone we abstain from them, in order to subdue the lusts of the flesh, or to do penance for our sins: and neither this great apostle, nor any one that understands and follows him, ever said, that this laudable and pious distinction is the doctrine of devils; it being manifest, that everyone can, for the good of his soul or body, lawfully abstain from what meat he pleases; nay, the apostle himself saith: "I shall never eat flesh, lest I should scandalize my brother."[182]

224. **How do you prove that it is against those heretics the apostle speaks?**

First, it is proved from the same place, where he saith, that "God created (all meats) to be received with thanksgiving"; and that "every creature of God is good":[183] we say the same thing, and none but heretics ever said the contrary.

Secondly, if all distinction of meats were unlawful, the great Saint John the Baptist had been guilty of the doctrine of devils; for he drank "neither wine nor strong drink":[184] he lived in the wilderness upon "locusts and wild honey";[185] and "came," says our Savior, "neither eating nor drinking."[186]

The prophet Daniel had been guilty; for he saith of himself: "Flesh and wine entered not into my mouth…for three weeks."[187]

The Rechabites and their posterity had been guilty; for by their father's command they abstained always from wine; yet they are highly commended by God, and rewarded for it.[188]

The apostles themselves, and the elders of the Church have been very guilty; for they have not only abstained, but have also, for good reasons, commanded the primitive Christians to abstain from meats offered to idols,

---

[182] 1 Cor 8:13
[183] 1 Tm 4:3, 4
[184] Lk 1:15
[185] Mt 3:4
[186] Mt 11:18
[187] Dn 10:3
[188] Cf. Jer 35

from blood, and from things strangled, yet they were guided herein by the Holy Ghost.[189]

225. **But doth not the apostle St. Paul say: "Eat all that is sold at the market, asking no question for conscience sake"?[190]**

Yes; for although it was prohibited to eat meats offered to idols, yet the apostle would not have the Christians to be so scrupulous as to ask whether this ox or this calf had been sacrificed to idols before it was carried to the market, it being certain, that the very meat offered to idols was created by God, and good in itself;[191] still he says, in the same place, that if anybody tells the Christian that the meat was offered to idols, he ought, for conscience sake, not to eat it;[192] that it was neither expedient nor edifying,[193] and that no offence should be given to either the Jews or the Gentiles, or the Church of God.[194] The apostle then is far from opposing the commandments of the Church; and so far is he from it, that he orders us to obey our prelates, and to be subject to them; for they watch as being to render an account of our souls.[195]

226. **What say you to this passage of the apostle: "Let no man judge you in meat, or drink, or in respect of a holy day or of the new moon, or of the sabbaths"?[196]**

I say that the words new moon and sabbath do manifestly show, that he speaks of a Judaical distinction of clean and unclean meats, conformable to God's commandment in the old law, which at that time was quite abolished, excepting still, as above, blood and strangled meat, though sold at

---

189 Cf. Acts 15:28-29
190 1 Cor 10:25
191 Cf. 1 Cor 10:26
192 Cf. 1 Cor 10:28
193 Cf. 1 Cor 10:22-23
194 Cf. 1 Cor 10:32
195 Cf. Heb 13:17
196 Col 2:16

the market; for this is not contrary to that which St. Paul said: eat all that is sold at the market.[197]

227. Doth not our Savior himself say, that "what entereth into the mouth, doth not defile a man"?[198]

Yes; those indeed are his words, but no way to the purpose here; and none surely will urge this text, which may seem to be against fasting in general, except libertines and impious persons, who give full scope to their evil inclinations, and would fain discredit all restraining and mortification of the flesh; who impose upon ignorant and weak people, and manifestly profane the word of God, in pretending to prove, that Christ declared fasting to be an idle and useless action; when our Savior commends St. John the Baptist's rigorous abstinence and other austerities,[199] and fasted himself forty days and forty nights for our instruction; when also he tells us, that certain devils (or strong passions) can be overcome by "nothing but by prayer and fasting";[200] and that the children, or companions of the bridegroom, that is, his own disciples, or followers, should fast when he would be gone from them,[201] which they undoubtedly did: witness what the apostle St. Paul, writing to the Corinthians, sayeth of himself and the preachers of the gospel.[202] In a word, the body of the scripture, the practice of the servants of God, nay, the liturgy or *Common Prayer Book* of the modern Church of England, will rise in judgment against these loose livers, "whose God is their belly, and whose end is perdition."[203]

228. What then is the meaning of Christ's words?

The Scribes and Pharisees, a set of carping hypocrites, were very careful to wash their hands, their dishes, and cups, before they eat or drank, lest they should be defiled, although they were inwardly full of uncleanness

[197] Cf. 1 Cor 10:25
[198] Mt 15:11
[199] Cf. Mt 11:11, 18
[200] Mk 9:28
[201] Cf. Lk 5:35
[202] Cf. 2 Cor 6:5; 11:27
[203] Phil 3:19

and iniquity: they saw our Savior's disciples eat bread without washing their hands, and boldly reproached him for it; he answered, saying: "What entereth into the mouth doth not defile a man, but what proceedeth out of the mouth (and cometh from the heart[204]) defileth a man";[205] "for from the heart proceed evil thoughts, murders, adultery, fornication, thefts, false witness," etc. "These are the things that defile a man; but to eat with unwashed hands defileth not a man."[206]

Now, it is plain, that our Savior says nothing here against fasting, which was purely instituted either to do penance, or to curb those inordinate passions which defile the soul; for after Christ had spoken the foresaid words, eating of hogs' flesh would have defiled the souls of the apostles and of the whole Jewish nation; the primitive Christians should have been denied by eating "blood or things strangled";[207] and, although all meats be clean in themselves, yet to eat meat that is forbidden, doth defile the soul, as the apple defiled Adam's soul, and as taking of drink to excess defiles the drunkard.

The meaning then of our Savior's words, and the wholesome instruction we are to draw from them, is, that if we do not seriously endeavor to fulfil the weightier points of the law, such as to bridle our evil desires, to purify our souls, and to love our neighbor, etc., it is in vain for us to purify our bodies, or even to observe either fast or feast: our fasting will be an abomination before the Lord,[208] and may be well compared to the fast of devils, who neither eat nor drink; but although fasting from sin be at all times the great and indispensable fast, Christ says: We ought to do the weightier matters of the law, and not to leave the rest undone;[209] for "he who is faithful in that which is least, is also faithful in a greater thing; and he who is unjust in a little thing is also unjust in a greater thing."[210]

---

[204] Cf. Mt 15:18
[205] Mt 15:11
[206] Mt 15:19, 20
[207] Acts 15:29
[208] Cf. Is 1:11; 58:3ff; Zac 7:5
[209] Cf. Mt 23:23
[210] Lk 16:10

229. **Now, although I clearly see that it is both lawful and laudable to fast, and even to abstain from certain meats, yet I do not well see that the Church can command us to fast.**

The Jewish church often ordained fasts;[211] the people of Nineveh ordered a universal fast;[212] the modern Churches of England and Holland do sometimes proclaim and ordain a general fast; it is therefore manifest, that the Catholic Church, to which Christ said, "Whatsoever you shall bind on earth, shall be bound in heaven,"[213] can more warrantably oblige us to fast after the example of the Council of Jerusalem, which commanded the primitive Christians to abstain from blood and strangled meat.

230. **Who are exempted from the fast?**

Sick people, weakly old persons, young people not past one-and-twenty years, women big with child, and people that labor hard.

231. **At what hour is the one meal to be made?**

About noon, or any hour after it.

232. **Is drinking a breach of fast?**

It is the general opinion, that it is no breach of fast to take a little drink for quenching a great thirst, for strengthening in weakness, or for some other real necessity; yet it is not to be supposed that it is permitted to sit or stand tippling, through an inordinate desire of drinking, or for the sake of company, for pastime or worldly affairs.

233. **Why do you think that drinking, without a real necessity, is not permitted?**

Because strong drink excites and inflames the inordinate desires of the flesh more than meat; and likewise because the Church instituted the fast, in order we should subdue our disorderly passions, do penance, and make satisfaction for our sins, by suffering hunger and thirst. Moreover, tippling, without any necessity, is contrary to temperance.

---

[211] Cf. 1 Esd 8:21; 2 Par 20:3; Jer 36:9; Jl 1:14
[212] Cf. Jon 3:5
[213] Mt 18:18

234. Is it permitted to take any nourishment but the one meal?

Yes, it is allowed to take a moderate collation at night, or in the evening of a long day; but it is not permitted to eat flesh, fish, eggs, or any milk-meats at this collation, without the spiritual superior's leave, or a custom sufficiently authorized.

235. Say the third commandment of the Church.

To keep the commanded days of abstinence.

236. Why did the Church forbid the eating of flesh meat on Fridays and Saturdays?

In order, no week might be free from the works of penance; and likewise to put us in mind of the death of our Savior on Friday, and of his being in the grave on Saturday.

237. Say the fourth commandment of the Church.

To confess our sins at least once a year.

238. What doth this commandment oblige us to?

To confess our sins once a year, at least.

239. To whom ought we make this yearly confession?

To our own priest, or to any other priest that has power and permission to hear this confession.[214]

240. Who is our own priest?

Our bishop or parish priest; in a word, our pastor, howsoever he be styled; for it is our pastor that is charged by God and the Church, to watch carefully over his flock, to lead them to eternal life, and to feed them diligently in the way to that life, with the word of God and the sacraments.[215]

---

[214] Cf. Fifth Lateran Council, Session 11; Fourth Lateran Council, Const. 21; Martin IV, Bull *Ad Fructus Uberes*; Bened. XI, *Extrav. Inter cunctos*

[215] Cf. Jer 3:15; Jn 10:3ff

241. **What obligation do we lie under to our proper priest or pastor?**

We are obliged to show him submission and obedience, to hear often his Mass and instructions, and to follow his counsel earnestly.[216]

242. **At what age are we obliged to go to confession?**

When we are come to the knowledge of good and evil, and fall into sin.

243. **Is it certain, we are not obliged to go to confession but once a year?**

The Church obliges us to no more: nevertheless, the sinner who would defer his welfare from day to day, and from week to week, is a great fool, void of reason and conscience, seeing it depends of himself, with the grace of God, to repent and confess his sins. Moreover, it is to be feared, and it commonly happens, that the senseless people, who confess their sins but once or twice a year, do make a bad confession.[217]

244. **Say the fifth commandment of the Church.**

To receive the Blessed Sacrament at Easter, or thereabouts.

245. **What doth this commandment oblige us to?**

It obliges us to receive the Blessed Sacrament devoutly from our parish priest, or from our pastor, whosoever he be, at the time of Easter.[218]

246. **At what age ought we to receive Christ's holy body?**

When we come to sense and understanding; but it is requisite to learn well beforehand, the catechism or Christian doctrine.

247. **What punishment doth the Church inflict on the person who fulfils not this commandment, and that which we spoke of last?**

She orders he should be banished from the communion of the faithful, and deprived of Christian burial. Yet this excommunication doth not fall upon

---

[216] Cf. Heb 13:17
[217] Cf. Ecclus 5:8-9; Lk 12:40
[218] Cf. Fourth Lateran Council, Const. 21

him whom the pastor puts off for a time, in order he should do penance, and duly prepare himself.

248. **Are we obliged to communicate but once a year only?**
The Church obligeth us to no more; yet she exhorts us to receive often our Savior's blessed body with the necessary dispositions.[219]

249. **Why doth the Church exhort us to receive often this Blessed Sacrament?**
Because great fruit is reaped from this heavenly nourishment; and that it is to be feared that he who makes use of the food of eternal life but once or twice a year, makes no great account of his own salvation.[220]

250. **What is forbidden in the sixth commandment?**
The celebration of marriage during Advent and Lent.

251. **Why did the Church forbid the celebration of marriage in the time of Advent and Lent?**
Because she appointed these times for prayer and penance.

252. **Did not the Church command us to pay tithes?**
She did certainly; but we cannot, at this time, pay them to our own clergy; nevertheless we are obliged to maintain and support our clergy by some other means: for our Savior commandeth us to give a livelihood to those who serve at the altar, and preach the gospel.[221]

253. **Are we obliged to fulfil any other commandments?**
Yes; we are commanded to fulfil the particular obligations of our trade or calling.[222]

---

[219] Cf. 1 Cor 11:28
[220] Cf. Mt 11:28
[221] Cf. Lk 10:7; 1 Cor 9:13-14; 1 Tm 5:17-18
[222] Cf. Col 4:17; 1 Thes 4:11

254. **Are we obliged to know the obligations of our trade or calling?**

Yes certainly: for ignorance in this point is very seldom excusable.[223]

255. **Did not our Savior give us, besides commandments, certain counsels, called evangelical?**

Yes; he gave us three principal counsels.

1. Voluntary poverty; that is, to forsake all worldly things to follow Christ.[224]

2. Perpetual continence, or an inviolable chastity until death; that is, renouncing entirely the pleasures and allurements of the flesh.[225]

3. Voluntary obedience to the will of another, in all that is not sin; that so we may the more perfectly deny our own will and inclinations.[226]

Chapter 4

LESSON 11

Of Sin

256. **What is sin?**

It is a disobedience to the commandments of God, of the Church, or of our superiors.

257. **Is it necessary to avoid sin above all things?**

Yes; for there is no evil so great as sin.

---

[223] Cf. Lk 19:44
[224] Cf. Mt 19:21
[225] Cf. Mt 19:12; 1 Cor 7:38
[226] Cf. Lk 2:51; Heb 13:17

258. Why so?

Because it is sin alone that makes us enemies to God, and damns us eternally.[227]

259. How many kinds of sin are there?

There are two, to wit, original, and actual.

260. What is original sin?

It is a sin in which we are all born, through the disobedience of our first father, Adam.[228]

261. Which are the evils we suffer by it?

Unavoidable death, much labor and sickness, an inclination and facility to do evil, a slackness and difficulty to do good works; and lastly, eternal damnation, unless we be cleansed by baptism.[229]

262. What is actual sin?

It is a sin we commit ourselves, such as lying, stealing, etc.

263. How many ways is actual sin committed?

Four ways: by thought, word, deed, and omission.

264. Which are the most dangerous sins?

The sins of omission: by reason they are more hidden, and less taken notice of than other sins.

265. What is it you call a sin of omission?

It is the sin we commit in neglecting our duty, such as a sin of a father and mother, who do not diligently instruct and correct their children and

[227] Cf. Jer 2:19; Jn 3:6, 8
[228] Cf. Rom 5:12; Eph 2:3
[229] Cf. Jn 3:5

family; who do not oblige them to morning and evening prayers, to hear Mass on holy days, to learn punctually the Christian doctrine.[230]

266. **Give us another example of that kind.**

Those children sin grievously, who act not according to the will of their parents, or do not assist them in their distress or old age.[231] Servants and laborers do likewise sin, when they do not diligently work for their wages, or hire.[232]

LESSON 12

Of Mortal and Venial Sin, and of the Means to Avoid Them

267. **How many kinds of actual sin are there?**

Two; mortal and venial.

268. **What is mortal sin?**

It is a sin whereby we lose the grace of God, and make ourselves liable to eternal damnation.[233]

269. **Why is it called mortal sin?**

Because it kills the soul.

270. **How can that be, whereas the soul is immortal?**

Because it is by sin, the soul loses the grace of God, which is its spiritual life.[234]

---

[230] Cf. 1 Tm 5:5
[231] Cf. Prv 19:26; Ecclus 3:14-18; Eph 6:1-2
[232] Cf. Eph 6:5-7
[233] Cf. Jas 1:15
[234] Cf. Rom 6:21, 23

271. Can a person be damned for one only mortal sin?

He can certainly, and the devils have been damned for one only bad thought.

272. What is venial sin?

It is a light sin, whereby the grace of God is not lost; but it lessens his love in our hearts.[235]

273. Ought we to avoid venial sin?

We ought certainly; because it weakens the will, and inclines it to mortal sin; and likewise because it diminishes the grace of God, and makes us liable to grievous torments, which we must suffer in purgatory, if we do not make satisfaction in this life.[236]

274. How many capital mortal sins are there?

Seven, to wit: pride, covetousness, luxury, envy, gluttony, anger, and sloth.

275. Why are they called capital mortal sins?

Because they are the source and root of all other sins.

Of Pride

276. What is pride?

It is an excessive love of one's self, and an immoderate desire of being above others.

277. Is pride a great sin?

There is no sin more ancient, more grievous or more dangerous; for it is the sin of the fallen angels, and of the first man;[237] it is the sin, which we

---

[235] Cf. Prv 24:16; Mt 12:36
[236] Cf. Ecclus 19:1; Apoc 21:27
[237] Cf. Ecclus 10:7, 15; 1 Pt 5:5

have the greatest difficulty to preserve ourselves from,[238] and the last we overcome.[239]

278. **How many kinds of pride?**
There are four: 1) First, to boast of, or glory in, any gift of body or mind, we have; whether by thought, word, or deed. 2) To conceit that we deserve any favor from God, or that he is any way indebted to us. 3) To desire that others would believe that we are more virtuous or accomplished than we really are. 4) To despise or undervalue any person.

279. **Which are the sins that proceed chiefly from pride?**
Although pride be the source of all sins, yet, there are certain sins which immediately spring from it; such as: vainglory, disobedience, desire of revenge, praising of oneself without great necessity; hypocrisy, which is an abominable sin in the sight of God; contention, scolding, defaming; and all variances or strifes begun, or maintained without necessity, truth, or charity; obstinacy, or too great a tie to one's own opinion or counsel, without much ground; haughtiness, pomp, ambition.

280. **What is the remedy against pride?**
Humility or submissiveness.[240]

281. **What is humility?**
It is a virtue, which inclines us to conceive a mean opinion of ourselves; to require neither esteem nor respect of others; to despise no person; and to suffer contempt and disrespect patiently and calmly.[241]

---

[238] Cf. Is 14:12-15; Gn 3:5
[239] Cf. Augustine, *Exposition on Psalm 18*
[240] Cf. Nm 11:20
[241] Cf. Gal 6:3; 1 Cor 4:7; Prv 14:21; 17:5; Lk 21:19

282. Is humility necessary?

It is so necessary, that no one can be saved without it, according to the express words of our Savior Jesus Christ himself.[242]

Of Covetousness

283. What is covetousness?

It is an immoderate love of the things of this life.

284. When is the love of worldly things immoderate?

When the heart of man is tied to them.[243]

285. How can it be known that the heart is tied to the world?

It is known by one of these four signs: 1) First, when a person is overjoyed for possessing, or over-sad for losing, any earthly thing.[244] 2) When he acquires, or keeps anything unjustly.[245] 3) When he seeks greedily after worldly goods, or retains them with too great an affection.[246] 4) When he is not bountiful to the poor, according to his ability.[247]

286. How can one know that his heart is not tied to the world?

By doing everything that is contrary to the signs we now spoke of.

287. If that be true, there are but few, who are not covetous.

There are but very few; for everyone is covetous, that is tied to his share of this world, although he came lawfully by it.[248]

---

[242] Cf. Lk 18:17
[243] Cf. Ps 61:6
[244] Cf. Ps 51:9; 2 Cor 7:10
[245] Cf. Is 33:1; Hb 2:6-7
[246] Cf. 1 Cor 7:30-31; 1 Tm 6:9-18
[247] Cf. Lk 11:41
[248] Cf. Jer 8:10; Phil 2:21

288. Can the poor be covetous?

The poorest person is covetous, if he loves the riches he has not; or if he thinks it is a misfortune for him to be poor, and is impatient in poverty.[249]

289. Is covetousness a grievous sin?

It is certainly; for the Holy Ghost sayeth, that it is the "root of all evil";[250] and particularly of breach of trust, lies, deceit, perjuries, violence, trouble of mind, hard-heartedness in regard of the poor.[251]

290. What remedy is there against covetousness?

Liberality and prayer.

291. What is liberality?

It is a virtue, which weans our hearts from earthly things, and inclines us to share our goods freely, not with the rich and persons in easy circumstances, but with the poor.[252]

292. How is prayer a remedy against covetousness?

Inasmuch as grace and the virtue of liberality are obtained from God by the means of fervent prayer.[253]

293. Is it a good prayer to think of death?

It is a very good prayer, if we think seriously and often of it: death will put us in mind, that we must part with all earthly things. "We brought nothing into this world, and doubtless we can carry nothing out of it."[254]

---

[249] Cf. Mt 13:22
[250] 1 Tm 6:10
[251] Cf. Eph 5:3, 5; Ecclus 29:13ff
[252] Cf. Ps 40:2; Lk 11:41; Is 58:7
[253] Cf. Jas 1:5-6
[254] 1 Tm 6:7-8; Cf. Jb 1:21

Of Luxury

294. What is luxury?

It is a desire of the sin of the flesh, an abominable sin, which ought not to be so much as named among Christians.[255]

295. When is it that a person is guilty of this odious sin?

We spoke of it at large, in explaining the sixth and ninth commandments; wherefore it is sufficient to say now, that a person is guilty of it, not only when he commits the fact, but likewise, when he willfully, with delight or pleasure, hearkens to, looks upon, or thinks of anything whatsoever, which any way moves him to this detestable sin.[256]

296. By what virtue is luxury overcome?

By chastity.[257]

297. What is chastity?

It is a purity of body and mind, an angelical virtue, which God bestows upon people of prayer, upon the obedient and humble.[258]

Of Gluttony

298. What is gluttony?

It is an immoderate desire of either meat or drink.

299. When does a person fall into gluttony?

1) First, when he eats or drinks too much.[259] 2) When he is greedy.[260] 3) When his meat and drink cost him too much, and that he will not be

---

[255] Cf. Eph 5:3
[256] Cf. Jb 31:1; Eph 5:4-5
[257] Cf. Gal 5:23-24
[258] Cf. 2 Cor 7:1; Ws 8:21; Jas 4:6
[259] Cf. Ez 16:49
[260] Cf. Gn 25:33-34; Ecclus 37:32

satisfied, without choice meat and drink.[261] 4) When an excess of meat or drink makes him sick.

300. **Which is the worst and most destructive kind of gluttony?**
Drunkenness.[262]

301. **What is drunkenness?**
It is to tipple or drink so as to lose any share of our reason, or senses.

302. **Is gluttony a grievous sin?**
It is; for the Holy Ghost says, that the god of gluttons is their belly, and that they are accursed by God.[263]

303. **How is gluttony overcome?**
By temperance.[264]

304. **What is temperance?**
It is a virtue which bridles the immoderate desire of meat and drink, and likewise all other disorderly passions.[265]

Of Envy

305. **What is envy?**
It is a sadness or repining at the worldly or spiritual good of our neighbor, or a rejoicing at his damage or distress.

306. **Whence does envy proceed?**
It ordinarily proceeds from pride; for the reason why we are sorry for our neighbor's welfare, or rejoice at his misfortune, is, because we think that

---

[261] Cf. Nm 11:5; Prv 21:17
[262] Cf. Prv 23:21, 30-32
[263] Cf. Phil 3:19
[264] Cf. 1 Thes 5:6-8
[265] Cf. Rom 12:3

the welfare and good luck of our neighbor lessen our own credit; and that his misery and misfortune increase it.[266]

307. Why are we obliged to bear great hatred against this sin?

Because it is it that makes us resemble the devils or evil spirits, who continually go about to hurt us; for it is a kind of death to them, that man is more fortunate and happier than themselves.[267]

308. By what virtue is envy overcome?

By charity or the love of our neighbor.

309. Wherein doth this charity consist?

In doing and wishing good to our neighbor, as we should have others do to ourselves.

310. By what other virtue is this odious vice overcome?

By humility; for whosoever is humble, is not sorry that his neighbor is more rich, more learned, and more esteemed than himself.

Of Anger

311. What is anger?

It is an immoderate or violent motion of the heart, against such persons or things as displease us.

312. May there not be a flashy motion without sin?

There may, when one falls into a moderate anger, in order to do good or hinder evil.[268]

---

[266] Cf. Gn 27:41; 37:4ff
[267] Cf. 1 Pt 5:8
[268] Cf. Ps 4:5; Jn 2:15-17

313. When is it proper to show this moderate flash of anger?

When there is a likelihood that it may turn to the advantage of any one; but it is fit to be very wary, for fear it should do more hurt than good.

314. Which are the vices that spring from anger?

Hatred, spite or grudge, strife, revenge, fury, clamors or uproar, threats, mutiny, affronts, slander, cursing, quarrels, beating, manslaughter and murder; all which are grievous sins in the sight of God.[269]

315. By what virtue is anger overcome?

By patience.[270]

316. What is patience?

It is a willful suffering of all injuries, hardships, miseries, troubles, labor and poverty for God's sake, as Christ has done.[271]

317. What other remedy is there against anger?

To consider and do all things rationally and discreetly with the eyes and light of faith; and to beg earnestly the grace of God to do so.[272]

Of Sloth

318. What is sloth?

It is a laziness and slackness, which make us omit the service of God, or do it slowly and negligently.

319. When is a person guilty of the sin of sloth?

1) First, when he does not take proper care of his own serious affairs.[273] 2) When he does not take pains to know the things that every Christian is

---

[269] Cf. Mt 5:22; Gal 5:20-21; Eph 4:31
[270] Cf. Lk 21:19
[271] Cf. Eph 4:32; 1 Pt 2:23
[272] Cf. 2 Cor 4:17-18; Jas 1:17
[273] Cf. Prv 6:6-8; 1 Thes 4:11

obliged to know, or that regard his calling; or when he acts not according to his knowledge, nor reaps any profit from it.[274] 3) When he refuses to embrace the calling which God calls him to, and whereof he is conscious.[275] 4) When he is given to idleness, laziness, or long sleeping.[276] 5) When he spends his time in insignificant and frivolous affairs, such as visiting, unprofitable discourses and play.[277] 6) When he neglects the service of God, and uses no diligence to overcome his failings, or to advance in virtue.[278]

320. Is sloth a great sin?

It is a sin which deserves hell fire; as our Savior says.[279]

321. By what virtue is sloth overcome?

By devotion.

322. What is devotion?

It is a godly endeavor and pious zeal for the service of God, and for every other business that regards our calling and duty.[280]

323. How shall we know we have this virtue?

There is no better sign of it than to fulfil our duty readily and cheerfully.[281]

LESSON 13

The Sins against the Holy Ghost

324. How many are the sins against the Holy Ghost?

Six: 1) First, despair of salvation. 2) Presumption of God's mercy. 3) To

[274] Cf. 1 Cor 14:38; Rom 1:21ff
[275] Cf. Prv 1:24; Jer 9:6
[276] Cf. Prv 6:9-10
[277] Cf. Gal 6:10; 1 Tm 5:13
[278] Cf. Mt 25; Heb 6:11-12
[279] Cf. Mt 25:24ff
[280] Cf. Mk 13:33; Lk 13:24
[281] Cf. 1 Par 28:9; 2 Cor 9:7; Phil 2:14

resist the known truth. 4) Envy at another's spiritual good. 5) Obstinacy in sin. 6) Final impenitence.

325. What is despair of salvation?

It is a distrust in the mercies and power of God, as also in the merits of Jesus Christ, as if they were not of force enough to save us.[282]

326. What is presumption of God's mercy?

A foolish confidence in the mercy of God, as if he should save us without a good life, or without any care to keep the commandments: such as they have, who pretend to be saved by faith only, without good works.[283]

327. What is it to resist the known truth?

To argue obstinately against any known point of faith; or to pervert the way of our Lord by false constructions and lies; as those do, who teach the ignorant people, that Catholics give to images, saints, and angels the honor which is due to God alone; or that the pope, for money, gives us leave to commit what sins we please: although they full well know, that all these are as great falsehoods as can be invented.

328. What is envy of another man's spiritual good?

A sadness or repining at another's advancing in virtue; as it is usual with all those who scoff and are troubled at the frequent fasts, prayers, feasts, almsdeeds and other pious practices of the Church.[284]

329. What is obstinacy in sin?

A willful persisting in wickedness, and running on from sin to sin, after sufficient instruction and admonition.[285]

---

[282] Cf. Gn 4:13; Mt 27:4-5
[283] Cf. Jas 2:14, 17ff
[284] Cf. Gn 4:3ff; 1 Jn 3:12; 3 Jn 1:10
[285] Cf. Heb 10:26; 2 Pt 2:21

330. What is final impenitence?

To die without confession or contrition for our sins.[286]

331. Why is it said, that the sins against the Holy Ghost shall never be forgiven, either in this world or in the world to come?

Because it is very difficult to obtain the forgiveness of them; for men very seldom do true penance for them.

332. God and the Church then can forgive them, if we truly repent?

Yes, without doubt; all, except final impenitence.[287]

LESSON 14

The Sins Which Cry to Heaven for Vengeance

333. How many sins are there that cry to heaven for vengeance?

Four.

334. Which is the first?

Willful murder.

335. What is the second?

Sodomy, that is, a horrible and unnatural sin of the flesh.[288]

336. What is the third?

Oppression of the poor, which is a cruel or unjust dealing with widows, orphans, or inferiors.[289]

---

[286] Cf. Acts 7:51
[287] Cf. 1 Jn 1:9
[288] Cf. Gn 19:13
[289] Cf. Ex 22:22; Is 10:1-2

337. **What is the fourth?**

To defraud workmen of their wages.[290]

338. **May not one make himself partaker and guilty of the sin of another?**

He may certainly; for everybody undoubtedly sinneth, who counsels, commands, consents to, commends or gives permission to commit sin; he also sinneth by provoking another to evil, by assisting him to do it, by defending the fact, or by not hindering it when he may and ought to prevent it.[291]

339. **What ought we to do, in order to shun the abominable sins we spoke of, and all other mortal ones?**

We ought to shun the occasions of sin; to frequent the sacraments, and to pursue the virtues that are contrary to them, to wit: humility, liberality, chastity, charity, temperance, patience, and devotion or piety.

340. **What else do you do, that you may not fall into sin?**

I consider that God beholds me; I likewise meditate on the passion of our Savior Jesus Christ, and on the four last things.[292]

LESSON 15

Of the Four Last Things

341. **What are the four last things?**

Death, judgment, hell and heaven.

342. **How ought we to think on death?**

1) We ought first to think and believe firmly, that we must certainly die.[293]

---

[290] Cf. Jas 5:4
[291] Cf. Rom 1:32
[292] Cf. Gn 17:1; Ecclus 7:40; Heb 12:2ff
[293] Cf. Heb 9:27

2) That the hour, the place, and the manner of our death is uncertain.[294] 3) That God commands us to be prepared and always on our guard; and assures us, that death will, without much delay, surprise those foolish people who sleep and dwell in sin.[295] 4) That we shall die but once.[296] 5) That it is most likely we shall die as we shall have lived; if we spend our life in the state of grace, we shall, according to all appearance, die in the state of grace; or, if we pass our life in the state of sin, we shall, in all likelihood, die in the state of sin.[297] 6) That the gaining or losing of the glory and everlasting bliss of the kingdom of God, depends on the hour of death.[298]

343. How ought we to think of judgment?

We ought to consider and believe firmly: 1) First, that we shall undergo a particular judgment at the hour of our death, and a general judgment at the end of the world.[299] 2) That all our thoughts, words, actions, and omissions since we came to the use of reason, shall be judged.[300] 3) That there can be no appeal from, nor revoking of either judgment.[301] 4) That the law of God, the life and words of our Savior Jesus Christ, are the rule of our judgment.[302] 5) That it will be put in execution upon the spot, without showing us either pity or mercy.[303] 6) That the punishment and reward appointed for us by our judge, shall be everlasting.[304]

344. How are we to consider on hell?

We ought to think, and firmly believe: 1) First, that the damned shall never see the face of God.[305] 2) That they shall burn and be tortured both in body

[294] Cf. Mt 25:13; Mk 13:35
[295] Cf. Eccles 9:12; Mt 24:44ff; Mk 13:13ff; 1 Thes 5:3; Apoc 3:3
[296] Cf. Heb 9:27
[297] Cf. Prv 1:24ff; Ecclus 41; Rom 2:5-8
[298] Cf. Eccles 3:3; 9:10
[299] Cf. Heb 9:27; Apoc 14:13
[300] Cf. Mt 12:36
[301] Cf. Mt 25:46
[302] Cf. Rom 2:16
[303] Cf. Heb 10:31
[304] Cf. Mt 25:46
[305] Cf. Ps 48:12

and soul during eternity.[306] 3) That they shall suffer all the evil, and all the misery, that can be thought of, without any comfort or rest.[307] 4) That the worm of their conscience shall be gnawing and tearing them, whilst God is God.[308]

345. How ought we to think on the kingdom of heaven?

We ought to think often: 1) First, that the blessed shall suffer no kind of evil, in regard of either body or soul.[309] 2) That they shall abound with all good things.[310] 3) That they shall see God face to face; Jesus Christ, the Virgin Mary, and all the saints.[311] 4) That their bodies shall be glorious, immortal, active, vigorous, and bright.[312] 5) That they shall possess everlasting joy and happiness, without any danger or apprehension of ever losing them:[313] in a word, that "the eye hath not seen, nor the ear heard; nor hath it entered into the heart of man what things God hath prepared for those who love him."[314]

The Fruit of These Considerations

1) First, O Lord, give me the grace to think with benefit every day, morning and evening, on these four last things. 2) Grant me through thy great mercy, to be prepared to die in the state of grace. 3) I shall endeavor to do penance for my sins in this life, in order to escape thy severe judgment, and that I may not be cast down into hell. 4) I shall mortify my inordinate passions, and strive to spend my life holily, to the end I may, through the merits of Jesus Christ, be worthy of enjoying the bliss and happiness of the kingdom of God, for ever and ever.

[306] Cf. Is 33:14; Apoc 20:10
[307] Cf. Apoc 20:10
[308] Cf. Mk 9:43, 45
[309] Cf. Apoc 7:16-17
[310] Cf. Ps 35:9
[311] Cf. 1 Cor 13:12; Heb 12:23, 28
[312] Cf. 1 Cor 15:42ff
[313] Cf. Jn 16:22
[314] 1 Cor 2:9

Chapter 5

LESSON 16

Of the Christian Virtues, and Good Works

346. **What is a Christian virtue?**

It is a power and facility which we acquire by the grace of God, to do good works and whatever is agreeable in the sight of God, with cheerfulness.

347. **How many theological or divine virtues are there?**

Three: faith, hope, and charity.[315]

348. **What is faith?**

We have already spoken of it; and shall speak of hope in the fourth part.

349. **What is charity?**

It is a virtue we receive from the Holy Ghost, which makes us love God above all things, for his own sake; and likewise our neighbor as ourselves, for God's sake.

350. **Are we bound to have this virtue?**

Yes, most certainly: for no one can be saved without it.[316]

351. **How shall we know that we have the love of God above all things?**

There is no better sign of it, than to love our neighbor as ourselves; for it is false to say that we love God, when we love not our neighbor.[317]

---

[315] Cf. 1 Cor 13:13
[316] Cf. 1 Cor 13
[317] Cf. 1 Jn 4:20

352. How yet shall we know, that we love God and our neighbor?
We shall know it by our good works: for as the tree is known by its fruit, so shall the righteous man be known by his obedience to the Church, and by his good works.[318]

353. How many kinds of good works are there?
There are three principal ones, to wit: fasting, almsdeeds, and prayer.

354. By which of these good works do we prove that we love our neighbor?
By almsdeeds; that is, by the works of mercy.

355. How many kinds of almsdeeds, or works of mercy, are there?
Fourteen, to wit: seven corporal works, and seven spiritual.

356. Say the seven corporal works of mercy.[319]
1. To feed the hungry.
2. To give drink to the thirsty.
3. To clothe the naked.
4. To harbor the harborless.
5. To visit the sick.
6. To visit and relieve the imprisoned.
7. To bury the dead.

357. Say the spiritual works of mercy.
1. To instruct the ignorant.[320]
2. To admonish the sinner.[321]
3. To give counsel to the doubtful.[322]
4. To suffer injuries patiently.[323]

---

[318] Cf. Mt 7:16ff
[319] Cf. Mt 25:35-36; 26:10
[320] Cf. Prv 14:33
[321] Cf. Gal 6:1
[322] Cf. Job 29:21
[323] Cf. Rom 12:17fff

5. To forgive offences.[324]

6. To comfort or encourage the afflicted.[325]

7. To pray for the living and the dead, and for our persecutors.[326]

358. **When is it that a work of mercy is most meritorious?**

When it is really done for God's sake, and applied to the person that stands most in need of it.

359. **What are the offences we ought to forgive?**

All offences and injuries, let them be never so great and so many.[327]

360. **What is the reward of the works of mercy?**

Mercy from God in this life and the kingdom of heaven in the other.[328]

361. **What shall be the lot of those who are hard-hearted to the poor?**

God affirmeth, that judgment without mercy, and the everlasting fire of hell are allotted to those who show no mercy to persons in distress.[329]

LESSON 17

Of the Cardinal Virtues

362. **How many cardinal virtues are there?**

Four: prudence, justice, fortitude, and temperance.

363. **Why are they called cardinal virtues?**

Because they are the hinges, as it were, or the fountains of many other virtues.

---

[324] Cf. Jas 5:16
[325] Cf. 2 Cor 1:4
[326] Cf. Mt 5:44
[327] Cf. Mt 18:21-22
[328] Cf. Mt 25:34-35
[329] Cf. Mt 25:41

364. What is prudence?

It is a virtue which makes us wary that we ourselves be not deceived, nor deceive others; and that we do all things in their proper time and manner.[330]

365. What is justice?

A virtue which makes us render his due to everyone.

366. What is fortitude?

A virtue which gives us courage to endure all hardships, dangers, and death itself, for our faith and the service of God.[331]

367. What is temperance?

A virtue whereby we bridle our inordinate desires.[332]

368. What are the other virtues which our Savior chiefly requires of us to pursue?

Humility, patience, meekness, chastity, and vigilance.[333]

LESSON 18

Of the Eight Beatitudes

369. What do you call the eight beatitudes?

The eight blessings which Christ gives to the virtuous, and to such as practice good works.

370. Say them, as they are set down in the gospel.[334]

1. Blessed are the poor in spirit: for theirs is the kingdom of heaven.
2. Blessed are the meek: for they shall possess the land.

---

[330] Cf. Prv 15:21; 16:16; Ecclus 3:32; Mt 10:16
[331] Cf. Prv 28:1; Mk 10:28
[332] Cf. Ecclus 37:34; 1 Thes 5:21; 1 Pt 2:11
[333] Cf. Mk 13:33-37; Mt 5:28; 11:25; Lk 21:19
[334] Cf. Mt 5:3-10

3. Blessed are they that mourn: for they shall be comforted.

4. Blessed are they that hunger and thirst after justice: for they shall be filled.

5. Blessed are the merciful: for they shall obtain mercy.

6. Blessed are the clean of heart: for they shall see God.

7. Blessed are the peacemakers: for they shall be called the children of God.

8. Blessed are they that suffer persecution for justice sake: for theirs is the kingdom of God.

371. Who are the *poor in spirit?*

Those that are humble of heart, and not tied to earthly things.

372. Who are the *meek?*

Those who patiently endure affronts and injustice; and whose reward is the land of the living, that is, the kingdom of heaven.

373. Who are those that *mourn?*

The people that bewail bitterly their own sins, and those of others; and who shall therefore receive unspeakable comfort in heaven.

374. Who are those that *hunger and thirst after justice?*

Those that have a great desire of advancing daily in virtue.

375. How will they be filled?

With the abundance of the riches and joys of the kingdom of God.

376. Whom do you call the *merciful?*

Such as forgive their neighbor, and are charitable, and serviceable to the distressed; and whose reward is forgiveness and mercy from God.

377. Who are the *clean of heart?*

The innocent and harmless, whose hearts are not tied to sin; and therefore shall see and possess God eternally.

378. **Who are the** *peacemakers?*

Those who subdue their passions so well, that they are in peace with God, with their neighbor and with themselves; and that endeavor to make peace among others; and who, upon that account, are called the children of God and co-heirs of Christ in heaven.

379. **Who are those that** *suffer persecution for justice sake?*

Such as are banished, or put to trouble for maintaining the true faith, and for following virtue; or that are ready to suffer death itself, sooner than offend against either.

380. **Does it depend of us to practice all these virtues and good works, and avoid the detestable sins, whereof we have spoken?**

It does, undoubtedly, with the assistance of God's grace.

LESSON 19

Of the Grace of God

381. **What means the grace of God?**

It means, in general, every gift freely bestowed upon us by God; and all the good he has liberally done us, and we have in no wise deserved of him.

382. **How many kinds of graces are there?**

They are many; some are natural, as life, health, strength, understanding, etc.; and others supernatural, such as the incarnation of the Son of God, the redemption of mankind, etc. Some are exterior, or outward, as the preaching of the gospel, our vocation to the faith, etc.; others are interior, or within us, as faith, hope, charity, etc.

383. **What do you chiefly understand by the grace of God?**

I understand the heavenly gifts, which God, through his own great mercy, and the merits of Jesus Christ, infuses into our hearts to cleanse us from sin, and enable us to work out our salvation.

384. **How many sorts of grace doth God infuse into our souls?**

Two sorts, to wit: habitual and actual grace.

385. **What do you understand by habitual grace?**

The graces which remain and dwell in our soul; such are the three divine virtues, faith, hope, and charity, or the graces which cleanse us from sin, and sanctify us.[335]

386. **What do you understand by actual grace?**

The transitory graces, which come and go; which enlighten our understanding, and move the will to shun evil, and do good.[336]

387. **Is grace necessary for every good work?**

It is absolutely necessary for every work and action that contributes to our salvation.[337]

388. **Cannot we, without the assistance of grace, receive the faith when it is preached to us?**

No: We can have neither faith, nor hope, nor charity, as it behooveth, without another grace, which prepares and strengthens the soul for receiving these divine virtues.[338]

389. **Cannot we, if we have faith, hope and charity, keep the commandments of God and the Church, without actual grace?**

We can neither begin nor finish any action, tending to our salvation, without an actual assistance from God, through Jesus Christ.[339]

---

[335] Cf. Jn 14:16-17, 26; Rom 8:9, 11; Eph 3:17; 2 Tm 1:5, 14; Jas 4:5
[336] Cf. Ps 22:6; 58:11; Phil 2:13; Jas 1:7
[337] Cf. Is 26:12; Jn 3:27; 1 Cor 4:7; 12:6
[338] Cf. Jn 6:44, 66; 15:5; 1 Jn 4:10; Acts 16:14; Council of Trent, Session 6, Can. 3
[339] Cf. 1 Cor 12:6; Phil 2:13

390. **Can we not at least, by our own proper force, pray to God, and beg and obtain grace of him?**

We cannot; for without the grace of the Holy Ghost, "we know not (even) what we should pray for, as we ought."[340]

391. **What! have we not free will?**

We have certainly; but since our first father Adam's fall, it is weak and prone to evil. Moreover, if our free will were in its first force, we could not make one step towards the kingdom of heaven, without a supernatural help; wherefore it is no wonder now, that "we are not sufficient of ourselves to think of any thing, as from ourselves, but that our sufficiency is from God."[341]

392. **If that be true, how have we free will?**

Chiefly, inasmuch as we can cooperate with the grace of God, or resist and reject it; for we are under no necessity in regard of either the one or the other.[342]

393. **Is it certain that we can resist the grace of God?**

It is most certain; for, alas! we resist it daily, and as often as we do not follow the good thoughts, which God inspires us with.[343]

394. **Is it in our power, with the help of grace, to fulfil the commandments?**

It is for certain; for we can do all things in Jesus Christ, who strengthens us.[344] Zechariah and Elizabeth "were both just in the sight of God, walking blameless in all the commandments and ordinances of the Lord."[345]

---

[340] Rom 8:26
[341] 2 Cor 3:5; Cf. Council of Trent, Session 6, Can. 1
[342] Cf. Gn 4:7; Dt 30:19; Jo 24:15; Ps 31:9; 89:3; Ecclus 14:16ff; Mt 6:33; Rom 8:13; 1 Cor 7:37
[343] Cf. Acts 7:51; 2 Cor 6:1; Heb 12:15
[344] Cf. Phil 4:13
[345] Lk 1:6

395. Does God give us sufficient grace to keep the commandments?

He does certainly; for God is too just and too merciful to lay any load upon us which we are not able to bear; but we cannot fulfil his commandments as we ought, nor overcome the temptations of the world, the flesh, and the devil, without a supernatural help from God, through Jesus Christ; whence it is evident; that God gives us sufficient assistance for accomplishing his law.

396. Could not God, without any injustice, have left us in darkness, and in the guilt of original sin; and therefore refuse us his grace and the knowledge of his law?

He could undoubtedly; just as he hath left the apostate angels: yet he hath not dealt so with mankind;[346] for "he spared not even his only Son, but delivered him for us all";[347] and "not only for our sins but for the sins of the whole world":[348] wherefore, he gives us his holy law, and grace to fulfil it.

397. Cannot God, even now, refuse us the knowledge of his law, and his grace, without doing us any injustice?

He can certainly; for grace would not be grace,[349] nor a free gift, but a debt or reward, if God were bound to grant it to us. Yet, through his own great mercy and the merits of Jesus Christ, he deals not so with us; but according to his promises, he invites us all, saying: "Come to me all you that labor, and are burthened, and I will refresh you. Take upon you my yoke, and learn of me, because I am meek and humble of heart: and you shall find rest to your souls; for my yoke is sweet and my burthen light."[350]

---

[346] Cf. Heb 2:16
[347] Rom 8:32
[348] 1 Jn 2:2
[349] Cf. Rom 11:6
[350] Mt 11:28-30

398. **Is it true that God doth not forsake us after he has thus called us, and adopted us for his children?**
It is certain that he doth not forsake us, until we have first forsaken him; for God is most merciful and most faithful in his promises.[351]

399. **For what doth God forsake us?**
For falling into mortal sin.

400. **Can the grace which God withdraws from us, be recovered?**
It can undoubtedly; but let nobody, therefore, rashly flatter himself; for it often happens that it is not recovered, because a great many do not repent as they ought.[352]

401. **Doth God forsake us entirely when we fall into mortal sin?**
No; we lose not our faith but by infidelity, nor our hope but by despair. Moreover, God recalls and excites us often by his grace to prayer and repentance.[353]

402. **Is it true that God doth often awake and excite the sinner to prayer and repentance?**
It is; as he affirmeth himself, saying: "I stand at the door and knock, if any man shall hear my voice, and open the gate, I will come in to him."[354] Besides, who is the sinner that hath no remorse of conscience, and that doth not perceive the voice of God awaking and moving him to prayer and penance?[355]

---

[351] Cf. Heb 10:23; 13:5; 1 Jn 1:9; Council of Trent, Session 6, Can. 11
[352] Cf. Mt 12:45; Heb 6:4ff; 10:26ff
[353] Cf. 1 Cor 13:2; Council of Trent, Session 6, Can. 15
[354] Apoc 3:20
[355] Cf. Rom 2:4

403. **What do you say of those who give a deaf ear to the voice and call of God; who offer an indignity to the spirit of grace, and despise the richness of the goodness and patience of the Lord?**[356]

The Holy Ghost saith, that "according to the hardness of their impenitent hearts, they lay up for themselves wrath in the day of wrath, and of the time that the just judgment of God shall be revealed";[357] and that "it is a dreadful thing to fall into the hands of the living God."[358]

404. **Do they deserve a great punishment for resisting continually the voice and grace of God?**

There is no punishment, be it never so great, but they deserve; for they despise God himself, when they make no account of his grace and mercy. They trample underfoot the Son of God, and undervalue his most sacred blood, which was shed for them; which cleansed them from sin and merited for them from his heavenly Father these gifts and graces which they impiously reject.[359]

405. **What do you say to those who receive a great deal of grace from God, and are always falling into mortal sin, and always rising out of it, as they pretend, without showing the fruit of grace or true repentance?**

The Holy Ghost compares them "to a man who beholds his countenance in a glass...goes his way, and presently forgets what manner of man he was";[360] and likewise to "the earth which drinketh up the rain that cometh often upon it," yet "bringeth forth thorns and briars," and "whose end is to be burnt."[361]

---

[356] Cf. Ibid.
[357] Rom 2:5
[358] Heb 10:31
[359] Cf. Is 1:2; Heb 10:29
[360] Jas 1:23-24
[361] Heb 6:7-8

406. **How can we avoid this just vengeance, and benefit as we ought of the grace of God?**

It is necessary we should readily and diligently cooperate with the grace of God, by following cheerfully the good thoughts we receive from him; never to harden our hearts against the call and voice of the Lord,[362] nor receive his heavenly gifts in vain,[363] lest we should grieve or offend the Holy Ghost,[364] lose the favors which he freely bestowed upon us,[365] and be delivered over to the shameful desires of our hearts.[366]

407. **What else ought we to do?**

It is necessary for us to give great attention to the thoughts and motions of our soul, and speedily to shut up our hearts against the evil inclinations which we feel springing up within us; for it is certain, that the most part of the world are lost for want of watching over and governing their own thoughts and hearts;[367] and that the grace of God doth not rest in a soul that is a slave to sin,[368] because there can be no communication or fellowship betwixt light and darkness, that is, betwixt grace and sin.[369]

408. **What more ought we to do?**

We have need to humble our hearts "under the powerful hand of God,"[370] who "resisteth the proud and giveth grace to the humble";[371] and to "work out (our) salvation with fear and trembling. For it is God who worketh in (us) both the will and the deed through his good will";[372] and no one knows "whether he be worthy of love or hatred."[373]

---

362 Cf. Ps 94:8
363 Cf. 2 Cor 6:1
364 Cf. Eph 4:30
365 Cf. Am 1:3; 2
366 Cf. Rom 1:24, 28
367 Cf. Jer 12:11
368 Cf. Ws 1:4
369 Cf. 2 Cor 6:14-16
370 1 Pt 5:6
371 1 Pt 5:5
372 Phil 2:12-13
373 Eccles 9:1

409. Lastly, what else ought we to do?

If we have a mind to draw the grace of God abundantly upon us, and to preserve and increase it in us, we must frequent the sacraments and pray often.

410. Did you not already say that we cannot merit the grace of God?

I said only, that we cannot merit it by our proper force; but it is certain that, with the assistance of grace, we can obtain more grace from God; and go on from grace to grace, and from virtue to virtue, by frequenting the sacraments, by prayer, and other good works.[374]

---

[374] Cf. Ps 83:8; Mt 25:16ff; Council of Trent, Session 6, Can. 10-24

SECTION III
Of the Sacraments

Chapter 6

411. What is the third thing necessary for salvation?

It is to receive the sacraments worthily; although they be not all necessary for all persons.[375]

412. What is a sacrament?

It is a sensible sign of an invisible grace, instituted by our Savior Jesus Christ, for our justification and sanctification.

413. How many sacraments are there?

Seven, to wit: baptism, confirmation, Eucharist, penance, extreme unction, holy order, and matrimony.

414. What ought we to do, in order to receive the sacraments with fruit or benefit?

We should prepare ourselves diligently, and come to receive them devoutly. We ought also to give great praise and thanks to our Savior, for having left these sacred fountains of grace to the Church, to cleanse mankind from the filth of sin, and strengthen them in the way of eternal life.[376]

---

[375] Cf. Jn 3:5; 20:22; Council of Trent, Session 7
[376] Cf. Mt 7:6; 1 Cor 11:28

LESSON 1

Of Baptism

415. What is baptism?

It is a sacrament which cleanseth us from original sin, and makes us children of God and of the Church.[377]

416. Doth not baptism cleanse one from other sins besides original sin?

It cleanses everyone from all the sins he committed before he received baptism, and from the punishment due to sin, provided he duly prepare himself; and it infuses many graces and virtues into the soul.[378]

417. Is baptism necessary?

It is undoubtedly; for without baptism, or the desire thereof, together with the fervent love of God, nobody can be saved, unless he be a martyr, who is baptized in his own blood.[379]

418. Can everybody confer the sacrament of baptism?

Yes, in time of need only, and when a priest cannot be had; but it is not permitted to a woman to baptize in the presence of a man, nor to a layman in the presence of a clergyman, etc.

419. What is requisite for the conferring of baptism?

It is necessary that one should have the intention of conferring it in earnest, and that he should sprinkle natural water on the head (if possible) of the person to be baptized, pronouncing these words: "I baptize thee in the name of the Father, and of the Son, and of the Holy Ghost. Amen."[380]

---

[377] Cf. Mt 28:19; Ti 3:5-6
[378] Cf. Rom 8:1-2
[379] Cf. Jn 3:5; Council of Trent, Session 7, "On the Sacraments in General," Can. 4; "On Baptism," Can. 5
[380] Cf. Mt 28:19

420. **Is it lawful to receive baptism twice?**

No, it is not lawful to receive it upon any account more than once; because it imprints a spiritual character in the soul, which shall never be blotted out.[381]

421. **What is required of him who has a mind to receive baptism?**

It is required of him, and he promises to God, to renounce the devil, his works, his pomps, and all his vanities. Moreover, it is necessary for him who is come to the use of reason before he receives baptism, to have faith, to do penance for his sins, and to begin to love God.[382]

422. **What do you understand by the works of the devil?**

All kinds of sin.

423. **What do you understand by the pomps and vanities of the devil?**

I understand vainglory, worldly ambition, and every other kind of pride.

424. **How are children baptized, since they neither believe, nor promise anything before baptism?**

The Church, and the godfathers and godmothers do believe and answer for them.

425. **For what are godfathers and godmothers given to us?**

That they may answer for, and instruct us, in case our parents should be negligent, or should die.

426. **How many godfathers and godmothers should we have?**

One godfather and one godmother at most; both Catholics, and of no bad reputation.[383]

---

[381] Cf. Heb 6:4-6; 2 Cor 1:22

[382] Cf. Acts 2:38; Rom 10:10; Council of Trent, Session 6, Ch. 6

[383] Cf. Council of Trent, Session 24, "Decree on the Reformation of Marriage," Ch. 2; Charles Borromeo, *Acts of the Church of Milan*

427. **Is there not a kind of spiritual kindred or affinity contracted by the god-fathers and godmothers, and also by the person who baptizes, with the party baptized?**

There is undoubtedly; and likewise with his father and mother; for which reason they are prohibited to marry one another.[384]

428. **Are we bound to fulfil faithfully all that our godfathers and godmothers have promised in our name?**

We are certainly; for it is upon that condition we were admitted to baptism, and were made members of the Church, and heirs of the kingdom of heaven.[385]

429. **What obligation doth baptism lay upon us?**

To spend our life in the Catholic faith, to keep the commandments of God, and to follow diligently the example of our Savior Jesus Christ, and of the saints.[386]

LESSON 2

Of the Sacrament of Confirmation

430. **What is confirmation?**

It is a sacrament which gives us an abundance of grace, courage, and spiritual force to confess our faith, and follow the example of Christ publicly, although we should be put to death upon that account.[387]

---

[384] Cf. Council of Trent, Session 24, "Decree on the Reformation of Marriage," Ch. 2

[385] Cf. Rom 6:3-4; Gal 5:3, 6

[386] Cf. Rom 6:3-4; 1 Pt 2:21; Heb 13:17

[387] Cf. Acts 8:14-17

431. **Doth not this sacrament imprint a character in the soul, as baptism does?**
It does for certain; and it is, therefore, unlawful to receive it more than once.[388]

432. **Who confers this sacrament?**
A bishop only.[389]

433. **How does he administer it?**
He lays both his hands upon the head of the person that is to receive this sacrament, and anoints his forehead with consecrated or blessed oil, pronouncing a set form of words, which signify the force and fruit of this sacrament.[390]

434. **Who ought to receive this sacrament?**
Everybody that has been baptized, if it can be done conveniently: for whoever slights this sacrament sins grievously.[391]

435. **At what time ought it to be received?**
When one is come to the years of discretion, and particularly when he is persecuted for his faith.

436. **What preparation is necessary for the person who desires to receive confirmation?**
It is requisite he should know the principal articles of faith; make an act of faith; and clear his conscience from all mortal sin.

437. **What ought to be done after receiving confirmation?**
We ought to give great thanks to God for the abundance of grace we have received from him; to take a firm resolution to spend our life christianly,

---

[388] Cf. 2 Cor 1:21-22
[389] Cf. Acts 8:14-17; Council of Trent, Session 7, "On Confirmation," Can. 3
[390] Cf. Acts 19:6; Heb 6:2
[391] Cf. Synod of Laodicea, Can. 48

and to profess our faith openly: "For with the heart we believe unto justice, and with the mouth confession is made unto salvation."[392]

438. What else ought we to do?

We ought likewise to ask earnestly of God, the fruits of the Holy Ghost, to wit: charity, joy, peace, patience, longanimity, goodness, benignity, meekness, faith, modesty, temperance, and chastity.[393]

439. What else ought to be done?

We ought to beg diligently the gifts of the Holy Ghost, to wit: wisdom, judgment, counsel, fortitude, knowledge, piety, and the fear of the Lord.[394]

440. What is wisdom?

Wisdom is a gift of the Holy Ghost, whereby we undervalue the things of this life, and give our affection and love to God and godly things.

441. What is judgment?

It is a gift of the Holy Ghost, by which we understand and readily embrace all mysteries and truths belonging to faith.

442. What is counsel?

A gift of the Holy Ghost, which enables us to choose the things that tend to the glory of God and the good of our soul, and to recommend them to others.

443. What is fortitude?

A gift which helps us to suffer all tribulations and hardships for Christ's sake; and to overcome the enemies of our soul.

---

[392] Rom 10:9-10
[393] Cf. Gal 5:22-23
[394] Cf. Is 11:2-3

444. What is knowledge?

A gift of the Holy Ghost, which shows us the way to the kingdom of heaven; and the obstacles which might lead us astray.

445. What is piety?

A gift of the Holy Ghost, by which we humbly and readily do all that tends to God's glory and praise.

446. What is the fear of the Lord?

It is a gift of the Holy Ghost, which makes us dread doing anything that is not pleasing to God.

LESSON 3

Of the Eucharist or Blessed Sacrament

447. What is the sacrament of the Eucharist?

It is a sacrament wherein the body and blood, the soul and divinity of our Savior Jesus Christ, are really and verily present, under the forms of bread and wine.[395]

448. What do you understand by the forms of bread and wine?

I understand that which works upon our corporal or outward senses; such are the taste, smell, color, and figure of bread.

449. Is there bread or wine in the sacrament of the Blessed Eucharist?

No; for the whole substance of the bread and wine is changed into the body and blood of Jesus Christ, by the virtue of the most holy words pronounced by the priest, when he consecrates the bread and wine in the name and person of Christ.[396]

---

[395] Cf. Mt 26:26-28; Jn 6:52, 55ff
[396] Cf. Lk 22:19; 1 Cor 10:16; 11:24

450. **How is the bread and wine changed into the body and blood of Christ?**
By the divine power, which made the world out of nothing, by which Moses turned rivers into blood, our Savior changed water into wine; and by which many wonderful things are daily done, which we can neither comprehend nor understand.[397]

451. **Is the blood of Christ under the form of bread, and his body under the form of wine?**
Yes; Christ is whole and entire under each form.[398]

452. **Is our Savior in every consecrated host?**
He is certainly; let the host be great or small.

453. **When the host is broken, is the body of our Lord also broken?**
Not at all; for although he died once of his own accord for our sake, his glorious body can no more be broken, wounded, or put to death.[399]

454. **Whereas the glorious and sacred body of our Savior cannot be broken: and that there is neither bread nor wine to be broken or divided, what else is broken or divided?**
The forms or outward appearances of the bread and wine are divided.

455. **Is the body of Christ, after the host is broken, in every part?**
Yes; Christ, both God and man, is wholly and entirely in every small particle, just as he is in the greatest.

456. **Doth Christ leave the kingdom of heaven when he comes to us in this sacrament?**
He does not; for he is at the same time both in heaven and on earth, wheresoever Mass is celebrated, and in every place where the sacrament of the Blessed Eucharist is.

[397] Cf. Gn 1:2; Jn 2:8-9
[398] Cf. Rom 6:9-10
[399] Cf. Ibid.

457. How can that be?

By the mighty power of God, to whom nothing is impossible, and who can easily do more than we are able to understand.[400]

458. Does he who receives this sacrament under the form of bread alone, or under the form of wine alone, receive Christ whole and entire, just as he who receives under both kinds?

He really does; because the body and blood, soul and divinity of our Savior, are inseparable from one another; "for death has no more dominion (or power) over him."[401]

459. Did not Christ command us all to receive under both kinds?

No; for when he instituted this sacrament, and bid those who were present drink of the chalice, none were there but the apostles; and lest it might be thought that he commanded us all to receive under both kinds, he promises life everlasting to him who receives under the form of bread alone, saying: "He that eateth this bread shall live forever."[402]

460. When did our Savior institute this sacrament?

The night before he suffered and died for mankind.[403]

461. Why did he give us this sacrament?

For four reasons; first, to signify unto us his great love.[404]

462. What is the second reason?

That we may be always mindful of the death he suffered for our sake.[405]

---

[400] Cf. Jb 9:10; Ecclus 11:4; Jer 32:18-19; Rom 11:33
[401] Rom 6:9-10; Cf. Jn 6:52
[402] Jn 6:59
[403] Cf. 1 Cor 11:23
[404] Cf. Jn 3:16; 13:1
[405] Cf. Lk 22:19; 1 Cor 11:25-26

463. How does the Blessed Eucharist put us in mind of the death of our Savior?

Inasmuch as our Lord is upon the altar as if he were dead; and the separation also of the form of bread, which represents his sacred body, from the form of wine, which represents his most precious blood, puts us in mind that his body and soul, his flesh and blood have been separated from one another on the cross.

464. What is the third reason for which our Savior left us this Blessed Sacrament?

That it may be a spiritual food to our soul, and that it may augment and strengthen the life of grace in us.[406]

465. What is the fourth reason?

That we may have a pledge and a sure token of his sincere desire of giving us a glorious resurrection and life everlasting.[407]

466. Why do you believe all these things?

Because God hath revealed them to our holy mother the Church.

467. What follows from what we have said?

It follows that we are obliged to adore, love, and praise our most merciful Savior Jesus Christ in this Blessed Sacrament, as the saints and angels do in heaven.[408]

468. What else follows from it?

It likewise follows, that we ought to prepare ourselves diligently, in order to receive often this Blessed Sacrament with faith and devotion.[409]

---

[406] Cf. Jn 6:56-57
[407] Cf. Jn 6:54-59
[408] Cf. Ps 115, 116; Heb 1:6
[409] Cf. Ps 110:5; Mt 11:28

Of the Preparation to Be Made before Communion

469. What do you mean by Communion?

I mean the receiving of the body and blood, soul and divinity of our Savior Jesus Christ, verily, under the form of bread or wine.

470. How many conditions necessary for making a good Communion?

There are two kinds of them, to wit: one which regards the body, and another which regards the soul.

471. What is that preparation which regards the body?

It is to take neither meat nor drink, nor medicaments from midnight; to be silent and discreet, and gravely and orderly clothed.

472. Is it not sometimes permitted to receive the Communion, although a person had broke fast?

Yes: he who is in danger of death, may receive the Communion as a viaticum for everlasting life, notwithstanding his having taken some nourishment before.

473. What preparation is necessary in regard of the soul?

It is necessary to be free from all mortal sin, to be in charity with God and our neighbor, and therefore to be reconciled with our enemies, if we can, and to approach the altar with gravity and devotion; for "whosoever shall eat this bread, or drink the chalice of the Lord unworthily, shall be guilty of the body and blood of the Lord."[410]

474. Do those who are in mortal sin receive the body of Christ?

Yes, but it is to their eternal damnation they receive it, just as Judas has done.[411]

---

[410] 1 Cor 11:27-31
[411] Cf. Jn 13:27; 1 Cor 11:27, 29

475. Why is it a cause of damnation to them?

Because they receive it in a bad state.

476. Is it a great sin to communicate in a bad state?

One cannot fall into a greater sin.[412]

477. Can he who is in venial sin receive the Communion with benefit?

Everyone ought to endeavor to be free from venial sin; and particularly not to be inclined nor tied to it, for fear he should lose the fruit of this godly work.[413]

478. What is that devotion with which a person ought to come to Communion?

It is requisite he should make certain acts before and after Communion.

Of the Acts That Are Proper to Be Made before Communion

479. Which are the acts that ought to be made before receiving the sacred body of Christ?

Acts of faith, humility, contrition, hope, and love.

480. Make an act of faith.

O Lord, my God, I do firmly and steadfastly believe from my heart, that thy entire body and blood, thy soul and divinity, are really and verily present in this Blessed Sacrament, under the forms of bread and wine; because thou hast said so thyself.

481. Make an act of humility.

O Lord, I am not worthy that thou, the King of heaven and earth, shouldst come to me; because I am a very poor, and a very contemptible creature; and have often deserved thy anger, through my own very great fault.

---

[412] Cf. Heb 10:29

[413] Cf. Francis de Sales, *Introduction to the Devout Life*, Pt. 2, Ch. 20; *Various Letters*, Bk. 2, Epistle 46

482. Make an act of contrition.

O Lord, I am very heartily sorry for having offended thee; because thou art infinitely good, and infinitely amiable; and art most gracious and merciful to me, a poor sinner. I firmly purpose, with the help of thy grace, not to provoke thine anger henceforth.

483. Make an act of hope.

O Lord, I expect and trust greatly, that by the means of this sacrament thou wilt deliver me from sin; that thou wilt replenish me with thy grace; and grant me the glory of heaven.

484. Make an act of love.

O Lord, I love thee from my whole heart and above all things, because thou art infinitely good and amiable, and that thou art my everlasting joy and happiness.[414]

Of the Acts Which Are Proper to Be Made after Communion

485. What acts are to be made after Communion?

Acts of adoration, thanksgiving, offering, supplication, and good resolution.[415]

486. How do you make an act of adoration?

I say: "O Lord, I adore and praise thee in this Divine Sacrament; and do acknowledge that thou art my Creator, my Savior, my supreme Lord, and the sovereign ruler of the whole world."

487. Make an act of thanksgiving.

O Lord, I render thee a thousand thanks, with all my heart, for having vouchsafed, through thy great grace, to give thyself to me.

---

[414] Cf. Ps 72:25ff
[415] Cf. Ps 61:9

488. Make an act of oblation.

O Lord, I offer and resign to thee my thoughts, my words, my actions, and myself entirely, that I may be wholly thine.

489. Make an act of supplication.

O Lord, I most humbly beseech thee to grant me all that I stand in need of; and particularly powerful graces, that I may never henceforth offend thee.

490. Make an act of good resolution.

O Lord, I would rather die than fall into sin, after all the mercy and love thou hast shown to me.

491. What is to be done on the day of Communion?

We ought to shun much company and discourse; watch carefully over our senses; assist at Mass, and at the instruction and public prayers of the parish or congregation, and spend the greater part of the day in silence and devotion.

492. What is the principal obligation of him who receives the Communion?

He is bound to spend his life and health piously, as Jesus Christ and the saints have spent their lives on earth.[416]

493. When are we obliged to communicate?

At the time of Easter at least, and when we are in danger of dying.[417]

494. Is it not proper to receive the Communion oftener than once a year only?

God and the Church would wish that every Christian were prepared to receive this Blessed Sacrament daily.[418]

---

[416] Cf. 1 Cor 6:19-20; 2 Pt 2:20-22

[417] Cf. 1 Cor 5:7; Fourth Lateran Council, Const. 21; Council of Trent, Session 13, Can. 9

[418] Cf. Council of Trent, Session 13, "Decree Concerning the Most Holy Sacrament of the Eucharist," Ch. 8

495. **Is it fit to counsel every Christian to communicate daily?**

No; for few prepare themselves as it becometh to receive this Blessed Sacrament often.[419]

496. **That being so, how ought one to behave himself in regard to the frequent receiving of this great sacrament?**

Let everyone earnestly endeavor to spend his life honestly and devoutly, that he may, in some manner, be worthy to communicate often. However, let him act in all according to the advice of a godly and learned ghostly father.[420]

497. **What ought we to do, when we do not receive this Blessed Sacrament?**

We ought to communicate spiritually.

498. **What do you understand by communicating spiritually?**

I understand by it, that we ought to have a desire to receive this Blessed Sacrament; to conceive also a sorrow for the sins which hinder us from receiving this heavenly food; and humbly beseech our Savior to come unto us, and dwell in our hearts by his grace.

LESSON 4

Of the Sacrament of Penance

499. **What is the sacrament of penance?**

It is a sacrament whereby the sins we commit after baptism are forgiven us.

500. **How are sins remitted by this sacrament?**

They are remitted through the repentance of the sinner, and by the absolution of the priest.[421]

---

[419] Cf. Charles Borromeo, in Instruct. Euch. Tit. de freq. Comm.; Francis De Sales, *Various Letters*, Bk. 2, Epistle 40

[420] Cf. Ps 101:5; Charles Borromeo, Instruct, ad Confess., p. 58

[421] Cf. Mt 4:17; Apoc 2:5

501. Can the priest forgive sins?

He can; because Jesus Christ gave him this power.[422]

502. Is the sacrament of penance necessary for salvation?

Yes; it is as necessary as baptism in regard of all those who fall into mortal sin after they were baptized.[423]

503. Doth God forgive us our sins by this sacrament, upon the same condition that he hath forgiven them in baptism?

No, certainly; for according to the just judgment of God, the mortal sins we committed after baptism are not forgiven us without great sorrow and pains.[424]

504. What! doth not everyone that approacheth this sacrament obtain the forgiveness of his sins?

No; because they do not come with the conditions which our Savior requireth of them.

505. How many conditions are necessary for the penitent?

There are five: 1) First, to examine his conscience. 2) To conceive a hatred against sin, and a sorrow for having fallen into it, and incurred the wrath of God. 3) To make a firm resolution of sinning no more against God's holy will. 4) To make a good confession of all his sins to a priest that is approved by the Church. 5) A resolution to make satisfaction to God and his neighbor according to his ability.

---

[422] Cf. Jn 20:23

[423] Cf. Ibid.; Cyprian, *Epistle 54*, To Cornelius; Pacian, *Epistle 1*, To Sympronian; Chrysostom, *On the Priesthood*, Bk. 3; Ambrose, *On Repentance*, Bk. 1, Ch. 2; Cyril of Alexandria, *On the Gospel According to John*, Bk. 12; Augustine, *Epistle 228*, To Honoratus; Leo, *Epist. 83, alias 91*, c. 2; Council of Trent, Session 6, "Decree on Justification," Ch. 14

[424] Cf. Ps 6:7; 2 Cor 7:9-11; Council of Trent, Session 14, "Doctrine on the Sacrament of Penance," Ch. 2

Of the Examination of Conscience

506. **What is an examination of conscience?**

It is a diligent search which one makes in his own mind, in order to re-member his sins, to conceive a detestation and aversion for them, and to declare them in confession.[425]

507. **What endeavors are we obliged to use herein?**

The same endeavor and diligence which we would use in great and prof-itable worldly affairs.[426]

508. **Do those make a good confession who do not examine their conscience?**

No; for it is not at all likely that they can have the knowledge of their sins, or declare them in confession.[427]

509. **What ought we to do that we may get a thorough knowledge of our sins?**

We ought to beseech God to give us the grace to know our sins; and then to make an exact examination of our conscience, in regard to the com-mandments of God and the Church; and in regard of the seven capital sins, whereof we have already treated at large.

510. **How do you make this examination?**

If I confess but seldom in the year, I do quietly and steadily consider of every point of these in particular, and closely observe wherein, and how often I have offended God by thought, word, deed, or omission.[428]

511. **Are there not certain sins which we ought to examine our conscience upon very diligently?**

There are; to wit: the sins which regard our profession or calling; and the sins to which we are most inclined or given.

---

425 Cf. Is 38:15
426 Cf. Prv 2:4
427 Cf. Is 46:8
428 Cf. Ps 76:6

512. What should we do that we may the better call to mind our sins?

We ought to think of the places and companies we have been in; and likewise how we spent our time, or fulfilled the duties of our calling, in respect of God and our neighbor.[429]

LESSON 5

Of Contrition

513. What is the second thing necessary for the sacrament of penance?

Contrition.

514. What is contrition?

It is a hearty sorrow for having fallen into sin; and detestation thereof, together with a firm purpose of amendment.[430]

515. Do those make a good confession who are not sorry for having fallen into sin?

They do not; for this sorrow is absolutely necessary.[431]

516. What conditions doth this godly sorrow require?

It is necessary: 1) First, that it should be interior. 2) Supernatural. 3) Universal. 4) Supreme, or above all other grief.

517. What means saying that this sorrow ought to be interior?

It means that it must proceed really from the heart.[432]

---

[429] Cf. Rom 12:2; 1 Thes 5:21

[430] Cf. Ez 18:30-32; Ps 6:7; Jn 8:11

[431] Cf. Jas 4:2; Council of Trent, Session 14, "Doctrine on the Sacrament of Penance," Ch. 4

[432] Cf. Jl 2:12-13

518. What means supernatural?

It means that this sorrow must proceed from the inspiration of the Holy Ghost, and from the motives which faith teacheth us.[433]

519. What are those motives which faith teacheth us?

The fear of hell fire; a hatred of the baseness of sin; the loss of the kingdom of heaven; and the goodness of God.[434]

520. Is it not enough for one to have a sorrow for sin because it draws the reproach and contempt of his neighbor, or some worldly inconvenience upon him?

By no means; because the motive of this mean sorrow is neither God, nor the things which faith teacheth us, but the world.[435]

521. Why do you say that it ought to be universal?

Because it is necessary that this sorrow should be for all mortal sins at least.[436]

522. Why do you say that it ought to be supreme?

Because it is necessary we should hate sin above all other evils; for there is no other evil so great as sin.[437]

523. How many kinds of contrition are there?

Two: perfect and imperfect contrition.

524. What is perfect contrition?

It is a sorrow for having offended God, because he is sovereignly good in himself, and has an abhorrence for sin.

---

[433] Cf. Jn 15:5; Council of Trent, Session 6, Can. 2; Session 14, Ch. 4

[434] Cf. Council of Trent, Session 6, "Decree on Justification," Ch. 6; Session 14, "Doctrine on the Sacrament of Penance," Ch. 4

[435] Cf. 2 Cor 7:10

[436] Cf. Ez 18:30-31

[437] Cf. Dt 30:15ff; Mt 25:41; Rom 5:12; 6:23

525. Make an act of perfect contrition.

O Lord, it grieves me to the heart to have deserved thine anger, because thou art infinitely good and amiable. I am resolved, with the help of thy grace, to amend my life.

526. What is imperfect contrition?

It is a hearty sorrow for having fallen into sin, because of its baseness; or for fear of hell fire; together with a detestation of sin, and with the hope of obtaining pardon of God.[438]

527. Make an act of imperfect contrition.

O Lord, I am extremely sorry for having offended thee, because sin is very odious, and puts me in danger of forfeiting eternally thy sight, and thy heavenly kingdom; and of damning myself forever. I am resolved, with the assistance of thy grace, to amend my life.

528. Does he who is perfectly contrite obtain the remission of his sins, when it is not in his power to confess them?

He does; provided he be resolved to confess them.[439]

529. Is imperfect contrition, together with the sacrament of penance, sufficient for obtaining the remission of our sins?

It is, when none of the four conditions we spoke of above is wanting; and provided the penitent "begin to love (God) as the fountain of all justice."[440]

---

[438] Cf. Council of Trent, Session 14, "Doctrine on the Sacrament of Penance," Ch. 4
[439] Cf. Ibid.
[440] Council of Trent, Session 6, "Decree on Justification," Ch. 6

Of Certain Things Which Greatly Serve to Strengthen and Move the Sinner to Contrition

530. **What ought the sinner do in order to be truly sorrowful and contrite for his sins?**

He ought to beg earnestly of God, to grant him this heavenly sorrow, and diligently to reflect on the things which may excite him thereunto.[441]

531. **What are those things which he ought to reflect upon?**

Let him consider: 1) First, the majesty and goodness of God, whom he has offended. 2) Let him consider all the good he has done him. 3) Let him lay before his eyes the passion or sufferings of Jesus Christ for his sake.[442]

532. **What else ought he to do towards moving himself to a true sorrow for his sins?**

Let him think: 1) First, on the number and baseness of his sins. 2) On his ingratitude and unreasonable boldness in committing sin.[443]

533. **Is there not still some other means from which he can draw advantage?**

Yes; he can consider that he has deserved the divine vengeance, and the torments of hell.[444]

534. **What else ought he to do, after having diligently considered and weighed in his mind these things we spoke of?**

He ought to excite himself earnestly to praise and love God above all things, the Father of all mercy, his Maker, his Savior, and his preserver; not only on account of the time he gave him to repent, and of all his other gifts, but also because he is infinitely good and amiable in himself.[445]

---

[441] Cf. Jn 15:5
[442] Cf. Ps 47:2; Dt 32:6ff; Phil 2:5ff
[443] Cf. Jer 2:12ff; Heb 10:28-29
[444] Cf. Jer 2:19; Heb 10:27
[445] Cf. Ps 33; Lk 18:19

Of a Firm Purpose of Amendment

535. What is the third thing that is necessary for receiving the sacrament of penance with benefit?

A firm and strong resolution to do nothing against the will of God, henceforward.

536. What do you say of him who has not this firm resolution?

His confession is good for nothing; because this resolution is absolutely necessary.[446]

537. Make an act of firm purpose?

O Lord, I am resolved, and have strong hopes, by the help of thy grace, not to deserve thine anger anymore; I would rather die than fall henceforth into sin.

538. How shall one know that he had this resolution?

He will know it by two principal signs, to wit: the shunning of the occasions of sin, and amendment of life.[447]

LESSON 6

Of Confession

539. What is the fourth thing that is necessary for the sacrament of penance?

Confession.[448]

540. What is confession?

It is an accusation and declaration of sins, made by the penitent against

---

[446] Cf. Ps 118:106; Mt 10:37-39; Council of Trent, Session 14, "Doctrine on the Sacrament of Penance," Ch. 4
[447] Cf. Mt 7:20; Lk 6:44; Col 3
[448] Cf. Nm 5:7; Jn 20:23; Acts 19:18; Jas 5:16

himself, in the presence of a priest, who has power to enjoin him penance, and to give him the remedy and absolution thereof.[449]

541. **How ought this declaration to be made?**

We are obliged, after a diligent and exact examination of ourselves, to tell every mortal sin we remember, without adding or diminishing, and likewise every kind of sin; how often we fell into it, and every circumstance thereof which doth considerably aggravate the sin.[450]

542. **Is it certainly necessary to mention in confession all the mortal sins which we have committed and call to mind?**

It is undoubtedly; for whosoever conceals any one sin, addeth a grievous mortal sin to the rest of his offences, by abusing this sacrament, and by lying not to man, but to God himself.[451]

543. **What hinders us to declare all our sins in confession?**

It is commonly either fear or shame.

544. **Is it necessary for us to renounce this criminal fear and foolish shame?**

Yes; for unless we do so, we shall be damned forever; and instead of the shame we refused to endure in private, we shall suffer shame and reproach publicly, before the whole world, on the day of judgment.[452]

545. **Is it not to be feared that our ghostly father may discover our sins to somebody else?**

No; for he is bound, under pain of eternal damnation, to suffer death

---

[449] Cf. 1 Jn 1:9

[450] Cf. Council of Trent, Session 14, "Doctrine on the Sacrament of Penance," Ch. 5; *Catechism of the Council of Trent*, "The Sacrament of Penance"; Charles Borromeo, *Acts of the Church of Milan*

[451] Cf. Jas 2:10; Acts 5:4; Council of Trent, Session 14, "Doctrine on the Sacrament of Penance," Ch. 5

[452] Cf. Na 3:4ff; 1 Cor 4:5; Council of Trent, Session 14, "Doctrine on the Sacrament of Penance," Ch. 5

sooner than reveal any one sin; moreover, he would fall from his degree or rank in the Church.[453]

LESSON 7

Of the Manner in Which Confession Is to Be Made

546. **After you have recollected your sins, and fixed them in your memory, after you have also stirred up and excited yourself to true sorrow for having fallen into them, how do you behave yourself in the presence of the priest?**
I fall upon my knees full of heaviness and sorrow, I bless myself, and humbly ask the ghostly father's blessing.[454]

547. **What words do you make use of, when you ask his blessing?**
I say, *Benedic mihi, Pater, quia peccavi*; that is, "Bless me, Father, for I have sinned."

548. **What do you do afterwards?**
I say the *confiteor* in Latin, to *mea culpa*, if I understand Latin; if not, I say it in English, to these words, "through my fault."

549. **Say the *confiteor* in Latin.**
Confiteor Deo omnipotenti, Beatae Mariae semper Virgini, beato Michaeli archangelo, beato Joanni Baptistae, sanctis apostolis Petro et Paulo, omnibus sanctis, (et tibi, Pater,) quia peccavi nimis cogitatione, verbo et opere, mea culpa, mea culpa, mea maxima culpa. Ideo precor Beatam Mariam semper Virginem, beatum Michaelem archangelum, beatum Joannem Baptistam, sanctos apostolos Petrum et Paulum, omnes sanctos (et te, Pater) orare pro me ad Dominum Deum nostrum.

550. **Say it in English.**
"I confess to Almighty God, to the Blessed Virgin Mary, to the blessed

---

[453] Cf. Thomas Aquinas, *Quodlibetal Questions*, q. 12, a. 16; Fourth Lateran Council, Const. 21

[454] Cf. Ps 50; Jas 4:10

Michael the archangel, to the blessed John Baptist, to the holy apostles Peter and Paul, to all the saints (and to you, Father), that I have sinned in thought, word, and deed, through my fault, through my fault, through my most grievous fault. Therefore I beseech the Blessed Virgin Mary, the blessed Michael the archangel, the blessed John the Baptist, the holy apostles Peter and Paul, and all the saints, (and you, Father,) to pray for me to our Lord God."

551. **What are you to do next?**
I must tell how long it is since I confessed last, and accuse myself particularly of all the mortal sins which I have committed since that time; and likewise of the mortal sins which I forgot before.

552. **What ought you to do when the ghostly father asks you questions?**
I am obliged to answer him faithfully and submissively.[455]

553. **What do you do after you have confessed your sins?**
I finish the *confiteor*, and listen attentively to the counsels which the confessor gives me, and to the penance which he enjoins me.

554. **How do you behave yourself when the confessor is giving you the absolution?**
I make at the same time an act of contrition; that is, I conceive great grief and sorrow for my sins, and receive the absolution with the head bowed down, and with a humble heart.

555. **What are you to do after confession?**
I ought to give great thanks to God for having forgiven me my sins; I ought likewise to renew my good resolutions, and to perform my penance devoutly and thankfully as soon as possible.[456]

---

[455] Cf. Eph 4:24-25
[456] Cf. Lk 15:16ff; Jas 1:24

556. **Is it not sometimes profitable to the sinner that the absolution should be deferred?**

It is sometimes profitable, and even absolutely necessary for him that it should be deferred.[457]

557. **For whom is it necessary that the absolution should be deferred?**

For those who are ignorant of the things which every Christian is obliged to learn and know, or that are ignorant of the duties of their calling; for those also, who, after admonition, neglect to instruct and govern their children and family Christian-like; for those, likewise, that are not willing to avoid the immediate occasions of sin.[458]

558. **What means the immediate occasion of sin?**

Everything that is wont to draw one into sin; as for example, the frequenting of a house or company which commonly draws one into sin, the reading of love-books, the following of a calling or trade by which a person is accustomed to fall into sin.

559. **Is it possible that we are obliged upon any account, to avoid and forsake our kindred, companions, or the calling we live by?**

It is very possible; for it is certain that we are under an obligation of shunning them when we see that after all the admonitions we have received, and after all the endeavors we have made, they continually draw us into sin; for it is necessary for us either to cease from sinning or to avoid the occasions.

560. **Who gave us this commandment?**

Our Savior, saying if thy right eye or hand scandalize thee, pluck out the

---

[457] Cf. Mt 7:6; 2 Cor 7:8-9; *Rituale Romanum*; Charles Borromeo, *Acts of the Church of Milan*, Pt. 4, "Instructions for Confessors"

[458] Cf. Innocent XI, Decret. contra 65 Propos. 2 Martii, 1679; Charles Borromeo, *Acts of the Church of Milan*, Pt. 4, "Instructions for Confessors"; *Rituale Romanum*

eye, or cut off the hand, and cast it from thee; "for it is better for thee that one of thy members perish, than that thy whole body be cast into hell."[459]

561. For whom else is it necessary that the absolution should be deferred?

For those who are in a habitual or customary sin, until such time as they mend their life; for those also that have not the will to forgive their neighbor, nor to make peace with him.[460]

562. For whom still is it necessary that the absolution should be refused or deferred?

For those who have their neighbor's goods, or that have hurt their neighbor either in his goods or reputation, and have no mind to make restitution according to their ability.[461]

563. To whom else is it fit to refuse or delay the absolution?

To those who have sinned publicly, and refused to make satisfaction or do penance openly, according to the custom of the country, and the injunction of the bishop or superior.[462]

564. For whom, lastly, is it necessary that the absolution should be deferred?

For those who come to confession without preparation, without an examination of conscience, without sorrow for their sins, without a true resolution of correcting themselves; and likewise for those who make not a full confession; or that are not willing to perform the penance which the priest enjoins them.

---

[459] Mt 5:29-30; Cf. Mk 8:36; Lk 9:25; Gregory the Great, *Can. Falsas de Pœnit.* dist. 2; Innocent II, *Can. Fratres de Poenit.* dist. 5; Alex. VII. Innocent XI, Decret. contra 65 Propos., 1679.

[460] Cf. Charles Borromeo, *Acts of the Church of Milan*, Pt. 4, "Instructions for Confessors"; Second Lateran Council, Can. 22; *Rituale Romanum*

[461] Cf. Ibid.

[462] Cf. Council of Trent, Session 24, "Decree on Reformation," Ch. 8; *Rituale Romanum*

565. **Is it enough for all these people to knock their breasts hard, and positively promise to do all things that are necessary?**

It is not enough for the ignorant people who come to confession without preparation, nor for those who by their promises have already deceived their confessor, or rather themselves, unless they be in danger of death, and that such as are ignorant be actually instructed, and duly disposed before they get absolution; for it is not by words or promises, but by works, the kingdom of God is obtained.[463]

566. **What would happen if the director should absolve those whom he sees to want the necessary conditions?**

It would happen that this absolution would be of no force nor value; and that both the confessor and sinner would commit a great crime against God.[464]

567. **What should be said to the senseless people who would take ill the confessor's severe sentence or refusal; and would say that they are afraid to die suddenly in their sins?**

They ought to be made sensible, that far from their receiving any benefit by an absolution given against all rule, it would draw the curse of God upon them;[465] and that God will not abandon them in the time of necessity, if they themselves endeavor to repent and make their peace with the Lord of mercies.[466]

---

[463] Cf. Mt 7:21; 1 Cor 4:20; Ti 1:16; Second Lateran Council, Can. 22; Charles Borromeo, *Acts of the Church of Milan*, Pt. 4, "Instructions for Confessors"; Innocent XI

[464] Cf. Mt 15:14

[465] Cf. Jer 4:14; Ez 13:10, 19; Gregory the Great, *Homily 26 on the Gospels*

[466] Cf. Fourth Council of Carthage, Can. 2; Council of Arles, Can. 12; Cyprian, *Epistle 18*

LESSON 8

Of Satisfaction

568. **What is the fifth thing necessary for the sacrament of penance?**
Satisfaction, that is, a reparation of the injury offered to God by sin; and of the injustice done to our neighbor.

569. **Can we not make a good confession without having a resolution of making satisfaction according to our power?**
We cannot; for this resolution is absolutely necessary.[467]

570. **Is not the punishment due to sin forgiven, when the sin itself is remitted?**
The everlasting punishment is forgiven; but the temporal punishment is not usually forgiven.[468]

571. **Did not Christ make satisfaction for us?**
He did, certainly; however, his superabundant satisfaction will not avail us, unless we ourselves cooperate with his grace, and use our endeavors to satisfy God in Christ and through Christ, who renders our actions agreeable and meritorious before God, and in whom we put all our hope and confidence; for although our Savior suffered and humbled himself to death for our sake, still we must humble ourselves and suffer in union with him, if we have a mind to be conformable to him, or to be made partakers of his resurrection and everlasting bliss.[469]

572. **How is satisfaction made to God?**
By performing the penance enjoined us by our ghostly father; and also by

---

[467] Cf. Ex 22; Rom 13:7; Council of Trent, Session 14, "Doctrine on the Sacrament of Penance," Ch. 8
[468] Cf. 2 Kgs 12:13-14; Heb 12:6; Council of Trent, Session 14, "Doctrine on the Sacrament of Penance," Ch. 8
[469] Cf. Rom 8:17-18, 29; Col 1:24; 2 Tm 2:11-12

a voluntary mortification of the flesh, by almsdeeds, fasting, and prayer; and by suffering patiently all affronts and troubles for God's sake.[470]

573. **Have priests power to enjoin us penance?**
They have truly; for Christ gave them power not only to loose us, but likewise to bind us.[471]

574. **What do you say of those who find fault with, and blame their ghostly father for laying a heavy penance upon them; although it be proportionable to their transgressions, and in their power to perform it?**
I say, they do a great wrong to the ghostly father; and that it is likely they know not what is good for themselves.

575. **Why do you say they wrong the ghostly father?**
Because it is certain, that he is bound to enjoin a penance proportionable to the sins and evil inclinations of the penitent, in order not only to preserve him from relapsing into the same faults, but likewise to punish past offences; and in case he were too indulgent or easy to the penitent, he would become partaker of his sins.[472]

576. **Why do you say that it is likely they know not what is good for themselves?**
Because it is much better for them to endeavor, with God's grace, to make satisfaction in this life for their sins, than to undergo the punishment due to them, in the fire of purgatory. Moreover, a proportionable and wholesome penance greatly contributes to put them upon their guard, and to preserve them from fatal relapses, and from eternal damnation.[473]

---

[470] Cf. Rom 8:17; Col 1:24; 1 Cor 5:3; Council of Trent, Session 14, "Doctrine on the Sacrament of Penance," Ch. 8-9

[471] Cf. Mt 18:18; 1 Cor 5:3ff

[472] Cf. Council of Trent, Session 14, "Doctrine on the Sacrament of Penance," Ch. 8-9; *Catechism of the Council of Trent*, "The Third Part of Penance"

[473] Cf. Council of Trent, Session 14, "Doctrine on the Sacrament of Penance," Ch. 8-9

577. **Is it a great sin not to perform our penance?**

It is; because we are obliged to bring forth worthy fruits of penance;[474] and that God is despised, when the ghostly father, who represents him, is not obeyed.[475]

578. **How is satisfaction made to the neighbor?**

By restitution, or a reparation of the hurt done to him in his goods, in his credit, or reputation.[476]

579. **Are there no means in the Church, which help us to satisfy the divine justice?**

There are, to wit, indulgences.

LESSON 9

Of Indulgences

580. **What is an indulgence?**

It is a gift or grace from the superiors of the Church, whereby we receive the remission of the temporal pains, which we are obliged to undergo either in this world, or in the other, for the sins which were forgiven us by the sacrament of penance.[477]

581. **Doth not a plenary indulgence remit us all our sins?**

No; it remits only the temporal punishments; for no mortal sin ever was, or ever shall be forgiven to any one, after baptism, without a hearty sorrow for having fallen into it; and likewise without a firm purpose of amending his life for the future.[478]

---

[474] Cf. Mt 3:8
[475] Cf. Lk 10:16; 1 Thes 4:8
[476] Cf. Rom 13:7
[477] Cf. 2 Cor 2:6ff; Chrysostom, *Homily 4 on 2 Corinthians*; Ambrose, *On Repentance*, Bk. 2, Ch. 7; Pacian, *Epistle 1*, To Sympronian; Cyprian, *Treatise 3*
[478] Cf. Council of Trent, Session 14, "Doctrine on the Sacrament of Penance," Ch. 4

582. **Doth every indulgence release entirely the temporal punishments due to our sins?**

It does, according to the generality of divines, if it be a plenary indulgence; but if it be not, it remits only a part of the temporal punishment.

583. **Doth the Church therefore exempt us from making satisfaction, when she grants us a plenary indulgence?**

Not altogether; for our holy father the pope commands us to give alms, to fast and to pray devoutly; we are likewise obliged to perform diligently and piously the penance which our ghostly father enjoins us; and to make satisfaction, or restitution to our neighbor in his goods and reputation, according to our ability. Moreover, as nobody knows whether he has the necessary conditions for gaining the indulgence, the prudent Christians do, at the same time, endeavor to make satisfaction for their sins.[479]

584. **Are we not also obliged to be resolved to satisfy and serve God until death?**

We are undoubtedly; for God commands us to "endeavor to enter in at the narrow gate,"[480] "to work (our) salvation with fear and trembling,"[481] and to love him with our whole heart, and above all things.[482] Moreover, the life of a Christian, upon earth, "ought to be a perpetual penance."[483]

585. **Doth a plenary indulgence free us from fulfilling the commandments, and from subduing our disorderly passions?**

It is unreasonable and damnable to say or think that it exempts us from either of them; for it is certain and manifest, according to the express words of the Holy Ghost, that "man's life upon the earth is a warfare"[484] and temptation; and it is also certain, that neither the sin, nor the temporal punishment, is forgiven to those who have not a sincere resolution at the

---

[479] Cf. Bellarmine, *De Indulg.*, c. 12
[480] Lk 13:24; Cf. Mt 7:13
[481] Phil 2:12
[482] Cf. Mt 22:37
[483] Council of Trent, Session 14, "On the Sacrament of Extreme Unction," Introduction
[484] Jb 7:1

time of the indulgence, to employ their goods, their life, and their health according to the law of God and the Church.[485]

586. **Is it certain that the Church has power to grant indulgences?**
It is very certain; for Christ gave her this power, when he said, "Whatsoever you shall bind upon earth, shall be bound in heaven, and whatsoever you shall loose upon earth shall be also loosed in heaven."[486]

587. **Who are those in the Church that have power to grant indulgences?**
The bishops have power to grant some of them; but the pope hath full power to grant all indulgences, according to the promise made by Christ to Saint Peter in particular.[487]

588. **How doth the Church by indulgences forgive the punishment due to sinners?**
By applying liberally to us the benefit or fruit of the superabundant satisfaction and merits of Jesus Christ and of the saints, which is called the "treasure of the Church."[488]

589. **What ought to be done to gain an indulgence?**
It is necessary to perform diligently and devoutly, according to the intention of the Church, everything that she orders for that purpose; and to be in the state of grace.[489]

590. **Why is it necessary that one should be in the state of grace, in order to gain the indulgence?**
Because the temporal punishment due to us for sin, is not remitted us until we have made our peace with God.[490]

---

[485] Cf. Mt 3:8-10; Gal 5:24; 1 Jn 3:14
[486] Mt 18:18; Cf. Council of Trent, Session 25, "Decree Concerning Indulgences"
[487] Cf. Mt 16:19
[488] Council of Trent, Session 21, "Decree on Reformation," Ch. 9; Cf. 1 Cor 1:30; Col 1:24
[489] Cf. 1 Cor 13:1-3; Bellarmine, *De Indulg.*, c. 13
[490] Cf. Jb 9:4; Rom 5:1; Bellarmine, *De Indulg.*, c.13

591. **Can those who are not actually prepared, and that are put off or delayed by their ghostly father, gain the indulgence at another time?**

They can undoubtedly gain the indulgence called jubilee, if according to the directions of the confessor, they prepare themselves for it, as they ought.

592. **What doth the Church command, in order to receive the indulgence with benefit?**

She orders us to repent sincerely, to confess, to communicate, and to perform diligently certain other good works.

593. **What is the intention of the Church in granting indulgences?**

Her intention is to assuage the wrath of God; to make him satisfaction for our sins, by applying the merits of Christ to us; and to obtain grace from him both for us, and for the whole Church.

594. **What benefit ought we to reap from this exposition of indulgences?**

1) First, we ought to make a great account of indulgences. 2) To render thanks to God for having given us such easy means of applying to us the merit of his most precious blood. 3) To endeavor to receive indulgences as often as possible; particularly at the hour of death, in order to be freed from the fire of purgatory.[491]

LESSON 10

Of the Defects Which Render Confession Void, and of the Manner of Repairing It by a General Confession

595. **When is a confession void?**

When any of the five conditions necessary for receiving the sacrament of penance lawfully, is wanting.

---

[491] Cf. 2 Cor 6:12

596. **When has one reason to fear that his confessions are void and of no effect?**
When he has not shunned the immediate occasions of sin; and has not used either diligence or endeavors to amend his life, or to learn the duties of a Christian, and of his proper calling.[492]

597. **Is there anything else which gives one room to doubt that his past confessions were of no effect?**
There is, to wit: when he has not made peace with his enemy or adversary; or has not made restitution of his neighbor's goods when in his power.[493]

598. **What are the necessary means whereby bad confessions can be repaired?**
A good general confession.

599. **What ought to be done to attain to it?**
It is necessary to renew the past confessions, and to let the ghostly father know all the defects thereof; and to fulfil whatever he will order.

600. **How is one to make this general confession with order and benefit?**
He should retire to a private place, and divide his life into parts, according to the variety of the affairs he has been engaged in; and of the places of his abode.

601. **What else is he to do?**
It is necessary, he should take time, not one day nor two, but the time that is necessary for examining closely his conscience according to the division we spoke of above, and according to the extent or scope of the commandments of God and the Church, and of the deadly sins.

602. **What else is he still to do?**
He ought, humbly and diligently, to beg the light of the Holy Ghost, that he may see his faults: after this prayer, let him earnestly endeavor to call

---

[492] Cf. Charles Borromeo, *Acts of the Church of Milan*, Pt. 4, "Instructions for Confessors"
[493] Cf. Rom 3:17; 13:7-8; Second Lateran Council, Can. 22

to mind the companies which he frequented from time to time, and from place to place; and in what, and how often he transgressed the law of God.

603. **What else, lastly, is he obliged to do?**

Let him, as well as he can, sum up in his memory, or write down, if he be a scholar, the kinds and number of all his sins; let him beg mercy of God; and let him stir himself up to great grief and sorrow for them; let him firmly resolve to amend his life; let him confidently approach the throne of mercy, in order to obtain pardon for all; and let him devoutly perform the penance which shall be enjoined him.

LESSON 11

Of Extreme Unction

604. **What is extreme unction?**

It is a sacrament instituted by Jesus Christ; which enables us to overcome the wiles and temptations of the devil, at the hour of death, and likewise helps us to die well.[494]

605. **Doth not this sacrament sometimes restore corporal health to the sick person?**

It does, when it is expedient for the salvation of his soul.[495]

606. **How ought one to prepare himself for this sacrament?**

He must confess, if he be in mortal sin; he ought also to make an act of contrition at the time he receives it; and to beg of God to forgive him the sins, which he hath committed by every organ or part that is anointed.

---

[494] Cf. Jas 5:13-15
[495] Cf. Mk 6:13; Jas 5:13-15; Council of Trent, Session 14, "On the Sacrament of Extreme Unction," Ch. 2

607. **How ought those, who are present at the administration of this sacrament, to behave themselves?**

They ought to be attentive to the prayers of the Church, and to pray for the sick person; they should afterwards enter into themselves, and consider the frailty of this life, and the great need they have to prepare themselves betimes, for eternity.

608. **At what time ought the extreme unction to be received?**

In every dangerous sickness: yet it ought not to be administered to infants, fools, or to such as are always mad.[496]

609. **Is it fit to wait until the hour, or agony of death?**

No; for it is much more profitable for the sick person to receive it whilst he has leisure, reason, and memory to prepare himself for it as becometh, than to receive it late and unseasonably.[497]

610. **Suppose one had lost his speech, and could not therefore confess his sins, what ought he to do?**

Let him make an act of contrition or sorrow for his sins, and give signs that he hath a desire to obtain the forgiveness of them, and to receive the extreme unction.

611. **From whom ought we to receive this sacrament?**

From the parish priest, or from another priest, with his permission, if it be possible.[498]

612. **How is this sacrament administered?**

The priest anoints with consecrated oil, the eyes and the other organs of our corporal senses, saying: "By this holy anointing, and through his own

---

[496] Cf. Council of Trent, Session 14, "On the Sacrament of Extreme Unction," Ch. 3

[497] Cf. Charles Borromeo, *Acts of the Church of Milan*, First Provincial Council, Pt. 2; *Catechism of the Council of Trent*, "The Sacrament of Extreme Unction"

[498] Cf. *Catechism of the Council of Trent*, "The Sacrament of Extreme Unction"; Charles Borromeo, *Acts of the Church of Milan*, Fifth Provincial Council, Pt. 1, tit. ult.

most tender mercy, may the Lord forgive thee every sin thou hast committed by seeing," and so of the other senses.

613. **How many corporal senses are there?**
Five; to wit: feeling, smelling, taste, hearing and seeing.

614. **Why are those parts anointed rather than any other parts of the body?**
Because it is by our corporal senses we sin oftenest.

615. **How ought the sick person to behave himself after receiving the extreme unction?**
He ought to trouble himself no more with worldly affairs; to be patient and mild to those who serve, or attend him; and to conform his will to the will of God, in all things; for "whether we live or die we are the Lord's."[499]

616. **What else ought he to do?**
He ought to employ the remainder of his strength and time, in prayer and godly thoughts, and in actions of thanksgiving to God, for having given him the benefit of this sacrament; in meditating on death and eternity; in putting his entire confidence in the mercy of God, and in the sufferings of Jesus Christ for his sake.[500]

LESSON 12

Of the Sacrament of Holy Order

617. **What is holy order?**
It is a sacrament which gives power and grace to clergymen to offer holily the Sacrifice of the Mass; and to administer the sacraments, and the word of God, with diligence and devotion.[501]

[499] Rom 14:8
[500] Cf. 1 Pt 4:2
[501] Cf. 1 Tm 4:14; 2 Tm 1:6

618. From whom comes this power?
From Christ, who first gave it to the apostles, with authority and command to give it to other men.[502]

619. Who administers or gives this sacrament?
A bishop only.[503]

620. How many conditions should he have who is upon receiving this sacrament?
There are many; but it is most necessary he should have five principal conditions.

621. What is the first condition?
It is necessary that he be called by God, or by the person who represents God, and that he choose not this holy state of his own head;[504] for, as our Savior sayeth: "He that entereth not by the door into the fold of the sheep, but climbeth up another way, the same is a thief and a robber."[505]

622. Is it not enough, that he has a great desire to be of the Church?
No; for it often happens, that this great desire comes not from God, but either from the love of idleness and ease, or from an expectation of gaining honor and esteem in the world; or from some other disorderly passion, which deserves the curse of God.[506]

623. Is it sufficient that his parents design him for the Church?
No; for parents are often as worldly and as vain as their children; moreover, they are commonly ignorant of the obligations of clergymen, and of the dangers of this high calling; so that, as our Savior said to the children of Zebedee, and to their mother: they know not what they ask.[507]

---

[502] Cf. Lk 22:19; Jn 20:23; Acts 13:2-3; Ti 1:5
[503] Cf. Council of Trent, Session 23, "Decree on Reformation," Ch. 8
[504] Cf. Heb 5:4
[505] Jn 10:1
[506] Cf. Is 30:1-2; Os 8:4-5; Mt 8:19-20; Phil 3:18-19; Gregory the Great, *Pastoral Rule*, Bk. 1, Ch. 1; Sixtus V, Bul. edit. 1588
[507] Cf. Mt 20:22; Council of Bordeaux in 1624

624. How then can one know that God calls him?

If he has the conditions we are going to speak of here, and if the person who represents God, doth, after a long and due trial, either call him, or even counsel him to be of the Church, it can be well presumed that he is called by God; yet, after all that, let him fear and tremble; for Judas, although called by God himself, was miserably lost.[508]

625. Whom do you mean by the person who represents God?

The bishop chiefly, and every pious and learned man to whom he gives power to instruct and conduct his people to everlasting life, and who likewise has no worldly motive or interest whatsoever in the person whom he directs being or not being advanced to orders.[509]

626. What is the second condition?

A resolution and sincere desire of spending his life and health in promoting the glory of God, and in working his own salvation, and that of his neighbor.[510]

627. What is the third condition?

An honest, virtuous, and exemplary life.[511]

628. What is the fourth condition?

He must be free even from all hidden mortal sins, at least for a long time before he receives this sacrament, and be in love and peace with God and man; for it is to clergymen God speaks, saying: "Be ye clean, who carry the vessels of the Lord."[512]

---

[508] Cf. Mt 10:4; Jn 17:12

[509] Cf. Acts 9:10ff; 13:2ff; Ti 1:5

[510] Cf. Ps 15:5; 68:10; Lk 16:13; 1 Cor 9:16; 2 Tm 2:4

[511] Cf. Lv 20:7; Mt 5:13; 1 Tm 3:2ff; Council of Trent, Session 23, "Decree on Reformation," Ch. 12; *Catechism of the Council of Trent*, "The Sacrament of Holy Orders"; Benedict XIV, *Ubi Primum*

[512] Is 52:11; Cf. Lv 21:8; 1 Tm 3:8-10; Gregory the Great, *Pastoral Rule*, Bk. 3, Ch. 25; Bk. 3, *Epistle 26*; Council of Trent, Session 23; *Catechism of the Council of Trent*, "The Sacrament of Holy Orders"

629. What is the fifth condition?

Learning and knowledge, enough to instruct and guide others both by word and example,[513] according to the law of God and the Church; for God warns the ignorant, saying: because thou hast rejected knowledge, I will also reject thee, that thou shalt not be a priest to me;[514] and it is to the clergy Christ says: "You are the light of the world…let your light shine before men, that they may see your good works, and glorify your Father, who is in heaven."[515]

630. Which are the virtues that are most requisite in the person who aspires to the ecclesiastical state?

The spirit or love of prayer, chastity, temperance, prudence, humility and docility; contempt of the world, patience in adversity, fortitude or strength of mind, love of retirement, to be laborious and given to study.[516]

631. What followeth from all we have said here?

It followeth: 1) First, that parents are strictly obliged to take a special care to give a godly and truly Christian education and solid learning, to such of their children as they would fain engage in an ecclesiastical state; for as the great pope, who sits today in the chair of Saint Peter, sayeth: it cannot be expressed, how important it is to train up such as are called to the inheritance of the Lord, to piety, good manners, and ecclesiastical discipline from their infancy.[517] 2) That, far from so much as counselling those of their children, who are not witty, pious, and studious, to embrace the ecclesiastic state, they are obliged, by all means, to hinder them from engaging therein; for no greater evil or misfortune can befall their children, than to enter into sacred orders without the necessary qualifications.[518]

[513] Cf. Mal 2:7
[514] Cf. Os 4:6
[515] Mt 5:14, 16; Cf. 1 Cor 9:16; *Catechism of the Council of Trent*, "The Sacrament of Holy Orders"; Council of Trent, Session 22, "Decree on Reformation," Ch. 1; Session 23, "Decree on Reformation," Ch. 14; Benedict XIV, *Ubi Primum*
[516] Cf. 1 Tm 3:8-10; 2 Tm 3:17
[517] Cf. Benedict XIV, *Ubi Primum*
[518] Cf. 1 Kgs 2, 3, 5; Mt 27:3ff

3) That, if they have a mind that any of their children should be clergymen, they ought to present God with the most witty, the most pious, and the most studious; for it is not pleasing to either God or the Church, to offer them the dull-witted, the impious, the maimed, the infirm, or the refuse of their children.[519] 4) That they ought to lay no obligation whatsoever on those, even of their children, whom they look upon as pious and studious, either to engage or not engage themselves in the ecclesiastical state, but leave them at full liberty, and commit them entirely to the bishop and their spiritual director's hands and charge; for it belongeth to God and the Church, and to no one else, to call them to this holy state.

5) That every youth, who thinks of entering one day or other into the ecclesiastical state, is strictly bound to learn his religion well; to fly sin, and avoid bad company; to choose a godly confessor, and be obedient to him in all things; to frequent the sacraments; to pray much, that he may find out the will of God, and be not deceived in his choice, saying often in the day: "Show me thy ways, O Lord; teach me thy paths: direct me in thy truth, and teach me; because thou art my God and my Savior."[520] 6) It is necessary he should learn and closely consider the advantages and disadvantages, or dangers of this state; lest he should enter blindly upon it, and repent too late; for although its advantages be many, its obligations, disadvantages, or dangers are likewise many.[521]

7) That it is absolutely necessary for him to ask counsel often, not of the first man that comes in his way, but of "one among a thousand,"[522] one that has the conditions we have already spoken of, and to whom he will discover, from time to time, his motives, his difficulties and inclinations, whether good or bad; to be obedient to his bishop until death; to have only in view to do the will of God, and to save himself and his neighbor: in a word, to pass his life piously, to labor earnestly for science; and to be persuaded that "it were better for him," as our Savior sayeth, "that a millstone

---

[519] Cf. Lv 21:17ff; Decret. Greg. IX. lib. 1, Tit. 20
[520] Ps 24:4-5
[521] Cf. Ws 6:6; Lk 12:48
[522] Ecclus 6:6

were hung at his neck, and that he were drowned in the depth of the sea,"[523] than to give scandal to anyone, either by his bad life, or by his ignorance.

LESSON 13

Of Matrimony

632. **What is matrimony?**

It is a sacrament, which sanctifies the lawful society of a man and a woman; and gives them grace to bring up their children in the fear and love of God; to support the difficulties of marriage; and to be faithful to one another until death.

633. **What are the conditions necessary for receiving this sacrament Christian-like?**

There are four very necessary conditions.

634. **What is the first condition?**

A conscience clear from all mortal sin; wherefore it is fit to confess and communicate a day or two beforehand.[524]

635. **What is the second condition?**

It is necessary to be free from all impediments of matrimony; such as the obstacles that arise from consanguinity, affinity, or spiritual kindred; want of age, a vow of chastity, and from some more of the like kind.[525]

636. **How shall one find out that he hath no impediment?**

Let him open his mind and condition to a learned director, sometime before the marriage.

---

[523] Mt 18:6

[524] Cf. Council of Trent, Session 24, "Decree on the Reformation of Marriage," Ch. 1

[525] Cf. Lv 18:6ff; Council of Trent, Session 24, Can. 3; "Decree on the Reformation of Marriage," Ch 2

637. What harm is it that a person who hath an impediment should marry?

It is a great sin; moreover, there are impediments, which entirely break the marriage, and draw a curse and much mischief upon the couple, if they cohabit.[526]

638. Why do you say, that it is fit to confess and ask counsel beforehand of a learned director?

Because a marriage impediment often comes from the hidden sins of the time past.

639. Why do you say, it is proper to do so, sometime before the marriage?

To the end, that one may have leisure to get a dispensation from the bishop; or to take some other course, according to the advice of the ghostly father.

640. What is the third condition?

It is to receive it with a resolution of fulfilling the law of God and the Church, in this state.[527]

641. What is the fourth condition?

It is to receive it with devotion, modesty, and shamefacedness.[528]

642. From whom ought this sacrament to be received?

From the parish priest in the presence of two or three witnesses, or from another priest with the express permission of the bishop or parish priest.[529]

---

[526] Cf. Council of Trent, Session 24, "Decree on the Reformation of Marriage," Ch. 4-5

[527] Cf. Tb 6:22; 1 Thes 4:3-5

[528] Cf. Tb 8:5; Charles Borromeo, *Acts of the Church of Milan*, Pt. 1, Fifth Provincial Council, Pt. 3, "De Matrimonium"

[529] Cf. Council of Trent, Session 24, "Decree on the Reformation of Marriage," Ch. 1

643. Do young people sin who marry or espouse each other unknown to the parish priest, without the consent of their parents, and without two or three witnesses?

It is certain that they sin grievously; and it is also certain, that the marriage contracted unknown to the parish priest, and without two or three witnesses, is neither lawful nor valid where the law of the Church is received in its full extent.[530]

644. What are the obligations of the married couple?

1) First, to be united and live together during life.[531] 2) To be faithful to one another, as they have promised in marriage.[532] 3) To assist one another in their distress; to bear patiently the indiscretion, weakness and burthens of each other.[533] 4) To get their children baptized as soon as possible; and to instruct and bring them up Christian-like.[534]

645. What are the faults or vices which the married couple ought to avoid?

Jealousy, bitterness, hatred, reproaches, contentions, scolding, fretfulness, abuse, an excessive love of their children, or of the world; and likewise an immoderate affection, without reason or decency, for one another, whereby they make slight account of the law and love of God.[535]

646. What are the obligations of the married woman in particular?

1) First, she is obliged to be obedient to her husband in everything, that is not contrary to the will of God; for the man is the head of the woman, as Christ is the head of the Church.[536] 2) To beware of miscarrying through her own fault. 3) To bear patiently, and as a punishment of sin, the uneasiness of her pregnancy, and the pains of childbirth.[537] 4) Not to permit

---

[530] Cf. Ibid.
[531] Cf. Mk 10:6-9; 1 Cor 7:10ff
[532] Cf. 1 Cor 7:3; Heb 13:4
[533] Cf. Gal 6:2; Col 3:18-19; 1 Pt 3:8
[534] Cf. Eph 6:4; *Catechism of the Council of Trent*, "The Sacrament of Baptism"
[535] Cf. Col 3:19; 1 Pt 3:1
[536] Cf. Eph 5:22-24; Ti 2:5
[537] Cf. Gn 3:16

that the infant should sleep in one bed with herself or its nurse, within the space of a twelve-month, for fear it should be overlaid, and that the nurse or mother should be guilty of the child's death.[538] 5) She ought, if possible, to nurse her own children, after the example of the holy women of ancient times, and as the holy fathers earnestly recommend to them.[539]

647. What else is she obliged to?

As the man is obliged to provide for his family, and often look after his business abroad, she is in like manner bound to take good care of her family affairs within doors; and not to go about tattling from house to house, nor do, nor suffer anything to be done, which may offend God;[540] for "whosoever takes not care of his own, and especially of those of his own house, he hath denied his faith, and is worse than an infidel."[541]

648. What else are both of them obliged to do?

To give good example to their children and to their whole family; and to engage all to serve God, and pray to him, especially morning and evening.[542]

[538] Cf. *Rituale Romanum*

[539] Cf. Gn 21:7; 1 Kgs 1:22-23; 2 Mc 7:27; Lk 11:27; Basil, *Homily 21*; Ambrose, *Hexameron*, Bk. 5, Ch. 18; Chrysostom, *Homily on Psalm 1*; Gregory the Great, Bk. 2, *Epistle 64*

[540] Cf. Prv 31.13ff; 1 Tm 5:8, 13-14; *Catechism of the Council of Trent*, "The Sacrament of Matrimony"

[541] 1 Tm 5:8

[542] Author's note: Read Lesson 5 of Chapter 2, above.

SECTION IV

Of Hope and Prayer

Chapter 7

LESSON 1

Of Hope and Prayer in General

649. What is the fourth principal thing which every Christian is obliged to do, in order to save himself?

It is to put his hope in God, to crave his assistance, and praise his holy name.[543]

650. What is hope?

A divine virtue, which makes us expect with great confidence, to obtain from God mercy and grace in this life, and eternal bliss in the life to come.[544]

651. On what is our confidence or hope grounded?

Upon the promises of God, who affirmed, that he would give eternal happiness to such as fulfil his law or commandments.[545]

652. On what else is our hope grounded?

Upon the superabundant merits of our Savior Jesus Christ, for which God gives us his grace in this world, and promises us his kingdom and everlasting bliss in the world to come.[546]

---

[543] Cf. Ps 61:9; Rom 8:24
[544] Cf. Rom 8:24
[545] Cf. Heb 6:18-20
[546] Cf. Jn 10:10; Rom 8:32

653. On what condition did God promise us this everlasting happiness?

On condition we shall, with the help of his grace, keep his commandments, and do good works.[547]

654. How doth one sin against hope?

Two ways.

655. What is the first way of sinning against it?

By despair, when one falsely persuades himself that he cannot obtain eternal life, and that, therefore, it is in vain for him to do good works, or repent.[548]

656. What is the second way of sinning against hope?

By presumption, when one foolishly puts his confidence in his own strength, or in the mercy of God; and therefore defers his amendment, and so hardens on in sin.[549]

657. Make an act of hope.

O Lord, my God, I have great confidence that through thy great mercy, and through the superabundant merits of my Savior Jesus Christ, thou wilt give me the assistance of thy grace in this world, and life everlasting in the other, provided I fulfil thy commandments and law.

658. How is hope turned to use or profit?

By often making a humble prayer to God.

659. What is prayer?

Prayer is an elevation or lifting up of our heart to God, in giving him adoration, praise, or thanks; or in begging of him to grant us whatever is necessary, or even profitable for working our salvation.

---

[547] Cf. Mt 19:17; 25:34ff; Rom 2:6
[548] Cf. Jer 18:12; Mt 27:5; Eph 4:19
[549] Cf. Ecclus 5:5-7; Rom 2:4-5

660. **Is it not also permitted us to pray God to grant us the worldly things whereof we stand in need?**

Yes; provided we are resolved to make use of them to the glory of God, and for our own salvation.

661. **Is every Christian obliged to pray?**

Yes; for everybody is bound to honor, praise, and give thanks to God; and likewise to beg mercy and grace of him.

662. **Doth God always hear our prayers?**

No; because we do not always pray as we ought.[550]

663. **How ought we to pray?**

We ought to pray humbly, respectfully, attentively and devoutly.

664. **What do you understand by praying humbly?**

I understand by it, that we ought to think that we are not worthy either to speak to God, or to receive the fruit of our prayers from him; and that if we obtain anything of what we beg of him, it is through his great mercy he grants it to us.[551]

665. **What do you mean by praying respectfully?**

I mean by it, that we should pray to our Lord God, with great respect and reverence.[552]

666. **What do you understand by praying attentively?**

I mean that we are obliged, in the time of prayer, to guard our understanding and will, as well as we can, not only against the wiles and temptations of the devil, but also against worldly thoughts and inclinations, which might withdraw us from God, or distract us in our prayers.[553]

---

[550] Cf. Jas 4:3
[551] Cf. Gn 18:27; Is 66:2; Ps 33:19; Mt 8:8; Lk 18:13-14
[552] Cf. 1 Par 29:17-18; Ps 33:10; Heb 5:7; 12:28
[553] Cf. Is 29:13; Jn 4:23-24

667. **What ought we to think upon in time of prayer?**

Upon God, upon the meaning of the words we pronounce, or upon the things we beg of God.

668. **What do you understand by praying devoutly?**

I understand by it, that we are obliged to pray earnestly and with fervor, so that our heart may be warmly set upon God, or upon the things which dispose and lead us to everlasting life.[554]

669. **Are there not other conditions necessary for praying with benefit?**

There are still three conditions necessary.

670. **What is the first condition?**

To be in the state of grace, or at least to desire sincerely to be reconciled with God.[555]

671. **What is the second condition?**

To have great confidence, that God will give us what we beg of him, if it stands with his glory and the good of our soul.[556]

672. **Upon what should this great confidence of ours be grounded?**

Upon the superabundant merits of Jesus Christ; for it is in his name we make every request to God.

673. **Who taught us to pray in Christ's name?**

It was himself, saying in the gospel: "Whatsoever you shall ask the Father in my name, this I will do."[557] "Whatsoever you shall ask the Father in my name, he will give it you."[558] The Church likewise teacheth us to pray in the

---

[554] Cf. Ps 38:4; Lk 12:49

[555] Cf. Ps 144:18; Jn 15:7; Mt 11:28; Mk 9:23; Lk 18:9-11; Prv 28:9; Is 1:13ff; *Catechism of the Council of Trent*, Pt. 4, "Parts of Prayer"

[556] Cf. Ez 33:11; Mk 11:24; Jas 1:5ff

[557] Jn 14:13

[558] Jn 15:16

name of Christ; for she commonly finishes her prayers with these words: "Through our Lord Jesus Christ"; *Per Dominum nostrum Jesum Christum.*

674. **Why are we obliged to pray through Jesus Christ?**

Because he is our Savior, and that it is by him we have access to our heavenly Father.[559]

675. **What is the third condition?**

Perseverance in praying to God.

676. **What do you understand by perseverance in prayer?**

I understand that we ought to continue in prayer, and not to be weary of praying to God although he should defer granting our request.[560]

677. **Is it true that God always hears our prayer, when we pray to him as we ought?**

It is certain that when we are in the state of grace, God gives us everything that is necessary for our salvation, if we ask it for ourselves with perseverance and as we ought.[561]

678. **Who promised that on these conditions our prayers shall always be heard?**

Our Savior Jesus Christ himself promises it to us; for he says in the gospel: "Ask, and it shall be given you; seek, and you shall find; knock, and it shall be opened to you."[562]

679. **Why do you dwell so long on this lesson of prayer?**

Because there is no instruction whatsoever more necessary than it; for not one of those that were baptized ever was, or ever shall be damned, but either for want of praying as it behoveth, or for want of praying sufficiently.[563]

---

[559] Cf. Rom 5:2; Eph 2:18
[560] Cf. Lk 18:1; 1 Thes 5:17; Eph 6:18
[561] Cf. Ecclus 2; Lk 11:5-13; Jn 15:7
[562] Mt 7:7; Cf. Mt 7:8, 11.
[563] Cf. Ps 144:18; Rom 10:13

680. **What is it we ought oftenest to beg of God?**

The fear and love of God during the whole course of our life, and at length a good end, or happy death.[564]

681. **To whom do we direct our prayers?**

To God, and even to the saints; but not after the same manner.

682. **How do we direct our prayers to God?**

As to the sovereign Lord and supreme ruler of all things, who is able to grant us everything we call for, by his own almighty power.

683. **How do we pray to the saints?**

As to the servants and friends of God, who can obtain grace and mercy for us from God, through the superabundant merits of Jesus Christ.[565]

684. **Is not this praying to saints contrary to the honor we owe to God, and likewise to the great confidence which we are obliged to have in our Savior Jesus Christ?**

By no means; for if the invocation of saints were dishonorable to God or to our Savior, as those who are astray would fain make the ignorant people believe, the apostle Saint Paul had not desired the faithful to pray for himself, and for one another.[566]

685. **For whom ought we to pray?**

For mankind in general; for our spiritual and temporal superiors; for the righteous and for the wicked; for pagans, and for all such people as are astray from the faith; for our friends, and for our enemies; for the living also and for the dead.[567]

---

[564] Cf. Lk 10:42
[565] Cf. Gn 48:16; Lk 15:10; Apoc 1:4; 2:26-27; 5:8; 8:4
[566] Cf. Rom 15:30; Eph 6:18-19; 1 Tm 2:1; Heb 13:18
[567] Cf. 1 Tm 2:1-2; Mt 5:44; 2 Mc 12:46

686. **Whether is it better to pray in private, all alone, or to pray in public, or along with others?**

It is generally better to pray in public, or in society with others.

687. **Why so?**

Because Christ says, that he is in the midst of two or three who are gathered together in his name.[568]

688. **For what other reason is public prayer to be preferred?**

Because when many join together in prayer, they offer, as it were, a holy violence to God, and obtain their request more easily.

LESSON 2

Of the Lord's Prayer

689. **What is the best and most powerful prayer?**

The Lord's Prayer.

690. **Why is it called the Lord's Prayer?**

Because it is our Lord Jesus Christ himself that made it.[569]

691. **Say it in Latin.**

Pater Noster, qui es in coelis, sanctificetur nomen tuum; adveniat regnum tuum; fiat voluntas tua, sicut in coelo, et in terra. Panem nostrum quotidianum da nobis hodie; et dimitte nobis debita nostra, sicut et nos dimittimus debitoribus nostris; et ne nos inducas in tentationem; sed libera nos a malo. Amen.

692. **Say it in English.**

Our Father which art in heaven, hallowed be thy name; thy kingdom come; thy will be done on earth, as it is in heaven. Give us this day our

---

[568] Cf. Mt 18:20
[569] Cf. Mt 6:9-13

daily bread; and forgive us our trespasses, as we forgive them who trespass against us; and lead us not into temptation; but deliver us from evil. Amen.

The Lord's Prayer Expounded

693. **How many petitions are there in the Lord's Prayer?**
There are seven.

694. **Whom do we call *Our Father*?**
God the Father, God the Son, and God the Holy Ghost.

695. **Why do you not say *My Father* instead of *Our Father*?**
Because he is our common Father, and we are all brethren; and even because we are obliged to pray for ourselves and for our neighbor.[570]

696. **How is God our Father?**
Because it is he who created, redeemed, and chose us for his children.

697. **Why do you say, *which art in heaven*, whereas God is everywhere?**
Because it is in heaven he chiefly manifests his glorious majesty; and because the kingdom and inheritance of his children are in heaven.[571]

698. **What do we ask in the first petition, *hallowed be thy name*?**
We desire that God may be known throughout the whole world; and that he may be honored, praised, and loved for ever and ever.

699. **Who are they that hallow or sanctify God's name?**
Those who believe in, and obey him.

700. **Who are they that abuse the name of God?**
Those who break his law, or sin against his commandments.[572]

[570] Cf. 1 Tm 2:1
[571] Cf. Heb 13:14
[572] Cf. 2 Kgs 12:12; Rom 2:23-24

701. What do we beg in the second petition, *thy kingdom come?*

We beg of God to pour his grace into our hearts in this life, and to give us everlasting glory in the life to come.

702. What do we beg in the third petition, *thy will be done on earth as it is in heaven?*

We beg of him, to give us grace to do his will in this world, as the angels do in heaven.

703. What means to do the will of God?

It means to fulfil his commandments, and to bear patiently all the troubles and adversities that befall us.[573]

704. What ought we to consider or think, when God afflicts us with troubles or crosses?

We ought to consider, that God is most just, and that we deserve a great deal more of that kind.[574]

705. What ought we to say in time of trouble, or adversity?

O Lord, thy will be done; blessed be thy name.

706. What do we beg in the fourth petition, *Give us this day our daily bread?*

Everything we stand in need of, in regard to both soul and body; that is, the sacraments, the word and grace of God, even food and rayment.[575]

707. Why do you say, *Give us this day?*

To put us in mind that it is not lawful to be solicitous for tomorrow; and that we ought to put our confidence in the providence of our heavenly Father, who feeds the birds of the air.[576]

---

[573] Cf. Lk 21:19
[574] Cf. Jb 15:15; Lk 23:41
[575] Cf. Mt 4:4; Jn 6:34ff; 1 Tm 6:7ff
[576] Cf. Mt 6:25ff

708. **What do we beg in the fifth petition,** *forgive us our trespasses, as we forgive them that trespass against us?*

We beg that our sins may be forgiven us, according as we forgive our enemies: for we cannot obtain forgiveness from God unless we forgive others all injuries be they never so great.[577]

709. **What does he beg who has no mind to forgive his enemies?**

He begs of God not to forgive him his sins.[578]

710. **What means to forgive him, who did us hurt?**

It means to renounce all desires of revenge, and to be willing to render good for evil.[579]

711. **Can we forgive our enemy, and yet demand some satisfaction for the damage he has done us?**

We can, provided we require it rationally and according to law; and that our hearts be free from hatred and aversion to the people whom we pursue.[580]

712. **Does he, who endures not the sight or company of those who did him hurt, truly forgive them?**

He does not; for he followeth not God's example, who regards us with affection and receives us compassionately and lovingly when he forgives us.[581]

713. **What do we beg in the sixth petition,** *lead us not into temptation?*

We beg of him, to give us victory over the temptations of the world, the flesh, and the devil.

---

[577] Cf. Mt 18:21-22; Mk 11:25-26
[578] Cf. Mt 7:2; 18:32-33
[579] Cf. Rom 12:20-21
[580] Cf. 1 Cor 6
[581] Cf. Mt 18:35; Eph 4:32; Col 3:12-13

714. Is it true that God tempts us sometimes?

It is not; on the contrary, it is damnable to say or think that God tempts anyone to evil;[582] yet it is true that God tries us sometimes by poverty, by sickness, or by some other tribulation.[583]

715. Why does he try us by affliction and calamity?

In order to purify us from the filth of sin, as gold is purified by fire; or else to give us an unspeakable reward in heaven for our patience.[584]

716. Doth God try us any other way?

He likewise tries us by riches, by long life, by health, and by the other favors he confers upon us, as means to do good works, and to merit life everlasting.[585]

717. Which are the causes of the temptations that move us to evil?

The world, the flesh, and the devil.[586]

718. Why doth God suffer the enemies of our souls to tempt us?

In order to give us means of meriting much, by fighting courageously against our enemies.[587]

719. Does he sin, whom the world, the flesh, or the devil provokes to evil?

No, unless he draws these temptations upon himself; or unless he consents to them.[588]

720. How shall one know that he has not consented to the temptation?

If he renounced it quickly; or if he endeavored without delay, to give attention to something else; if he was troubled or grieved whilst the evil thought

---

[582] Cf. Ps 5:5; Rom 9:14; Jas 1:13
[583] Cf. Jb 7:1
[584] Cf. Jas 1:2-4; 1 Pt 1:6-7
[585] Cf. Ecclus 15:14ff; 1 Tm 6:17-19
[586] Cf. Mt 4:3; Rom 7:23; Jas 1:14; Jn 2:15-16
[587] Cf. Apoc 2:10-11
[588] Cf. Rom 7:17ff

lasted; or if he earnestly begged the assistance of God, or the intercession of either saint or angel, it is certain he did not consent to it.

721. **How shall one know that he consented?**
If after he perceived the evil thought, he quietly suffered it, it is true that he consented to it.

722. **What do we beg in the seventh petition,** *but deliver us from evil?*
We beg of God to free us from everything that would do us hurt or mischief, in regard of either body or soul; and particularly from whatever is contrary to our salvation.

723. **What means the word,** *Amen?*
It signifies, so be it.

724. **Why do you finish the Lord's Prayer with these words,** *so be it?*
To show that we desire to obtain all these petitions from God.

LESSON 3

Of the Ave Maria, *or the Angelical Salutation*

725. **What understand you by the** *Ave Maria,* **or Angelical Salutation?**
I understand that it is a prayer composed of the words of the angel, likewise of the words of St. Elizabeth, and of the Church; a prayer which is very pleasing to the Blessed Virgin Mary, and is commonly said after the Lord's Prayer.

726. **Why is it called the Angelical Salutation?**
Because it is the angel Gabriel that made the first part of it, saluting and congratulating the Virgin Mary, when he came with a message to her from

God, that the second Person of the Trinity would be made man in her womb.[589]

727. **Say the Angelical Salutation in Latin.**

Ave Maria, gratia plena, Dominus tecum: benedicta tu in mulieribus, et benedictus fructus ventris tui, Jesus. Sancta Maria, Mater Dei, ora pro nobis peccatoribus, nunc et in hora mortis nostrae. Amen.

728. **Say it in English.**

Hail Mary, full of grace, our Lord is with thee: blessed art thou among women, and blessed is the fruit of thy womb, Jesus. Holy Mary, Mother of God, pray for us sinners, now and in the hour of our death. Amen.

729. **Which is the angel's part of this prayer?**

Hail Mary, full of grace, our Lord is with thee: blessed art thou among women.[590]

730. **What did Saint Elizabeth say to the Blessed Virgin Mary?**

Blessed art thou among women, and blessed is the fruit of thy womb, Jesus.[591]

731. **When did she speak so?**

When the Blessed Virgin went to visit her.[592]

732. **Which is the Church's part of this prayer?**

Holy Mary, Mother of God, pray for us sinners, now and in the hour of our death. So be it.[593]

---

[589] Cf. Lk 1:29
[590] Cf. Lk 1:28
[591] Cf. Lk 1:42
[592] Cf. Ibid.
[593] Cf. Council of Ephesus

733. **Why did the angel say that the Virgin Mary was *full of grace?***

Because she received greater gifts and favors from God, than any angel or saint whatsoever.[594]

734. **For what else did he say that she was full of grace?**

Because she conceived immediately, and carried the author of grace in her womb.[595]

735. **Why did the angel say to her, *our Lord is with thee?***

Because God preserved her from all sin, and always guided her.[596]

736. **How is the Holy Virgin Mary *blessed above all other women?***

Because God preserved her from all sin; and that she was both a Mother and a Virgin at the same time, without losing her virginity in any wise, before or after childbirth; a favor which God never did, nor will grant to any woman whatsoever.[597]

737. **Why do we say that the fruit of the womb of the Holy Virgin Mary is *blessed?***

Because Christ her son is the fountain of all holiness and blessings.[598]

738. **Why do we call the Blessed Virgin, *Mother of God?***

Because it is she alone that is the true Mother of Jesus Christ, who is both God and man.[599]

---

[594] Cf. Lk 1:30ff; S. Epiphan. tom. 2. p. 292, etc.

[595] Cf. Lk 16

[596] Cf. Augustine, *On Nature and Grace*, Ch. 42, n. 36; Council of Trent, Session 5, "Decree Concerning Original Sin"

[597] Cf. Jerome, *Against Jovinianus*, Bk. 1, n. 31; Bk. 13, *On Ezechiel* 44; Bernard, Sermon 4, *Upon the Assumption*

[598] Cf. Col 2:9

[599] Cf. Mt 1:20-21

739. **Why do we beseech the Blessed Virgin to pray for us *at the hour of our death*, especially?**
Because we stand in much greater need of the grace and mercy of God at that time than at any other.

740. **How so?**
Because the temptations of the devil are stronger and more dangerous at the hour of death than at any other time; and likewise, because God decrees the kingdom of heaven, or everlasting punishment for everyone, when the soul parts from the body.[600]

741. **Why is it recommended to us to say this prayer often?**
That we may frequently think on three things.

742. **Which is the first?**
The incarnation of God's only Son in the womb of the Virgin Mary for our sake.

743. **Which is the second thing?**
The virtues of the Blessed Virgin, to wit: her faith, her charity, her patience, her chastity, her humility, and obedience.

744. **Which is the third thing?**
The powerful intercession of the Mother of God, in behalf of those who invoke her, and sincerely endeavor to imitate her behavior.

745. **Who are those among the Catholics themselves that dishonor the Blessed Virgin, and lose the benefit of the few prayers they direct unto her?**
The foolish people, who imagine that to gain heaven it is enough for them to have a great confidence in her, on account of the little fasting or lukewarm prayers they offer unto her; although they be at the same time given

---

[600] Cf. Eccles 11:3

up to their inordinate passions, and do not so much as propose sincerely to amend their lives, nor in any wise follow the example of the Blessed Virgin.

Of the Time of Prayer

746. **When are we obliged to pray to God?**
In the time of temptation, danger, and every necessity of soul or body; and also when God confers any new favor upon us.

747. **On what days are we most obliged to pray to God?**
On Sundays and on all other holy days; because these days are exempted from worldly business, in order to pray, praise, and serve God.

748. **Is it not also necessary to pray to God every day?**
It is certainly; for it would be a great and ungrateful forgetfulness in us to let any one day pass without praying or praising God diligently.[601]

749. **At what hour of the day ought we chiefly to offer our prayers to God?**
Morning and evening, before and after meat, and when we begin any work, as hereafter set down.[602]

---

[601] Cf. Lk 18:1; Eph 6:18
[602] Cf. Ecclus 39:6-7; Ws 16:27-29; Ps 140:2; 1 Cor 10:31

Chapter 8

LESSON 4

Of a Christian, and of the Sign of the Cross

750. **Are you a Christian?**

Yes, by the grace of God.

751. **Why do you say, "by the grace of God"?**

Because I did not, neither could I deserve this great benefit of God, who made me a Christian through his great mercy.[603]

752. **Who is a Christian?**

Everyone who, being baptized, inwardly believes, and outwardly professes the doctrine and law of Jesus Christ.[604]

753. **Of what advantage is it for one to be a Christian?**

He receives three great advantages thereby.

754. **What is the first advantage?**

It is that the Christian is delivered through the grace and superabundant merits of our Lord Jesus Christ, from sin and from the power of the devil, who held him in hard bondage.[605]

755. **What is the second advantage?**

He is regenerated or new born, not unto his earthly, but unto the heavenly Father; so that he can confidently say, "Our Father, which art in heaven."[606]

---

[603] Cf. Rom 9:15ff; Ti 3:5-7
[604] Cf. Rom 10:10
[605] Cf. Rom 7:4, 6
[606] Cf. Rom 8:14ff; Ti 3:6-7

756. What is the third advantage?

It is, that the Christian is heir of the kingdom of heaven, and hath a right to everlasting life.[607]

757. What do you mean by the doctrine or law of Christ?

I mean by it all the truths which Christ revealed, and the holy Catholic and Roman Church teacheth us.

758. Are we obliged to know the Christian doctrine?

We are undoubtedly obliged to believe all, and to know distinctly the principal articles thereof.[608]

759. What are those principal articles of the Christian doctrine which we are obliged to know punctually?

The mysteries of faith, which are contained in the Creed of the Apostles; the commandments of God and the Church; the things which regard the sacraments that we are bound to receive, together with the dispositions that are necessary for receiving them; the Lord's Prayer, and the particular duties of our profession, trade, or calling.

760. Is he who is ignorant of these things obliged to seek earnestly for knowledge?

He is certainly; and that under pain of damnation.[609]

761. Is it not enough, that one should assist at sermons and Mass?

No certainly; for he who is ignorant of the principal articles of the Christian doctrine, doth not commonly understand the sermon itself, nor any other profound instruction.

762. What is the sign of a Christian?

The sign of the cross.[610]

---

[607] Cf. Rom 8:17; Jas 2:5
[608] Cf. Council of Trent, Session 24, "Decree on Reformation," Ch. 4, 7
[609] Cf. Is 5:13; Prv 15:14; 19:2; 1 Cor 14:38
[610] Cf. Basil, *De Spiritu Sancto*, Ch. 27, n. 66

763. **How is the sign of the cross made?**

By putting the right hand to the forehead, from thence below the breast, to the left shoulder, and to the right, saying: "In the name of the Father, and of the Son, and of the Holy Ghost. Amen."

764. **What doth the sign of the cross put us in mind of?**

It puts us in mind of the most Holy Trinity; that the second Person of the Trinity was made man; and that he redeemed us from the bondage and slavery of the devil, and of sin, by suffering death for us on the cross.

765. **At what time is it fit to make the sign of the cross?**

At our rising in the morning, going to bed at night, when we begin prayer and every other work.[611]

766. **Is it not useful to make the sign of the cross at other times?**

Yes; and particularly in time of temptation, or of any danger whatsoever.

767. **Was the sign of the cross used in the primitive Church?**

Yes; as it plainly appears from Saint Augustine: "If the sign of the cross of Jesus Christ," says this great father of the Church, "be not applied to the foreheads of the believers, to the water with which they are baptized, to the chrism with which they are anointed, to the sacrifice with which they are fed, none of these things is duly performed."[612] The reason is, that all the sacraments have their whole force and efficacy from the cross; that is, from the death and passion of Jesus Christ on the cross.

768. **Did the primitive Christians only make use of the sign of the cross in the administration of the sacraments?**

Not only then, but upon all other occasions: "At every step," sayeth the ancient and learned Tertullian, "at every coming in and going out, when we put on our clothes or shoes, when we wash, when we sit down to table,

---

[611] Cf. Gal 6:14; Jerome, *Letter 22*, To Eustochium, n. 37; Cyril of Jerusalem, *Catechetical Lecture 4*, n. 14; Ambrose, *Sermon 43*

[612] Augustine, *Tractate 118 on John*, n. 5

when we light a candle, when we go to bed…whatsoever conversation employs us, we imprint on our foreheads, the sign of the cross."[613]

769. **Why do we make the sign of the cross?**

1) It is, first, to give to understand, that we are Christians; and that we are no more ashamed of the cross of Christ, than the apostle St. Paul, who gloried in the cross of our Lord Jesus Christ.[614] 2) It is to profess openly that we believe in a crucified God; although it is a "scandal to the Jews, and a folly to the Gentiles,"[615] to do so. 3) It is to help us to be always mindful of our Savior's death and passion. 4) It is to chase away the devil; and dissipate his illusions; for the cross is the standard of Christ, and the evil spirit trembles at the very sign of the instrument of our redemption.[616]

770. **Can you prove, that by means of the sign of the cross, we receive any favor from God?**

There are innumerable instances of it in ancient Church history, and in the writings of the holy fathers, which would be too tedious to relate here. I shall only recount, that the cross was given by our Lord Jesus Christ to Constantine, the first Christian emperor, as a token and assurance of victory, when he and his whole army, in their march against the tyrant Maxentius, saw a cross formed of pure light above the sun, with this inscription: "By this conquer"; and that by it, he forthwith conquered his enemies; which account the ancient historian Eusebius, in his book of *The Life of Constantine*, declares he had from that emperor's own mouth.

771. **How comes it then that it is of little advantage to a great many to make the sign of the cross often?**

Because they only carry it on their forehead, and not in their heart; for, as

---

[613] Tertullian, *De Corona Militis*, Ch. 3

[614] Cf. Gal 6:14

[615] 1 Cor 1:23

[616] Cf. Mt 24:30; Cyril, *Catechetical Lecture 13*; Athanasius, *On the Incarnation of the Word*, Ch. 27; Augustine, *Sermon 19*

St. Augustine assures, it availeth little to have the forehead covered with the cross, and the heart full of crimes.[617]

772. **With what disposition ought it to be made?**
With a spirit of prayer and devotion; with great faith and confidence in the merits of Jesus Christ.

LESSON 5

Of Morning Prayer and Good Purpose

773. **What is a Christian to do at his rising in the morning?**
He ought to give God the first thought, the first word, and the first action.

774. **How is that to be performed?**
After making the sign of the cross, let him say: "O Almighty God, I offer thee my whole heart; O Jesus, assist me; Blessed Virgin Mary, pray for me."

775. **What doth the good Christian do whilst he is putting on his clothes?**
He behaves himself decently and modestly; and lifts up his heart, now and then, to God.

776. **What ought he to do after dressing?**
Having sprinkled himself with holy water, he ought to put himself upon his knees, and offer up devoutly his morning prayers to God.

777. **How is it you pray in the morning?**
I make acts of adoration, love, thanksgiving, oblation, good purpose, and supplication.

778. **Make an act of adoration.**
O Almighty God, I adore and praise Thy Divine Majesty; I acknowledge

---

[617] Cf. Augustine, *Sermon 215, de Temp.*

that thou art my Maker and my sovereign Lord; I entirely submit myself to thy power.

779. **Make an act of love.**

I love thee, O Lord, with my whole heart, above all things; because thou art infinitely good and amiable.

780. **Make an act of thanksgiving.**

O Lord, I give thee infinite thanks for having preserved me last night; for having created and redeemed me; for having made me a Christian; and for all the graces thou hast granted me hitherto.

781. **Make an act of oblation.**

I consecrate to thee, O Lord, my thoughts, my words, my actions, and myself entirely; that all may tend to thy praise and glory forever.

782. **Make an act of good resolution.**

I purpose, O Lord, with the assistance of thy grace, to keep thy commandments this day better than I have hitherto done; and to shun all sorts of sin, particularly the sins I am most inclined to.

783. **Make an act of supplication.**

O Lord, grant me assistance, through thy great mercy, in all my necessities both of soul and body; and deliver me from all sin. O great God, I earnestly beg this of thee, through the merits of the most precious blood of Jesus Christ; and through the intercession of the Blessed Virgin, and of all the saints and angels.

784. **Do not you say some other prayers?**

Yes; I say, at least, the Lord's Prayer, the Angelical Salutation, the Creed, and the commandments of God; and I crave the assistance of my angel guardian, and of my holy patron.

785. **How do you crave the assistance of your angel guardian?**

I say: "O angel of God, who, through the mercy of the Lord, watchest over me, enlighten, guide, protect, and defend me this day. Amen."

786. **What other prayer is to be said in the morning?**

It is very meritorious to say the litanies of Jesus devoutly every morning.

787. **How do you finish the morning prayer?**

I call to mind and reflect for some time on the four last things, or upon some other godly subject; and lastly, I humbly beg of God to deliver me from all evil, but especially from sin, through Jesus Christ our Lord.

LESSON 6

Of Evening Prayer and Examination of Conscience

788. **How do you pray and examine your conscience at night?**

After giving thanks to God, I beg the grace of him to know my sins; I examine my conscience, and make an act of contrition.

789. **How do you beg of God the knowledge of your sins?**

I say: "Grant me, O Lord, through thy great mercy, the light of thy grace, that I may see my faults, and conceive a thorough detestation and perfect hatred of them."

790. **How do you examine your conscience?**

I consider the sins I have committed by thought, word, deed, or omission; and particularly the sins I am most inclined to.

791. **How do you make an act of contrition?**

I say from my heart: "O Lord, I am very sorry for having offended thee, because thou art infinitely good and amiable, and because sin displeaseth thee. I resolve, by the assistance of thy grace, not to incur thy anger for the future, and likewise to go to confession as soon as I can."

792. What do you say after that?

I say the *confiteor*.

793. What other prayers do you say?

I say the Lord's Prayer, the Angelical Salutation, the Creed, the commandments of God, the litanies of the Blessed Virgin Mary, the prayer to my angel guardian, and to my holy patron.

794. Do you not pray for the souls that are in purgatory?

I say the psalm, *De profundis*,[618] etc., or at least, "Grant, O Lord, through thy great mercy, succor and eternal rest to the souls in purgatory."

795. What else do you do?

I think and meditate for some time on the four last things, especially upon death and judgment.

796. How do you finish the evening prayer?

I offer my rest to God, saying: "O Lord, I offer unto thee my sleep; it is to satisfy thy holy will that I desire to take this rest. Preserve me this night from my enemies, through Jesus Christ, our Lord. Amen."

797. What do you do whilst you are taking off your clothes?

I beg of God, through the stripping of Jesus Christ before he was crucified, to strip me entirely of the inordinate desires of the world and the flesh.

798. On what do you think as you lie down in your bed?

I consider that perhaps I shall never rise out of it; and as I settle myself to sleep, I say from my heart: "Into thy hands, O Lord, I commend my soul, since it is thyself, O King of heaven, that hast redeemed me."

---

[618] Ps 129

LESSON 7

Of the Prayers Said before and after Meat, and at Other Times

799. **Ought we to pray before and after meat?**

We ought; for otherwise we should behave ourselves like brute beasts.

800. **What prayer do you say before meat?**

I say: "Bless, O Lord, this food, which we are to receive for strengthening ourselves, in order to fulfil thy holy will. Amen. In the name of the Father," etc.

801. **What prayer do you say after meat?**

I say: "O Lord, we give thee thanks for this nourishment, which thou hast given us; grant us, through thy grace, to spend our lives, our health, and our strength, so that every favor which we receive from thee may tend to thy glory and praise, through Jesus Christ our Lord. Amen." I also say the Lord's Prayer and the Angelical Salutation.

802. **What is proper to be done at the beginning of every work?**

It is fit we should lift up our hearts to God, saying: "O Lord, I offer thee my work: it is for thy sake I desire to perform it; bless both me and it, through thy great mercy."

803. **What prayer do you say in order to keep yourself from sin?**

I say: "Enlighten me, O Lord, with thy holy light; sustain me by thy grace, and suffer me not to fall into any sin; through Jesus Christ our Lord. Amen."

804. **What should one do when he is tempted?**

He ought to beg assistance of God, and to renounce courageously the temptation.

805. What do you say in order to overcome the temptation?

I say: "Assist me, O Lord, with thy grace; I renounce these temptations: I would sooner suffer death than consent to them."

806. What ought one to do when he thinks he has fallen into sin?

He ought to make an act of contrition, and say: "O Lord, I am very sorry for having offended thee: I purpose, with thy assistance, to be more upon my guard for the future."

807. Are we not obliged to pray at other times?

Our Savior says that it is necessary to pray always, and not to grow slack therein.[619]

808. How can we fulfil this commandment?

We shall in some measure fulfil it, if we often in the day lift up our hearts to God, and if we devoutly offer up our actions to him.

809. Is it difficult to do so?

No; it is so easy a work, that no one can truly say he has not both time and leisure for it. The gentleman, the scholar, the merchant, the tradesman, the shepherd, the ploughman, the servant, the sick, everyone may, frequently in the day, think of God and godly things, and sanctify all his actions by offering them piously to his Maker and Redeemer.

LESSON 8

Of the Holy Mass, and of the Manner of Hearing It

810. What is the Mass?

It is both a choice prayer and a sacrifice, wherein the body and blood of our Savior Jesus Christ are really offered to God, under the forms of bread

---

[619] Cf. Lk 18:1

and wine, in remembrance of his holy passion and death on the cross, for our sake.

811. **What is a sacrifice?**

It is an offering of sensible or corporal things, which God ordained to be offered to himself alone; and also to be slain, or some way changed, in public acknowledgment of his sovereign dominion over the living and the dead.

812. **How is the Mass a true sacrifice?**

Because the true body and true blood of Jesus Christ are therein offered and sacrificed to God, under the forms of bread and wine.[620]

813. **Can it be said or imagined, that the glorious and immortal body of our Savior is sacrificed in the Mass?**

It can and should be said, and firmly believed; for, when the priest consecrates the bread and wine, Christ verily offers himself to his heavenly Father; and it is thereby represented to us, that by the sword of the words, his body and blood are separated from one another,[621] as they were really separated upon the cross.[622]

814. **How yet can it be said, that the sacred body and blood of Christ are sacrificed, or mystically destroyed in the Mass?**

Because the priest consumes the most precious body and blood of the Son of God; and that this consumption puts us likewise in mind of Christ's death and passion upon the cross.[623]

815. **To whom is this sacrifice offered?**

To Almighty God only; because it is he alone that is King of kings, Lord of lords, and sovereign Prince of heaven and earth.

---

[620] Cf. Gn 14:18; Ps 109:3-4; Heb 7; Mal 1:10-11; Mt 26:26ff; Heb 13:10
[621] Author's note: See q. 463, above.
[622] Cf. 1 Cor 11:24ff; Apoc 5:6
[623] Cf. 1 Cor 11:26

816. Is not the Sacrifice of the Mass sometimes offered to the saints?

No; nor is it lawful to offer it to either saint or angel; but it is offered to God alone, in thanksgiving for his great favors to the saints; and there is a commemoration made of them in the Mass, to the end that this most precious sacrifice may tend to their honor, and that they pray for us in heaven at the same time that we celebrate their memory upon earth.[624]

817. Who said the first Mass?

Our Lord Jesus Christ.

818. At what time did he say it?

The same night he was betrayed to be crucified.[625]

819. Who says the Mass, or offers this sacrifice now to God?

Christ, our eternal high priest, says it, and offereth himself daily in the Mass to his heavenly Father for us.[626]

820. Do not the other priests also say Mass?

They do undoubtedly; and they offer it to God in Christ's name, whose servants and ministers they are.[627]

821. Who is it that has power to say Mass?

Those only whom God and the Church have appointed to say it, to wit: bishops and priests.[628]

---

[624] Cf. *Canon of the Mass*; Council of Trent, Session 22, "Doctrine on the Sacrifice of the Mass," Ch. 3

[625] Cf. 1 Cor 11:23

[626] Cf. Ps 109:4; Heb 6:20; 7:24-25; Council of Trent, Session 22, "Doctrine on the Sacrifice of the Mass," Ch. 2

[627] Cf. Lk 22:19

[628] Cf. Heb 5:5

822. **Since it is certain that Christ offers his own body and blood in the Mass to his eternal Father, is it not likewise certain that the Sacrifice of the Mass is the same with the sacrifice of the cross?**

It is verily certain that they are the same, save only, that the sacrifice of the cross was bloody, and that the Sacrifice of the Mass is unbloody; that is, that Christ's precious blood was spilt, and that his body and soul were really separated from one another on the cross; and that now his blood is not spilt, nor is he put to death, only mystically, and in appearance or representation.[629]

823. **For whom is the Mass offered?**

For the living and the dead.[630]

824. **Of what advantage is the Sacrifice of the Mass to the living?**

It procures them from God the merits and fruit of the sacrifice of the cross, that is, the graces we stand in need of.

825. **Who are those among the living that benefit by the Mass?**

The members of the Church in general, and especially the person for whom it is said, the priest who says it, and those who assist at it.

826. **Of what advantage is it to the dead?**

It lessens their pain in purgatory, and hastens their deliverance out of it.[631]

827. **Are we bound to hear Mass often?**

We are not obliged to hear it, but upon Sundays and holy days only; yet it is very good and commendable to hear Mass as often as it can conveniently be done.

---

[629] Cf. Rom 6:9-10

[630] Cf. Council of Trent, Session 22, "Doctrine on the Sacrifice of the Mass," Ch. 2

[631] Cf. 2 Mc 12:43-46; Augustine, *Confessions*, Bk. 9; *Enchiridion*, Ch. 110; Council of Trent, Session 22, "Doctrine on the Sacrifice of the Mass," Ch. 2; Can. 3

828. Should one endeavor to hear Mass every day, or often?

He should indeed; because it is very pleasing in the sight of God, and very beneficial to him who heareth it.

829. Is it not hurtful to the people that the Mass should be celebrated in a language which is not understood by all of them?

It is not; for the Mass is only a prayer and sacrifice, which the priest alone is obliged to offer for the people. Moreover, the Church commands every parish priest to expound often some part of the Mass to the people, or to get it expounded for them, and particularly on Sundays and holy days.[632]

Again, it is manifest, although the Latin be a dead language, that there is no language in Europe more universally understood, there being scarce a village without somebody that understands it; so that it cannot truly be said that it is an unknown tongue.

830. Why doth the Church make use of the Latin preferably to any other language in Europe?

First, it is more universally understood than any other language. In the next place, because it is a dead language, not subject to change, it is in the liturgy, or common prayers of the Church, which can thus be best preserved from alteration and corruption; a thing which could hardly be done, if the Mass were turned into all the different and variable jargons spoken not only in each country, but also in many provinces and remote districts of almost each nation throughout all Europe.

Besides that, it is a great advantage and comfort to travelers and foreigners, to find the public prayers of the Church uniform, or the very same, both at home and abroad; so that they must indeed be very idiots, if they know not when to say "Amen," when to kneel, when to stand, or do anything else that concerns them, or that is proper for them to do.

---

[632] Cf. Council of Trent, Session 22, "Doctrine on the Sacrifice of the Mass," Ch. 8

831. **How ought we to hear Mass?**
We should hear it entirely, attentively, respectfully, and devoutly; for "cursed is he who doth the work of God negligently."[633]

832. **Who are they who hear Mass carelessly?**
Such persons as sleep at it, or that give attention to idle or worldly things.

833. **Who are they who hear it with disrespect?**
Those who gaze or look about, talking to one another, or amuse themselves with trifles during a considerable part of the Mass, and also those who hear it upon one knee, or leaning half stretched upon anything.

834. **What is to be done in order to hear Mass devoutly?**
One ought to behave himself modestly and gravely, and to pray to God with all his heart and soul; for "God is a spirit, and they who adore him, must adore…in spirit and in truth."[634]

835. **What do you, when the priest begins the Mass?**
I make the sign of the cross, and offer the holy sacrifice to God with the same mind and intention with which Jesus Christ first offered it, and with which the Church offers it in his name.

836. **With what intention did our Savior offer it?**
His intention was, and still is, to adore and praise God, to give him thanks, and to merit for us grace, and the remission of our sins.[635]

837. **What do you, at the elevation of the blessed host, that is, the body of Christ?**
I say: "O Lord, I verily believe that thy body and blood, thy soul and divinity also, are really present in this sacrament. I do with all my heart adore and praise thee herein."

---

[633] Jer 48:10
[634] Jn 4:24
[635] Cf. Mt 26:28

838. What do you say at the elevation of the chalice?

I say: "O Lord, I adore thy most precious blood: I give thee infinite thanks for having shed it for my sake on the cross. Suffer me not, by my sins, to lose the fruit thereof."

839. What do you do afterwards until the Mass is ended?

I continue in adoring, praising, and loving our Lord, and also in humbling myself before him.

840. What do you do at the end of the Mass?

I give thanks to God for his great favors, particularly for the Mass I heard; and I beg pardon for the faults I committed whilst I was hearing it.

841. How do you give thanks to God for having heard Mass?

I say: "O Lord, I give thee infinite thanks for having, through thy great mercy, vouchsafed me to hear this Mass, and for the graces which I have received thereat."

842. Is it not the custom to take holy water at Mass?

Yes, it is; and even to carry it home, in order to take it now and then, particularly morning and evening, and before prayers.

843. What is holy water?

Water sanctified by the word of God and prayer.

844. Is it not a superstitious practice to bless water or inanimate things, or to attribute any virtue to them?

No; it is no superstition to look for heavenly favors from the prayers of the Church of God; and it is in virtue of these prayers, that we hope to reap advantage from these things, when we use them with faith; and many a fact proves that our hopes are not in vain.[636]

---

[636] Cf. S. Epiphan., *Haer. 30*; Jerome, *The Life of Hilarion*; Theodoret, *Ecclesiastical History*, Bk. 5, Ch. 21

Moreover, God himself ordered holy and purifying waters to be made in the old law; and that, assuredly, without witchcraft or superstition.[637]

845. **Can you show from holy writ that water, salt, oil, and the like may be lawfully used to obtain any favor from God?**

I can; for we read, in 4 Kings 2 and 5, that the prophet Elisha miraculously healed the noisome waters of Jericho by casting salt into the spring;[638] and cured Naaman the Syrian of the leprosy by the waters of the river Jordan.[639]

Our Savior himself, who had by his sole word created heaven and earth, "spit on the ground, made clay of (his) spittle," and spread it upon the eyes of a man born blind, "saying unto him: 'Go, wash in the pool of Siloe.'…He went, therefore, and washed, and came back clear sighted."[640]

The apostles also "anointed with oil many that were sick, and healed them."[641]

846. **Can water and the like be capable of blessing or any holiness?**

It can, as well as meat and drink, which all those who live like Christians do bless every day; for our Savior sayeth, that "the altar sanctifies the gift"[642] that is upon it; and the apostle, St. Paul, assures us, that "every creature…is sanctified by the word of God, and prayer."[643]

847. **What is the use of holy water?**

The Church blesses it with solemn prayer, to beg God's protection and blessing upon those who use it, and particularly that they may be defended from the powers of darkness.

Moreover, it may well serve to put us in mind of the covenant we made with God, against the devil, when by the water of baptism, we were

---

[637] Cf. Nm 5:17; 19:9ff
[638] Cf. 4 Kgs 2:19-22
[639] Cf. 4 Kgs 5:10, 14
[640] Jn 9:6-7
[641] Mk 6:13
[642] Mt 23:19
[643] 1 Tm 4:4-5

mercifully cleansed from sin; and of renewing our promise, or of making an act of contrition.

848. **Are the prayers of the Church so prevailing with God as to obtain us his assistance against the wiles and power of the enemy of our salvation, when we use holy water with faith?**

Nothing prevails more upon God than prayer in general; and the apostle St. James, exhorting us to pray for one another, assures us, "that the assiduous prayer of a just man availeth much"; that "Elias was a man subject to the like passions as we are; and prayed earnestly that it might not rain upon the earth, and it rained not for three years and six months"; that "he prayed again, and the heaven gave rain, and the earth yielded her fruit."[644]

Now, if the prayers of particulars be so powerful, it is manifest that the constant prayers of the whole Church, from the rising of the sun to the going down thereof, are always graciously heard; and that God granteth to all those who cooperate with his grace, the fruit of the perseverant prayer of that Church, to which Christ said, "Verily, verily, I say unto you, if you ask the Father anything in my name, he will give it you."[645]

849. **Is the use of holy water ancient in the Church of God?**

It is very ancient, seeing it is mentioned in the *Apostolical Constitutions*, and in the writings of holy fathers and ancient Church historians.[646]

850. **Why is salt blessed, and mingled with the water?**

To signify unto us, that as salt preserves meat from corruption, and gives it a relish, so doth the grace which we receive in virtue of the prayers of the Church, when we use this water with faith, defend us from unclean spirits, and give us a taste for heavenly things.

---

[644] Jas 5:16-18

[645] Jn 16:23

[646] Cf. *Apostolic Constitutions*, Bk. 8, Ch. 29; Cyprian, Bk. 1, *Epistle 12*; Jerome, *The Life of Hilarion*; Basil, *De Spiritu Sancto*, Ch. 27, n. 66; Gregory the Great, Bk. 9, *Epistle 71*; S. Epiphan. ib.; Theodoret, *Ecclesiastical History*, Bk. 5, Ch. 21; Palladius, *The Lausiac History*, Ch. 17

851. **Why doth the Church make use of the sign of the cross in blessing the salt and water, and in all her other consecrations?**
To let us understand that all our good must come through Christ crucified for us on the cross.

852. **What advantage ought we to draw from what is here said upon holy water?**
First, we ought to look upon it, and upon all the other sacred rites and ceremonies of the Catholic Church with due reverence and esteem, to be persuaded that they are all instituted to help on the great affair of salvation, either by putting us in mind of the unspeakable favors which we have already received from God, or by raising our affections to heaven, humbly begging the divine assistance, whereof we stand in need every moment of our life, and ought never to imitate those mistaken people, who rail against "all things which they understand not."[647]

Secondly, we ought to use holy water with attention and devotion, always endeavoring to make an act of contrition, or some other act of religion, and to sprinkle ourselves, and even our dwellings with it from time to time, saying, without making any other sign but that of the cross: "Thou shalt sprinkle me, O Lord, with hyssop, and I shall be cleansed; thou shalt wash me, and I shall be made whiter than snow."[648]

LESSON 9

Of the Beads, or Crown of the Blessed Virgin

853. **What prayer are you accustomed to say in honor of the Blessed Virgin; and in order to deserve and obtain her intercession?**
I say the beads.

---

[647] Jude 1:10
[648] Ps 50:9

854. **Is this prayer agreeable to our Savior, and to his Blessed Mother?**

It is; because it consists only of the Creed, the Lord's Prayer, and Angelical Salutation, which are most pleasing prayers in the sight of God.

855. **For what end are the beads said?**

To praise our Lord and the Blessed Virgin, and to obtain grace and mercy from God, through the merits of the Son, and the intercession of the Mother.

856. **How do you say the beads?**

After making the sign of the cross, I say the Creed in Latin, or in English at the cross of the beads; the Lord's Prayer at every great bead, and the Angelical Salutation at the small ones.

857. **What do you do whilst you are saying the beads?**

I heartily and humbly beg every petition that is contained in these prayers.

858. **On what else may one think when he says his beads?**

On the following mysteries, to wit: the nativity, poverty, and tribulations; the life and death, resurrection and ascension of our Savior; or on the joys and sorrows of the Blessed Virgin in this life.

859. **May not one sometimes entertain other good thoughts?**

He may undoubtedly; wherefore it is very profitable for us to bewail our sins, to form a resolution of not falling into them anymore, and to beg the assistance of God, through the intercession of the Blessed Virgin, for putting this good resolution in practice.

860. **How do you finish the beads?**

I say the Lord's Prayer thrice, and the Angelical Salutation thrice, and the Creed; and I make the sign of the cross, saying, as I did in the beginning: "In the name of the Father," etc.

861. **Is it advantageous to repeat often the same prayer?**
It is certainly, provided that the heart earnestly desires the contents of it.

862. **Is it to be supposed that there is any virtue in the number of *Paters* and *Aves* whereof the beads are composed?**
No: such an opinion is both vain and superstitious.

863. **To whom can the beads be beneficial?**
To all Christians; for there is no prayer whatsoever more necessary, and more pleasing to God, than the prayers whereof the beads are composed.

864. **To whom are the beads of the greatest use?**
To those who cannot read, or that are not as yet trained up or used to prayer.

865. **What prayer, besides those we have already spoken of, would you have people to practice?**
Meditation or mental prayer.

LESSON 10

Of Meditation or Mental Prayer

866. **What is that prayer you call meditation or mental prayer?**
Meditation or mental prayer is a serious and frequent reflection, which is made in the presence of God, and by the assistance of his grace, on the truths of salvation, to know them well, to love them, and to put them in practice.

867. **Is this prayer of great benefit?**
It is of very great benefit; for by practicing it, we learn to know solidly the truths of salvation, to love them warmly, and to put them in practice faithfully. These are the three effects of meditation, which can hardly be sufficiently esteemed, because they comprehend all that is necessary for salvation.

Moreover, meditation teaches us to speak to God, and to hear God, when he does us the favor to speak to us. We speak to God when we pray, and when we beg of him to grant us those things we stand in need of. God speaks to us when he enlightens our understanding by good thoughts, excites our will by his holy inspirations, and animates us to put them in execution. In speaking to God, we beseech him that he will come to us by his grace; in hearkening to him, we open our hearts for him to enter there. In speaking to him, we demand his lights and favors; in hearkening to him, we receive them, and enclose them in our hearts, to conserve and practice them. Upon these two actions, speaking to God from our heart, and hearkening to him when he speaks to our heart, depends absolutely our salvation, that is, the beginning, progress, and perfecting of our sanctification.

868. Doth it not belong only to recluses or people, who have quitted the world, to use this prayer?

Not only to them, but also to others; it is the business of everybody to learn well the truths of salvation, to love them, and to put them in practice. It is the business of everyone to speak to God from his heart in prayer, and to hearken to him attentively when he vouchsafes to speak to his heart. It is for that reason, the royal prophet begins his psalms, with the praise of meditation, saying: the affection of the righteous is "in the law of the Lord, and he shall meditate on his law, day and night."[649] He adds, that this meditation will make the righteous resemble a fair tree planted by the water side, which will bear fruit in its time:[650] because as the water, in moistening the root of the tree, makes it fertile and abounding in fruit, so meditation upon holy things, in filling the heart with good thoughts and pious affections, renders the soul rich in virtue and good works. And although the prophet says, that it is the righteous man that will meditate so, it is most certain that the sinner stands in much greater need of it; wherefore, the prophet Isaiah says: "Return, ye transgressors, to your heart."[651] That is to say: you breakers of the law, think and reflect in your heart, repent and take a firm resolution to serve God.

[649] Ps 1:2
[650] Cf. Ps 1:3
[651] Is 46:8

869. Who is the author of meditation or mental prayer?

God himself; for when he gave the law to his chosen people, he commanded them to meditate on it continually, saying: "The things which I command thee this day, shall be in thy heart, and thou shalt teach them to thy children, and thou shalt meditate on them, whether sitting in thy house, or walking on the way, lying down, and rising up. And thou shalt have them in thy hand, and they shall be before thine eyes."[652] And a little after, sayeth the Lord: "Lay up my words in your hearts, and in your minds; and they shall be in your hands, and before your eyes; and teach them to your children, that they may meditate on them."[653]

870. Is not meditation or mental prayer a difficult exercise?

It is not, as it can be easily made manifest; but it is a very strange thing that men should account that hard, which is performed daily in all sorts of business, except that of salvation. What merchant is there who doth not seriously and often think on the affairs of his traffic? Who is it, that has a process, or suit at law, and doth not daily cast up in his mind the means to gain it? And that not lightly and hastily, but seriously, with attention, with affection, and putting in execution all the means he finds? To act in this manner, in the affair of salvation, is what we understand by meditation. Who is the housekeeper that doth not think seriously and often, both night and day, on the affairs of his family?

Doth not the good student meditate? Does he not think and re-think, when he is at his book, composing anything, or learning any difficult question? He applies his mind to comprehend it, to remember it, and to reap profit from what he learns. All this is nothing else but meditation, or a serious consideration.

Doth not the bad scholar, even when he seems to be at his book, continually think on pastime and divertissement with so much application, and so frequently, that he gives no attention to anything else?

Doth not the wicked man, as the scripture sayeth, meditate iniquity?[654]

---

[652] Dt 6:6-8
[653] Dt 11:18-19
[654] Cf. Ps 139:3; Mi 2:1

When he has an ill design to put in execution, he takes no greater pleasure than in seeking and finding the means to effect it. Cannot and should not the Christian meditate on virtue, as the impious do meditate on vice and wickedness? Can he not, and ought he not, to do so much for his eternal salvation, as people daily do for worldly interest and pleasure? Let it not therefore be imagined that meditation or mental prayer is difficult.

871. **Can we not easily work our salvation without meditation or mental prayer?**
Not easily indeed; for seeing meditation, or mental prayer is nothing else but a serious and frequent reflection upon the truths of salvation, to know them, to love them, and to practice them, it is certain that it is a very difficult thing to effect our salvation without meditation, as it is very hard to practice the truths of the same salvation without knowing them, and to know them without thinking seriously and frequently on them, and without often and humbly demanding of God the grace to know them, to love them, and to practice them. The scripture for this reason attributes the corruption of manners, and the frequent loss of the salvation of men to the want of reflection: "The earth is replenished with desolation, because there is no person who revolves in his heart"[655] the truths of salvation.

It is indeed for want of considering seriously and frequently in our heart, why we came into the world, that we forget the errand upon which we are come hither, which is: to know God, to love him, and to serve him faithfully. It is for want of reflecting seriously and often on the vanity and inconstancy of this world, on death, judgment, heaven, and hell, that people love the pleasures, riches, or goods of this poor life, more than Jesus Christ and the life everlasting. It is for want of thinking daily and in good earnest on the mysteries of our redemption, to wit: the incarnation, life, passion, death, glorious resurrection, and the triumphant ascension of our Savior Jesus Christ, that men do take so much pains for this mortal life, that they scarcely even think of doing anything for him, who created, and redeemed them by suffering an ignominious death on the cross for their sake. It is for want of

---

[655] Jer 12:11

thinking earnestly and often on the great mercies and severe judgments of God, that neither his love nor fear hinders us from offending him.

It is for want of considering earnestly and often that it is necessary that we should be humble, obedient, chaste, patient, temperate, liberal to the poor, and honest in all our dealings, that the far greater part of the world is proud, disobedient, unchaste, impatient, choleric, quarrelsome, revengeful, given to gluttony, hard-hearted to the poor, unjust and unfaithful to one another, or addicted to some vice or other. It is for want of thinking often and deliberately, that we are all under an indispensable obligation of loving God with our whole heart, and above all things, and our neighbor as ourselves for his sake; of fulfilling his commandments, and the duties of our calling; of begging humbly and often the assistance of his grace, without which we cannot make one step towards heaven; of speaking to God from our heart, and of hearkening to him attentively, when he does us the honor to speak to our heart. It is, I say, for want of meditating and revolving in our minds seriously and frequently, these most important points of our religion, that young and old, poor and rich, gentle and simple, in a word, the much greater part of mankind, are in love with this deceitful world, backbiters, enslaved to their disordinate passions, plunged and drowned in ignorance and sin.

Now, it is certain, that it is neither easy, nor ordinarily possible for us to work out our salvation without mental prayer, or meditating one way or other, it being certain, that the sole knowledge of virtue doth not suffice, except we be inclined with affection to the good we know; and the love of good is not enough, unless we proceed to the execution. It is also certain, that ordinarily we cannot fulfil, love, and learn well our duty, without reflecting or thinking seriously and often on it, and without humbly begging the divine assistance to perform all.

872. **Is it not sufficient we should say our ordinary prayers, such as the Lord's Prayer, the Angelical Salutation, the Creed, and other vocal prayers?**
It would indeed suffice to say them often from the heart, if we also hearkened to God, when he does us the favor to speak to our heart; if we seriously endeavored to find out the will of God; if we took a firm resolution to accomplish his will; and if we faithfully executed this resolution. But alas! it falls out

very frequently that people recite the above prayers by rote, and with so much precipitation, that they do not think on what they say; their tongue talks, and goes on like a stream, but their heart is silent and without motion; so that the same reproach may be justly made this day to the greater part of Christians, which God made to the Jews, saying: "This people honoreth me with their lips, but their heart is far from me."[656] Yet it is the heart alone that prays and obtains; it is that alone to whose voice and language Almighty God gives ear; and indeed it is unreasonable to expect that God will listen to those who do not listen to themselves. Now, there is no better remedy against this too common abuse than the exercise of meditation, whereby we learn to speak to God from our heart, and to hearken to him when he speaks to our heart.[657]

873. **After what method or order are we to meditate?**
Many good prayer books treat very amply of the method of meditation; let them be consulted: this is no place to make a long dissertation upon mental prayer.

874. **What do you say to those who have neither books nor learning?**
1) First, I say to them, and to others too, that they ought to ask and receive instruction from their spiritual directors as affectionately, at least, as they seek and receive silver and gold,[658] or other earthly things; and that there is not a more effectual means for learning mental prayer, and a method of meditation, than a great desire and affection for salvation. Whosoever loves his salvation will think freely and often on it; he will seek with much care the means to obtain it, and will easily put them in practice: nothing is difficult to him who loves.[659] 2) That, as they tender their eternal salvation, they ought to accustom themselves to mental prayer; and that the frequent exercise of this godly action will make it obvious and easy; for exercise and practice makes us overcome in all things the greatest difficulties, and render easy that which before appeared impossible. 3) That as it is most certain that nobody

---

[656] Mt 15:8
[657] Cf. Is 29:13
[658] Cf. Prv 2
[659] Cf. Cant 8:6

can have either good thoughts for salvation, or pious affections, or any good resolution, except he be inwardly enlightened[660] by the grace of "the Father of lights,"[661] and author of all pious affections and good resolutions, they ought to rely upon the divine assistance more than upon all human industry. But that this great confidence in the grace of God above all things, may not be presumptuous and unreasonable, it is very necessary they should beg it humbly and often of Almighty God, saying from the bottom of their heart, after the example of the apostles: "Lord, teach us to pray."[662]

It is likewise necessary they should be as solicitous about God's grace, which is the life of the soul, as men commonly are about the nourishment of the poor corruptible body, which shall shortly be the food of worms; and that they should take special care not so much as to think deliberately on doing or saying anything that would offend God, and stop the current of his grace. If they act thus, the holy unction of God's grace, as the apostle assures,[663] will teach the method of meditation, or mental prayer; and that shall be fulfilled in them which the prophets foretold,[664] and Christ promises in the gospel, saying: "They shall be all taught of God,"[665] notwithstanding their want of learning and books; it being very certain, that it is the grace of God and a sincere desire to advance in virtue, and obtain life everlasting, that are requisite for meditation or mental prayer, and not great wit, nor any other learning, besides the knowledge of the duties of a Christian.

875. **What advice do you give concerning mental prayer?**

I would advise everyone to bestow about half an hour a day on this prayer, and that in the morning, as it is recommended to us in many passages of the holy scripture.[666]

---

[660] Cf. 2 Cor 3:5
[661] Jas 1:17
[662] Lk 11:1
[663] Cf. 1 Jn 2:20, 27
[664] Cf. Is 54:13; Jer 31:34
[665] Jn 6:45
[666] Cf. Ecclus 39:6; Ps 62:7; 118:148

876. What do you say to those who find no leisure for it?

I say, that it is a wonderful and dreadful thing that Christians do daily find leisure for doing all affairs, except the one only necessary affair,[667] for which they were created and placed in this world; and that they grudge bestowing one half hour only in twenty-four hours, on the affair of salvation, or the service of God, to which their whole time, their substance, their labor, and life ought to be entirely consecrated; for the first and great commandment is, to love and serve God with our whole heart, with our whole soul, with our whole mind, and with our whole strength.[668] All other lawful affairs may, and ought to be rationally and moderately looked after, inasmuch as they serve and help us to carry on the great affair of salvation, and to pay daily that tribute which our Maker and Savior justly demands of us; and ought consequently to be laid aside, when they are a hindrance to the faithful discharge of that great and necessary duty, which no business, nor power either in heaven or on earth, can exempt us from.[669]

All this visible world was created for the service of man, in order he should love and serve God, and work out his own salvation; no worldly business then ought to be put in balance with that only necessary business; no business whatsoever ought to take place of it: for if it be well done, all is well done; if it be neglected, all is lost forever.

But the case is, that this vain and deceitful world, or some corrupt passion, is the god of a vast number of the Christians of these times. "They confess," as the apostle says, "that they know God, but in their actions they deny him."[670] It is for this reason alone they find no time for prayer, although it be presumption and madness to pretend to obtain life everlasting without pains, without thinking seriously and frequently on the affair of salvation; without speaking often to God from the heart; and without hearkening to him when he speaks to the heart.

As to those, who are in great distress, or under the command of others, and have not much time at their own disposal, let them endeavor to

---

[667] Cf. Lk 10:42
[668] Cf. Dt 6:5; Mt 22:37; Mk 12:30
[669] Cf. Mt 16:26
[670] Ti 1:16

meditate as often as they can, and particularly on Sundays and holy days, and on days of confession and Communion. Every head of a family is obliged to allow his servants time, and even to engage them to pray every day; and if he does not, how can he expect that his servants will be faithful to him, when neither he nor they are faithful to God?

Besides that, grant that servants and workmen, who are under subjection, should get no set time, yet they can and ought to practice mental prayer; for everyone, as he awakes in the morning, can give his first thought and his first word to God; he can beg his grace and give him thanks; he can, whilst he is putting on his clothes, revolve or repeat the same good thoughts, or the like again and again in his heart; then he should and can in a short time, consider what he should do throughout the day, with relation to God, his neighbor, and the duties of his calling, and offer up himself entirely, his labor and his work, from his whole heart to Almighty God, and beg his grace humbly and affectionately, that he may spend the day inoffensively and Christian-like. Everyone can, at all hours in the day, dedicate whatever work he takes in hand, to his Maker, as the apostle St. Paul recommends to all Christians, saying: "Whether you eat, or drink, or do anything else, do all things to the glory of God."[671]

There is nobody but can beg God's grace, and make acts of contrition, faith, hope, and charity from time to time. Everyone can, in the course of the day, bewail his sins, take a resolution not to commit them for the future, and beseech the Father of mercies to forgive him his offences, to enlighten his understanding, to strengthen his will, to purify his heart, to confirm his good resolutions, and bring them to a good issue. Everyone may and has need, at all hours to watch well over his own thoughts, and either to reject them when he perceives they are bad, by humbling himself in the presence of God, and by demanding his assistance; or to open his heart to them, when he knows they are good, saying along with young Samuel, "Speak, Lord, for thy servant heareth (thee)."[672] Thus, everyone may, by ejaculatory or short prayers, speak to God seriously and frequently from his heart: he may, at

[671] 1 Cor 10:31
[672] 1 Kgs 3:10

any time, even in company, have one eye, the eye of the body, on his worldly business, and the eye of the heart on God, after the example of the holy king David, who says of himself: "Mine eyes are always towards the Lord, because he will pull my feet out of the net."[673] Still this great king had many wars and weighty affairs on his hands. But this pious practice, far from hindering either king, or servant, or laborer, or others from their business, will draw the blessing of God on them, and on whatever they undertake.

The time which many spend in idle discourse, or in thinking and judging uncharitably of their neighbor, will serve to think and reflect on themselves; to examine and condemn their own thoughts, words, and actions; to consider that they are in the presence of God; that he sees the most secret motions of their heart; and that they shall render him a strict account of every bad thought, and even of every idle word, at the day of judgment. The awful presence of Almighty God, and this severe account are a subject of continual meditation, and of fear and trembling to all, and especially to those who are not upon their guard.

Once more, to finish the day, everyone may and should, at night, humbly beg the grace of God, and give him thanks for his creation, redemption, preservation, and all the favors he conferred on him since he came into the world, especially that day; he may and ought to examine his conscience, to make an act of contrition, and to resolve firmly to labor against his failings; he may say some prayers, or think seriously on the four last things, or on some pious subject; and then resign his soul and body, his repose and sleep, to his Maker and Redeemer; he may, even in bed, entertain himself with some pious thoughts; and ought not to count on seeing the day following, for many were disappointed.

Now, all this is mental prayer, and no one can truly say but he has leisure for it, since those, who are obliged to get their livelihood by the sweat of their brow, may easily find time to stick to this Christian practice every day of their life. "He that shall persevere to the end shall be saved."[674]

THE END

---

[673] Ps 24:15
[674] Mt 24:13

A
CATECHISM
MORAL
AND CONTROVERSIAL

Proper for fuch as are already advanced to
Some Knowledge of the Chriftian
Doctrine.

TO WHICH

Is annexed by Way of an Appendix a
Practical Method of preparing for Sacramental Confeffion.

DEDICATED

To His Eminence.

CARDINAL MANOEL

By T...s M...s B...ke O. P.

Superiorum Permiffu.

✠

LISBON.

PRINTED IN THE YEAR 1752.

Original Title Page

A

Catechism
Moral
and Controversial

Proper for such as are already advanced to
Some Knowledge of the Christian Doctrine.

TO WHICH

Is annexed by Way of an Appendix a
Practical Method of preparing for Sacramental Confession.

DEDICATED

To His Eminence,
CARDINAL MANOEL

By T... s M... s B...ke O. P.
Superiorum Permissu.

✠

LISBON.

PRINTED IN THE YEAR 1752.

Author's Introduction

The sum, of what a Christian is bound to know, may be reduced to five general heads, viz: what he is to believe, what to receive, what to do, what to avoid, and what to pray for.

The first is comprehended in the knowledge of the nature of faith, and of the mysteries contained in the Apostles' Creed. The second, in a due understanding of the nature of the sacraments, and the dispositions of soul required for the worthy receiving of them. The third, in a knowledge of the enormity of sin and a right understanding of its different kinds, and of the difference between mortal and venial sin. The fourth is included in the knowledge of the ten commandments, the six precepts of the Church, and of the works of mercy. The fifth is contained in a knowledge of the nature of prayer, and of the form and manner, in which we must pray.

All these truths, which we must know to be saved, are either points of doctrine not known by the light of nature, but by revelation only; or moral precepts: these last are either first principles of reason, as, "Do not to another what you would not have done to yourself," or are immediate consequences from them, as: the ten commandments, or remote consequences, as: all those precepts and ordinances of the Church or state, that are founded in right reason and the nature of the thing. In the three first, viz: revealed truths, first principles of reason, and the more immediate consequences of them, all Catholic divines agree, though they differ very much as to the remote consequences which they judge may be deduced from them, as well as in their decisions of moral and practical cases concerning them. Hence it is, that in laying down revealed truths, the more general moral precepts, and their more immediate consequences, I merely relate what Catholic divines say; but in my resolutions of practical and moral cases, I am obliged out of many opinions to choose that which seems most reasonable to me, and that without any design of disparaging the judgments of those who are of a contrary opinion.

My method is as follows. First, I explain in a moral sense: faith in general, the mysteries contained in the Apostles' Creed, the seven sacraments, the ten commandments, the six principal precepts of the Church, the fourteen works of mercy, sin in general, and its different kinds, particularly the seven capital sins, prayer, devotion, meditation, and contemplation in general, the Lord's Prayer, the principal forms of prayer prescribed by the Church, the chief parts and ceremonies of the Mass, and also the ceremonies of the Holy Week. Secondly, I distinguish counsels from precepts, what is advised as best, from what is strictly commanded. Thirdly, I resolve the common moral cases relating to all Christian duties either according to the unanimous consent, or more probable opinions of divines.

If the Catholic Church had no enemies, I might have stopped here; but misrepresentation of Catholic tenets is so common a practice among protestants as well in their pulpits, as in their printed works, that something farther seems necessary to remove those false notions, those disadvantageous impressions of the doctrine of Catholics, which protestant teachers are so industrious in spreading, to keep the ignorant still in the dark, to prevent their seriously examining the grounds of the Catholic religion, and to strengthen that aversion to Catholic tenets, which they have imbibed from the prejudices of education. In these unhappy circumstances it is as necessary for us, according to St. Peter's directions, to be "ready to give satisfaction to every one that asketh us, a reason of the hope that is in us";[1] as it was in the beginning of the Church, when St. Peter gave this advice.

For these reasons, I thought it might be beneficial to adjoin (in different chapters or sections, as the subject required it) to the moral part of this work, a kind of controversial exposition of the Catholic doctrine according to the solemn declarations of the Catholic Church in her general councils, authentic catechisms, and public professions of faith; as also briefly to prove the said tenets by testimonies of scripture and tradition, and to answer in short some of the chief objections usually made against the doctrine and discipline of the Catholic Church; that thus the Catholic Christian being fully instructed in the belief and knowledge of his religion, may be able to give to everyone that asketh him, a solid reason of that hope, which is in

---

[1] 1 Pt 3:15

him; that he may rather pity than envy the miserable state of protestants, who, to defend a bad and weak cause, are forced to recur to the poor shift of misrepresentation and calumny. Finally, that thus instructed he may evade their fallacious objections and false accusations, which lose all their force, when objected against the Catholic tenets understood according to the true and genuine sense of the Church; for an argument against a question misstated loses all its force, when the same question is fairly stated.

In this work I pretend to no other merit than that of a compiler. I am sensible I say nothing but what has been often said before, but scattered in many books, or at least put together in other works of a much greater bulk. I hope the usefulness of this work, or at least the good intention of it will plead my excuse for the inaccuracy or meanness of the language, the former of which is owing to my not having had the opportunities I could wish of acquiring an exact knowledge of the force or propriety of English expressions; and the latter may with great truth be in a great measure ascribed to the desire I had of being understood by persons, who have not had the advantage of the best education, for whose use this work was principally designed, though perhaps the better instructed may find it worth their perusal.

Chapter 1

Of Faith in General

Faith Explained in a Moral Sense

1. **What is faith in general?**

   It is the belief or assent that the mind gives to a proposition advanced by another, upon the authority of the proposer, or some other, and not upon any certain knowledge, that it is really and absolutely so.

2. **What is divine faith?**

   It is a theological virtue, whereby we are persuaded to assent to all those truths relating to God, which he has revealed to us, either by scripture or apostolical tradition.

3. **What is supernatural faith?**

   It is the belief of a thing out of, or above the common course of nature.

4. **What is the Catholic faith?**

   It is that universal faith, which is proposed and approved by the apostolic Roman Church.

5. **What articles doth this Catholic faith contain?**

   All those which God has revealed, either by scripture or apostolical tradition, when they are proposed by the Church to her children to be believed.

6. **Are we all bound to believe and know all the particular articles of the Catholic faith?**

   We are not bound to know them all explicitly and distinctly, though we are obliged to believe them all with an implicit faith.

7. **What is an implicit faith?**

It is a belief of all the articles in general, without knowing them in particular.

8. **What is an explicit faith?**

It is a belief accompanied by a distinct knowledge of the articles of faith in particular.

9. **What articles is every Christian bound to believe with an explicit faith?**

All the articles and mysteries contained in the Apostles' Creed, which may be reduced to three general heads viz: the articles relating to God's divinity and to the mystery of the Blessed Trinity; the articles concerning Christ's incarnation, death and passion; the article of believing the Catholic Church implies the belief of the sacraments, the nature of which each person is bound to know, according as it is his duty to receive or administer any of them.

10. **Can anyone be saved or justified without an explicit faith of all these mysteries?**

He cannot, if he has an opportunity of learning them; because every Christian is bound by a divine and ecclesiastical precept to know them explicitly and distinctly.

11. **Is the knowledge of any of these mysteries so absolutely necessary to justification, that without it, we cannot be justified or saved, even in case of invincible ignorance?**

A distinct knowledge of some of these mysteries is not only obligatory, so that our ignorance may be in some case excusable; but is also so absolutely necessary to salvation that without it we never can be saved.

12. **How many are the mysteries which we must necessarily know to obtain salvation?**

Three viz: the unity of God, "who will render to every man according to his works,"[2] the mystery of the Blessed Trinity, and that of the incarnation, wherever the gospel is sufficiently published according to the more probable opinion of divines: "For he that cometh to God must believe that he is, and that he is a rewarder of them that seek him."[3] Wherefore all confessions made by a sinner, though invincibly ignorant of these mysteries, are void and null, and consequently must be made over again.

13. **Is it enough to know these mysteries by heart, so as to be able to rehearse them in English or Latin?**

That is not enough, for we must also understand the true meaning of them.

14. **What kind of knowledge is necessary?**

There are two sorts of people in the Church, the one, prelates, masters and confessors, the other, the inferior clergy and laity. The first are bound to know what belongs to their respective functions, and the mysteries of faith, so as to be able to defend them against all heretics; the second are only bound to know the meaning and signification of each mystery, and the difference of one from the other, and may leave all the difficulties and subtleties relating to them, to be discussed by divines.

15. **Are there not some so dull and stupid, as not to be capable of learning these mysteries?**

No one come to the use of reason is so stupid, or otherwise so lawfully employed, as not to be able to know the mysteries of faith absolutely necessary to salvation, if he uses proper diligence to be instructed. Nay, those born and bred among infidels may beg of God to enlighten them, and give them grace to observe the law of nature; and if they do this, God will use means to instruct them in the mysteries necessary to salvation, either by some interior illumination of their minds, or by the ministry of some preacher, as he sent Peter to instruct Cornelius.[4] For as no one is so stupid or busy as not to know how to seek his daily bread, so there is no one who is not

---

[2] Rom 2:6
[3] Heb 11:6
[4] Cf. Acts 10

capable of learning the mysteries of faith which he is obliged to believe, if he be willing to examine, inquire, and implore God's assistance to be instructed therein. It is our own negligence and carelessness that persuades us to the contrary, but this pretext will not avail us at the day of judgment.

16. **How can a person subject to temptations against faith overcome them?**
If he doubts obstinately by not submitting his judgment to what he knows to be an article of faith, he sins against faith; if he only feels doubts and temptations, not by judging any mystery of faith to be false or uncertain, but merely on account of some difficulty in comprehending and reconciling the mysteries of faith with the principles of reason, in this case (I say) he does not sin against faith. On the contrary, he is like the man in the gospel who said: "I believe, O Lord help my incredulity."[5] Yet he should endeavor to reject and cast away these doubts and temptations, which often disturb the mind without affording any benefit or advantage to it.

17. **What are the best remedies against those temptations?**
We are first of all to beg of God, to strengthen and increase our faith. Moreover, a person is tempted to doubt of either all the articles of faith, or of some particular one. If he be tempted with regard to all the articles, he is to apply the means commonly used to persuade infidels of the truth of the Christian religion, by considering that we cannot live in this world without faith; whereas we believe several things upon the testimony of men, viz: that we descend from such ancestors; that there are such and such kingdoms and cities, which we have never seen.

Moreover, if he should change from the Catholic religion to any other sect of Christians, he cannot be better off, seeing that, in every sect there are several things above reason to be believed upon weaker grounds than in the Catholic religion, wherein the mysteries of faith are proposed as revealed by God, by a learned and holy Church, whose doctrine (though contrary to the bent of corrupt nature) has been defended by the ablest pens, confirmed with thousands of miracles, and sealed with the blood of

[5] Mk 9:23

a million martyrs; a Church, that in spite of the bloody persecutions of the heathen emperors for above the three first centuries of Christianity, and of the violent opposition and calumnious misrepresentations of her doctrine, which she has met with from her own rebellious children, still endures, and preserves the unity of her doctrine; whence we may reasonably infer that nothing less than the almighty hand of God has instituted, established, and preserved among so many various nations such a perfect harmony and unanimity in faith and doctrine.

If a person be tempted with regard to any particular mystery, he is to repel the temptation, by considering that if he believes all other mysteries to be revealed by God, because they are so proposed to him by an infallible Church, he should also believe this article, as being equally proposed by the same unerring authority.

18. **When is every Christian bound to make an act of faith?**

As often as he is in imminent danger of death or grievously tempted against faith, and at least once a year; but observe that this last obligation is complied with by receiving worthily any sacrament, because such a reception always implies an act of faith. Moreover, every Christian is obliged to make an act of faith, when he is bound to make acts of hope, charity, penance, or an exterior profession of faith, all which require an interior belief of the mind.

19. **When are we bound to make an external profession of faith?**

As often as God's honor, our own, or neighbor's spiritual good require it; viz, in three cases. First, when our not professing our faith would give occasion to others to despise it, or to judge us to have none at all. Secondly, when by professing our faith, others may be very probably converted to it. Thirdly, when our neighbor is in imminent danger of denying his faith, and this may be prevented by our professing it.

20. **If a person questioned about his faith be silent, does he transgress this precept?**

He does, if he be questioned by a magistrate, or one of public authority;

but if by a private person, he may evade the question by telling him it is not his business, or by some such ambiguous answers. But observe that he never can positively deny his faith. We shall treat of the vices opposite to faith in Chapter 4.

Faith Explained in a Controversial Manner

21. **Is faith necessary to salvation?**

It is, because "without faith it is impossible to please God."[6] And because, "He that shall not believe, shall be condemned."[7]

22. **Are we bound rather to lose our lives, fortunes, and friends, than to deny our faith?**

We are, because Christ sayeth: "Whosoever shall deny me before men, I will also deny him before my Father in heaven."[8]

23. **Is faith alone, (excluding good works) sufficient to salvation?**

It is not, because "man is justified by works, and not by faith only."[9]

24. **Why then does St. Paul say: "We esteem a man to be justified by faith without the works of the law"?[10]**

St Paul only excludes the works of the law of Moses, as insufficient to a true justification, to show that the Jews cannot be justified, sanctified, nor saved by the works of the written law of Moses, but by the faith and grace of Jesus Christ. St. Paul does not pretend that the virtue of faith alone will justify and save a man. Nothing can be more opposite to his own doctrine elsewhere, for he tells us that, God "will render to every one according to his deeds."[11] And that "not the hearers of the law…but the doers…shall be

---

6 Heb 11:6
7 Mk 16:16
8 Mt 10:33
9 Jas 2:24
10 Rom 3:28
11 Rom 2:6

justified."[12] He teaches us, that the faith by which we must be saved, must be a faith, "which worketh by charity."[13] He also tells the Corinthians that "circumcision is nothing, and uncircumcision nothing: but the keeping of God's commandments."[14] That though a man should have faith, so that he could remove mountains, it would avail him nothing without charity.[15]

25. Is it enough to believe all that is written in the Bible?

It is not, for we must also believe all apostolical traditions, because St Paul sayeth: "Brethren stand firm: and keep the traditions, which you have learned, whether by word, or whether by our epistle."[16] Whence it appears, that the apostles did not deliver all things that were to be believed, by writing.

26. But does not Christ say: "You have made void the precept of God, on account of your traditions,"[17] and, "In vain do they worship me, teaching the doctrines and precepts of men"?[18]

It is evident that Christ there speaks of such traditions, as were contrary to the law of God, or of nature, such as: not assisting our parents in need, under the specious pretext of giving our substance to the Temple, and that whatsoever gift we make to God will be profitable to our parents, as well as to ourselves, and therefore that we are no farther obliged to assist them.[19] Or Christ speaks of vain and frivolous traditions, such as not washing their hands, when they eat bread.[20]

27. Is tradition a necessary rule of faith?

It is, because without it, it is impossible to know what books of the old or new testament are true and genuine, or to understand the real sense of them.

[12] Rom 2:13
[13] Gal 5:6
[14] 1 Cor 7:19
[15] Cf. 1 Cor 13:2
[16] 2 Thes 2:14
[17] Mt 15:6
[18] Mt 15:9
[19] Cf. Mt 15:5-6
[20] Cf. Mt 15:2

28. **Are there not several pious or at least indifferent traditions, which are no points of faith?**

There are.

29. **How then shall I be able to know when a traditional fact or doctrine is a point of faith?**

It is a point of faith, when it is unanimously held to have been so delivered by the apostles, and when it is so declared by the major part of the holy fathers succeeding them; but if the fathers differ among themselves, then it must be declared a point of faith by the Church, and the contrary doctrine censured as erroneous.

30. **How shall I be able to know when the Church has received any doctrine or discipline by tradition from the apostles?**

By that golden rule of St. Augustine, viz: that what is found not to have had its institution from any council, but to have been observed by the universal Church, that same must needs have come from the first fathers and founders of the Church, that is, from the apostles.[21]

31. **May not everyone be saved, that lives in any faith according to his conscience?**

No; because a man's conscience itself is often a grievous sin, when it proceeds from obstinacy, neglect, unjust prejudices, or any wicked passion. Thus, a pagan thinks it no sin to worship his false gods; a Jew, to blaspheme Christ; a Turk, to believe the Alcoran[22] and not the Bible, and yet their impieties will not save them.

32. **Is moral honesty sufficient to salvation?**

It is not, though it were joined to a belief in Christ, because many other duties are necessary, such as: baptism,[23] the avoiding of heresy and schism.[24]

---

[21] Cf. Augustine, *On Baptism, against the Donatists*, Bk. 4, Ch. 24
[22] Editor's note: the Quran.
[23] Cf. Mt 28:19
[24] Cf. Gal 5:20

33. **If there be so many Christian duties necessary to salvation, why does St. Paul say: "If you shall confess with your mouth the Lord Jesus, and shall believe in your heart that God has raised him from the dead, you shall be saved"?**[25]

St. Paul does not there exclude the other necessary duties, which he has often recommended elsewhere. His meaning then, is that whereas to confess Christ in a persecuting age is a most difficult act of religion, and Christ's resurrection startled the Athenian philosophers;[26] supposing a compliance with these two duties, St. Paul did not fear but the rest would be observed.

34. **Can a person, who is out of the Catholic faith, be saved in any communion of Christians, who believe the Trinity and incarnation?**

He cannot, if he be but vincibly ignorant of the heresy in which he is engaged. Hereafter, I shall explain vincible and invincible ignorance.

35. **Is it charity to suppose all men saved, whose lives are morally honest?**

It is not, because divine revelation tells us, that several other duties besides moral honesty are necessary to salvation; wherefore though it be charity to desire the salvation of all men, yet it is downright nonsense to think that all are saved, who only comply with one duty necessary to salvation.

36. **Is it not inconsistent with the infinite goodness of God to suffer the greatest part of mankind to perish?**

No one perishes who fears and loves God above all things; for though in respect of those who perish, few are saved,[27] yet God neither made the greatest, nor any part of mankind to be eternally miserable, but to be forever happy; so that if few are saved, it is because the greatest part of mankind will not observe the conditions on which heaven is promised.

---

[25] Rom 10:9
[26] Cf. Acts 17:32
[27] Cf. Mt 20:16; 22:14

37. **If protestants judge more favorably of the salvation of Catholics, than Catholics do of theirs, are not protestants the more charitable of the two?**
The protestant's judgment is less charitable and more favorable; and that of Catholics is more charitable and less favorable.

38. **How do you prove that?**
A favorable judgment is that which is given in a person's favor, be it right or wrong. A charitable judgment is that which is grounded on truth, and proceeds from the love of God, and our neighbor; so that a charitable judgment may be very unfavorable and a favorable judgment may be very uncharitable. Thus, to judge with St. Paul that adulterers, drunkards and idolaters "shall not obtain the kingdom of God";[28] though this judgment be less favorable to these miserable wretches, yet it is in itself more charitable, (because it is grounded on God's infallible truth) than the contrary judgment, which allows that such profligate livers can be saved; otherwise, libertines, who maintain that drunkenness and lasciviousness are no sins, would be more charitable than St. Paul, who judged the contrary.

39. **Has the faith of the Catholic Church been the same in all ages?**
It has always been the same; for the Church has no articles of faith, but what were revealed to the apostles, and these she knows, not by any revelation made immediately to her, but by scripture, which she sees and reads, and by apostolical tradition, which is conveyed to her, either by oral tradition, which she hears, or by the writings of Catholics of former ages, which she reads and sees.

40. **But did not the Catholic Church coin new articles of faith, when she settled the whole canon of scripture; when she defined against the Donatists the validity of baptism administered by heretics? For the second was no article of faith in St. Cyprian's time; nor the first, even in the fourth century.**
It is true, she made those and other articles formerly doubted of known to the faithful, but she did not make them articles of faith, for this is more

28 Gal 5:21

than the apostles themselves could do; because God only can make articles of faith by revealing them to the apostles, who were the authentic publishers of divine revelation to the Church, as she is commissioned to publish them to her children, when called in question; as English laws are made only by the king and Parliament, but printers and criers make them known to the subjects, without derogating in the least from the supreme authority of king and Parliament; so that though the two abovementioned articles, and several others since defined were revealed to the apostles, they were not articles known to all the faithful. For it is not requisite, that every mystery of faith in particular should be always proposed to them to be believed. It is enough for them to believe as much as they have an obligation and opportunity to know.

41. **What was the Church's motive for deferring to settle the whole canon of scripture, till after the fourth century?**

That was owing to the prudent economy of the Church, who seeing several apocryphal books, and corrupt editions of the scripture forged and handed about by divers heretics of those times in favor of their respective errors, prudently waited to compare and examine those books and editions by the test of tradition, and thereby declared true and canonical, such as she found conformable to her universally received doctrine, and rejected as spurious and apocryphal, such as were contrary to her universal tradition; which plainly evinces the necessity of tradition both for the expounding of the scripture, and distinguishing the true and genuine from the false and adulterate.

42. **Has the language of the Church been as unchangeable in all ages, as her faith?**

It has not, because the new-growing heresies obliged her to use new words to express more dogmatically and emphatically her faith, thereby to distinguish true believers from miscreants. Thus, the name of divine Persons was unknown till Sabellius, by denying the distinction of the Father, and Son, and Holy Ghost, obliged in a manner the Church to use it. Thus, also the word *consubstantial* was added to the Nicene Creed, to explode the error of Arius, who held that Christ was a pure creature; and the word *transubstantiation* was used in the eleventh century, when Berengarianism required it, to distinguish Catholics from dissenters, but to conclude from hence, that the real presence or change of the substance of the bread and wine into the body and blood of Christ signified by the word *transubstantiation* was not held by the Catholic Church before the eleventh century, is as great an absurdity as to think that the Trinity of the divine Persons was unknown to the apostles, because they never used the word *person*, or that the divinity of Christ was unknown to the Antinicene fathers, because they did not use the word *consubstantial*.

43. **Is the discipline of the Church as unchangeable as her faith?**
It is not, for her discipline, (by which are meant the particular forms, practices, and ceremonies in her public prayers, sacrifices, and sacraments, or in her government, which in regard to the law of God are neither forbidden nor commanded) all these (I say) may be changed according to the will of the Church's pastors.

44. **What does the Church propose to her children to be believed in particular?**
All things, which are clear in scripture, or defined in general councils approved by the Church, and also all the articles contained in the Apostles' Creed, which must be explicitly believed by every Christian, as I have already explained.

The Creed Expounded

A Short Preamble to the Creed

45. **What is the Creed?**
It is the sum of our belief made by the twelve apostles, before they separated and divided themselves into the several countries of the world, to preach the gospel; that so they might be able to teach one and the same doctrine in all places.

46. How many articles of faith does the Creed contain?

According to some catechists, it contains twelve, and according to others fourteen, viz: seven relating to God's divine nature and the Blessed Trinity; and seven more relating to the incarnation of Christ; besides which it contains five mysteries necessary to be believed.

47. What is the difference between a mystery and article of faith?

A mystery is a supernatural truth revealed by God and proposed by the Church; but an article of faith besides all this, must contain a new and special difficulty to be believed. Thus, the passion, death and burial of Christ are three different mysteries, though but one only article of faith; because, supposing the belief of Christ's passion, there is no special difficulty in believing his death and burial, but as there is a new difficulty in believing Christ's resurrection, this is a different article of faith from that of his death and burial.

48. What is the difference between a miracle and a mystery?

Both are supernatural, but a mystery is essentially obscure, and a miracle may be visible. Thus, that Christ was born of a Virgin, was a miracle but no mystery, because his birth was visible; but the hypostatical union, or the union of the divine and human nature together in the Person of Christ, (in which the mystery of the incarnation consists) was both supernatural and invisible.

The Articles Relating to the Divine Nature and to the Blessed Trinity, Expounded

49. How many articles are there in the Creed, relating to the divine nature?

Seven, viz: the belief of one God only, of God the Father, of God the Son, of God the Holy Ghost, of his being our Creator, our Savior, and our Glorifier.

50. **What means the article:** *one God?*

It means that there are not many gods, because there are not different divine natures.

51. **Why are there not three gods, since there are three different divine Persons, each of which is a substance or essence?**

Because the divinity, substance, and all absolute perfections are neither divided, nor multiplied in God; for such a division or multiplication would argue an imperfection in him, because then one Person would have some perfection, which the other would not have; but the divine Persons are distinct from one another by their mutual opposite respects to each other, and as these relations are three, the Persons are three, though the divine essence be one and the same in them all. As there are three different powers in one soul, though this example falls short of an exact comparison.

52. **Are the three divine Persons equally immense, eternal, and omnipotent?**

In those and all other absolute perfections, they are not only equal, but also consubstantial and the very same, so that one Person cannot be without the other, for the least space or duration of time.

53. **Since these three Persons are one only God, why may not the Father be called the Son, and the Son, the Holy Ghost?**

Because they are three different Persons by the mutual opposite relations of the Father, Son, and Holy Ghost, though their essence be one and the same.

54. **How shall I know these Persons to be different?**

By their respective distinguishing marks, viz: the Father proceeds from no other Person, and the two others proceed from him; the Son proceeds from the Father, as an idea or conceit of his intellect; and the Holy Ghost proceeds from the Father and the Son, as the object of their mutual and infinite love and affection.

55. **Does the Holy Ghost proceed from the Father and the Son, as from one origin, or as from two?**

He proceeds from them as from one origin and one indivisible love, though the lovers be two.

56. **Why cannot the Holy Ghost be called the Son, since he proceeds from the Father?**

Because he does not proceed as a similitude or likeness of the Father, but only as a propension or attraction of his will; and the Son proceeds as the similitude and likeness of the Father's intellect and understanding; and it is proper to the understanding to conceive and produce a similitude or likeness of the conceived object (hence the idea is said to be born or to be the offspring of the understanding) but the will is only an inclination or propension towards its beloved object.

57. **What means the article: *Creator of heaven and earth?***

It means, that all creatures had a beginning, that God made heaven and earth, all creatures visible and invisible therein, out of nothing, through his own power and goodness.

58. **What means the article: *Savior of mankind?***

It means, that God forgives offences, gives grace, and furnishes all mankind with means necessary to salvation.

59. **Can we be positively certain, that God furnishes everyone with that grace, and those means?**

We cannot be positively sure that he actually gives that grace, or furnishes everyone with those means; but we are to confide in his mercy, and believe that he offers it to them, and is willing to save all, if they observe the conditions on which salvation is promised.

60. **What are the conditions on which salvation is promised?**

Faith alone is not sufficient; for besides faith, which is requisite as a foundation, charity and good works are necessary as a superstructure, and the sacraments are needful as means to apply to us the merits of Christ's death and passion.

61. Is God Savior of the living and of the dead?

The living only can be saved; those in heaven are already saved; in hell there is no redemption; whilst we are in this life, we are in the road to either salvation or damnation.

62. What means the article: *Glorifier?*

It means, that God gives endless glory to those that fear and love him above all things.

63. In what does that glory consist?

In a clear sight of God, and of all his attributes, and in an eternal enjoyment of him.

64. Is that glory conferred upon the soul immediately after it goes out of this life?

The souls that depart this life in the state of grace, and have fully satisfied for the temporal punishment due to sin, are immediately glorified; such as die in actual mortal sin go to hell; those that die in venial sins only, or without having fully satisfied for the temporal punishment due to mortal sins, go to purgatory. The souls of infants that die unbaptized, go to *limbus.*

65. Where are these places: hell, purgatory, *limbus,* and the bosom of Abraham?

The three first are within the different concavities of the earth, in the most dark and tormenting places of the universe. The bosom of Abraham is over these three prisons, but under the surface of the earth; though now the bosom of Abraham commonly means, celestial paradise.

66. Will the bodies also of the blessed be glorified?

They will at the day of universal judgment, because then they shall be united to their glorified souls.

67. **In what will that glory consist?**

Chiefly in four qualities, viz: impassibility, whereby the body shall be exempt from all pain, sickness, or death, according to that: "This corruptible must put on incorruption, and this mortal put on immortality";[29] agility, whereby it can move from one place to another with the same swiftness that an angel can, according to that: "It is sown in infirmity, it shall rise in power";[30] subtlety, whereby it shall be cleansed and purified from the gross matter in which it was immersed, according to that: "It is sown a natural body," but "it shall rise a spiritual body";[31] and clarity, whereby it will appear as bright and splendid as the sun, according to that: for as "one star differeth from another in glory; so also is the resurrection of the dead."[32]

68. **Can a glorified body penetrate or get through any material thing without breaking it?**

It can, as Christ raised himself from the sepulchre, and entered the house where the disciples were, without breaking or opening the doors or windows.

69. **Where do the blessed souls reside?**

In the imperial or uppermost heaven, where they enjoy the beatific vision.

70. **What punishments do the damned undergo?**

Two sorts of punishment: the one of loss, whereby they shall be perpetually deprived of the sight of God; the other of sense, which is the never-ending torments of the fire of hell.

71. **Do children that die unbaptized, undergo these two sorts of punishment?**

No; but they are deprived of the sight of God; for, "Unless a man be

---

[29] 1 Cor 15:53
[30] 1 Cor 15:43
[31] 1 Cor 15:44
[32] 1 Cor 15:41

born again of water, and the Spirit, he cannot enter into the kingdom of heaven."[33]

72. **What pains do the souls undergo in purgatory?**
Both the pain of sense and of loss, till they have fully suffered for the punishment due to their sins; and according to the diversity of their offences, they are differently punished.

73. **Are there different degrees of glory in heaven, and of punishment and torments in hell?**
There are, according to the merits and demerits of each person there.

74. **Are these three titles: Creator, Sanctifier, and Glorifier, common to the three divine Persons?**
They are, because all external operations, or such as proceed from God in regard to any object different from the three divine Persons; these (I say) are common to all the Blessed Trinity; but the title of Redeemer is peculiar to the Son, who alone was made man, to redeem lost man.

75. **How do you prove, that there are three different divine Persons, and one only God?**
Out of 1 John 5: "There are three that give testimony in heaven, the Father, the Word, and the Holy Ghost. And these three are one."[34]

The Articles Relating to the Humanity and Incarnation of Christ, Expounded

76. **How many articles are there in the Creed, relating to the humanity and incarnation of Christ?**
Seven. The first is that Christ as man was conceived by the Holy Ghost. The second, that he was born of the Virgin Mary. The third, that he

---

[33] Jn 3:5
[34] 1 Jn 5:7

suffered bitter torments, a true and real death, was crucified and buried. The fourth, that he descended into *limbus*, to free the holy fathers who waited there for the redemption of mankind. The fifth, that the third day he rose again from the dead. The sixth, that he ascended into heaven, and sits at the right hand of God the Father Almighty. The seventh, that from thence he shall come to judge the quick and the dead.

77. **What is the incarnation?**

It is the act of assuming human nature, and adding to it, by uniting the Godhead and manhood in one divine Person.

78. **How is God made man called?**

Jesus Christ, true God, and true man.

79. **Why did he make himself man?**

To save lost man, for the honor and glory of God.

80. **Was the incarnation necessary for the salvation of man?**

It was not absolutely necessary for that end, because God might redeem man by several other means, but it was necessary for a condign and rigorous satisfaction; for our offences being against God's infinite goodness required an infinite satisfaction, which no one could make but God made man; because his being man rendered him capable of suffering, and his infinite Person rendered his sufferings infinitely valuable, satisfactory, and acceptable to God.

81. **How many persons are there in Christ?**

One only divine Person, and no created one.

82. **How many natures are there in Christ?**

Two, the one divine, the other human. The first he has as the true and real Son of his eternal Father from all eternity; not by choice or adoption, but by nature. The second he has, as being born of the Virgin Mary; and for this reason, he is sometimes called a double or compounded Person, because he has two different natures, though in himself he is one indivisible Person.

83. **Which of the three Persons was made man?**
The second Person only.

84. **To be made man, did he separate himself from the Father, or cease to be God?**
He did not; for he cannot lose the divine nature, and therefore must be always with his Father, whose nature he has.

85. **Was the incarnation the work of one Person only?**
It was the work of all the three, because it was wrought by the same omnipotence, which is common to the three divine Persons, though one of them only assumed human nature; as if two should cooperate to clothe a third Person, and he himself should concur to the same effect.

86. **Why then do we say in the Creed, that Christ was conceived by the Holy Ghost, rather than by the three divine Persons?**
Because the incarnation was a work of excessive love for man, it is in a particular and especial manner appropriated and ascribed to the Holy Ghost, who proceeds from the mutual and reciprocal love of the Father and Son.

87. **What means the article: *Who was conceived by the Holy Ghost?***
It means, that the body of Christ was framed, not by human generation, but by the work of the Holy Ghost.

88. **How did the Holy Ghost effect the incarnation?**
First, he framed Christ's body of the blood of the Blessed Virgin. Secondly, he created the soul of Christ. Thirdly, he united the soul to his body. Fourthly, he hindered the natural result of a human person, in lieu of which he united Christ's human nature to the divine Person of the Son.

89. **What means the article:** *Born of the Virgin Mary?*
It means, that Christ as man had a real Mother, in whose womb he was conceived, and of whom he was really born, and that this Mother was a Virgin not only before, but also in, and after her childbirth.

90. **How could a child be born without opening the bars of nature?**
To be really born, it is enough that the child should come into the world, out of the womb in which he was conceived, without opening the bars of nature; for God can make one body pass through another without breaking or opening it, as Christ came to the disciples, the doors being shut.[35]

91. **What means the article:** *He suffered under Pontius Pilate, was crucified, dead, and buried?*
It means, that Christ as man, not as God, suffered both in his soul and body most bitter torments and grievous afflictions under Pontius Pilate, president of Judea.

92. **What were those torments and afflictions?**
He suffered in his mind excessive grief, affliction, and anguish; in his delicate body, most bitter torments, such as: his bloody sweat, his scourging at the pillar, his crown of thorns, his carrying the cross, his being nailed thereto, and dying thereon. In his credit and reputation, he suffered the most opprobrious injuries and affronts, such as: his purple garment, his scepter of a reed, and his being deemed an impostor possessed by an evil spirit.

93. **How could Christ's soul suffer, whereas it was glorified from the first instant of its creation?**
Though it was glorified from the very first instant of its creation, and by consequence had a clear sight of God, yet as Christ was willing that his body should remain passible, in order to suffer for our sins, his soul, as to

[35] Cf. Jn 20:19

the inferior part thereof, or inasmuch as it animated his passible body, was subject to pains and afflictions.

94. **If Christ was true God, and intended to manifest his infinite goodness to mankind by his incarnation, why did he humble himself so as to submit to so many injuries and afflictions, which seem to derogate in a great measure from the glory and greatness of God?**

Christ's sufferings and afflictions are so far from debasing him, that on the contrary, they are a strong indication of his glory and greatness; because they were intended to make a rigorous and adequate satisfaction to God for our sins, whereby we have offended an infinite goodness, which satisfaction no creature (though never so perfect) could make but God made man. Moreover, we should consider not only what Christ suffered, but also the cause, motive, infinite value, and the end of his sufferings; which were to satisfy an offended deity out of an excessive love for man, and that without the least constraint or obligation. To suffer in this manner, is a most glorious and honorable death.

95. **What means the article: *He descended into hell?***

It means, that Christ's blessed soul being separated by death from his body, but still remaining united to his divine Person, descended into *limbus*, to free the holy fathers, who waited there for the redemption of mankind, according to that: "Whom God raised up again, the sorrows of hell being loosed,"[36] as it was foretold by David: "Because thou wilt not leave my soul in hell, nor suffer thy holy one to see corruption."[37] And, "Ascending on high, he hath led captivity captive; he bestowed gifts on men. And that he ascended, what is it, but that he also descended first into the lower parts of the earth?"[38]

96. **Did Christ's humanity descend?**

From the time of his death to that of his resurrection, there was no

[36] Acts 2:24
[37] Ps 15:10; Acts 2:27
[38] Eph 4:8-9

humanity which consists of soul and body united; so that his soul only descended, and his body remained dead in the sepulchre.

97. **Did Christ's divinity remain united to his soul and body, when these were separated from each other by death?**
It did, as a person who has his sword sheathed, by unsheathing it, does not lose either sword or scabbard, though the sword be separated from the scabbard.

98. **Did Christ descend into the hell of the damned and into purgatory?**
He descended in Person into *limbus* only, but the effects of his descent reached purgatory and the hell of the damned.

99. **What were the effects caused by Christ in purgatory and in the hell of the damned?**
In purgatory, he freed from their captivity the souls there detained that were sufficiently purified according to the order of divine justice; and also comforted the souls that remained there with the happy news of the great work of their redemption being accomplished. In the hell of the damned, he weakened the devil's power, who was greatly afflicted to see Christ's soul so victorious and triumphant; and also severely reprimanded the devils and damned souls, as their just judge.

100. **Did any souls remain in *limbus* after Christ raised himself from death?**
It is certain that Christ preached to the souls there detained, according to that, "He preached to the spirits that were in prison."[39] That is, he brought them this agreeable news, that he, who was their Redeemer, was now to come to be their deliverer, and that at his glorious ascension, they should enter with him into heaven, where none could enter before our Redeemer, who opened, as it were, heaven's gates; Christ then freed all the souls in *limbus* from their captivity, and led them at his ascension, triumphant with him into heaven. So that since Christ's ascension, *limbus* is a place where

[39] 1 Pt 3:19

the souls of infants only that die without baptism go, as not being guilty of personal crimes to condemn them to the fire of hell or purgatory, and not free from original sin, and pure enough to go to heaven.

101. **What means the article: *The third day he rose again from the dead?***
It means, that Christ after being dead almost three days, by his divine power raised himself again from death, by uniting together his soul and body heretofore separated, and thus rose to an immortal life by his glorious resurrection.

102. **Is the resurrection a second incarnation?**
It is not, because Christ's soul and body during the time of his death remained united to his divine Person. And by his resurrection he only united together his soul and body heretofore separated from each other. But before the incarnation, neither soul nor body were united to his divine Person.

103. **Did Christ reassume all the parts of his body?**
He did, even the least drop of his vital blood, and the very scattered hairs of his head.

104. **How could Christ rise glorious and immortal, whereas after his resurrection he appeared to his disciples in the same passible state as before his death?**
Though Christ raised his body to a glorious and immortal life, yet he could temper this glory, so as not to make it visible to all, that thus he might confound the incredulity of some of his disciples, and retain the marks of his wounds, to present them often to his Father as a propitiation for our sins.

105. **What means the article: *He ascended into heaven?***
It means, that Christ as man ascended by his own power into heaven, forty days after his resurrection, his apostles being eyewitnesses.[40]

---

[40] Cf. Acts 1:9-10

106. **What means:** *He sitteth at the right hand of God the Father Almighty?*

Nothing of that is to be understood literally, for God the Father, who is incorporeal and a pure Spirit, has neither right nor left hand; neither does Christ now glorious and impassible want a seat to rest on; but it is said, that *Christ sitteth at the right hand of God*, to signify to us that as God, he is equal to his Father in power and glory, and as man, he has a preeminence in glory above all other creatures.

107. **What means the article:** *From thence he shall come to judge the quick and the dead?*

It means, that besides the sentence which is pronounced upon everyone at his death, there shall be a general judgment at the end of the world, when our bodies shall be raised from death to life, and Christ will come in great power and majesty accompanied with legions of angels, to sentence in the Valley of Jehosaphat[41] both our souls and bodies, according to our deeds, either to eternal happiness, or to everlasting torments.

108. **Why is it said that he shall** *judge the quick and the dead?*

To signify that he shall judge not only the damned, but also the blessed souls; for though the whole race of man shall be raised from death to life; yet the blessed souls are called "the quick" or living, because they shall enjoy everlasting life, and because they died in the state of grace, which is the life of the soul; but the damned souls are called "the dead," because the life they shall hereafter enjoy is everlasting death and torments, and because they died in mortal sin, which is death to the soul.

The Mysteries of Faith Contained in the Apostles' Creed, Expounded in a Moral Sense

109. **Are there any mysteries of faith in the Creed besides the abovementioned articles?**

There are five, viz: I believe the holy Catholic Church, the communion

---

[41] Cf. Jl 3:2

of saints, the forgiveness of sins, the resurrection of the flesh, and life everlasting.

110. **What means: *I believe the Catholic Church?***

It means, that I believe the Church in all things appertaining to faith, with the same divine faith wherewith I believe in God; but with this difference, that I believe in God as the object, motive, and end of my belief, but I believe the Church as my guide, and as an infallible proposer of all points of faith, wherefore we say in the Creed: *I believe in God*, but we do not say, *I believe in the Church*, but only *I believe the Church*.

111. **What is the Church?**

It is the congregation of all the faithful, under Jesus Christ their invisible head and his vicar upon earth, the pope.

112. **Why is the Church said to be one?**

Because all her members worship one God, profess one law, use the same sacraments, believe the same articles of faith, and obey one supreme head.

113. **How is the Church holy?**

Because she has holy laws, professes a holy faith, has holy sacraments, which are means of sanctification, is guided by the Holy Ghost, has several saints in heaven, and many holy good livers on earth.

114. **What means: *The communion of saints?***

There are two sorts of communion in the Church: the one of faith only, the other of faith, charity, and good works. The first is common to all the faithful within the pale of the Church, and by it they partake of the public prayers and suffrages of the Church; for none is excluded from this communion, but pagans, heretics, and those who are excommunicated by name. The second is peculiar to such as are in the state of grace; by it they may have a share in the merits of each other, satisfy for the temporal punishments due to the sins of each other, and also be aided and assisted by the intercession of the saints in heaven.

115. **What means:** *The forgiveness of sin?*

It means, that Christ has instituted sacraments as means of grace, and left the Church power to forgive all kinds of sins though never so enormous, provided there be a right disposition on the sinner's side.

116. **Can we have an absolute certainty of our final perseverance, or that our sins are forgiven us?**

We cannot without a special revelation; because a "man knoweth not whether he be worthy of love, or hatred."[42] And St. Paul exhorts us to work out our salvation with fear and trembling.[43] Neither is that certainty necessary for the peace of our conscience, because for this it is enough to have a moral certainty, and a most lively hope, that our sins are forgiven us by the due use of the sacraments.

117. **What means:** *The resurrection of the flesh?*

It means, that these bodies in which we now are, the same in substance, though different in qualities, shall be raised in a moment by God's command, at the day of universal judgment, according to that: "At the command given, and at the voice of the archangel, and at the trumpet of God, the Lord himself shall come down from heaven; and the dead, who are in Christ, shall rise first."[44] Not as to time, but in dignity.

118. **At what age and stature shall men rise?**

Some conjecture, that all the elect shall have bodies every way perfect, and shall seem to be about thirty-three, of the stature and age of Christ when he suffered, according to that: "Till we all meet in the unity of faith, and of the knowledge of the Son of God, unto a perfect man, unto the measure of the age of the fulness of Christ."[45]

---

[42] Eccles 9:1
[43] Cf. Phil 2:12
[44] 1 Thes 4:15
[45] Eph 4:13

119. **What means:** *Life everlasting?*

It means, that after this life there is another which shall last forever. Our souls are in themselves immortal, our bodies shall be also so, when they shall rise at the general resurrection from death to life. The just shall live with God in glory, which is properly life everlasting, and the wicked shall live in never-ending torments.

120. **In what does life everlasting chiefly consist?**

In a fruition of God, and a clear vision of him and of all his divine attributes and processions, according to that: "This is life everlasting: that they know thee the only God, and whom thou has sent Jesus Christ."[46] Whence will follow an ardent love, steadfast possession, unspeakable joy, and everlasting thanksgiving.

121. **Hitherto you have sufficiently expounded in a moral sense the articles and mysteries contained in the Apostles' Creed. But as protestants and Catholics differ chiefly about the true meaning of two, viz: the Catholic Church and the communion of saints, I would willingly hear you explaining these two mysteries in a controversial manner.**

I shall endeavor to comply with your request to the utmost of my power, in the two following sections.

The Church Expounded in a Controversial Manner

122. **Has Christ commanded us to believe and obey the Church?**

He has; out of Matthew 18, where he sayeth: "He (that) will not hear the church, let him be unto you as a heathen and a publican."[47]

123. **Are bishops of divine institution?**

They are, because "the Holy Ghost has placed (them) to rule the church of God."[48]

---

[46] Jn 17:3
[47] Mt 18:17
[48] Acts 20:28

124. **How do you prove St. Peter, and the pope his successor to be the supreme visible head of the Church?**

First, out of Luke 22, where Christ commanded St. Peter to strengthen his bretheren,[49] that is the apostles. Secondly, out of John 21, where Christ in the presence of seven apostles commissioned St. Peter to feed his lambs and sheep;[50] which words must needs import a power superior to that of the apostleship, which Christ had conferred on him in common with the other apostles after his resurrection.[51]

125. **How does the Catholic Church believe the pope as St. Peter's successor to be heir of the promises made to St. Peter?**

She believes the pope to have a just claim by divine right to all the promises made to St. Peter, which belong to his pastoral office, but not to his impeccability or power of doing miracles; wherefore the pope's deposing power, his indirect sovereignty over kings, and the like questions controverted in the schools are not points of the Catholic faith.

126. **If some popes have abused their power by carrying their claims higher than justice or conscience would allow, have they not thereby forfeited their supremacy?**

Whilst men are peccable (as popes are) they may abuse their authority; but to infer from the abuse of power, a forfeiture of all just authority granted by God, is as downright nonsense as to think that parents have forfeited all divine and natural right over their children, because many have exceeded in the exercise of it.

127. **Why has Christ instituted the supremacy of St. Peter?**

To maintain in the Church a perfect unity of faith, which is a mark of the true Church, according to that: there is but "one Lord, one faith, one baptism."[52] Therefore unity of faith and baptism are parallel cases.

---

[49] Cf. Lk 22:32
[50] Cf. Jn 21:15-17
[51] Cf. Jn 20:21-23
[52] Eph 4:5

128. **Can protestants and other sectaries pretend to possession, and prescription in matters of the Church?**

They cannot, because Catholics can show when they began, and also prove that the Catholic Church was both at their beginning, and is still in a more quiet possession than they yet are, or ever can be.

129. **What if protestants should say, that they differ not from us in fundamental points of faith, but only in indifferent ones, which do not exclude them from being united to us in the same Church?**

I would answer, that they contradicted their own tenets; for they accuse us of idolatry in worshipping saints, in holding transubstantiation, the pope's supremacy, and many other points, which are not indifferent matters, but of great importance.

130. **Are not protestants guilty of a great incoherency, in freeing the Church of Rome from fundamental errors, and at the same time traducing her as an idolatrous body?**

They are thereby guilty of so palpable a contradiction, as suffices to startle any thinking man: for how can a Church that errs in the true worship of God not err in fundamental points of faith, whereas the true worship of God is the first and chief fundamental point of faith in all churches? Or can the same Church teach that divine worship is to be paid to God alone, and at the same time teach that salvation is consistent with idolatry, which is as opposite to the true worship of God as light is to darkness?

131. **But how comes it, that protestants, who neither want wit nor learning, should be guilty of such a palpable contradiction?**

Truly, I know not, unless it be through a blind persuasion that it is lawful to blacken papists by any methods whatsoever, whether fair or foul; and both parts of the contradiction are very proper to answer that unjust end; for idolatry is an abominable crime, therefore papists must be charged with it, for it will render them very odious and contemptible; yet salvation must not be denied them, because this charitable opinion (the incoherency of which will not be perceived by the vulgar) will serve to show the uncharitableness of papists, who deny salvation to all that are out of their communion.

132. **Is the dead letter of scripture interpreted by any man of judgment, a decisive judge of controversies?**

It is not, for all heretics (as we see by experience) pretend equally to interpret the scripture, and yet are damning one another for miscreants; no one of them submitting to the authority of the Church for deciding their doubts, but appealing to the letter of scripture as interpreted by their own idle brain.

133. **How then can we be assured of the truth of controverted points?**

By the infallible authority, definition, and proposition of the Catholic Church.

134. **Is the Church infallible in all matters of faith?**

She is, because she is "the pillar and ground of truth,"[53] by the promises of Christ to send to his apostles the Holy Ghost to "teach (them) all truth,"[54] and to be with them all days, even to the end of the world.[55] Not with the apostles only, who were but to live a few years, but with their successors, whom Christ appointed to govern his Church to the end of the world.

135. **Are the definitions of a general council approved by the pope, infallible in matters of faith?**

They are, because such a council is the Church representative, and its definitions are directed by the Holy Ghost, according to that of the apostles defining in the first general council: "It hath seemed good to the Holy Ghost and to us."[56]

[53] 1 Tm 3:15
[54] Jn 16:13
[55] Cf. Mt 28:20
[56] Acts 15:28

136. **Is the Church visible?**

She is, because she consists of apostles, evangelists, doctors, and pastors given her by Christ,[57] all which are visible things.

137. **Why then would protestants have the Church to be invisible?**

Because our controvertists have proved against them, that there was no visible society of Christians, (besides heretics condemned by the Church) in which protestancy could be, before Luther's pretended Reformation.

138. **Is the Church universal both as to time and place?**

She is, because Christ hath said: "Go therefore, teach all nations…and behold I am with you all days, even unto the end of the world."[58]

139. **How does the Church behave with regard to the interpretation of scripture?**

She is so far from making herself mistress of her faith, (as protestants calumniously accuse her) that on the contrary she has done what she could to bind and deprive herself of all means of innovation, for in the Council of Trent, Session 4, she not only submits herself to the holy scriptures, but to the end that she might forever banish all arbitrary interpretations, which make men's imaginations pass for articles of faith, she has obliged herself to interpret the scripture, in what relates to faith and manners, according to the sense of the holy fathers, from which she professes never to depart, declaring in all her councils and professions of faith, that she does not receive any doctrine which is not conformable to scripture and the tradition of former ages.

140. **Can the Church err in matters of faith?**

She cannot. First, because she would then cease to be that one, holy, Catholic, and apostolic Church, the belief whereof we profess in the Nicene Creed, and by consequence that Creed would be false; but the Creed cannot be false, even according to most protestants, who allow that no

---

[57] Cf. Eph 4:11
[58] Mt 28:19-20

corruptions in faith began in the Church of Rome till after the fifth or sixth century; therefore, the Church cannot err in her faith.

Secondly, if the Church in her decisions of faith should err against any part of the Christian revelation, she would not be the pillar and support of truth.[59] She would not retain the word of God in her mouth forever.[60] She would not be the true Church of Christ, against which the gates of hell shall not prevail.[61] She would not have those pastors, with whom Christ promised to remain all days, even unto the end of the world.[62] Her decisions would not be such, that he who will not hear them, is to be accounted no better than a heathen and a publican.[63] Her pastors and teachers could not secure her children from errors.[64] She would not have the Spirit of truth remaining with her forever.[65] But all these consequences are false, and contrary to the express words of scripture, therefore the Church cannot err in her decisions of faith.

141. **But how do you prove from the abovementioned texts, and the Nicene Creed, that the Church of Rome is the only true Church of Christ, to which all the said promises were made, and which we profess in the Nicene Creed; and consequently, that all novelists and heretics are cut off from the true Church of Christ upon earth?**

By this unanswerable dilemma: before the Reformation, the Church of Rome with all the churches in communion with that see either was that one, holy, apostolic Church, to which Christ made all the abovementioned promises, and which we profess in the Nicene Creed; or was not. If she was not, then both the Creed and Christ's promises were false, because protestants cannot show any other society of Christians before the Reformation, (except heretics who have been condemned by the Church; nay, and who have always, and even now differ from protestants in several

---

[59] Cf. 1 Tm 3:15
[60] Cf. Is 59:21
[61] Cf. Mt 16:18
[62] Cf. Mt 28:20
[63] Cf. Mt 18:17
[64] Cf. Eph 4:11-12
[65] Cf. Jn 14:16-17

points of faith, such as: transubstantiation, purgatory, etc.) which was that true Church of Christ upon earth; but if the Church of Rome was that one Church, which we profess in the Creed, and to which Christ made all the abovementioned promises, then that Church with all the churches in communion with her, was the sole and only true Church of Christ upon earth, and consequently all novelists who differ from that Church in matters of faith, are cut off from the sole and only Church of Christ upon earth.

142. **Might not some errors in faith have crept insensibly into the whole Church, without being perceived by anyone?**

That is impossible, for nothing causes more grievous disturbances, or is more taken notice of, than any public change in matters of religion.

143. **But protestants say, that the Church of Rome has erred in her faith, and that they have only reformed the errors introduced by the power and prevalence of some popes, and the connivance of temporal princes.**

They say so indeed, and so did all heretics before them; but thereby they expose themselves to the laughter of all men of learning; because they never could produce any authentic history in which there is an account of the beginning, the author, time, place, or progress of any disturbances caused by, or councils called to condemn any one article, which the Catholic Church now holds to be a point of faith; which is a moral demonstration to any thinking man, that the belief of all those articles has been handed down to the Church from the very time of the apostles till now.

144. **How do you prove that to be a moral demonstration?**

Because all changes in religion are constantly attended with such a train of remarkable circumstances and events, as cannot possibly escape the notice of historians of the times in which they were broached. Thus we have the histories of the Arian, Nestorian, and Berengarian heresies; that of the Greek schism, and also the history of the English Reformation, of that of Luther and Calvin, with a particular account of the names and personal qualities of the authors of them, of the very year and place, wherein they were first broached, of the progress they made, of the opposition they met with, of the disturbances they occasioned, of the books wrote for and against them, and of the councils that were called to condemn them.

We have also the authentic history of the personal faults and misdemeanor of some popes, of their having abused their power, of their negligence in their pastoral duty, of the reproaches and opposition they met with on account of their neglect, and some private opinions, such as: Liberius signing the condemnation of St. Athanasius and an equivocal profession of faith in order to be restored to his see; the criminal connivance of Honorius with regard to the Monothelites; the opposition John XXII met with from the greater part of the Church, for holding as a private doctor that the blessed souls were not to enjoy the beatific vision till after the day of judgment.

Since therefore no one of the articles of faith now held by the Roman Catholic Church is recorded by any authentic historian of past ages as a novelty brought into the Church, it is a moral demonstration to any thinking man that those articles are not novelties, but revealed truths delivered to the Church by Christ and his apostles; for it is as morally impossible that the historians of the times should pass over in silence the noise, disputes, and troubles which attend the bringing of any new doctrine into the Church; as that the changes of religion in the reigns of King Henry VIII and Queen Mary should be wholly omitted by any historian writing the reigns of these two royal persons.[66]

The Communion of Saints Expounded in a Controversial Manner

145. How does the Church teach us to pray to saints?

She teaches us to pray to them in the same spirit of charity, and according to the same order of fraternal society, which moves us to ask the prayers of our brethren living upon earth; and as the intercession made to the faithful living with us does not prejudice the quality of mediator, which

---

[66] Author's note: See in Chapter 1, how the new-growing heresies obliged the Church to use new words, to express her faith more dogmatically and emphatically.

the scripture gives to Christ, so neither does the intercession of the saints prejudice it.

146. **Is there any difference between the manner of imploring God's assistance, and that of saints?**

There is a vast difference between them; for we pray to God, either to give us good things, or to deliver us from evil; but because the saints are more acceptable to him than we are, we beg of them to undertake our cause, and to obtain for us those things we stand in need of. Wherefore, the proper manner of praying to God is: "Have pity on us, hear our prayers"; whereas we only desire the saints to pray for us.[67]

147. **Are we bound to pray to the saints?**

The Church enjoins no such obligation, but only recommends as good and profitable our invoking the saints, and having recourse to their prayers, to obtain of God his benefits through Jesus Christ, who is the one and only mediator of redemption, because he "gave himself a redemption for all."[68] As the saints are our advocates or mediators of intercession; so that in reality we do not obtain those benefits, which we receive by the intercession of saints, otherwise than through Jesus Christ, seeing the saints themselves pray in no other manner than through Jesus Christ, and are not heard but in his name.[69]

148. **Does the Church offer sacrifice to the saints?**

She does not, but to God alone, who has crowned them; wherefore the priest does not address himself to St. Peter or St. Paul saying: "I offer up to you this sacrifice"; but rendering God thanks for their victories, he asks their assistance to the end, that those whose memory we celebrate

---

[67] Cf. *Catechism of the Council of Trent*, Pt. 4, "To Whom We Should Pray"; Editor's note: The *Catechism of the Council of Trent* is included in Volume VII of the Tradivox series.

[68] 1 Tm 2:6

[69] Cf. Council of Trent, Session 25, "On the Invocation, Veneration, and Relics, of Saints, and on Sacred Images"

upon earth, may vouchsafe to obtain for us the grace of God, particularly the benefit of imitating them; to which we are excited by their example, and by the honor which we render in the presence of God to their happy memories.[70]

149. **Are Catholics idolaters by attributing to saints the knowledge of their necessities, and of their secret thoughts, which scripture seems to ascribe to God alone?**

They are not, because they do not attribute that knowledge to saints by their own power, but by a light communicated to them by God; and the example of the prophets clearly proves, that to have a knowledge of future or of secret things in this manner, is not to raise a creature above his condition.

150. **By what means do the saints hear our prayers?**

The Church has decided nothing about that; whether it be done by the ministry of angels, as some divines think; whether by a particular revelation made to them, or whether in the divine essence, in which all truth is comprised; but let the means be what they will, it is certain the Church does not attribute to the greatest saints any divine perfection, as idolaters do; seeing she does not permit us to acknowledge in them any excellency, nor any knowledge of things transacted amongst us, nor any power to assist us, but what proceeds from God.

151. **All religious worship then terminates in God, as in its necessary end, and the honor we pay to the Blessed Virgin, and to other saints, is religious merely on account of its necessary relation to God.**

What you say is all right, wherefore though the saints should neither hear our prayers, nor pray for us; yet it is good to invoke them, as it is good to desire the prayers of an absent friend, though he should not receive the letter whereby we desire his prayers; because this is an act of humiliation

---

[70] Cf. Council of Trent, Session 22, "Doctrine on the Sacrifice of the Mass," Ch. 3

and diffidence of our own acceptableness in the sight of God, which act terminates in God alone.

152. **How do you prove that we may pray to saints in the abovementioned manner?**

Out of Genesis 48, where Jacob taught his children to do it saying: "Let my name be invoked upon them, the names also of my fathers Abraham, and Isaac."[71]

153. **How do you prove that the saints and holy angels pray for us?**

First out of Zacharias 1, where an angel prayed for Jerusalem, and the cities of Juda in the following manner: "O Lord of hosts, how long wilt thou not have mercy on Jerusalem, and the cities of Juda, against which thou hast had indignation these threescore and ten years?"[72] Secondly, out of Apocalypse 5: "The twenty-four elders fell down before the Lamb, having every one harps, and vials full of odors, which are the prayers of the saints."[73]

Chapter 2

The Sacraments in General Expounded in a Moral Sense

154. **What is a sacrament?**

It is a visible or sensible sign of the sanctifying grace, which is thereby given to the soul of him that worthily receives it.

155. **Were there sacraments from the beginning of the world?**

Since the fall of Adam there were some sacraments, or outward ceremonies,

[71] Gn 48:16
[72] Zac 1:12
[73] Apoc 5:8

by which grace was communicated to the souls of those who performed or received them.

156. **Are the sacraments of the new law more perfect than those of the old law?**
They are, because those of the new law confer the grace which they signify, in virtue of Christ's passion already accomplished; but the sacraments of the old law gave grace in proportion to the disposition of the receiver, and this in virtue of a lively faith in Christ, who was then expected.

157. **How many things are necessary for a sacrament to be valid?**
Three, viz: matter and form as essential and constituent parts, and the intention of the minister as a necessary condition, without which a sacrament cannot subsist. The matter is the sensible thing whereof the sacrament consists. The form are the words pronounced by the minister, who must have an intention to do by that outward ceremony what Christ has instituted and the Church appoints. There are two sorts of matter in each sacrament, the one called remote, the other, immediate. The first is that between which and the form something intervenes; the second is that between which and the form nothing is intermediate. For example, the remote matter of baptism is water, because the ablution or washing comes in between it and the form of baptism, but the washing is the immediate matter, because between it and the form nothing intervenes.

158. **Is the intention of the receiver also necessary for the validity of a sacrament?**
It is, if the receiver be come to the use of reason, excepting the Eucharist given to the laity; and in baptism administered to infants, the intention of the Church or of their godfathers and godmothers will suffice.

159. **Who is the ordinary minister of a sacrament?**
A priest, excepting holy orders and confirmation which are reserved to bishops only. And baptism, in case of necessity, (when a priest cannot be had, and a child is in immediate danger of death,) may not only validly, but also lawfully be administered by any person whatsoever; in which case a

cleric, though only in lesser orders, is to be admitted preferably to a layman, and a man preferably to a woman, and a Catholic preferably to a heretic.

160. **In what disposition of soul is the ordinary minister of a sacrament obliged to be, in order to administer any sacrament?**

He (and also the receiver that is come to the years of discretion) is obliged to be in the state of grace or at least to prepare himself by faith and repentance; otherwise, they incur the guilt of a grievous sacrilege.

161. **Do all the seven sacraments give grace?**

Baptism was instituted to give grace; penance, to restore the grace lost by sin; and the other five sacraments were instituted to increase the grace that is already in the soul of the receiver.

162. **How do the sacraments cause grace?**

Instrumentally only, for God is always the principal cause of grace.

163. **What is grace?**

It is a supernatural quality produced in our souls, and inherent in them, by which we are made and called the adopted children of God, and like to him in some degree; as iron is made like to fire by heat.

164. **Do the sacraments cause any other effects?**

Three of them, viz: baptism, confirmation, and holy orders (which cannot be received any more than once) imprint a character or spiritual mark in the soul, whereby we are marked for God's servants, and which always remains. Moreover, each sacrament communicates to the soul some special kind of grace, whereby we obtain of God some special remedy or preservative against different kinds of sin. Thus, baptism gives a regenerating grace, by which we are regenerated unto God, freed from original sin, and born again by a spiritual birth to be heirs of God, and co-heirs of Christ. Confirmation gives a fortifying grace, to strengthen the soul against all visible and invisible enemies of the Christian faith. The Eucharist gives a nourishing grace, by which our souls are fed with divine grace, against all passions and concupiscences, maintained at present in the life of grace, and brought to life everlasting, according to that: "He that eateth of this bread, shall live for ever."[74]

Penance gives a healing grace, by which the sores of sin are healed and cured. Extreme unction gives a restorative grace, whereby the soul is strengthened in her last agonies against the violent onsets of the devil. Holy orders gives to the persons ordained grace and a spiritual power to exercise worthily their respective functions, and to rule and govern others in all things belonging to their souls. Matrimony gives grace to the married couple to love one another according to God, to restrain the violence of concupiscence, to bear with one another's weakness, and to bring up their children in the fear of God. By these effects you easily know the necessity of, and the ends for which the seven sacraments have been instituted by Christ.

Baptism Expounded in a Moral Sense

165. **What is baptism?**

It is an exterior washing of the body, under a set form of words. This is called the first sacrament, because before it a man is not capable of receiving any other.

166. **In what manner must baptism be administered so as to be valid?**

It must be administered in true natural water, (such as rain water, that of the sea, river or fountain) if it be administered in rose-water, or any of the like artificial waters, it is no baptism. It must also be administered under this or the like form of words, "I baptize thee in the name of the Father, and of the Son, and of the Holy Ghost,"[75] which words ought to be pronounced at the same time as the water is applied to the person that is baptized, and by the same minister. If these words, *I baptize thee*, or any of the names of the three Persons should be left out, the baptism would be invalid, but the omission of other ceremonies does not render baptism

[74] Jn 6:59
[75] Cf. Mt 28:19

invalid. Baptism may be validly administered by dipping, by pouring of the water, or by sprinkling with the water, but the custom of the Church is to administer this sacrament either by dipping in the water, which is used in the East, or by pouring of the water upon the person baptized, which is more customary in the West.

167. **Who are capable of receiving this sacrament?**
Both infants and adults, if they have not already received it.

168. **What think you of an infant, who is not quite out of his mother's womb, and is in immediate danger of death?**
If the head appears, he may be baptized, and this baptism ought not to be done over again; if any other part of his body be visible, and seems to be alive, he may be baptized under a condition, and if the child should afterwards come alive into the world, he ought to be baptized under this condition: "If thou be not baptized, I baptize," etc.

169. **Is it a grievous sacrilege to baptize a person twice?**
It is, when there is not a prudent motive to doubt of the baptism already administered, "For it is impossible for those who have been once illuminated…and have been made partakers of the Holy Ghost (by baptism according to the best interpretation)…to be again renewed unto penance,"[76] that is, to be renewed again by baptism, which is also called a "renovation."[77] If it be evident that the baptism already administered was invalid, to repeat it again is not administering the sacrament twice; but if there be a prudent doubt concerning the validity of the baptism administered, then it ought to be repeated again under the abovementioned condition.

[76] Heb 6:4, 6
[77] Ti 3:5

170. **What think you of a person come to the years of discretion, who has committed mortal sins, and receives baptism without repentance, though with an intention?**

I think that he receives the sacrament and character of baptism, but not the grace of the sacrament, nor the remission of his sins, which he cannot obtain till by a sincere repentance he detests all his mortal sins.

171. **Is original sin and also all actual sins, both as to the guilt and temporal punishment, remitted in baptism?**

They are, according to that: "I will pour clean water upon you, and you shall be cleansed from your filthiness."[78] Hence no penance is enjoined in baptism.

172. **Is baptism necessary to salvation?**

It is, because: "Unless a man be born again of water, and the Holy Ghost, he cannot enter into the kingdom of God."[79]

173. **May not a person obtain the remission of his sins, and eternal salvation, without being actually baptized?**

He may in two cases. First, when a person not yet baptized, but heartily desiring baptism, is put to death for the faith of Christ, before he can have this sacrament administered to him; for such a one is baptized in his own blood. Secondly, when a person that can by no means procure the actual administration of baptism, has an earnest desire of it, joined with a perfect love of God and repentance of his sins, and dies in this disposition. Hence there are three sorts of baptism: that of water, which is the usual one; that of the Spirit or Holy Ghost, which is an act of charity or contrition joined with a desire of receiving baptism; and that of blood, which is martyrdom suffered for Christ. The first only is a real sacrament, the other two are called baptisms, because they produce the same effect as the baptism of water does as to the remission of sin.

[78] Ez 36:25
[79] Jn 3:5

174. **Can the children of infidels be baptized against the consent of their parents?**
If they be come to the years of discretion and have a desire of baptism, they may be lawfully baptized though their parents should not agree to it; but it is unlawful to baptize them whilst they are infants without the consent at least of one of the parents.

175. **How many godfathers and godmothers may a person have in baptism?**
The Council of Trent,[80] considering that a spiritual affinity, which is an impediment of marriage, is contracted between the gossips and the child, and also between the gossips and the parents of the child; the council (I say), to prevent too great an extent of this affinity, orders that no one should have any more than one godfather and one godmother; whose duty it is (in case of a neglect or death of the children's parents) to bring up their godchildren in the true faith and fear of God, to instruct them timely in the Christian doctrine. Upon this account, according to the *Roman Ritual*, none are to be admitted for godfathers and godmothers that are not members of the Catholic Church, none whose lives are publicly scandalous, none who are ignorant of the Christian doctrine.

176. **For what baptism has the Church appointed godfathers and godmothers?**
For solemn baptism only; wherefore this ceremony may be lawfully omitted in a baptism administered in a case of necessity; in which case if there should be godfathers or godmothers, it is very probable that they do not contract a spiritual affinity. As to the meaning of the ceremonies of baptism, see *The Catholick Christian Instructed*, Chapter 3, and the *Doway Catechism*, Chapter 4.[81]

Confirmation Expounded in a Moral Sense

177. **What is confirmation?**
It is a sacrament by which the faithful after baptism receive a fortifying

---

[80] Cf. Council of Trent, Session 24, "Decree on the Reformation of Marriage," Ch. 2

[81] Editor's note: The catechisms here mentioned by the author are included in Volumes III and I of the Tradivox series, respectively.

grace by the imposition of the hands of the bishop and prayer, accompanied with the unction of their foreheads with holy chrism.

178. What is the matter and form of this sacrament?

The remote matter is chrism, which is a compound of oil of olives and balm solemnly consecrated by the bishop on Maundy or Holy Thursday. The immediate matter is the unction or outward anointing of the forehead with chrism; and the form are the words pronounced by the bishop, when he makes the sign of the cross with holy chrism upon the forehead of him that is to be confirmed.

179. At what age may a person be confirmed?

Confirmation may be validly administered to the faithful after baptism at any age, though, commonly speaking, the Church does not give confirmation till a person is come to the use of reason, (unless in case of immediate danger of death) that thus it may be received with more devotion, because it can be received but once; for it imprints an indelible character or spiritual mark in the soul, which makes those that receive it soldiers of Christ, and arms them to make an open profession of Christ's doctrine, and not to flinch from this profession for fear of anything that the world can either say or do. Hence the unction is made on the forehead of him that is confirmed.

180. May a person have a godfather or godmother in confirmation?

He may; and this godfather or godmother contracts the like obligations and the same spiritual affinity as in the sacrament of baptism.

181. May a person that is confirmed take a new name?

It is usual so to do, not by way of changing one's name of baptism, but by way of adding to it another name of some saint, to whom one has a particular devotion, and by whose prayers he hopes to acquit himself more faithfully of the obligations of a soldier of Christ.

182. **Is it a mortal sin to neglect receiving this sacrament, when a person might conveniently receive it?**

It is not, unless he omits receiving it out of contempt, or is in imminent danger of denying his faith for want of receiving it, or unless he be dangerously sick and in the state of mortal sin, and has not an opportunity of receiving any other sacrament; in which cases he sins mortally by not receiving confirmation, when he might conveniently have it.

The Eucharist Expounded in a Moral Sense

183. **What is the Blessed Eucharist?**

It is a sacrament instituted by Christ at his last supper, which contains the true body and blood of Christ under the accidents or outward forms of bread and wine, and which gives a nourishing grace to the soul of the worthy receiver.

184. **What is the necessary matter of this sacrament?**

True and real bread and wine. True bread is that which is made of wheaten flour only, not that which is made of any other grain besides wheat. True wine is that which is pressed from ripe grapes, not verjuice, nor that which is become vinegar; for the sacrament to be valid either leavened or unleavened bread will suffice, but the custom of the Latin Church is to use unleavened bread, and the Greek Church makes use of leavened bread. The water mingled with the wine is not a necessary matter of this sacrament, but only a ceremony instituted by the Church (though a willful omission of this ceremony would be a grievous sin) to represent to us: first, the union of the divine and human nature in the Person of Christ; secondly, the union of the faithful with Christ in the Eucharist; thirdly, the blood and water that flowed from the side of Christ.

185. **What is the form of this sacrament?**

The words that Christ said at his last supper: "This is my body";[82] "This is the chalice of the new testament."[83]

186. **Why are bread and wine, (which are different things) the matter of this sacrament?**

For two reasons: first, that the nourishment and refection given by the Eucharist should be perfect and complete, by consisting of meat and drink; secondly, to represent perfectly the passion of Christ, (of which the Eucharist is a remembrance) by separating the accidents containing the blood from those containing the body, to represent to us that Christ's blood has been really shed and separated from his body on the cross.

187. **Do the consecrated bread and wine make two sacraments?**

No, but one only, for meat and drink make but one complete entertainment.

188. **What do you understand by the accidents or outward forms of bread and wine?**

The color, savor, quantity and the other qualities of the bread and wine.

189. **Is Christ himself, true God and true man, truly, really and substantially present in the Eucharist?**

He is; for the bread and wine are truly, really, and substantially changed by consecration into the real body and blood of Christ; and this change is called by the Catholic Church transubstantiation.

190. **In what then does the Catholic doctrine of transubstantiation differ from the Lutheran doctrine of consubstantiation?**

In this, that Luther and his followers maintain the real presence of the body and blood of Christ in the bread and wine, or with the substance of the bread and wine; whereas the Catholic Church believes that the bread

---

[82] Mt 26:26
[83] Lk 22:20

and wine are changed into the body and blood of Christ, so that there remains nothing of the inward substance of the bread and wine after consecration, but only the outward appearances or accidents.

191. Do the accidents of bread and wine remain without the substance?

They do, by the almighty power of God; for according to the Aristotelian philosophers, accidents are really distinguished from substances; or, according to modern philosophy, are the affections of our senses, which remain and affect our senses in the same manner after consecration, as before it.

192. Does Christ's body descend from heaven to be present in this sacrament?

It does not descend, as if it were, by moving from one place to another, or by quitting heaven its proper place or residence; as Christ's body did not move at his last supper to be under the outward forms of bread and wine. But it may be said that Christ's body descends virtually or in effect, because it is as substantially present in this sacrament as if it had really descended from heaven.

193. Is Christ's body whole in the whole host, and whole in every part of it?

It is; as the soul of man is whole in the whole body and whole in every part of it; in the like manner God by his almighty power can make Christ's body (now immortal and impassible)[84] to be substantially, (though in a spiritual and indivisible manner) whole in the whole host, and whole in every particle thereof; wherefore the body of Christ in the sacrament cannot be hurt, divided, digested, or corrupted, the outward forms only are liable to these changes.

194. Are Christ's soul and divinity in the Blessed Sacrament?

They are; for where the body and blood of Christ are, there his soul and his divinity must needs be by concomitancy or a natural union, but with this difference: that Christ's body only is under the accidents of the bread,

[84] Cf. Rom 6:9

in the manner of signifying it, and his blood, soul and divinity are there by concomitancy or the natural union of body, blood, soul and divinity in Christ's divine Person. In the like manner, Christ's blood only is under the accidents of wine in the manner of signifying, because the words whereby the wine is consecrated, signify as if Christ's blood only was there; though his body, soul, and divinity are there by concomitancy or a natural union.

195. **What think you if the bread and wine had been consecrated when Christ was really dead?**

In that case, Christ's body would be dead in the host, and his blood without life in the wine; for as Christ's body and blood are in themselves, so they are under the forms of bread and wine.

196. **What are the effects of the Eucharist?**

It increases grace in the soul of the worthy receiver; it nourishes and strengthens his soul: by repairing its forces; by arming it against its passions and concupiscences; by maintaining it at present in the life of grace, and bringing it to life and glory everlasting, according to that: "If any one shall eat of this bread, he shall live for ever; and the bread which I will give, is my flesh for the life of the world."[85]

197. **In what disposition of soul is a person to be, in order to receive worthily the Eucharist?**

He is obliged to examine diligently his conscience, and if he finds it charged with any mortal sin, he is bound to discharge it by a sincere sacramental confession, otherwise he commits a grievous sacrilege. If upon examination, he finds his conscience free from the guilt of any mortal sin, he may worthily receive the sacrament, as to the increase of grace which it gives, and without committing a mortal sin, though he should be somewhat distracted and retain an affection for venial sins; which indispositions deprive the soul of the other graces and comforts, which it would have received, had it been perfectly disposed.

[85] Jn 6:52

198. **What is the best disposition and preparation for receiving worthily the Blessed Sacrament?**

Besides clearing the conscience from mortal sin by a sincere confession, I should recommend to the communicant to think well on what Christ said: "Do this in remembrance of me";[86] or as St. Paul expresses it: "As often as you shall eat this bread, and drink the chalice, you shall show the death of the Lord until he come."[87] That is: as often as you receive, it shall be with a devout and grateful remembrance of Christ's sufferings and death for your sake; for Christ absented himself from us by dying on the cross for our sins. A devout remembrance then of Christ's death and passion is the best disposition to receive him present to us in the Blessed Sacrament.

199. **If the person who is to receive this sacrament finds his conscience charged with any mortal sin, is it enough that he should make an act of attrition or contrition?**

That is not enough, for he must go to confession or abstain from receiving, except in a case of great necessity; when for example, he is at the Communion table, finds himself guilty of some grievous sin, and cannot retire without giving scandal to the beholders, and by consequence without endangering his own character; in which or the like cases he may communicate without going to confession, by first making an act of contrition.

200. **What other disposition is required of a person that is to receive the Eucharist?**

He must be fasting, that is without having taken from the midnight before one drop or crumb, even by way of medicine, except the case of approaching death; for then persons are permitted to communicate by way of viaticum, though they are not fasting. But observe that if a person washing his mouth or picking his teeth, should through inadvertence let a drop of water or a little of the remains of the victuals between his teeth, fall to the

---

[86] Lk 22:19
[87] 1 Cor 11:26

stomach, or by breathing, swallow a fly or the like insect, these things (I say) do not hinder him from receiving the Blessed Sacrament.

201. **Are all Christians that are come to the years of discretion under a mortal obligation of receiving the Eucharist?**

They are, first, by a divine precept;[88] which precept obliges them to receive the Eucharist sometimes at least in their life, and at their death. Secondly, by a precept of the Church, which obliges them to receive once a year, but of this more in Chapter 4.

202. **At what age are Christians obliged to communicate?**

By a precept of the Church they are bound to communicate once a year, when they have the perfect use of reason, and are so well instructed in their duty as to be able to discern the body of Christ, and to receive it with due reverence and devotion; which happens in some earlier, in others later, but commonly about ten years of age. If a child be between seven and ten years of age, and in evident danger of death, some divines think that he is obliged by a divine precept to communicate.

203. **Can a person come to the years of discretion be saved without receiving the Blessed Sacrament at his death?**

He cannot without receiving it either really, or in desire, that is, without a will and desire to receive it, when he can conveniently so do.

204. **Is it better to communicate daily, than to put it off for a long time?**

It is better to communicate daily, if the communicant be rightly disposed.

205. **What is the best disposition for daily Communion?**

Priests who offer the Sacrifice of the Mass not only for their own but also for the benefit of others, to which communicating is annexed, these (I say) may be allowed to communicate daily, though this very obligation should induce them to lead very holy lives.

[88] Cf. Jn 6:54

As to the laity, to communicate daily requires in them something more than an ordinary disposition, such as: not only refraining from mortal sin, but also a constant practice of prayer, fervent acts of charity, and other pious works; which were very common among the primitive Christians that communicated daily, but now alas are rarely practiced by Christians deeply involved in worldly concerns; wherefore I should recommend to the most devout layman what St. Bonaventure did to the most religious novice that observed the strict rule of St. Francis to a tittle,[89] viz: not to communicate oftener than once a week, unless in case of sickness or some great solemnity, that thus he may receive the sacrament with more fervor and devotion. But in this as well as in all other affairs of conscience he may follow his confessor's advice. I shall only observe that the Eucharist is solid and substantial food for the strongest stomachs, which if frequently taken by weak stomachs, it may do them more hurt than benefit.

206. Who is the ordinary minister of this sacrament?

A priest only, whose ministry consists in consecrating the bread and wine, and in administering this sacrament to the laity.

207. Is the Eucharist a sacrifice?

It is the unbloody sacrifice of the body and blood of Christ, the same in substance as that which Christ offered on the cross, but different in the manner of offering it, for this is a commemoration of that; and the sacrifice of the cross was offered by a real separation of Christ's blood from his body, but in the Eucharist, Christ's blood is separated from his body sacramentally only, or in the manner of signifying, as I have already explained.

208. For what ends is this sacrifice available?

It avails the offerer and those for whom it is offered (if they be rightly disposed) as a propitiation for the remission of sin, as a thanksgiving to God, and as an impetation for obtaining benefits spiritual and temporal conducive to their eternal salvation.

---

[89] Cf. Bonaventure, *De Profectu Religiosorum*, Ch. 77

Of Penance in General

The Sacrament of Penance Expounded in a Moral Sense

209. **What is the sacrament of penance?**

It is a sacrament instituted by Christ, to restore to us the grace lost by sins committed after baptism.

210. **What is the matter of this sacrament?**

The remote matter are all sins committed after baptism, or in the actual reception thereof; and the immediate matter are the acts of the penitent, viz: contrition, confession, and satisfaction.

211. **What is the form of this sacrament?**

These words: "I absolve thee from thy sins."

212. **Is there a virtue of penance different from the sacrament so called?**

There is, and it consists in a sorrow for having offended so good a God, which sorrow may be practiced out of confession.

213. **Can any mortal sin committed after baptism be remitted without this sacrament?**

It cannot without this sacrament either actually received, or in desire, that is, without an act of contrition attended with a desire of receiving it.

214. **How many parts hath this sacrament?**

Three, viz: contrition, confession, and satisfaction. The two first must necessarily precede the absolution; the last may be afterwards performed, for it is only required that the resolution of performing it should precede the absolution.

Contrition and Attrition Expounded in a Moral Sense

215. **What is contrition?**
It is a sorrow for having offended God, arising from the love of him, with a firm purpose of amendment.

216. **What is a firm purpose of amendment?**
It is a full determination to avoid to the utmost of our power mortal sin, and all the immediate occasions of it.

217. **What do you mean by the immediate occasions of sin?**
All such company, places, conversations, etc. which frequently draw a person into mortal sin either in deed or in thought.

218. **What is attrition?**
It is a sorrow for sin, arising from the consideration of the enormity of sin, the loss of heaven or the fear of hell.

219. **Can a sinner be justified by an act of charity, as well as by contrition?**
He can, because an act of charity implies a detestation of sin for the love of God.

220. **If a person detests sin, because it has deprived him of health, riches, or lodged him in a goal, has he a true attrition?**
He has not; for true attrition requires a detestation of sin out of some supernatural motive, such as the dread of hell, or the loss of heaven.

221. **Why must the motives of attrition and contrition be supernatural?**
Because contrition and attrition are founded on, and regulated by supernatural faith, whereby we know God's infinite goodness and strict justice, the consideration of which excites us either to detest our sins for the love of him above all things, or to abhor sin for fear of the everlasting punishment due to it.

222. Is attrition alone sufficient to justification?

It is not, unless it be accompanied by the sacrament of penance actually received; and even then, many great divines judge it absolutely necessary, that attrition should be accompanied with a certain love of God above all things, which they call initial charity; but perfect contrition with a desire of the sacrament of penance is sufficient to salvation.

223. What are the necessary conditions required for the sorrow of the sinner, (be it contrition or attrition) in order to obtain forgiveness of his sins in the sacrament of penance?

Three, viz: it must be a true sorrow, efficacious, and supernatural.

224. How is contrition or attrition a true and sincere sorrow for sin?

That does not consist in any sensible pain or affliction of the body, nor in the intenseness of our grief; nor in the pleasure or satisfaction which we find in the love or motive, whence that sorrow arises. It therefore consists in a deep consideration, and in a due sense of what it is to have offended an infinitely good and just God, and that from this consideration there should arise in the will a sincere detestation of sin either for the love of God's goodness, or for fear of his just judgment. Thus, we grieve more for sin than for any temporal loss, though this sorrow is sometimes less sensible to us, and less intense, than that which we have for temporal losses.

225. Why is that sorrow supernatural?

Because it is regulated by supernatural faith which teaches us that God is to be loved and feared above all things.

226. How can we obtain that supernatural sorrow?

By faith and prayer; for faith enables us to know the infinite goodness and the just judgment of God, as also how much we are indebted to him both as to our natural and supernatural being, he having created and redeemed us; wherefore we ought to love and fear him above all things. By prayer we may solicit and beg of God to give us that knowledge, love, and fear.

227. **How is that sorrow efficacious?**

That is a point hard to be decided with any certainty, and a difficulty which makes many penitents very uneasy about the validity of their confessions for want of an efficacious sorrow; for the will is deemed to be efficacious when it actually operates and effectually removes all the obstacles to its operating. The sorrow then of the penitent is efficacious when he sincerely grieves for past crimes, fully determines to fly for the future all willful sin, and firmly purposes to sacrifice all that is dear to him, rather than to return to sin.

228. **But though the penitent cannot be positively assured of the efficacy of his sorrow, are there not at least some signs or indications whereby he may probably conjecture it to have been efficacious?**

There are six. The first is when he cuts off all desire of whatever is a mortal sin, hence that sorrow is called contrition, because it grinds and crumbles all criminal desire of sin. The second is when he avoids all immediate occasions of sin. The third is when he undergoes the penalties and austerities of penance with pleasure and satisfaction, and mortifies his appetite by denying it the use of what is pleasing and agreeable. The fourth is when he is willing to be humbled, despised and contemned, because by sin he has arrogantly pretended to raise himself above his condition, and has rebelled against God. The fifth is when his will is inflamed with the love of God, and desires his honor and glory preferably to all things. The sixth is when he endeavors to persevere in any of these holy purposes, and in a word, when he hates his life in this world, that he may preserve it unto life everlasting.[90]

229. **If a person often relapses into the same sins which he has confessed, has he not reason to doubt or suspect that his sorrow at confession was not true and sincere?**

If he neither has an intention to sin, nor continues in the immediate occasions of it, he may relapse several times, and yet his sorrow at confession

---

[90] Cf. Jn 12:25

might have been true and sincere; for Christ commanded St. Peter to for-give his brethren not only seven times, but also "seventy times seven."[91] It is true that frequent relapses into the same sins soon after confession, particularly into those of deed or action, may justly alarm his fear about the sincerity of his precedent sorrow.

Confession Explained in a Moral Sense

230. **What is sacramental confession?**
It is a full and sincere accusation made to God's minister, of all mortal sins, which after a diligent examination of conscience a person can call to his remembrance, in order to obtain pardon and absolution.

231. **Is a confession made to an absent priest by a letter or messenger good and valid?**
It is not.

232. **Has every priest power to hear confessions?**
No, but only such as have either ordinary or delegate jurisdiction over the penitent. The bishop has ordinary jurisdiction over all that reside or are in his diocese, and every parish priest over his parishioners; all other confes-sors approved by the ordinary have a delegate jurisdiction over the laity.

233. **But does not that rule admit of some exception?**
It does in case of necessity, when a person is in evident danger of death, and cannot find an approved confessor, he may confess to any priest, who is empowered by the Church in this case to absolve him from all censures and reserved cases. But observe that if in this case he has been absolved from reserved cases, and afterwards recovers, he is bound to appear and present himself to the superior to whom the cases have been reserved.

[91] Mt 18:22

234. **If a person in evident danger of death cannot find a priest, and confesses his sins to a layman or to a clergyman that is not a priest, does he make a sacramental confession?**

He does not, but only expresses his desire to make one, in which case contrition will suffice for the remission of his sins, but attrition alone will not.

235. **What are the necessary conditions of a good confession?**

That it be true, sincere, and entire.

236. **When is a confession true and entire?**

When a person after using a moral diligence to find out the sins he has committed, and the number of times he has been guilty of any of them, confesses all to God's minister without concealing any through shame or fear, and without accusing himself of any, which he has not really committed; for to conceal a mortal sin in confession, and to accuse ourselves of one which we have not committed, are equally criminal; only with this difference, that he that does the latter, does it commonly through an anxiety of conscience and with a desire to make a complete confession; wherefore he is commonly ignorant of the fault he commits, and consequently does not make an invalid confession; whereas he that does the former commits a horrid sacrilege and makes an invalid confession.

237. **Are there any cases in which a person may leave out some mortal sins in confession, and yet make a true and sincere confession?**

There are three. First, when a person is in evident danger of dying before he can confess all his sins, he may confess some of them, and be immediately absolved; in which case he is not obliged to make an examination of conscience. Secondly, when the confessor is in evident danger of being infected by the penitent's contagious sickness, if he stays to hear all his sins. Thirdly, when the penitent is under a necessity of going to confession, and reasonably apprehends that some considerable detriment may ensue either to himself or to his neighbor from declaring certain sins to some particular confessor, and no other can be found. In these and the like cases the penitent may leave out some sins, and yet make a good confession.

238. **If a person conceals through shame or fear any mortal sin in confession, what is he bound to do?**

To confess the sin he concealed, and all the others which he has confessed, and also the sacrilege he committed by concealing it.

239. **But what if through forgetfulness or some little negligence in examining his conscience, he should pass over some mortal sin in confession?**

He is bound to confess the sin thus omitted afterwards when he remembers it; and if he remembers it before Communion, it ought to be confessed before he goes to Communion; if he remembers it not till after Communion, he must confess it in his next confession. But he is not obliged to confess in his next confession those sins which he has confessed before, unless his having taken no care to examine his conscience gave occasion to his forgetfulness, or his forgetfulness has been affected; in which cases the whole confession must be made again.

240. **When is a confession invalid or nothing worth, and consequently must be made again?**

In five cases: first, when the priest to whom it was made had not the necessary faculties and approbations, or when he had not an intention to absolve the penitent; secondly, when any mortal sin is concealed through shame, fear, or affected ignorance; thirdly, when the penitent has taken no care to procure the necessary sorrow for his sins, and a true purpose of amendment; fourthly, when the penitent has taken no care to examine his conscience; fifthly, when the penitent is ignorant of those mysteries of faith, the knowledge of which is absolutely necessary to salvation, as I have explained in Chapter 1.

241. **By what has been said, it is evident that to conceal a sin in confession is not only a horrid sacrilege, but also a great folly and madness.**

It is so. First, because such offenders, if they have not renounced their faith, know very well that these sins must be confessed, or that they must burn for them; and they cannot be ignorant that these bad confessions do but increase their burthen, by adding to it the dreadful guilt of repeated sacrileges; for a sacrilegious confession is generally followed by a sacrilegious Communion, and what is still worse, such sinners seldom stop at the first bad confession and Communion, but usually go on a long time in these sins, all which they will have far more difficulty of confessing than these very sins, of which they are now so much ashamed. Secondly, because the greater the penitent's sins have been, the greater will be the joy of his confessor, to see the penitent's sincere conversion to God testified by the humble confession of his most shameful sins.

Thirdly, because by the law of God and his Church, whatever is declared in confession can never be discovered directly nor indirectly to anyone; of which the confessor cannot speak to the very penitent without his express leave, nor even to save his own life, make any use at all to the penitent's discredit, confusion, or disadvantage.[92] Fourthly, because besides the present comfort and ease of conscience which a humble confession brings along with it, by a short confusion which will last but a moment, the penitent will escape the dreadful shame of having his sins written on his forehead at the day of judgment to his eternal confusion.

242. **If a person has made a bad confession by concealing some mortal sin, and afterwards confesses to the same confessor, is he obliged to confess again those sins which he has confessed before?**

If the confessor has a confused remembrance of the sins before confessed, it is probable that it may suffice for the penitent to accuse himself in general terms of all that has been confessed before; and then to specify in particular the sins that have been omitted, together with the number of the bad confessions and Communions that have been made.

243. **How must a person examine his conscience, in order to make a good confession?**

He must use a moral diligence to find out the sins he has committed; that is, such a diligence as a prudent person uses in examining into any affair of great moment. This requires more or less time and care according to

---

[92] Cf. Innocent XI, *Ex Decreto*, Anno. 1682

the length of time from his last confession, according to the greater or less facility he has in calling to mind past things, and according to the occasions of sin in which he has been; but to pretend to determine what time each particular must spend in examining his conscience, is above the reach of the most able divines. I shall therefore only observe, that if a person be of a middling capacity, and has not been deeply engaged in worldly affairs, which frequently induce to sin, ten or twelve hours examination will suffice for his yearly confession.

But as this is a point in which some are careless and negligent and others overnice and scrupulous, it may not be improper to lay down the following rules: first then, the careless and negligent ought to consider that the Council of Trent[93] requires that the penitent should examine strictly and look narrowly into the hidden corners and private recesses of his conscience; secondly, the scrupulous and overnice should observe, that an examination of conscience is made in order to call to mind past sins, which is what we can scarce do with any great exactness; because it often happens that the more we endeavor to call to mind past things, the less we can remember them; for which reason the said council in the same session supposes, that after a sufficient examination is made, some sins cannot be called to mind, which yet are included in the penitent's confession; wherefore when the penitent uses a moral diligence to find out the sins he has committed, and is ready to use more diligence had he thought it necessary, he ought to quiet his mind and depend entirely upon the judgment of his confessor, who ought to help the penitent by asking him what questions he thinks most necessary, and who (generally speaking) ought to suppose scrupulous penitents to have made a sufficient examination of conscience.

244. **What does the Council of Trent mean by saying that the penitent ought to look narrowly and search closely into the hidden corners and private recesses of his conscience?**

It means, that the penitent ought to examine the passions and evil inclinations to which he is most inclined, the bad company he has kept, the

---

[93] Cf. Council of Trent, Session 14, "Doctrine on the Sacrament of Penance," Ch. 5

immediate occasions of sin in which he has been, the good or bad intention of his actions, the care he has taken of resisting the temptations that commonly persecute and attack him. But of this, more in the Appendix.

245. **Is the penitent obliged under mortal sin to confess all his sins?**

He is obliged to confess all such sins as are mortal, or of which he has reason to doubt if they be mortal, as also such circumstances of sin as quite alter the kind or nature of it; and according to the most able divines, such circumstances as considerably aggravate the guilt of mortal sin; but he is not obliged to confess venial sins, nor mortal sins confessed before, though it is very recommendable so to do; as also a laudable custom to confess some mortal sin confessed before, when a person goes to confession without finding his conscience charged with any mortal sin committed since his last confession, that thus he may avoid all danger of making a sacrilegious confession for want of a sincere sorrow and a firm purpose of amendment; for we are easier moved to grieve for, and to avoid mortal, than venial sins; for this reason if he cannot remember any mortal sin which he has committed all his life time, he ought to confess and specify some particular venial sin to which he has the greatest abhorrence.

246. **Is the penitent obliged to examine his conscience as to the number of times that he has been guilty of this or that sin?**

He is, as also to confess, as near as he can, the number of his sins. But of this more in the Appendix.

247. **By what rule shall I be able to know when one mortal sin is of a different kind or nature from another?**

Sins are of different kinds when they are immediately opposite to different virtues. Thus, perjury and theft are different kinds of sin, because the first is immediately opposite to the virtue of religion, and the second, to that of justice; but two different thefts are not different kinds of sin, because they are both opposite to the same virtue, and in the same manner.

248. **How shall I be able to know when a circumstance quite alters the kind or nature of sin, and when it only aggravates considerably the guilt of sin?**

A circumstance alters the nature of sin, when it multiplies the sin and makes it to be opposite to another virtue. Thus, to steal in the Church is a circumstance that makes the theft not only a sin of injustice, but also of sacrilege; because theft committed in any place is a sin of injustice, and the circumstance of committing the theft in a sacred place makes it to be a sacrilege opposite to the virtue of religion.

A circumstance considerably aggravates the guilt of sin, when it does not make the sin to be opposite to another virtue, but only increases its opposition to the same virtue. Thus, to steal at once eight or ten shillings is a circumstance that considerably aggravates the sin of theft, because supposing one shilling to be a sufficient matter for a sin of injustice, to steal eight or ten shillings at once (though in itself but one mortal sin) is equivalent to eight or ten thefts of a shilling, each committed eight or ten different times; but the theft of fifteen pence does not add a considerably aggravating circumstance to the stealing of a shilling; because supposing three pence not to be a sufficient matter for a mortal injustice, this added to a shilling does not make the theft equivalent to two grievous thefts committed at different times. But though it be very easy to know in all matters of injustice, when a circumstance considerably aggravates or not; yet to pretend to determine which circumstances considerably aggravate the guilt of other sins, and which not, is above the reach of the most able divines; and therefore, a prudent Christian will not easily pass over the circumstances of his sins, under pretense of their not being aggravating, unless he be certain of it.

249. **How shall I be able to determine the number of my sins, when they are of the same kind or nature?**

Sins are as many in number, and of the same kind, as there are different deliberate acts of the will or different exterior actions, whereof one has no connection with the other if they be all opposite to the same virtue: for example, three different thefts are three mortal sins of the same kind, because one has no connection at all with the other, and they are all opposite to the virtue of justice.

250. **Does a person commit a different sin as often as he deliberately wills the same unlawful object?**

He does, if there be a moral interruption between the different deliberate acts of the will; but he does not, if there be a moral union between them.

251. **By what rule shall I be able to know when the different deliberate acts of the will are morally interrupted, or morally continued?**

Observe that some sins are consummated in the mind or by a deliberate thought, such as: envy, heresy, ambition, the hatred of God or of our neighbor, lustful desires without a design of putting them in execution. Others again are completed by words, such as: perjury, blasphemy, detraction, or bearing false witness against our neighbor. Others in fine are consummated by some exterior action, such as: murder, adultery, theft and the like. If the sins be of the first kind, they are as many in number as there are different deliberate acts of the will; but sins of the second and third kind are not as many in number as there are different deliberate acts of the will, unless there be a new deliberate act of the will after the sin is completed, or before its consummation a considerable space of time intervenes between the different deliberate acts of the will.

252. **Be pleased to explain that a little more by some examples.**

First, as often as a person makes a different deliberate act of envy, or any other sin that is consummated in the mind, he commits a new sin. Secondly, if a person intends to commit murder, or any other sin that is completed by words or exterior actions, and to this end procures arms or undertakes a journey, though he should repeat the same evil intention, he commits but one sin, (though a long continuance in this intention may be an aggravating circumstance necessary to be declared in confession). But if after having intended to murder or steal, he applies his mind for a considerable time (such as one or two hours) to other things no way conducive to the accomplishment of his intended design, and afterwards renews the same intention, he commits a different sin from the first; as also by intending to commit a second theft, after the first is completely accomplished.

253. May not a person commit many sins by one deliberate act of the will, and but one sin by different deliberate acts?

Yes, he may.

254. How does that happen?

If he wills either by one or many deliberate acts many unlawful objects completely distinct, whereof one has no moral connection with the other, he commits as many sins as there are objects willed by him; but if he wishes for one object only, or different ones, whereof one has a connection with the other, he commits but one sin.

255. Explain that by some examples.

First, if a person upon the same occasion and in the same violence of anger utters different opprobrious expressions prejudicial to one man's character, he commits but one sin, because though the expressions be different, the object is but one; but if he utters but one only expression hurtful to the credit of three different persons, he commits three sins, because the honor and reputation of one man has no connection with that of another.

Secondly, if a person kills three men with one shot, scandalizes three by the same action, or steals the property of three different owners, by each of these actions he commits three different sins, because the life, spiritual good, and property of one man have no connection with those of another.

Thirdly, lustful kisses and immodest touches immediately preceding a criminal complete act are not sins different from the act, nor notoriously aggravating circumstances necessary to be declared in confession, because they are ordained to the same end and object. But observe that if a person first only intended lustful kisses, and upon a second consideration, proceeds to a complete act, he commits two mortal sins.

256. If a person be guilty of a crime that is prohibited by different laws, does he commit different sins?

He does not, if the different laws forbid it out of the same motive, but if they forbid it out of different motives, he commits different sins: for example, theft though prohibited by the divine, civil, and ecclesiastic law, is but one sin, because all these laws forbid theft out of the same motive of justice; but to steal in a Church adds a sin of sacrilege to that of injustice, because the ecclesiastic law forbids theft in the Church out of deference to that sacred place, which is a different motive from that of the divine and human law.

Satisfaction and Indulgences Expounded in a Moral Sense

257. **What is sacramental satisfaction?**

It is a faithful performance of the penance enjoined by the confessor.

258. **For what does that penance avail?**

For releasing the debt of temporal punishment which remains due to our sins, after the sins themselves, as to the guilt and eternal punishment, have been already remitted by the sacrament of penance. It also avails for preserving the penitent from future sins.

259. **Why are not the public penances practiced in the primitive Church now enjoined in confession?**

Those penances were not private nor sacramental but were imposed publicly in the Church on those that misbehaved themselves to any scandalous degree, according to some divines. But the penance enjoined in confession is a part of the sacrament, and therefore imposed in a private manner; though it is good that the confessor should make the penitent sensible of the severe penance due to his sins, had it been imposed according to the ancient canons of the Church.

260. **Ought the penance to be proportioned to the sins?**

It ought, otherwise the deficiency must be made good by performing other good works in the state of grace, by undergoing penalties in this life or in purgatory, or by gaining indulgences.

261. **Is the penitent obliged to be in a state of grace, in order to perform the penance enjoined by the confessor?**

To comply with the confessor's command, so as not to be obliged to per-form the penance again, it will suffice for the penitent to perform it at any time within the time limited by the confessor, though it should be performed by him after making another confession, or when he finds his conscience charged with a mortal sin; but to obtain a release from the temporal punishment due to sin, the penance must be performed by the penitent in the state of grace.

262. **Is it a mortal sin to omit or not to perform the penance enjoined within the time limited by the confessor?**

It is, if there be not some urgent necessity, (such as a grievous sickness) for omitting or deferring it.

263. **Can one confessor change the penance enjoined by another?**

He can, provided the penitent declares to him the same sins, for which the penance was imposed; but the penitent himself cannot change it into any other penitential works, because sacramental penance is not only a release from the temporal punishment due to sin, but also a part of the sacrament of penance.

264. **Which are the penitential works, whereby the temporal punishment due to sin is released?**

Prayer, fasting, and almsgiving, to which all others may be reduced.

265. **Is an indulgence, when duly obtained, a release from the debt of temporal punishment due to sin?**

It is.

266. **Why is the temporal punishment due to sin remitted by an indulgence?**

Because when the Church grants an indulgence to her children, she offers to God an equivalent for the punishment which was due to the divine justice; for the merits and satisfaction of Christ are of infinite value, and never to be exhausted; and the merits, satisfactions, and sufferings of the Blessed Virgin and other saints, who have suffered more than their sins deserved, these merits and sufferings (I say) as they have their value from Christ and through him, are applied by the Church and accepted by God as an equivalent for the temporal punishment due to the sins of the faithful upon earth, who are in the same communion with the saints in heaven; for as God leaves no merit unrewarded, nor no sin unpunished, so neither will he let any penitential works remain without some advantage or relief either to the sufferer, or to his brethren in the same faith and charity with him. These merits and satisfactions are called the treasure of the Church, out of which indulgences are said to be granted.

267. **What is an indulgence?**
It is a remission of the temporal punishment due to sins already remitted as to the guilt and eternal punishment, granted to the faithful by some prelate of the Church, who applies to them the treasure of the Church.

268. **Why is it a remission of the temporal punishment due to sin?**
Because it is not a pardon for the eternal guilt or punishment due to mortal sin, nor for sins to come, nor a leave to commit sin, (as the generality of protestants falsely imagine) it being only a release from, or a commutation of the temporal punishment due to sin into some penitential works.

269. **Why do you say that it is granted by some prelate of the Church?**
Because he that grants an indulgence must have sufficient authority for so doing, such as: the pope, who can grant plenary indulgences to the whole Church; and his legates, according to the power wherewith they are invested; cardinals, who can grant indulgences of 120 days; and bishops, indulgences of 40 days. Besides this authority, for the validity of an indulgence it is necessary (according to the most able divines) that there be a just cause or motive for the grant; so that indulgences granted without a just cause will not be ratified by Almighty God who made his ministers stewards, not squanderers of his gifts and favors.

270. **What conditions are necessary for gaining an indulgence on the part of him that is to obtain it?**

Four: first, that he be baptized; secondly, that he be not excommunicated; thirdly, that he duly perform the conditions prescribed; fourthly, that at least the last condition or work prescribed be performed by him when he is in a state of grace, for it is in vain to expect the remission of the temporal punishment due to sin, whilst a person continues in the guilt of mortal sin.

271. **Is it enough that he be in a state of grace when he performs the last condition prescribed, though he has been in a state of mortal sin when he performed all the other conditions?**

Divines are not perfectly agreed in the resolution of this query, though all are perfectly agreed in advising everyone to perform all the conditions prescribed when he is in the state of grace, or to discharge his conscience of the guilt of mortal sin, either by going to confession, or by an act of contrition; for some divines are of opinion, that to obtain any indulgence, it is requisite that all the conditions be performed in a state of grace, or with a disposition to do penance in this life. Others again think that to gain any indulgence it will suffice to perform in a state of grace the last condition prescribed. Others in fine (whose opinion is highly probable) distinguish between indulgences granted merely for obtaining the remission of sin, and those granted for some charitable end, (such as the building of a Church or hospital, the relief of the poor, and the like) and maintain, that to obtain the first kind of indulgences, it is requisite that all the conditions prescribed be performed in a state of grace; but to obtain the second, it is enough that the last condition be performed in a state of grace.

272. **What is a plenary indulgence?**

It is, when duly obtained, a remission of all the temporal punishment that remained due upon account of past sins.

273. **Does a plenary indulgence so far remit all temporal punishment as to free a penitent from all obligation of doing any farther penance for his sins, and from all necessity of obtaining other indulgences?**

It does not. First, because the obligation of doing penance for sin is an indispensable duty; hence the Church usually enjoins penitential works for the obtaining of indulgences. Secondly, because according to some eminent divines, one condition required for obtaining by a plenary indulgence the remission of all the punishment due to sin, is some proportion between the penitential works to be done for the obtaining the remission of temporal punishment, and the temporal punishment itself; so that if the temporal punishment due to sin greatly exceeds the works done for the obtaining of a plenary indulgence, a penitent does not thereby obtain a remission of the whole punishment, but only of a part of it, in proportion to the penitential works performed: and this opinion I take to be highly probable, for indulgences are intended by God and granted by the Church for the relief of the indigent; yet not so as to encourage the lazy, who refuse to labor at all for their own salvation.[94]

274. **You are then of opinion, that a Christian receives no farther benefit by an indulgence than he would by the penitential works which he performs for the obtaining of that indulgence?**

I am far from being of that opinion; for according to that way of thinking, no benefit would be reaped from an indulgence, but only from the works performed for the obtaining of it; which is contrary to the Council of Trent[95] where it has declared that indulgences are very wholesome to Christian people. But what I think with some able divines is that for obtaining the remission of temporal punishment by penitential works, there must be an equality between the works and the punishment; but for the obtaining

---

[94] Cf. St. Bonaventure, 4. *Sent. Dist.* 2. Q. 6.; Charles Borromeo, *Pastoral Epistle to his Suffragans*; Cardinal Cajetan Tract. 10. *de Suscipientibus Indulgentias.* Q. I. Baronius, ad Annum 1073; Cardinal Casimirus Denof, *Pastoral Instructions*; Seto in 4. m. *Dist.* 21. Q. 2. Art. 2; Sylvius, Eflius, Navarrus, Hesselius, Molanus, Fejoo, Gobar. Natal, Alexandre, Geneti, Pontas

[95] Cf. Council of Trent, Session 25, "Decree Concerning Indulgences"

of a plenary indulgence, some proportion, though not an equality, is required between the works to be done for the obtaining of an indulgence, and the indulgence itself.

275. What is meant by an indulgence of so many years, months, or days?

The remission of the punishment corresponding to the sins, which by the canons of the primitive Church would have required so many years or days of penance. And thus, if it be true that there ever were any grants of indulgences of a thousand years, (which some call in question) they are to be understood with relation to the punishment corresponding to the sins, which according to the ancient penitential canons would have required a thousand or more years of penance. For since by these canons, seven or ten years of penance were assigned for one very heinous sin, it follows, that habitual sinners, according to the rigor of the canons, must have been liable to great numbers of years of penance. And though it could not be expected that they could live so long as to fulfil this penance; yet as by their sins they had incurred a debt of punishment proportionable to so long a time of penance, these indulgences of so many years (if ever granted) were designed to release them from this debt.

276. What is an indulgence for the dead?

It is not granted by way of absolution, since the pastors of the Church have not jurisdiction over the dead; but the living may perform penitential works for the spiritual succor of the faithful departed, which by way of suffrage are applied to their souls out of the treasure of the Church.

277. What is the meaning of the jubilee or holy year?

Among the Jews, it was every fiftieth year when no one either sowed or reaped, and those who had sold or mortgaged their lands entered into free possession again, and all Hebrew slaves were set at liberty.[96] In imitation of which, the pope grants a jubilee or plenary indulgence. Boniface VIII first instituted a jubilee in 1300 and ordered it to be observed every 100

---

[96] Cf. Nm 36; Lv 25, 27

years. Clement VI considering the shortness of man's life, reduced it to 50 years. Urban VI to 30 and Sixtus V to 25, where it now continues. Besides which, the popes upon their exaltation to St. Peter's chair grant a jubilee, and also upon other extraordinary occasions.

The meaning of it is a plenary indulgence or release from all temporal punishment that remained due upon account of past sins according to the canons of the Church, which required so many years or days of penance. This jubilee is a remission of all this penance, to be obtained by performing certain penitential works. It also grants power to every approved confessor to absolve penitents from all excommunications and other reserved cases, and to change their vows into the performance of other works of piety, as specified in the bulls of every jubilee. And these certain privileges, which are not usually granted upon the occasions of other indulgences, are the chief difference between a jubilee and any other plenary indulgence.

278. **If Christ has superabundantly satisfied for all the temporal punishment due to our sins, where is the necessity of our endeavoring to satisfy for it by obtaining indulgences?**

It is true that Christ has paid the full price of our redemption, so that nothing is wanting in this price, because it is infinite; wherefore the remaining punishment comes not from any defect in the payment, but from a certain order which God has established, viz: to apply to us the infinite satisfaction of Christ by the sacraments and good works, which works being done by God's grace, are no less his than what he does alone by his absolute power.

Wherefore, though Christ has paid a superabundant price for our redemption, yet as he has determined to apply it to us by the worthy use of the sacraments, one of which, viz, baptism, causes a perfect remission of sin without reserving any temporal punishment; another again, viz, penance, remits sin as to the guilt and the eternal punishment in hell due to mortal sin, but still leaves the debt of temporal punishment due to God's justice (particularly when the repentance is not very perfect) which the penitent must either discharge in this life by the way of satisfaction and penance, or suffer for it hereafter. And God is moved to act in this manner by the ingratitude of those who have abused the baptismal grace; that thus they may be retained in their duty, lest if they should be too speedily freed from the bonds of justice, they would abandon themselves to a temerarious confidence, abusing the facility of pardon.

279. **Is an absolution from an excommunication or any other ecclesiastic censure a part of this sacrament?**

It is not, for a person may be absolved from it without going to confession.

280. **What does a major or greater excommunication deprive the excommunicated of?**

Of the power of either administering or receiving any sacrament, of the benefit of the public prayers and suffrages of the faithful, of being eligible to any ecclesiastic dignity, and of being capable of having any benefice conferred upon him. It also deprives the excommunicated of the benefit of hearing Mass, and excludes him the society of the faithful, except in case of some great necessity, or some notable detriment either to the excommunicated or to the faithful.

281. **If a person communicates without any great necessity with an excommunicated, does he sin mortally by so doing?**

He does in three cases. First, if he communicates with him out of contempt of the excommunication. Secondly, if he communicates with him in spirituals, such as prayer, divine service, or the canonical office. Thirdly, if he has been an accomplice of the crime, for which the excommunication is denounced. To communicate in temporals with the excommunicated is not a mortal, but only a venial sin, unless the excommunication has been denounced against such as any way communicate with the excommunicate, in which case it is a mortal sin to communicate with him.

282. **Is the excommunicated deprived of all jurisdiction, so that the faithful cannot receive any sacrament from him, even in case of necessity?**

He is, if he be not tolerated; but he is not, if he be tolerated. The excommunicate not tolerated are those who are denounced by name, or who openly lay violent hands upon a clergyman; all others are tolerated, though we should know them to be under an excommunication.

283. **What does a minor or lesser excommunication deprive the excommunicate of?**

Of the power of receiving the sacraments, but not of that of administering them.

Extreme Unction Explained in a Moral Sense

284. **What is extreme unction?**

It is the anointing of the sick with oil of olives blessed by the bishop under a set form of words.

285. **What is the matter and form of this sacrament?**

The remote matter is oil of olives solemnly blessed by the bishop; the immediate matter is the anointing of the sick person upon his eyes, ears, nose, mouth, hands, and feet. And the form are these words: "Through this holy unction and his own most tender mercy, may the Lord pardon thee whatsoever sins thou hast committed by the sight. Amen"; which words are said by the priest at the anointing of the eyes, and so of the hearing, and the rest, adapting the form to the several senses.

286. **To what kind of people is this sacrament to be administered, and what disposition of soul is required for the worthy receiving of it?**

To those that are in danger of death by sickness, but not to persons sentenced to death, nor to children not come to the use of reason, nor to idiots, nor to such as are constantly deprived of the use of reason. The disposition required in the worthy receiver is the same as that which is required for the worthy receiving of the sacrament of confirmation or the Eucharist.

The Sacrament of Holy Orders Expounded in a Moral Sense

287. **What is this sacrament?**

A sacrament by which the ministers of Christ are consecrated to their sacred functions, and receive grace to discharge them well.

288. **How many degrees are there in holy orders?**

Seven, viz: four called minor or lesser orders, and three called major or greater orders; for tonsure is not properly an order, but only a preparation for orders, and episcopacy is not a different order from that of priesthood, but only an extension of the power received by priesthood to certain privileges of governing the Church and administering some sacraments, viz: confirmation and holy orders. The four minor orders are: porter, or doorkeeper of the church; lector, or reader of the lessons in the divine service; exorcist, whose function is to read the exorcisms and prayers of the Church over those who are possessed or obsessed by the devil; and acolyte, whose function is to serve at Mass, light the candles in the church, etc. The first of the greater orders (which are properly called holy) is subdeacon, whose function is to sing the epistle in the Mass and to assist the deacon; deacon, whose office is to sing and preach the gospel, to baptize, and to assist the bishop or priest in the Sacrifice of the Mass; and the order of priest, whose function is to offer sacrifice to God and celebrate Mass as well for the living as for the dead, as also when duly approved, to absolve sinners from their sins.

289. **What is the matter and form of each of these orders?**

The remote matter is the different instruments or books belonging to the respective functions of each; and the immediate matter is the actual delivery and receiving of the said instruments; as also the imposition of hands, according to some divines. The form are the words said by the bishop when he applies the remote matter.[97]

---

[97] Editor's note: The essential matter required for valid sacramental ordination was given further precision under Pope Pius XII (cf. *Sacramentum Ordinis*, 1947) as being specifically the *impositio manus* (laying on of hands), long occurring in the Roman Rite amid the conferral of liturgical instruments (*traditio instrumentorum*) as described here. See also q. 349 below.

290. **Are there any particular obligations annexed to the receiving of holy orders?**

Those that are admitted into any of the three holy or greater orders are tied forever to the service of God and his Church, in a state of perpetual continence, and also obliged to the canonical hours of the Church-office; but such as have only received minor orders are at liberty to quit the ecclesiastical calling, and engage themselves by marriage in the world.

The Sacrament of Matrimony Expounded in a Moral Sense

291. **What is the sacrament of matrimony?**

It is a mutual contract between man and woman, and an indissoluble conjunction which cannot be dissolved but by the death of one of the parties, and which gives graces to the worthy receivers.

292. **What kind of grace does matrimony give to the married couple?**

If they receive it in the dispositions that they ought, it gives them grace to love one another according to God, to restrain the violence of concupiscence, to bear with one another's weakness, and to bring up their children in the love of God.

293. **If matrimony gives so great a grace, how comes it that so many marriages are unhappy?**

Because the parties seldom receive it in the dispositions they ought: they consult not God in their choice, but only their own lust or temporal interest; they do not prepare themselves for it, by putting themselves in the state of grace, and very often are guilty of freedoms before marriage, which are not allowable by the law of God.

294. **What is the matter and form of this sacrament?**

The remote matter is the mutual consent of the parties, and the immediate is the delivering of the power of their bodies to one another; and the form are the words or signs that express or signify the said consent and delivery.

295. **Who is the minister of this sacrament?**

According to the best divines, the parties themselves; but in any place where the Council of Trent is received with regard to discipline, the presence of the parish priest of one of the parties and of two witnesses is required for the validity of the marriage.

296. **If the Church can neither determine nor alter the matter or form of sacraments, how comes it that the Council of Trent declared void and invalid all marriages done without the presence of the parish priest and two witnesses? For these marriages before the said council were deemed valid, though unlawful.**

Marriage is not only a sacrament, but also a contract, or more properly a contract raised by Christ to the dignity of a sacrament. Though then the Church can neither determine nor alter the matter or form of the sacraments; yet to prevent frauds, she may add some conditions necessary for the validity of marriage; as any state, to prevent frauds and circumventions, may add to a contract, which is valid according to the law of nature, some conditions without which the contract cannot subsist. For example, a contract made by a minor without his guardian's consent is null. Now, when the contract of marriage, which is the foundation of the sacrament, is invalid, the sacrament founded thereon cannot subsist.

297. **What think you of two Catholic parties, or of one Catholic party and another protestant, who are married not by the parish priest, but by the parish minister in a country subject to a protestant government, where the Council of Trent has been received?**

I think them to be validly, though unlawfully married. Thus Cardinal Gotti and others.

298. **But what if they should be married in that manner in a Catholic country, where the said council is received?**

If they be married by the parish priest of any of the parties, doubtless the marriage is valid. If they be married by the parson of a factory, and both parties be protestants, the marriage is valid. But if both or one of the parties be Catholics, the marriage is invalid and nothing worth; for the Church, for weighty reasons, tolerates protestant ministers as parish priests in Catholic countries with regard to those of their own communion, not with regard to Catholics.

299. **But what think you of two Catholics, and of a protestant and Catholic, who are married not by the parish priest of any of the parties, but by some other clergyman in a country where the Council of Trent is received; for example, in Spain and Portugal?**
I take all such marriages to be both unlawful and invalid or nothing worth.

300. **If the parties be absent, can they marry?**
They can by their proxies, who are empowered to act for or in behalf of them.

301. **What is the difference between betrothing and marriage?**
Betrothing is a mutual promise and agreement of a future marriage between two persons. And marriage is the actual putting of one another into the possession of the power of their bodies.

302. **Do the betrothed sin mortally by cohabiting before they are married, or by taking any carnal delight in their future enjoyment?**
They do.

303. **What is the nuptial benediction?**
It is not an essential part of the sacrament, but a mere ceremony; wherefore the married couple may lawfully cohabit without receiving it. The Church does not give the nuptial benediction when the man or woman has been once married before, because the second marriage does not so perfectly represent the union of Christ and his Church, which is an eternal tie of one to one. But to omit in the first marriage the nuptial benediction, when it may be easily had, is a venial sin.

304. **What are the duties of married people to one another?**

To love, honor, and reverence one another. As also to render mutually the marriage-duty.[98]

305. **Is it a mortal sin not to render the marriage-debt after the marriage is once consummated?**

It is, if any of the parties demand it as a strict debt, or be in evident danger of otherwise violating chastity; unless one of the parties be sick or disabled, or it is not demanded as a strict debt but rather as a favor, nor is it positively refused, but only put off in a courteous manner; in which cases it is not a mortal sin, not to render it.

306. **Can a married couple be divorced without a crime and a juridical sentence?**

They cannot; unless in case of manifest adultery or heresy, in which case the innocent party is not obliged to cohabit with the guilty.

307. **Does a divorce free both parties from all obligation?**

It frees them from the obligation of bed and board; but not from the tie of matrimony, which cannot be dissolved but by the death of one of the parties.

308. **Do children sin mortally by marrying against their parents' will?**

They do according to the best divines; unless their parents give them cruel usage, neglect to get them married in proper time, or would endeavor to have them married to persons below their rank and condition, when they can be married according to their birth and rank. In these cases, children may lawfully marry without the consent of their parents.

309. **Is it lawful for parents to force children to marry against their will?**

It is not.

---

[98] Cf. Eph 5:25; 1 Cor 7:3

310. **What are the principal impediments of marriage which render it invalid?**
There are twelve in the canon law, to which the Council of Trent has added the presence of the parish priest and of two witnesses as a condition without which marriage is invalid. The most common impediments are consanguinity and affinity, which in all degrees in a right line are prohibited by the law of nature, and consequently indispensable by the Church. Collateral consanguinity to the fourth degree inclusively renders matrimony invalid; as also affinity, if it be contracted by a lawful marriage; but if by a criminal commerce, it annuls matrimony to the second degree only.

311. **If a married person has had a criminal commerce with one that is related to his spouse within the forbidden degrees of matrimony, can he demand the marriage-debt without committing a mortal sin?**
He cannot; but he may render it when it is demanded by the innocent party, who is not to suffer for crimes of the guilty.

The Sacraments Explained in a Controversial Manner

Of the Sacraments in General, and of the Three First in Particular

312. **Why are the sacraments seven, neither more, nor less?**
Because there are only seven outward or visible signs of Christ's institution, by which grace is given to the soul of the worthy receiver of them.

313. **Are there any other visible means of grace besides the seven sacraments?**
There are not, if the means of grace be strictly taken; for the sacraments only give grace *ex opere operato* (as the Council of Trent[99] terms it) that is, independently of the minister's sanctity; but not of the disposition of the receiver, if he be an adult (as some protestants misinterpret the council's words). But there are several other means of grace, if the word be taken in a larger sense: thus praying, fasting, and almsgiving are means of grace, because they move God to bestow his grace upon us. Thus also, hearing

[99] Council of Trent, Session 7, "On the Sacraments in General," Can. 8

sermons, reading pious books, seeing good example or a moving picture of Christ's sufferings may in a large sense be called means of grace, because they excite us to the practice of virtue by which we obtain an increase of grace.

314. **But what think you of those things which divines call sacramental, viz: the Lord's Prayer, holy water, an episcopal benediction, and saying the general confession; do not all these, by the mere performance of the work, give grace which remits at least venial sins?**

They do not; for they only incite us to the practice of some virtue, by which we obtain an increase of grace, which remits venial sins; but because they are immediate causes of this incitement, whereof other pious works are only remote causes, for this reason they are called sacramental, because they resemble in some measure the sacraments in their manner of giving grace.

315. **How do you prove that baptism is a sacrament?**

Because it has the three conditions required for a thing to be a sacrament. For first, it is a visible sign consisting in the washing with water under a set form of words. Secondly, it has a power of communicating grace to the soul, in the way of a new birth, according to that: "He saved us by the washing of regeneration, and renovation of the Holy Ghost."[100] And, "He that shall believe and be baptized, shall be saved."[101] Thirdly, it was instituted by Christ.[102]

316. **How do you prove against the Anabaptists, that infants may be baptized who are not capable of being taught or instructed in faith?**

First, by a tradition which the Church has received from the apostles.[103]

---

[100] Ti 3:5
[101] Mk 16:16
[102] Cf. Mt 28:19
[103] Cf. Irenaeus, *Against Heresies*, Bk. 2, Ch. 2; Origen, *Commentary on Romans* 5:9; Cyprian, *Epistle 58*; Chrysostom, *Ad Neophytos*; Augustine, *The Literal Interpretation of Genesis*, Bk. 10, Ch. 23

Secondly, I prove it from scripture by comparing together two texts thereof, one of which declares that without baptism no one can enter into the kingdom of heaven: "Unless a man be born again of water and the Holy Ghost, he cannot enter into the kingdom of God."[104] The other text declares that infants are capable of the kingdom of God: "To such belongeth the kingdom of God,"[105] and consequently they must be capable of baptism. Hence it is evident that when Christ said, "Teach all nations, baptizing them,"[106] and, "He that shall believe, and be baptized,"[107] he only spoke with regard to persons who are already come to an age in which they are capable of being instructed before their baptism.

317. **How do you prove against Quakers that baptism is to be given with water?**
From Acts 8: "Behold here is water, what hindereth me from being baptized…and they both went down into the water, Philip and the eunuch, and he baptized him."[108] Hence St. Paul exhorts us to "approach with a true heart in a full faith, having our hearts sprinkled from an evil conscience, and our body washed with pure water."[109]

318. **How do you prove that confirmation is a sacrament?**
Because the visible sign of the imposition of hands has annexed to it an invisible grace, according to that: "Then they (Peter and John, two bishops) laid their hands upon them (the baptized by Philip[110]), and they received the Holy Ghost,"[111] or invisible grace, but not the baptismal grace which they had received at their baptism. Therefore, they received at their confirmation a fortifying grace; and consequently, confirmation is a sacrament or visible sign of invisible grace. Hence it is also plain that the ordinary minister of confirmation is a bishop only, for the apostles "sent Peter and

---

[104] Jn 3:5
[105] Lk 18:16
[106] Mt 28:19
[107] Mk 16:16
[108] Acts 8:36, 38
[109] Heb 10:22
[110] Cf. Acts 8:16
[111] Acts 8:17

John"[112] to administer confirmation to those that were baptized by Philip, because he, being but a deacon, had not power to administer it. As St. Chrysostom observes in *Homily 18*.

319. **If the apostles gave confirmation by laying their hands upon those that were to be confirmed,[113] why does the bishop not only extend his hands towards them, but also sign their foreheads with holy chrism?**
For two reasons. First, to signify the efficacy of confirmation by a more express representation of the interior unction of the soul, which is made by the Holy Ghost at confirmation. Secondly, to signify the principal effect of confirmation, for chrism is a compound of oil of olives and balm: oil signifies an undauntedness to profess our faith before persecuting tyrants; and balm signifies the good odor of a Christian name, according to that: "We are a sweet odor of Christ to God."[114]

320. **How do you prove that the Eucharist is a sacrament?**
Because it is a visible sign consisting in the outward forms of bread and wine, and also of Christ's institution, by which spiritual life or grace is given to the soul of the worthy receiver, according to that: "If any one shall eat of this bread, he shall live for ever; and the bread which I will give, is my flesh, for the life of the world."[115]

321. **How do you prove the real presence of the body and blood of Christ in the Eucharist?**
From the plain words of Christ: "This is my body";[116] "This is my blood."[117]; which words if taken in a figurative sense would be contrary to the laws of speech; for the laws of discourse teach us, that a sign which represents naturally often borrows the name of the thing represented. The same

[112] Acts 8:14
[113] Cf. Acts 8:17
[114] 2 Cor 2:15
[115] Jn 6:52
[116] Mt 26:26; Mk 14:22
[117] Mt 26:28; Mk 14:24

sometimes happens to instituted signs after they are instituted and people are accustomed to them. Thus, Christ is called a "door,"[118] because he has in himself the property of a door, inasmuch as it is by him that we enter into his sheepfold; and is also called a "vine,"[119] because he has the property of the vine, in giving life and fruit to its branches.

But that in instituting a new sign which has no relation at all to the thing signified (for example a morsel of bread, to signify the body of a man), the name of the thing signified should be given to it without any explication or warning beforehand (as Christ has done at his last supper), is as repugnant to the common conceptions of mankind and to the laws of discourse, as if a person to deceive his company by concealing the true meaning of his words, should appoint within himself that an oak tree should be a sign of Alexander the Great, and pointing at the tree should gravely tell his friends (who were not acquainted with his design), "This is that hero that conquered Darius." Nor is the impropriety of speech avoided by answering that the bread is called Christ's body, and the wine his blood, because they convey Christ's body and blood to the soul of the worthy receiver. For what can be a greater impropriety of speech, than to say in a sober manner, that a fork is a capon, or a spoon good broth, because forks and spoons are means of conveyance and signs of what is served up?

322. **But we have instances in scripture of signs being called by the names of the things signified; as when Joseph interpreting the dream of Pharaoh says the seven good kine are seven years;[120] and Christ interpreting the parable of the sower says: "The seed is the word of God";[121] and St. Paul says, "The rock was Christ."[122]**

When a thing is already known to be a sign or figure of something else which it represents, it may indeed, according to the common laws of speech,

[118] Jn 10:9
[119] Jn 15:1
[120] Cf. Gn 41:26-30
[121] Lk 8:11
[122] 1 Cor 10:4

be said to be such or such a thing, as in the interpretation of dreams, parables, and ancient figures, where when a thing is said to be this or that, the meaning, by a long use, explication, or forewarning, is evident, viz: that it represents this or that. But it is not the same in the first institution of a sign or figure, for the reasons already alleged.

323. **How do you prove that the bread and wine are substantially changed by consecration into the body and blood of Christ?**

Because Christ did not say: "In this"; or "With this, is my body and blood"; but he said: "This is my body,"[123] and "This is my blood";[124] which words could not be verified without a substantial change. Thus, if Aaron, when he threw down his rod,[125] had said, "This is a serpent," the sentence would not be true without a substantial change. It is true that this sacrament after consecration is called "bread,"[126] because it still retains the qualities, accidents, and all the outward appearances of bread, as angels are called "men,"[127] because they appeared in the shape of men. And also, because it was made from bread, as man is called "dust,"[128] because he was made out of dust; and the serpent is called a "rod,"[129] because it was made from a rod.

324. **But do not all our senses bear testimony that the bread and wine sill remain?**

No; they only bear testimony that the accidents remain, but as to the inward substance, this is not the object of any of the senses, nor can it be perceived by any of them.

325. **But must we not believe our senses, and make a judgment of a thing's being in effect that which it has all the appearances of?**

We must indeed, unless either faith or reason makes an exception. But to

[123] Mk 14:22
[124] Mk 14:24
[125] Cf. Ex 7:10
[126] Cf. 1 Cor 10:16
[127] Cf. Lk 24:4
[128] Cf. Gn 3:19
[129] Cf. Ex 7:12

believe them in all cases is evidently repugnant to faith, to experience, to reason, and to our senses themselves. For then we must suppose, that he whom Joshua saw was a man,[130] that the stars are no bigger than walnuts, and that an oar, by being put into the water, is bent. It seems indeed so whilst in the water to all men's eyes, but both reason and experience correct them. The stars never appear in their true bigness, but reason corrects the mistake which sense cannot. And a rational faith in Joshua corrected the error of his senses. Christ to the apostles' eyes appeared to be a creature, but they did not judge of him according to the information of their senses, because the authority of him who said: "I am the Son of God,"[131] interposed, to oblige them to make another judgment. In the like manner, the testimony of him that said: "This is my body";[132] "This is my blood,"[133] interposes to make us believe that which appears to the senses to be bread and wine, to be, as to the substance contained, the body and blood of Christ.

326. **Are the body and blood of Christ naturally and corporally present under the sacramental signs?**

They are as to the matter, (that is: Christ's true body and blood are present); not as to the manner, which is spiritual, supernatural, and contrary to the usual laws of bodies. In this spiritual manner, Christ's body came into the world without opening the bars of nature.

327. **Are they present visibly or invisibly?**

The substance which appears to be bread and wine is Christ's body and blood, but the senses do not perceive it to be so. Wherefore by faith only, we know Christ's body and blood to be really present, though they are not present by faith only, for to be present by faith only imports no more than a moral presence, and Christ's body is not only morally but also really present in the Eucharist, though this is not known but by faith; just as the

130 Cf. Jo 5:13-14
131 Jn 10:36; Cf. Mt 16:15-17
132 Mk 14:22
133 Mk 14:24

apostles by faith only knew the hypostatical union, though this union of the divine and human nature in Christ's person was not only a union by faith, but also a real and substantial one.

328. How can Christ's body and blood be in different places at the same time?

They can be by divine power, in a supernatural manner, not only in different, but also in distant places; as well as two bodies can be in the same place by penetration, as appears from John 20.[134]

329. Is the eating of Christ's body literal or figurative?

It is literal as to the action, and figurative as to the effects; for common food is divided, digested, and consumed, of all which Christ's immortal body is incapable; yet it remains as long as the substance of bread (if there had been no consecration) would have continued.

330. Do we eat in this sacrament the same flesh which the Jews saw, and drink the same blood which was spilt upon the cross?

We do as to the matter, but not as to the visible and bloody manner; in which sense the Capharnaites understood Christ's words: "The bread which I will give, is my flesh, for the life of the world."[135] To correct this gross imagination, that Christ meant to give them his body and blood to eat in a visible and bloody manner, Christ said: "It is the spirit that quickeneth: the flesh profiteth nothing."[136] That is: The flesh (says St. Augustine) profits nothing, as the Capharnaites understood it, "for they understood flesh as it is torn in pieces in a dead body, or sold in the shambles, and not as it is animated by the Spirit."[137] But the flesh profits much, as united to Christ's soul and divinity, and as truly and really, though in a spiritual manner, present under the sacramental signs. Hence Christ subjoined: "The words that I have spoken to you, they are spirit and life,"[138]

---

[134] Cf. Jn 20:19, 26
[135] Jn 6:52
[136] Jn 6:64
[137] Augustine, *Tractate 27*, n. 5
[138] Jn 6:64

to insinuate to them that they should receive in the Eucharist this spirit and life in its very fountain, because they were to receive therein Christ's body and blood verily and truly.

331. **How can Christ's body and blood be really present under the sacramental signs, whereas he has said: "Do this in remembrance of me"?**[139] **For the remembrance of a thing supposes it to be absent.**

The meaning of Christ's words (as St. Paul explains them[140]) is to offer up and to receive his body and blood for a perpetual commemoration of his death. Now, though Christ's body and blood be really present in the Eucharist, yet his death is not a thing really present, but really past, and consequently a proper subject for our remembrance.

332. **How can the Eucharist be a sign if it really contains the thing signified?**

It is a sign, because the exterior and sensible part appears always the same to our senses, though our minds judge otherwise of the substance contained; because the authority of him who said: "This is my body,"[141] interposes.

333. **Have you any other argument in favor of the real presence of Christ's body in the Eucharist?**

I have the perpetual consent of all the oriental Christians, confirmed by the authentic testimonies of their patriarchs, archbishops, bishops, abbots, by the decrees of their synods against Cyril Lucar, by the writings of their ancient and modern divines, and by all their liturgies, all which may be seen in Monsieur Arnauld's *Perpetuite de la Foy*, Volume III, in the appendix to the first volume, and in the two additional volumes of Abbé Renaudot to the *Perpetuite de la Foy*.

---

[139] Lk 22:19
[140] Cf. 1 Cor 11:26
[141] Mk 14:22

334. **What think you of the custom of the Catholic Church to administer the Blessed Sacrament to the laity in one kind only, viz, under the form of bread?**

I look upon it as a matter of discipline which is neither forbid nor commanded by Christ; because Christ has promised eternal life to those who eat the bread only;[142] as well as he has promised it to such as eat his flesh and drink his blood.[143] Wherefore when Christ said, "Drink you all of it,"[144] he meant the apostles then present, and their successors, the bishops and priests of the Church, whom he has commanded to offer this sacrifice in remembrance of his death.[145] Now the nature of this sacrifice requires the separate consecration of both kinds, because it requires a representation of the real separation of Christ's blood from his body at his death and passion; and consequently the separate consecration of both kinds, which being consecrated, must be received by someone, and by no one more properly than by the minister.

But the laity, by communicating, do not offer a sacrifice, but only receive a sacrament, which sufficiently subsists in either kind, because in either kind there is a sufficient sign and cause of grace, which is annexed in this sacrament to the real presence of Christ. And Christ being as truly and really present in one kind as in both, he brings with him the same grace to the soul when received in one kind, as he does when received in both; and consequently, the faithful are not deprived of any part of the grace of this sacrament by receiving in one kind only.

335. **If Communion in both kinds be an indifferent thing, why did not the Council of Trent condescend so far with the Lutherans as to allow it to them?**

The Lutherans demanded both kinds as essential parts, without which the sacrament could not subsist; lest then the Church, by granting their request, might seem to patronize their error, she prudently denied it to them; for though it be a matter of discipline whether the Blessed Sacrament

---

[142] Cf. Jn 6:52, 58-59
[143] Cf. Jn 6:55
[144] Mt 26:27
[145] Cf. Lk 22:19

should actually be administered to the laity in one kind or in both; yet it is and ever was the faith of the Catholic Church, that, under one kind, we receive Christ whole and entire, and a true sacrament, and consequently that there is no command of Christ for all the faithful to receive in both kinds.

The Other Four Sacraments Explained in a Controversial Manner, as Also Indulgences and Purgatory

336. **How are our sins forgiven us?**

Freely by the divine mercy of Jesus Christ.[146]

337. **How do we merit by good works?**

In virtue of the promise of God, who has promised his children eternal life as a recompence, which is faithfully rendered to their merits and good works.[147] So that all the price and value of our merits proceed from the sanctifying grace, which is given us *gratis* in the name of Jesus Christ, as well as it is the effect of the continual influence of this divine head upon its members.

338. **How do you prove that penance is a sacrament?**

Because it has all the conditions and parts required for a thing to be a sacrament. For first, it is an outward sign, consisting in the sinner's confession and the form of absolution pronounced by the priest. Secondly, to this outward sign is annexed an inward grace, or the remission of sins promised by Christ.[148] Thirdly, it was ordained by Christ, when he said: "Receive ye the Holy Ghost. Whose sins you shall forgive, they are forgiven them; and whose you shall retain, they are retained."[149] By which we see that to the apostles, and to their successors, bishops and priests is given by Christ a power to be exercised, not only by forgiving, but also by retaining; not only by absolving and loosing, but also by binding, by refusing, or deferring

---

[146] Cf. Council of Trent, Session 6, "Decree on Justification," Ch. 9
[147] Cf. Council of Trent, Session 6, "Decree on Justification," Ch. 16
[148] Cf. Jn 20:22-23
[149] Jn 20:22-23

absolution according to the dispositions that are found in sinners, when they accuse themselves of their sins. From hence must needs follow an obligation on the sinner's part to declare and confess their sins in particular to God's ministers, who are appointed the spiritual judges and physicians of their souls; for a judge must know the cause to pronounce a just sentence, and a physician must know the distemper to prescribe suitable remedies.

339. **How do you prove, that after the guilt of sin and the eternal punishment has been remitted, there remains oftentimes a debt of temporal punishment due to the divine justice?**

First, from Genesis 3:24, where we find that Adam, after his sin was forgiven him, was cast out of paradise, made subject to death and other miseries. Secondly, from 2 Kings 12, where we read that although upon David's repentance the prophet Nathan assured him, that "the Lord had put away his sin";[150] yet he denounced unto him many temporal punishments, which should be inflicted by reason of his sin, which accordingly afterwards ensued.[151]

340. **Did the apostles ever impose any temporal punishment for sin?**

They did, as appears from St. Paul, where we find that he "delivered (the incestuous Corinthian) over to Satan,"[152] by a sentence of excommunication, depriving him of the sacraments, the prayers, and communion, and even of the conversation of the rest of the faithful, according to St. Chrysostom, *Homily 15*. And this is said to be done "for the destruction (or punishing) of the flesh, that (his) spirit, (or soul) may be saved in the day of our Lord Jesus Christ."[153]

341. **When did Christ give the Church power to grant indulgences?**

When he said to St. Peter: "Whatsoever thou shalt bind on earth, shall

---

[150] 2 Kgs 12:13
[151] Cf. 2 Kgs 12:10-14
[152] 1 Cor 5:5
[153] Ibid.

be bound in heaven; and whatsoever thou shalt loose on earth, shall be loosed also in heaven."[154]

342. **Did the apostles ever discharge a penitent sinner from the debt of temporal punishment, which remained due upon account of his sins?**

They did, as appears from St. Paul saying: now to him "to whom you have pardoned any thing, I also pardon: for…if I pardoned any thing, I pardoned for your sake in the person of Christ."[155] And this is said to be done in the Person of Christ, (says St. Chrysostom[156]) to signify that the temporal punishment due to sin was pardoned not only in the sight of men, but also in the sight of God, who gave his apostles this power.

343. **Whither go such as die in venial sin, or without having fully satisfied for the temporal punishment due to mortal sin remitted as to the guilt, and as to the everlasting punishment?**

To purgatory, where they must suffer, in proportion to the debt which they owe to the divine justice.

344. **What do you understand by purgatory?**

A middle state of souls who have neither lived so innocently as to go straight to heaven, nor so ill as to be condemned to eternal torments; which souls are helped by the acceptable Sacrifice of the Altar, and by the suffrages of the faithful. Not that the souls in purgatory can do penance for their sins, but that they must suffer for them till God's justice be satisfied; and that they are capable of relief, not from anything that they can do for themselves, but from the prayers and suffrages offered to God for them by the faithful upon earth, which God in his mercy is pleased to accept of, by reason of that communion which we have with them, by being fellow members of the same body the Church, under the same head Jesus Christ. The quality of the fire, the place where it is, the greatness of the torments, the terms of their duration are no points of faith with Catholics.

[154] Mt 16:19
[155] 2 Cor 2:10
[156] Cf. Chrysostom, *Homily 4 on Second Corinthians*

345. Can a mortal sin be forgiven after death?

It cannot, because when once a soul is come to heaven or to hell, its state is unchangeable, according to that: "If the tree falls toward the south, or toward the north, in the place where the tree falleth there it shall be."[157]

346. What say you, if we should pray for the release of souls that are in hell or in heaven?

Whereas God alone sees the hearts, and the Church has always prayed for all her children (infants and martyrs excepted) to whom she gave Christian burial, we hope the best, that our prayers will not be lost before God, but that they will return to us, if those for whom they are directed be either so miserable that they cannot be helped by them, or else so happy that they do not want them.

347. How do you prove that there is a purgatory?

First, from 1 Corinthians 3: "If a man's work abides, (as theirs do who deserve no purgatory) … he shall receive a reward. If a man's work burns (as theirs do who go to purgatory), he shall suffer detriment; but himself shall be saved, yet so as by fire."[158] But not by the fire of hell, from which there is no redemption, and by which there is no salvation; therefore, by the fire of purgatory. Secondly, because even those who live here in the faith and fear of God are often guilty of lesser offences; for "there is no man that sinneth not."[159] And if they die before they have duly repented of these lighter sins, they carry with them out of the world something which deserves punishment in the next, though it does not deserve hell. Either then we must say that God will not render to everyone "according to his deeds,"[160] which contradicts St. Paul, and that something that defileth enters into heaven, which is contrary to scripture;[161] or we must grant that

---

[157] Eccles 11:3
[158] 1 Cor 3:14-15
[159] 3 Kgs 8:46; Cf. Eccles 7:21
[160] Rom 2:6
[161] Cf. Apoc 21:27

some dying in the faith and fear of God have yet something to suffer, and some lighter sins to be forgiven after death.

348. **How do you prove that extreme unction is a sacrament?**

Because it is an outward sign of an inward grace, ordained by Christ; which is the definition of a sacrament. The anointing is the outward sign; the ordinance of God and the inward grace are found in James 5: "Is any one sick among you? Let him call in the priests of the church, and let them pray over him, anointing him with oil in the name of the Lord. And the prayer of faith shall save the sick man: and the Lord shall lift him up: and if he be in sins, they shall be forgiven him."[162]

349. **How do you prove that holy orders are a sacrament?**

Because they are a visible sign of an invisible grace by divine institution. The visible sign is found in the imposition of the bishop's hands and prayer, after which manner the seven deacons were ordained.[163] The invisible grace conferred by the imposition of hands is attested: "Stir up the grace of God which is in thee, by the imposition of my hands";[164] and consequently, this sacrament has been instituted by Christ, who alone can annex the gift of grace to any outward sign.

350. **How do you prove that bishops only can ordain priests?**

From St. Paul who said: "For this cause did I leave thee (Titus, the chief bishop of Crete) at Crete, that thou shouldest correct the things that are wanting, and establish priests in the cities."[165]

---

[162] Jas 5:14-15
[163] Cf. Acts 6:6; 13:3
[164] 2 Tm 1:6
[165] Ti 1:5

351. Can anyone take upon him priestly power without the ordination of the Church?

He cannot, for no man can "assume this honor to himself, but he who is called by God, as Aaron."[166]

352. Why cannot women preach or be ordained?

Because they are commanded "to be silent in the churches; for it is not permitted them to speak, but to be subject…For it is shameful for a woman to speak in the church."[167]

353. What is the doctrine of the Catholic Church concerning the celibacy of the clergy?

The Church considering that St. Paul advises married persons to abstain sometimes from what they may lawfully do, that they may "give themselves to prayer";[168] and that even the priests of the ancient law were to abstain from their wives, when they were employed in the functions of their ministry, as appears from Leviticus 15 and 1 Kings 21; for these and other weighty reasons the Church receives none to holy orders, but such as are willing to make a solemn vow of perpetual continence. For priests and deacons being daily to be employed in the functions of their ministry, if others be to abstain from the use of marriage for a time, then they always.

But the Church by this discipline is so far from absolutely forbidding marriage, as the Gnostics, Marcionites, and other heretics did, whose doctrine St. Paul calls "the doctrine of devils,"[169] that on the contrary she holds marriage to be a sacrament, and forbids it to none but to those that have voluntarily made a vow of perpetual continency; because St. Paul says of such as these that if they afterwards "marry, they incur damnation, because they have made void their first faith."[170] Hence it is evident that when St. Paul said to the unmarried and widows, "If they do not contain themselves,

166 Heb 5:4
167 1 Cor 14:34-35
168 1 Cor 7:5
169 1 Tm 4:1
170 1 Tm 5:11-12

let them marry; for it is better to marry than to burn,"[171] he speaks not of those who have already made a vow of living always a single life; for these, if they be in danger of burning, must use other remedies different from marriage, viz: fasting, self-denial and fervent prayers, to obtain the gift of continency; which remedies and no others must be often times used by married persons, when they are in danger of violating the chastity of the marriage bed. For example, when they are divorced from bed and board, when long absent from one another, when sick or disabled; they cannot marry another, but they can and must use the abovementioned remedies.

354. Has it been always the discipline of the Church that the clergy should abstain from marriage?

It has been at some times and in some places, as at present among the Greeks, permitted for priests and deacons to continue with their wives which they had married before their ordination; though even this was disallowed by many canons and holy fathers, such as: the twenty-seventh canon of the *Apostolic Canons* (if they be genuine); the Council of Neo-cesarea; the third canon of the Council of Nice; the third canon of the Second Council of Carthage; St. Epiphanius, *Haeresi 59*; St. Jerome, *Epistle 48*; and others.

But it never was the practice of either the Greek or Latin Church, that bishops, priests, or deacons should marry after their ordination; and we have not one instance in all antiquity of any such marriages being deemed lawful till the fifth century, when Jovinian and Vigilantius alleged against the celibacy of the clergy the same texts of scripture that are now brought by modern heretics, who have only picked up the ancient heretics' arguments, which have been already condemned by a council at Rome under Pope Siricius, and fully answered by St. Epiphanius, *Haeresi 59*; St. Jerome, *Against Jovinianus*, Bk. 1; Innocent I, *Epistle* to Victricius, Ch. 9; and St. Ambrose, *Epist. 6*.

---

[171] 1 Cor 7:9

355. **Why then does St. Paul say that bishops and deacons must be husbands of one wife?**[172]

The apostle's meaning is not that every bishop or deacon should have a wife, for he himself was a bishop and had none, as he declares.[173] His meaning then is that since, on account of the great scarcity of proper ministers in those days, there was a necessity of admitting married men to holy orders, this was to be done, provided the persons to be admitted had not been twice married.

356. **How do you prove that matrimony is a sacrament?**

Because it is a visible sign of invisible grace, and that by divine institution. The visible sign is the conjunction of marriage betwixt man and wife. The divine institution is found in Matthew 19: "What therefore God hath joined, let not man separate."[174] The grace conferred by this sacrament is gathered from its being "a great sacrament…in Christ and in the church,"[175] as representing the union or spiritual nuptials of Christ with his spouse the Church.

Chapter 3

Sin in General and Its Different Kinds Explained in a Moral Sense

357. **What is sin in general?**

It is a thought, word, or deed against the law of God or of our superiors.

358. **How is sin divided?**

Into original and personal. Original sin is a privation of original justice,

---

[172] Cf. 1 Tm 3:2, 12
[173] Cf. 1 Cor 7:8
[174] Mt 19:6
[175] Eph 5:32

which we inherit from our first parent Adam, being all by course of nature conceived and born in original sin; for "by one man sin entered into this world, and death by sin; and so death passed unto all men, in whom all sinned."[176] Personal sin is that which a person commits by his own free will.

359. What are the effects of original sin?

Concupiscence, ignorance, evil inclinations, proneness to sin, sickness, and death.

360. How is personal sin divided?

First, into actual and habitual. Secondly, into mortal and venial. Thirdly, into the sin of commission and that of omission.

361. What is actual sin?

It is the actual doing or omitting of anything that is commanded or forbidden.

362. What is habitual sin?

It is a vicious habit, or facility of sinning, acquired by many repeated criminal acts or omissions.

363. What is a sin of commission?

It is the doing of anything that is forbidden; or more properly, it is to act against a negative precept.

364. What is a sin of omission?

It is the omitting to do something commanded; or more properly, it is not complying with an affirmative precept.

365. What is the meaning of an affirmative and negative precept, and what is the difference between them?

An affirmative precept commands us to do something, and a negative

---

[176] Rom 5:12

precept forbids us the doing of something. The first is called affirmative, because it is delivered in the affirmative: "Do this or that." The second is called negative, because it is commonly intimated by the negative: "Do not this or that." The difference between them is that an affirmative precept obliges always, but not upon all occasions; but a negative precept obliges always, and upon all occasions. For example, the affirmative precepts of faith, hope, and charity, etc. oblige us always, so as not to do anything contrary to them, but yet we are not bound to practice these virtues upon all occasions, but only upon certain occasions when these precepts oblige us. But the negative precepts of not hating God, etc. oblige us always and upon all occasions, because there is no time nor circumstance in which the acts of hating God or our neighbor are not criminal.

366. What is a mortal sin?

It is any great offence against the love of God or our neighbor. It is called mortal, because it kills the soul,[177] by robbing it of grace, which is its spiritual life.

367. What is a venial sin?

It is a small and pardonable offence against God or our neighbor; such as an idle word,[178] and the like, into which even the just fall seven times a day,[179] which must needs be venial; for if they were mortal, the just that daily fall into them would be no longer just, but impious and wicked.

368. What are the effects of venial sin?

It does not rob the soul of grace, as mortal sin does, but only weakens the fervor of charity, and by degrees disposes a person to mortal sin, for "he that contemneth small things, falleth by little and little."[180]

---

[177] Cf. Rom 6:23
[178] Cf. Mt 12:36
[179] Cf. Prv 24:16
[180] Ecclus 19:1

369. **Is every personal sin voluntary and deliberate?**

It is, because no man sins by doing that which it is not in his power to avoid.

370. **By what rule shall I be able to know whether my sins be mortal or venial?**

For a mortal sin, three things are required, viz: a perfect advertency, a deliberate consent, and a weighty matter against the law of God; any one of these conditions being wanting, the sin is not mortal, but only venial.

371. **But how shall I know when there is a perfect advertency and a deliberate consent?**

There are three sorts of advertency on the part of the understanding, to which correspond three different consents of the will. For first, the understanding perceives the object to be agreeable to the senses without the least reflection of its being either forbidden or commanded; and the will consents to the object thus proposed. This advertency and consent are quite indeliberate, and consequently, excuse a person from the guilt of both mortal and venial sin.

Secondly, a person has an obscure notion or a glimmering knowledge of the unlawfulness of the object, (such as a person has when he is half asleep) to which corresponds a consent of the will to the object thus proposed. This advertency is imperfect, and the consent somewhat though not quite indeliberate, and consequently, will suffice for a venial but not for a mortal sin.

Thirdly, a person has a clear and distinct knowledge of the unlawfulness of the object, or at least of the danger of its being unlawful; and if this advertency be joined with a deliberate consent of the will to the object thus proposed, the person sins mortally if the object be a weighty matter against the law of God or of his superiors, but if the matter be trivial, he sins but venially.

372. **How shall I be able to know whether the matter be weighty or trivial, and consequently mortal or venial in itself?**

The matter is esteemed weighty, when the word of God represents it to us as hateful to God, against which God pronounces a woe, or the Church denounces an excommunication; and when the scripture declares that such as do those things shall not enter into the kingdom of heaven; as also, when the thing commanded or forbidden is very conducive to the honor of God, to the good of our neighbor, to the end intended by the lawgiver, or on the contrary, directly opposite to these ends. But if the thing forbidden or commanded do but slightly conduce to, or deviate but a little from these ends, the matter is to be esteemed trivial, and consequently the sin is not mortal, but only venial, though there should be a perfect advertency and a deliberate consent.

But though it be easy to know by these rules that some sins are mortal, and others but venial, yet to pretend to be able to distinguish in all practical cases which are mortal and which are not, is above the reach of the most able divines.

373. **May not a person do a thing that is a mortal sin in itself, and yet sin but venially by so doing?**

He may in three cases. First, when he has not a perfect advertency, nor a doubt of its being mortal. Secondly, when he has a perfect advertency of its being mortal, but yet his will does not fully consent to what is proposed, though he may be somewhat careless and negligent, by not using sufficient endeavors to resist and repel evil thoughts, if it be only some small neglect. Thirdly, when the sin is in a divisible matter. For example, theft is in itself a mortal sin, but as another man's property which is the matter of theft may be of either a great or small value, to steal a thing of no great value is but a venial sin.

374. **But are there not some sins which are always mortal in themselves?**

There are, viz: all those sins that are immediately opposite to the virtues that immediately relate to God or to any of his divine attributes, such as: infidelity, heresy, despair of God's mercy, the hatred of God, perjury, simony, and according to the best divines, all sins of impurity. So that a person never sins venially in these matters for want of a weighty matter, though he may often sin therein but venially, for want of a perfect advertency or a deliberate consent.

375. **Do many venial sins make one mortal?**

They do, if the different matters of them be morally united; but they do not, if the matters be morally discontinued.

376. **When are the different matters of venial sins morally united and morally discontinued?**

They are morally united by reason of the same time, precept, or person. On the contrary, they are morally discontinued by reason of different times, precepts, or persons.

377. **Explain that by some examples.**

First, if a person upon a fasting day takes at different times so many small quantities of victuals, that all put together they make up a considerable quantity sufficient to break the fast, by taking the last small quantity he sins mortally; because the time, precept, and person are the same. The same happens to him who works upon a Sunday or holy day at different times, or is willfully distracted for different small spaces of time in hearing a Mass of obligation or saying prayers of the same nature; if all these small transgressions being joined together make up a weighty matter, with regard to any one precept. The same also may be said of a person who at different times steals from the same or different owners so many trifles, that all being put together they make up a sufficient matter to do the owners a considerable prejudice.

Secondly, if a person takes different small quantities of fasting-food upon different fasting days, he commits different venial sins, all which will not make one mortal sin; because though the precept be the same, yet the times are different, and one day's fast has no connection at all with that of another. In the like manner, a person bound to hear Mass, abstain from servile works, and to say the divine office on the same day; if he should slightly transgress each of these precepts, he does not sin mortally; because though the time be the same, yet the precepts are different. Thus also, if you should induce different persons to work for a short time upon a Sunday or holy day, for different persons, you do not sin mortally; because though the time and precept be the same, and the work done by them be as much as could be done by one person in five- or six-hours' time; yet the persons are different, and one man's work has no connection at all with that of another.

378. **When is a person guilty of another man's sins?**
As often as he is an effectual cause of sin in others, by any of these nine means, viz: by counsel, by command, by consent, by provocation, by praise or flattery, by silence, by connivance, by participation, and by defense of the ill done.

379. **Does ignorance excuse a person from all guilt of sin?**
It does, if it be invincible; but it does not, if it be but vincible.

380. **How shall I know whether my ignorance be vincible or invincible?**
If no knowledge, doubt, or suspicion occurred to you concerning the unlawfulness of the action or omission, or, if any such thing has occurred, you have used proper diligence to depose your doubt or suspicion, then your ignorance is esteemed invincible and inculpable. But if any doubt or remorse has occurred, and you do not use proper diligence to depose it, then your ignorance is vincible and culpable.

381. **Supposing that some doubt has occurred, what diligence am I obliged to use in order to depose it?**
You are not obliged to use an extraordinary diligence, or that which is often used by over-nice and scrupulous people. It is enough that you use a moral diligence, or that which is commonly used by prudent and conscientious Christians on the like occasions, according to the importance of the matter and the quality of their persons; so that the diligence that will suffice for deposing the doubts of an illiterate person, and for resolving a common moral case, will not suffice for deposing the doubts of a learned man, nor for resolving a very intricate moral case.

382. **Give me some examples of an ordinary or moral diligence.**
When you buy anything, you are not obliged to ask the seller whether it be stolen; unless you have some strong motive to suspect that it was stolen,

by seeing that it is a chalice or some very valuable thing which is not commonly sold by such kind of sellers. In the like manner, though you should foresee that you may forget some sins at confession, you are not obliged to pen down your sins in order to remember them at confession, because this is an extraordinary diligence. Thus also, an illiterate person may depose his doubts, in virtue of what he is told by his parish priest, and all penitents (generally speaking) may do the same, in virtue of what they are told by their confessors, whom they should suppose to know their duty, unless the contrary appears evident to them.

383. **How is vincible ignorance divided?**

Into affected and supine. The first is a desire of being ignorant of our duty, that we may sin with less check and remorse of conscience. The second is a neglect, carelessness, or slothfulness to know our duty.

384. **If a person be under an unavoidable necessity of transgressing either of two precepts, for example of leaving a dying man alone or of omitting to hear Mass on a Sunday, and has nobody to consult with, what is he obliged to do in this or in the like cases?**

He ought of two evils to choose the least, and as it is a less evil not to comply with the precept of hearing Mass which is merely human, he ought to omit hearing Mass, and to assist the dying man, to which he is obliged by a natural and divine precept. For when two different precepts bind at the same time, so that one cannot be observed without omitting the other, the lesser precept ceases to oblige that the greater may be observed.

The Seven Deadly or Capital Sins, Explained in a Moral Sense

385. **How many capital sins are there?**

Seven, viz: pride, covetousness, lechery, gluttony, envy, anger, and sloth.

386. **Are they always mortal sins?**

They are vulgarly so called, though in themselves they are very often but venial.

387. Why then are they called capital sins?

Because from them, as from so many heads or sources, all other sins proceed and flow; for the matter of these sins is either pleasant or profitable, and pleasure or profit are the end of the sinner's actions.

388. What is pride, when it is a mortal sin, and when but venial?

Pride is an inordinate desire of our own excellency. If this desire be accompanied with a design of not subjecting ourselves to God or to our superiors in any weighty matter, it is always a mortal sin, and cannot be venial, unless a perfect advertency or consent be wanting; that is, when it is a sudden emotion of the mind, which we cannot speedily suppress. But observe, that pride is not the same as vainglory or vanity, which is either a desire of praise, or an ostentation of our own perfections without forfeiting the subjection due to God and to our superiors, and without a formal contempt of others. This is in itself but a venial sin; unless the vainglorious place their last end in their vanities, or boast of something that is mortally injurious to God, or very prejudicial to their neighbors, in which case they sin mortally.

389. What is covetousness, when is it a mortal sin, and when but venial?

Covetousness is an inordinate desire of riches. It is mortal in three cases. First, when we desire to acquire riches by unjust means, such as: usury, simony, fraud, rapine, or theft. Secondly, when we refuse to give of that which is our own, to such as are in any extreme or moral necessity. Thirdly, when we refuse to pay debts of some considerable value. Covetousness is a venial sin in two cases. First, when what a person covets is of no great value. Secondly, when a person is over-desirous to heap up riches, but yet does not intend to acquire them by unjust means, nor refuses to pay his debts, nor to give of that which is his own, to such as are in extreme or moral necessity. Prodigality is a less grievous sin than covetousness, though it is a mortal sin to squander away a considerable part of our substance.

390. What is lechery, when is it a mortal sin, and when but venial?

Lechery is an inordinate desire of delights of the flesh. It is always in itself a mortal sin (according to the best divines) and can never be venial for want of a weighty matter, but only for want of a perfect advertency or consent. Wherefore, not only fornication, adultery, and willful pollution are mortal sins, but also unchaste sights and touches, wanton speeches, and lustful kisses; unless kisses be given by way of civility, according to the custom of some countries, and not with any desire of sensual pleasure, in which case kissing is no sin.

391. **What is gluttony, when is it a mortal sin, and when but venial?**

Gluttony is an inordinate excess in meat or drink. It is mortal in three cases. First, when a person exceeds so far as to transgress the law of God or of the Church in a weighty matter. Secondly, when it does a considerable prejudice to our health, or deprives us of the use of reason. Thirdly, when it is an immediate occasion of other mortal sins, such as: lechery, blasphemy, perjury, theft, and many others, which are very often the effects of drunkenness. Gluttony is a venial sin, when thereby we only exceed the bounds of temperance, but yet do not act against the law of God or his Church in any weighty matter, nor deprive ourselves of the use of reason, nor do a notable prejudice to our health.

392. **What is envy, when is it a mortal sin, and when but venial?**

Envy is a sadness or repining at another man's good, inasmuch as it seems to lessen our own excellency. So that when we cannot endure to see our neighbor excel us, and therefore repine at his excelling us in any weighty matter, we sin mortally. When this sadness is fixed in the will, it is commonly attended with a hatred of our neighbor, because we consider him as a person that surpasses us, and as such we abhor him; though we would fain persuade the world to the contrary by saying that we do not abhor our neighbor's person, but only his disagreeable qualifications. It is true the envious do not abhor their neighbor's person, but only their excellencies, because they cannot abide to see their neighbor surpass themselves in any perfection. But observe that envy is different from emulation, which is a noble and praiseworthy striving to do something better than others, without repining at their good. Envy is not a mortal sin, when what we envy a person in is of no great moment, and when it is a sudden emotion of the mind which we do not speedily suppress.

393. What is anger, when is it a mortal sin, and when but venial?

Anger is an inordinate desire of revenge. It is mortal in two cases. First, when we deliberately desire any grievous and unjust revenge, such as: to take away another man's life, fortune, or reputation, or to do him any mischief, which if executed, would be a mortal sin. Secondly, when a person vents his anger in such an ungovernable manner, as not to mind whether or no what he says be highly injurious to his neighbor. Anger is a venial sin in two cases. First, when it is not perfectly consented to, but rather in some measure suppressed. Secondly, when the satisfaction required for the injury sustained is of no great moment, such as: pulling a child with some heat of passion by the hair of the head, or the like. It is no revenge to wish and desire the just punishment of an offence against God, ourselves, or our neighbors.

394. What is sloth, when is it a mortal sin, and when but venial?

Sloth is a laziness to begin or prosecute good things. This vice may be considered two ways. First as a sensitive passion, whereby the body has a reluctance to the practice of virtue on account of the labor and fatigue that attends it: "For the flesh lusteth against the spirit: and the spirit against the flesh; for these are adversaries one to another."[181] Secondly, this laziness may be in the mind or will, and if thereby we break any commandment that obliges under mortal sin, on account of the labor and difficulty annexed to the observance of it, in this case, sloth is a mortal sin. But if notwithstanding the unwilling disposition of the mind to observe any commandment, on account of the labor annexed to the observance of it, yet a person will undergo this labor, and observe the commandment, though with some little reluctance and tepidity, in this case (I say) sloth is a venial sin. Thus far of sloth, inasmuch as it is a capital sin.

Sloth, as a particular vice, is a sadness or repining at our own spiritual

---

[181] Gal 5:17

good. For example, to repine at our being rationals, and not beasts; at our being bred Christians and not infidels; as also to desire our own death for any of these motives; all which acts, if perfectly deliberate, are mortal sins.

Chapter 4

Of the Ten Commandments in General

A Short Preamble to the Ten Commandments

395. **How many commandments are there?**

Ten, whereof the three first relate immediately to the honor of God; and the other seven, to the good of our neighbor.

396. **Why are they called the commandments of God?**

Because God gave them to Moses on Mount Sinai in thunder and lightning, written in two tables of stone; those of the first table relate immediately to the honor of God; and those of the second to the good of our neighbor.

397. **Are these commandments either first principles of reason, or immediate consequences from them?**

They are, and have been observed before the written law, being the very immediate dictates of natural reason. But as the light of reason had been eclipsed in many by a continued course of vice, it was convenient to renew these commandments in the written law.

398. **Can anyone come to the use of reason be invincibly ignorant of these commandments?**

He cannot as to the substance, and but seldom as to the particular circumstances of them; though it is probable, that there may be some so stupid as to invincibly think, that some of these commandments do not oblige in some particular cases. Thus, though no one can be invincibly ignorant of the unlawfulness of perjury, theft, or murder; yet some may be so weak or ill-instructed as to invincibly think it lawful for them to forswear themselves, to save their innocent neighbor's life; to kill a dying man, to put him out of pain; to steal, to relieve their own or neighbor's grievous or moral necessity.

The First Commandment Explained in a Moral Sense

399. **What are we bound to by this commandment?**

To practice four virtues, whereof three, viz: faith, hope, and charity are called theological or divine, because they immediately relate to God's honor; the fourth is the virtue of religion which ordains and appoints the exterior worship due to God. We have explained faith in the first chapter.

400. **What are we commanded by the virtue of hope?**

Three things: first, to hope and confide in God; secondly, not to despair of his mercy; thirdly, not to presume too much either upon God's mercy, or on our own merits.

401. **What ought we to hope and expect from God?**

Principally everlasting glory, through the merits of Jesus Christ, and our own merits as proceeding from God's grace.

402. **Are our good works proceeding from the grace of God meritorious of an everlasting reward?**

They are, because "blessed are (they) who are reviled and persecuted...for very great is (their) reward in heaven."[182]

---

[182] Mt 5:11

403. Is it lawful to hope and expect from God temporal conveniences?

It is, and also to pray for them, inasmuch as they may be in some measure conducive to our spiritual good.

404. When are we bound to make an act of hope?

As often as we are obliged to reinstate ourselves in the state of grace, because it is impossible for us to dispose ourselves for receiving divine grace without hoping to obtain it from God. We are also bound to make an act of hope whenever we are obliged to implore God's assistance, and when we cannot resist vehement temptations against hope without the exercise of this virtue; and also once a year; but observe, that this last obligation is complied with by receiving worthily any sacrament, as I have explained in the first chapter.

405. What is required for a mortal sin of despair?

A positive judgment that God will not give us grace or glory, and that out of this erroneous principle we omit the means proper to obtain God's grace. Whilst we endeavor to seek and practice the means necessary for salvation, we do not despair of God's mercy, though we should be diffident of our own merits.

406. What is required for a mortal sin of presumption?

To expect glory without merits, the remission of sins without repentance, or to continue in sin merely on account of a temerarious confidence in God's mercy.

407. How then must our hope be balanced betwixt despair and presumption?

By a strong confidence in God's mercy, in Christ's merits, and a humble distrust of our own works, inasmuch as they are ours.

408. What are we commanded by the virtue of charity?

To love God above all things, and our neighbor as ourselves.

409. How do we love God above all things?

By loving him as the first cause and last end of all things and as our Lord, whose commandments we should keep even with the loss of our lives and fortunes, for: "This is the charity of God, that we keep his commandments."[183]

410. How do we love God with all our soul, with all our heart, and with all our might?

We love God with all our heart, when we love him with all our understanding. With all our soul, by loving him with all our will. And with all our might, when we love him with all our deeds or actions. So that nothing should be so dear to or esteemed by us in all our thoughts, words, and actions, as God's honor and the observance of his law. Thus, we love God above all things *appretiatively* (as divines term it), that is: as to the regard and esteem we have for him; though this love may be very often less intense and less sensible to us than that which we have for worldly affairs.

411. What do you understand by loving our neighbors as ourselves?

I do not understand thereby a perfect equality of love, but only a certain rule, whereby we should regulate our love so as to do to them as we would be done to by them.

412. Are we bound to love our enemies?

We are, according to that: "But I say unto you, love your enemies."[184]

413. How are we bound to love our enemies?

We are bound, first, not to hate them, nor to desire to revenge the injury or affront offered by them. Secondly, to pray for them in general, and to be civil and courteous to them in all public meetings, so as not to give them any motive of suspecting that we bear them any ill will. Thirdly, if the injury has been done in a public manner, and a public reparation be made

---

[183] 1 Jn 5:3
[184] Mt 5:44

by the aggressor, the injured is bound to a public reconcilement. Fourthly, we are bound to be in a preparation of mind to do any charitable office to them, when their extreme or moral necessity shall require it; as also to re-salute them, if they salute us first; but to show them particular signs of a special regard or esteem is not a work of precept, but of supererogation only.

414. **When does the precept of loving God bind us?**

As to the negative precept of not hating God, it binds us at all times and upon all occasions. As to the positive precept of making an act of charity, it binds us upon the same occasions, and is complied with in the same manner as the precepts of making acts of faith and hope, which I have already explained in the first and present chapter.

415. **How do we sin against charity?**

We sin against the love of God by hating him, and by not making acts of charity when we are bound to do so. We sin against the love of our neighbor by hating him, by injuring him, by not showing him a due respect and esteem, by not relieving him in an extreme or moral necessity; as also, by scandalizing him.

416. **What is scandal, and how do we sin against charity by scandalizing our neighbors?**

Scandal (in a moral sense) is any irregular word or action that occasions the spiritual ruin of our neighbor. It is a mortal or venial sin according to the prejudice done thereby. To be guilty of scandal, it is not required that we intend the spiritual ruin of our neighbor; it is enough that we say or do anything that is a strong provocation to sin, though the effect should not follow.

417. **If a person does a thing which in itself is no occasion of sin, and without an intention of scandalizing his neighbor thereby, but yet foresees that it will occasion his neighbor's spiritual ruin, does he thereby commit scandal?**

He does not, if he has any lawful necessity or conveniency in so doing.

Thus, a woman may dress herself according to her rank, and appear in public meetings, though she should foresee that her so doing may be an occasion of her being criminally admired by some amorous spark. Thus also, a man in necessity may borrow money from a usurer, though he foresees that the usurer will not lend it without committing usury. Thus likewise, a Christian may sell to a Jew a lamb, though he knows that the Jew intends it for a paschal sacrifice; and generally speaking, anything that is equally applicable to a good or bad purpose may be done by us without committing scandal, in case of any necessity or lawful conveniency. But all things that cannot be applied but to evil designs, (such as procuring for the criminal pleasures of others; conveying love-letters; harboring, aiding or encouraging thieves, loose women and the like) all these actions I say, though never so advantageous or beneficial for our temporal conveniences, are strictly forbidden by the precept of loving our neighbor.

418. **What is commanded by the virtue of religion?**

All things appertaining to the external worship and veneration of God. The reverence due to his holy name belongs to the second commandment, and the observance of his feasts, to the third.

419. **How ought we to worship and adore God?**

By consecrating and setting apart for a religious purpose, use, or intent, everything we have: our understanding, by prayer; our will, by devotion; our external actions, by humble adorations; our substance, by oblations, sacrifices, and tithes; and finally, by performing our vows; all which are acts of religion.

420. **If a person should firmly resolve to do a good thing without an intention of binding himself thereto either under a mortal or venial sin, is such a resolution a vow?**

It is not; neither does he sin mortally by not performing it, though it should be in a weighty matter.

421. **How do we sin against religion?**

Two ways, viz: by excess and by defect.

422. **How do we sin by defect?**

By tempting God; by not revering him; by profaning sacred places with theft, murder, or lascivious actions; by abusing the true use and intent of things consecrated to religious purposes, in order to make a scoff and derision of them; all which are heinous sacrileges.

423. **How do we sin by excess?**

By any superstitious or superfluous manner of worshipping God.

424. **How many kinds of superstitions are there?**

Two. The one is a mistake of the object, to which divine worship is due, such as: giving divine worship to the devil, saints, angels, or any created being. The other is a false opinion not of the object, but only of the proper manner of religious worship, such as: worshipping the true God with vain and superfluous ceremonies, which are neither instituted by God nor by the Church.

425. **Pray explain that a little more.**

The first kind of superstition is idolatry, or the superstitious worship which is paid to idols and false gods; as also the superstitious practice of consulting wizards, witches, or fortune-tellers (who make either an express or tacit compact with the devil) in order to learn from them past or future events.

The second kind of superstition is an indecent and unseemly manner of worshipping the true God, such as: preaching false miracles; exposing false relics to veneration; looking upon dreams, the flight of birds, or any other vain observations as certain omens or tokens of good or bad luck in any undertaking; of omitting to hear Mass because there is not a set number of candles upon the altar, or hearing it with more devotion merely on account of the number of candles; and finally, reposing any religious confidence in vain and superfluous ceremonies, which are not instituted by the Church to excite our devotion and reverence to the sacred mysteries; all which if perfectly deliberate and voluntary, are mortal superstitions.

426. **But may not a person be sometimes guilty of some of the abovementioned superstitions, and yet not sin mortally thereby?**

He may, when (for instance) he does not look upon dreams, or other vain observations as certain omens of future events, but is only fearful and apprehensive (as commonly happens to the simple and ignorant) of their being of an ominous nature.

427. **How many are the vices opposite to faith?**

Three, viz: heresy, Judaism, and paganism. Heresy is an obstinate assent to any error contrary to the faith, which we have professed at least by baptism; wherefore no one who has not received baptism is guilty of this vice. Paganism is an error contrary to the faith which was never professed, but always opposed and resisted, such as: Turkism, idolatry, and other kinds of infidelity. Judaism is an error contrary to the Christian faith not received in itself, but only in its types and figures, such as the ceremonial part of the Mosaic law, which is still professed by the Jews.

428. **What is the difference between heresy and apostasy?**

Apostasy sometimes means no more than leaving a religious order, whereof a man had made profession, without a legal dispensation; but the true difference between them is that heresy forsakes one part of the acknowledged faith, and apostasy forsakes the whole.

429. **What is the difference between heresy and schism?**

Though schism has often been the source of various heresies, yet it is different from heresy; for schism is the breaking off, or going from the one true visible head of the Church, but heresy denies and rejects some point of faith.

430. **Do Catholics subject to a protestant government sin mortally by assisting at the burials and marriages of protestants?**

They do not; because such acts are rather acts of friendship or courtesy conducive to public tranquility, than acts of religion or of joining with them in prayer.

431. **Has not the Catholic Church forbid her children to marry with those who are not of the same communion?**

She has for very just motives, viz: to remove all occasions of dissensions in families, of the Catholic party being perverted, or of the children being brought up in error. Though in some places the pastors of the Church, for weighty reasons, often dispense with this prohibition.

The Second Commandment Explained in a Moral Sense

432. **What is forbidden by this commandment?**

All false, rash, and unnecessary oaths.

433. **What is an oath?**

It is the calling of God to witness what we either affirm or deny.

434. **Is the calling of God's creatures to witness an oath?**

It is.

435. **How many sorts of oaths are there?**

Three, viz: an assertory, a promissory, and an execratory. The first is the affirming of anything with an oath. The second is either the promise of a reward, or the menace of some punishment upon oath. The third is the affirming or denying of anything, with an imprecation of some evil.

436. **Is an oath sometimes lawful?**

It is, when these three conditions, viz: truth, justice, and judgment are observed.

437. When do we swear in truth, justice, and judgment?

We swear in truth, when we swear to anything as it really is, or as we conceive it to be. We swear in justice, when we swear to nothing that is sinful in itself, nor hurtful to our neighbor. We swear in judgment, when we swear in our own, or neighbor's defense.

438. How is truth preserved in the three abovementioned kinds of oaths?

For the truth of an assertory oath, it is required that the thing affirmed or denied be so in reality, or at least in the opinion of the swearer. The chief truth of a promissory and execratory oath consists in the intention of performing what is promised or threatened; the performance of which binds the swearer, except in case of a moral impossibility; so that his not performing what he has swore to, is a mortal sin, if the matter be important, or the omission greatly prejudicial to his neighbor.

439. If a man swears to do an evil thing, is he bound to keep his oath?

He is not, for an oath is no bond of iniquity.

440. Is a false oath always a mortal sin?

It is, if it be perfectly deliberate and voluntary, though the matter be never so trivial; because the heinousness of a false oath is not to be computed by the matter to which we swear, but by the injury done to God, by calling him to testify a falsity.

441. Is it always a mortal sin not to perform our vows?

It is, if they be in any weighty matter; but if the matter be trivial, by breaking our vows, we sin but venially; because by making vows we do not call God's veracity to testify our performance.

442. What think you of a man, who swears that he will do a good action, though in a trivial matter?

If he swears without an intention of performing his promise, he sins mortally; if he had this intention when he swore, and afterwards fails in the execution, it is more probable that he sins but venially; because in a promissory oath, God's veracity is not called to testify the performance of the promise, but only the intention of performing it.

443. **Is it a mortal sin to swear falsely, even in defense of our own or neighbor's life or substance?**

It is.

444. **Is it as heinous a sin to swear without necessity, as it is to swear falsely or unjustly?**

It is not, for swearing falsely (or unjustly that is: to commit any sin) are mortal sins; but swearing without necessity is but a venial sin; though the evil habit of swearing frequently without necessity vehemently disposes to mortal sin, because it disposes to swearing falsely.

445. **If a man swears to every trivial thing without minding, whether what he swears to be true or false, though it should happen to be sometimes true, and sometimes false; does he sin mortally by every act of swearing in this manner?**

He does, on account of the danger he exposes himself to of committing perjury.

446. **Is it an oath to take God's name in vain, without affirming or denying anything?**

It is not, though it is a very bad habit, which greatly disposes to swearing, and also a want of the reverence due to God's holy name.

447. **Is every vicious habit of swearing, a mortal sin?**

The habit of swearing falsely, and that of swearing without minding, whether what we swear to be true or false, are mortal sins.

448. **If a man curses or wishes his neighbor any hurt or evil, does he sin mortally thereby?**

If he falsely affirms or denies anything with an imprecation of some evil, he sins mortally. If he curses his neighbor with a desire that some terrible evil or detriment may happen to him, he is guilty of a mortal revenge. If he curses his neighbor without wishing him any considerable hurt, but merely out of a little heat of passion and anger, he sins but venially; unless his passion be so violent, as to expose him to an imminent danger of committing scandal, or some grievous extravagancy.

The Third Commandment Explained in a Moral Sense

449. **What is commanded by this precept?**

To set aside a day for the worship and service of God. The keeping holy the sabbath-day began from the creation of the world,[185] and was afterwards renewed in the Mosaic law;[186] which sabbath was afterwards changed by the Christian Church into Sunday, because Christ fully accomplished the work of our redemption, by rising from the dead on a Sunday, and by sending down the Holy Ghost on a Sunday; the primitive Church then, judging the work of our redemption to be greater than that of our creation, thought the day in which this work was completely finished to be more worthy of her religious observance than that in which God rested from the creation.

450. **If the Jewish sabbath was the day which God appointed to be the day of religious worship, how could the Church, which has not power to dispense in the law of God, change the sabbath into Sunday?**

Jews and Christians are not equally tied to the commandments, for both the moral and ceremonial part of them obliged the Jews, but the ceremonial part being abrogated by Christ's death, ceased to oblige Christians; so that the commandments do not oblige Christians any farther than they are either moral precepts or approved in the gospel; hence though the deputing of some day or other to God's service be the law of God, and a moral precept indispensable by the Church; yet inasmuch as this precept prescribes the seventh day in particular for God's worship, it is a ceremonial precept,

---

[185] Cf. Gn 2:2
[186] Cf. Ex 20:8-11

which obligeth not Christians, and by consequence can be dispensed in, and changed by the Church into Sunday.

451. **Had the Church any warrant for enjoining other holidays besides Sunday?**
She had the example of God, who in the old law (besides the weekly sabbath in memory of our creation) appointed several other festivals to be kept holy, and forbid all servile work on them: as the feast of the Pasch or Passover, in memory of the delivery of the Jews from Egypt;[187] Pentecost, in remembrance of their receiving the law;[188] the feast of Trumpets, in memory of a ram being offered by Abraham instead of Isaac;[189] the feast of Expiation, in memory of the sin of worshipping the calf, and for all sins forgotten and unknown;[190] the feast of Tabernacles, to remember God's protection in the wilderness where the Jews dwelled in tabernacles forty years;[191] the feast of Collection, in memory of the peace given in the land of promise.[192]

Besides all those feasts, which were everlasting to the Jews and could never be altered by them, there were many others instituted long after Moses, as: the feast instituted;[193] and the restoration with the new dedication of the altar,[194] which was observed by Christ.[195] The Christian Church then, in imitation of the Jewish, can warrant the institution of other festivals besides the Sunday: in honor of God, of Jesus Christ, of his Blessed Mother, and of other saints, by whose intercession we expect to obtain benefits through Jesus Christ, particularly that of imitating them, to which we are excited by the honor which we render to their happy memories, by keeping a particular day holy in honor of them.

---

[187] Cf. Lv 23:5
[188] Cf. Lv 23:16
[189] Cf. Lv 23:18
[190] Cf. Lv 23:27
[191] Cf. Lv 23:34
[192] Cf. Lv 23:36
[193] Cf. Est 9:17
[194] Cf. 1 Mc 4:37ff
[195] Cf. Jn 10:22

452. **How are we commanded by the Church to keep holy the sabbath and other festivals?**

By hearing Mass and abstaining from servile works; as also by fasting Lent and the vigils commanded.

453. **How do we comply with the precept of hearing Mass?**

By assisting at that divine sacrifice with attention and devotion.

454. **Are we obliged to see the priest, or to hear him reciting the prayers used in the Mass?**

We are not, for all that the Church commands is a moral assistance, or our presence with attention and devotion to what is there performed; that thus we may be partakers of that sacrifice.

455. **Are we obliged to hear an entire Mass?**

We are, but if we should omit hearing, or be willfully distracted in hearing a small part of it, such as: from the beginning of the Mass to the beginning of the epistle, or from the consummation to the end; we sin but venially.

456. **How do we transgress this precept for want of a due attention?**

By doing anything that is incompatible with a due attention, such as: writing, reading profane books, conversing, or willfully thinking of and dwelling upon worldly affairs. But observe, that if a man be involuntarily distracted, and yet desirous to be attentive, though he should be somewhat negligent in expelling distractions, he sins venially, but yet complies with the precept; because the purpose of being attentive implies a virtual attention, as I shall farther explain in Chapter 5.

457. **When are we excused from hearing Mass?**

In case of any moral impossibility, that is: when we cannot hear it without a considerable loss or detriment to ourselves or neighbors, in our lives, fortune, or health.

458. **Is an excommunicated person bound to hear Mass?**

If he can get himself absolved from the excommunication, and neglects to do so, he sins mortally, both by hearing Mass and by not hearing it, because it was in his power to remove the impediment of not hearing it.

459. **If a man passeth through a town or village, where a particular fast or holy day is kept, is he bound to fast or to hear Mass?**

If he only passes through the place, without making any considerable stay therein, he is not bound either to fast or to hear Mass; though it is more probable that he is bound to do both, if he remains there the most part of the morning, though he should resolve to quit it that very evening.

460. **How ought we to employ our thoughts during the time of Mass?**

To fulfil the Church precept, it is enough to attend to God, the sacrifice itself, or to be employed in any prayers whatsoever; but the most profitable way of hearing Mass is to use such prayers as are best adapted to what the priest is then doing; and to meditate on the mysteries of Christ's passion, which are there represented.

461. **Are all the faithful obliged to hear three Masses on Christmas day?**

They are not, though it is very commendable to do so.

462. **Why then are three Masses said by every priest upon Christmas day?**

To denote three different births of Christ; his eternal birth from his Father, his temporal birth from his Mother, and his spiritual birth in the hearts of good Christians.

463. **If a man should hear Mass on a Sunday or holiday, without knowing that day to have been a feast commanded by the Church, is he bound to hear a second Mass?**

He is not; unless he had an express intention of not fulfilling the precept by hearing the first; nay even in this case, it is more probable that he is not obliged to hear another Mass.

464. **What has the Church prohibited upon Sundays and holidays?**

All servile works that have more toil and labor in them than recreation or diversion, or that belong rather to the condition of a servant than to the state of a master.

465. **Are not servile works sometimes allowed by the Church, upon Sundays and holidays?**

They are, in case of any moral necessity, such as: to dress victuals, clean the house, provide fodder for cattle, not having wherewith to support ourselves or families without working upon Sundays or holidays; and in fine, when we cannot abstain from servile works without some considerable detriment either to ourselves or to our neighbor. To work without necessity for the space of three quarters of an hour is but a venial sin; to work without necessity above an hour is a mortal sin, according to the more probable opinion of divines.

466. **Are we bound to spend the Sundays and holidays in reading good books, hearing sermons, or assisting at the vespers of the day?**

Though that has been partly the Church's motive in prohibiting all servile works, that thus the faithful may have nothing to hinder them from attending to God's service and the sanctification of their souls upon these days, yet the Church precept obliges us only to hear Mass and abstain from servile works, so that all other religious works are only works of supererogation, recommended, but not commanded by the Church.

467. **If a man sins on a Sunday or holiday, is the crime more enormous, or is it a more aggravating circumstance necessary to be declared in confession, than if he had committed the same sin on a weekday?**

It is not, unless the sin has been an occasion either to himself or others, of not keeping holy the Sunday or holiday.

468. **What think you of those who spend Sundays and holidays, in writing, teaching, or the like liberal works for lucre-sake?**

They do not transgress this commandment; but those (on the contrary) do transgress it, who spend a considerable part of Sundays or holidays in servile works, merely for their pleasure or diversion.

The Fourth Commandment Expounded in a Moral Sense

469. **What are we bound to by this commandment?**

First, to love, reverence, obey, and relieve our parents, who under God are the chief causes of our being, and who have power from God to direct, instruct, and correct us. Secondly, to love our relations on account of our parents. Thirdly, to love and obey our ghostly fathers in all things belonging to faith, doctrine, and the government of our souls; because, "They watch as being to render an account of your souls."[196] Fourthly, to obey princes and temporal magistrates in all things belonging to the good and peace of the commonwealth; for, "there is no power, but from God…He therefore that resists power, resists the ordinance of God."[197] But if they should command us to do things against the law of God, then God must be obeyed, rather than men.[198]

470. **How ought children to honor their parents?**

By relieving them in any sort of distress, trouble, or affliction; by concealing their faults, by taking care that they receive the rites of the Church in their last sickness, and that their wills be faithfully executed; as also, by praying for them both living and dead.

471. **What is prohibited by this precept?**

All sorts of injustice, abuse, contempt, and disobedience to our parents.

472. **Are we obliged to observe the laws and ordinances of our superiors?**

We are, for that is a part of the reverence due to them.

---

[196] Heb 13:17
[197] Rom 13:1-2
[198] Cf. Acts 5:29

473. **How shall I be able to know, when the laws and commands of my superior bind under mortal sin?**

The knowledge of that depends greatly upon the manner in which the law is received by the subjects, and upon the intention and declaration of the lawgiver. If the superior declares that his intention is to bind us under mortal or venial sin, we are bound accordingly; unless the law be in an insignificant matter, for no human law in a trivial matter can bind us under mortal sin. If the lawgiver has not declared his intention, we deem his law to bind under mortal sin. When he threatens the transgressors with inflicting some grievous punishment upon them, such as: death, excommunication, or perpetual banishment; as also, when the law is received by the subjects, as binding under mortal sin, or when the observance of it (though the matter be insignificant in itself) is very expedient, or necessary for the common good.

474. **Are parents, princes, and superiors bound to love their children and subjects?**

They are, for this obligation is reciprocal, wherefore as children are bound to honor their parents, so are parents obliged to give their children a competent education, maintenance, and instructions in the duties of a Christian. Princes are bound to consult the interest of their subjects, to support public tranquility, to have justice duly administered; to reward virtue, to punish vice, and not to over-burthen their subjects with taxes unnecessary for the support of the state.

475. **What are servants and masters commanded by this precept?**

Servants are bound to honor their masters, to execute their lawful commands; not to steal or embezzle their substance, nor to permit others to do it. Masters are bound to pay their servants just wages, not to give them less wages than their service deserves, by taking an advantage of their necessity, or want of service; and also to make them comply with the duties of a Christian, when they can conveniently do so without any considerable loss to themselves; that is, without enmity, ill will, or the loss of very useful servants.

476. **When do parents, children, princes, subjects, masters and servants, sin mortally against this commandment?**

They sin mortally, when the sin is in any weighty matter, that is: greatly afflictive or detrimental to the injured party; if the matter be insignificant, they sin venially.

The Fifth Commandment Explained in a Moral Sense

477. **What is prohibited by this commandment?**

All murder, anger, revenge, unjust shedding of blood, fighting, quarrelling, or affronting our neighbor, wishing him any evil, or rejoicing at his misfortunes. The injury done to our neighbor by detraction properly belongs to the eighth commandment.

478. **Is it sometimes lawful to kill?**

It is. First, in a just war, or when public justice requires it; for the magistrate "beareth not the sword in vain."[199] Secondly, against an unjust invader, in the blameless defense of our own or innocent neighbor's life or fortune. In all other cases, the willful killing of a man is a mortal sin, though it be done in a duel, out of a *punctilio* of honor; nay, the Church has excommunicated *ipso facto* all duelists, and has deprived such as die in duels of Christian burial, and of the public suffrages of the Church.

479. **When does a man kill in the blameless defense of himself or neighbor?**

When he has no other means of defending his own or neighbor's life or fortune, but by killing the unjust invader; though this ought to be his last refuge; for when he can preserve his life or fortune without killing the invader, he does not kill then in his own defense.

480. **Is it lawful for princes to order their subjects to be killed, banished, or punished, as they think proper?**

It is not, but only according to the course of justice, and when the common

---

[199] Rom 13:4

good of the state requires it; for "princes are not a terror to a good work, but to an evil one."[200]

481. **Are soldiers and executioners bound to know the justice of the war or sentence before they can do their duties?**

They are not; unless they have solid reasons to doubt of the justice of the war or sentence; in which case they ought to refrain, till they be better informed. For the executioners of the martyrs sinned mortally, because they might easily know the innocence and unjust condemnation of the martyrs. But in case any doubt should remain after having made a sufficient inquiry, the doubt should be deposed, and the superior's commands obeyed.

482. **What punishment does the Church inflict on murderers?**

An irregularity, whereby they are incapable of being either admitted to holy orders, or of exercising those already received. If the person murdered be a clergyman, the murderer incurs an excommunication, unless he be invincibly ignorant of the state of the person murdered, or kills him in his own defense, in which case he neither incurs an irregularity, nor an excommunication.

483. **If a man wounds another without killing him, does he incur any ecclesiastical censure?**

If he wounds or beats a clergyman, he incurs an excommunication; if he wounds a layman, he incurs no censure thereby, unless the person wounded be maimed in some one of his limbs, in which case he that wounds incurs an irregularity.

484. **What reparation is the murderer bound to make?**

To repair all the losses and damages that ensued to the necessary heirs of the person murdered, such as: his wife, parents, and children; though he should be punished with death for the murder, because by suffering death

---

[200] Rom 13:3

he only repaired the injury done to the commonwealth, not that done to the necessary heirs of the person murdered.

485. **Is it a mortal sin to make women with child to miscarry, and to wish and desire our own death, or to kill ourselves?**

They are all mortal sins; nay, the act of committing murder or any violence upon ourselves is more heinous than that of murdering our neighbor, because it is contrary to the natural law of self-preservation, for charity begins at home, and such as murder themselves commonly despair of the mercy and providence of God.

The Sixth Commandment Expounded in a Moral Sense

486. **What is prohibited by this commandment?**

All sorts of lechery either by thought, word, or deed.

487. **How many sorts of lechery are there?**

Eight, viz: simple fornication, adultery, debauching of a maiden, incest, sacrilege, pollution, sodomy, and bestiality.

488. **How does fornication differ from adultery?**

If both parties are single and sin by mutual consent, it is called simple fornication. If the woman be a maiden, it changes the nature of the sin, and makes it of a more grievous kind, and still more so, if she be forced against her will. If one of the parties be married, it is adultery, and doubly so, if both are married.

489. **How does fornication differ from incest and sacrilege?**

If the parties be related within the forbidden degrees of matrimony, that is, within four degrees of relation either by blood or marriage, it is called incest. If either of the parties be consecrated to God, either by receiving holy orders, by profession in a religious order, or by a vow of chastity, it is called sacrilege.

490. **Why are sodomy, bestiality, and pollution called sins against nature?**

Not only because all sins against chastity are contrary to the law of nature, but also because the very manner of committing these sins is contrary to the common and usual course of nature: wherefore each of them are two different mortal sins.

491. **What else is forbidden by this commandment?**

All unchaste touching of ourselves or others, and all carnal delights in lustful thoughts and kisses, because, "for fornication, uncleanness, lust, evil concupiscence...the wrath of God comes upon the children of incredulity."[201]

492. **Can anyone have an invincible ignorance of the unlawfulness of willful pollution or of the other kinds of lechery?**

He cannot, though he were bred among infidels; nay, though the committing of any of those sins should be necessary for the preservation of his life. For unless we shut our eyes against the light of reason, the very shame and confusion that attend the committing of any of those sins, sufficiently convince us of their heinousness and enormity.

493. **Are we bound to avoid all the occasions of lust?**

We are bound under mortal sin to avoid all the immediate occasions, but not the remote causes of it. The immediate occasions are such as are either impure in themselves, or cannot be put in use without an imminent danger of consenting to the impurity that follows, such as: unchaste touching of ourselves or others; beholding some immodest part of our bodies; unchaste discourse; reading lewd books; too much familiarity between persons of different sexes; their dwelling together without any great necessity or lawful motive, particularly such as have had a criminal commerce. The remote occasions are such as are not frequently attended with an imminent danger of sin; though they may be sometimes the occasion thereof, such as: modest conversation between persons of different sexes by way of courtesy,

---

[201] Col 3:5-6

pastime, or diversion; dressing in an over-gay, though modest manner; dancing, singing, or the like done without a lustful design.

494. **When is a person so miserably immersed in this vice, as to be incapable of receiving absolution?**

In three cases. First, when he cohabits with the accomplice of his sin, or is so familiar with him, as to have him at his beck and disposal. Secondly, when he refuses to forsake the immediate occasions of this vice, or his aiding and assisting others therein, by encouraging them or procuring lewd women to satisfy their lustful inclinations. Thirdly, when he frequently defiles himself with willful pollution, and seeks means to incite himself to that vile practice.

495. **Are deliberate lustful thoughts mortal sins?**

If there be a desire or intention of executing them, doubtless they are mortal sins; nay, without any such intention the sensual pleasure taken in lustful thoughts is a mortal sin. If there be no sensual delight, nor intention of executing lustful thoughts, but only a short dwelling of the mind upon the difficulty and contrivance of an intrigue, this (I say) is not a mortal sin; though it is very dangerous, because it vehemently disposes to a sensual delight of the object, which delight is a mortal sin.

496. **Are we bound under mortal sin to leave off the practice of all things or actions, whence pollution may follow either in our sleep, or when we are awake?**

There are two sorts of actions whence pollution may follow. Some are in themselves criminal, and vehemently dispose to pollution, such as: unchaste discourse, immodest touching of ourselves or others. Others are in themselves good and laudable, or at least indifferent, such as: hearing in confession the lewd actions of others; applying remedies to some immodest part of our bodies; regaling ourselves with delicious meat or drink. Now, that the pollution which follows from these things should not be imputed to us, two conditions are required. First, that it be merely permitted, and no way procured, nor intended. Secondly, that the will should not consent to, nor take any sensual pleasure in it; for if we find by experience that the vehemence of the temptation frequently overpowers the will, and forces it to consent, and take pleasure in the pollution that follows, we are bound to avoid all remote occasions thereof, though never so innocent or laudable in themselves. If a person finds himself defiled by pollution without concurring or consenting thereto, though he does not sin mortally, he has reason to doubt of his not having made a sufficient resistance.

497. **If a person addicted to this vice, through the absolute necessity of his circumstances, cannot forsake the occasions of it without exposing himself or his accomplice; what is he bound to do?**

To use proper means to prevent his relapsing into the same sin, such as: to implore God's grace; to frequent the sacraments; to break off all private communication with the accomplice. But if these means will not suffice, he is bound to avoid the occasion of his fall, even at the loss of his life and fortune.

498. **What think you of such as boast of their criminal intrigues?**

If they boast of any mortal sin, or willfully delight therein, or if their boasting be an inducement or occasion of a mortal sin to others, they sin mortally. If without any of these circumstances, they only boast of the manner, art, or dexterity wherewith they committed the sin, they sin venially.

499. **What think you of a person who praises another for having committed a mortal sin, or reproaches him for not having committed it?**

I think that he sins mortally in both cases.

500. **But what if he should boast of virtue or any other qualifications wherewith he is not endued, or vainly admit the false applause of others for them?**

If he does that without any considerable prejudice to his neighbor, he sins venially; if with an intent of doing any notable hurt to his neighbor, he sins mortally. Wherefore, unskillful physicians, lawyers, and ignorant clergymen who pretend to more knowledge or merits than they really have, to impose upon their patients, clients, or to get a Church-living, sin mortally;

as also, such as pretend to false revelations, to delude the ignorant, and impose upon their credulity.

The Seventh Commandment Expounded in a Moral Sense

501. **What is prohibited by this commandment?**
Three different kinds of theft, viz: simple theft, which is a secret taking away of another man's property; rapine, which is a violent open taking away, or keeping of another man's goods; and sacrilege, which is the stealing of sacred things, or of anything out of a sacred place.

502. **When is theft a mortal sin?**
When the thing stolen is of a considerable value, or causes a notable hurt to our neighbor. But observe that a thing which is insignificant in itself, may be of a very considerable value to some particular persons. Thus, a needle or a loaf of bread are insignificant things in themselves, though of very great importance to a tailor who has not another to work with, and to a poor man who has not another loaf to support nature. Wherefore the theft of such things from persons in these circumstances is a mortal sin, on account of the notable hurt that ensues.

503. **When is a thing of considerable value, so that the stealing of it is a mortal sin?**
The knowledge of that depends greatly upon a due consideration of the circumstances of time, place, and persons; for in some places where there is a great plenty of money, a greater sum is required for a mortal sin. In other places where there is a great scarcity of money, a less quantity will suffice. In the like manner, the circumstance of the person from whom the thing is stolen ought to be considered: for ten shillings are of no considerable value to a king, though they may be very considerable to a rich subject, and the third part of that sum, of great importance to a man of a moderate fortune; wherefore to steal that sum from him is a mortal sin. But observe that there are some matters of theft of a considerable value with regard to all sorts of people, such as a moidore or anything above it.

Others again are insignificant with regard to all degrees of people, such as three, or four pence.

504. **What think you of a man who by degrees steals or embezzles many trivial things, which put together amount to a considerable value?**
If at each time he stole a trifling thing, he had an intention of stealing a thing of considerable value, or of continuing to steal trifling things till they might amount to a considerable value, he sinned mortally by each theft. But if he only steals a trifling thing this day, and another tomorrow, without an intention of continuing in the same course, he sins venially by each theft, and mortally by stealing the last trivial thing which joined to the precedent makes up a thing of a considerable value.

505. **What think you of innkeepers, shopkeepers, or the like who defraud or overcharge their customers in things which are but mere trifles to each, though in themselves very considerable, if all were put together?**
I think that they sin mortally on account of the notable detriment done to the public.

506. **If a man receives anything of value for the loan of his money, does he sin mortally?**
He does, for he commits usury which is the receiving of money or money's-worth as gain above the principal, immediately out of the consideration of loan.

507. **What think you of a man who gets competent security for his principal, and besides receives interest for the use of it for a certain time?**
I think that he commits usury, because in this case he has no other title to receive anything above his principal but the loan of his money.

508. **If a person sells a thing for more than the just price, because he sells it upon trust, does he commit usury?**
He does; as also he that buys for less than the just price, because he pays beforehand.

509. **What is the just price of a thing?**

There are three prices: the highest, middle, and lowest; for example, 8, 10, and 12. When a fixed price is not set upon a thing by public authority, the buyer may buy at the lowest price, and the seller may sell at the highest.

510. **But is it not sometimes lawful for the seller to sell for more than the highest price, for the buyer to buy for less than the lowest, and for the lender to receive interest for the use of his money?**

It is in these cases. First, when there is a risk of danger or losing the principal. Secondly, when they sustain any loss by selling upon trust, paying beforehand, or lending their money. Thirdly, when they have a fair prospect of gaining by negotiating with their money, or of buying lands or tenements which may rent at the rate of 4, 6, or 8 percent, and these opportunities are missed by lending their money, selling upon trust, or paying beforehand.

511. **How do men generally sin against this precept?**

Princes, by imposing unjust taxes on their subjects; subjects, by not paying the taxes due to their princes; buyers and sellers, by selling with deceitful weights and measures, or by exceeding the just price; masters, by defrauding servants of their wages; servants, by embezzling their master's goods; simoniacs, by giving or receiving for money or money's-worth any Church-benefice, and by selling any sacred thing.

512. **Are we bound to restore whatever is acquired by theft, rapine, or any of the abovementioned frauds?**

We are, if we be able so to do; otherwise, the sin will not be forgiven.

513. **How many are the sources whence the obligation of restitution doth arise?**

Two, viz: the unjust taking way, and the unjust keeping of another man's property. For example, when I do any notable hurt to my neighbor by burning his house, destroying his lands, without any real advantage to myself, I am bound to make restitution on account of the unjust taking away of his property. If I buy a stolen thing without knowing that it was stolen, when I discover that it was stolen, I am obliged to restore it to the right owner, because it is his property.

514. **Who else besides the thief are bound to make restitution?**

All that any ways concur with him in committing the theft, by encouraging, accompanying, harboring or concealing him; as also by receiving the theft.

515. **If many persons concur in the different said ways to commit the same theft, is each of them bound to make restitution of the whole?**

If they all agree among themselves to restore their respective shares, this will suffice; but upon the failure of any of them, the rest, nay each of them is bound to restore the whole.

516. **What think you of a person who steals a thing of small value, and at the same time knows that others steal from the same owner several trifles, which put together amount to a considerable detriment?**

I think that he does not sin mortally, unless he concurs in some manner with the other thieves, in which case he sins mortally.

517. **Can a man who committed theft, or any other kind of injustice defer or be excused from making restitution?**

He cannot, unless he be either really or morally unable to make it, or the injured party forgives him.

518. **When is a person really or morally unable to make restitution?**

He is really unable, when he has not wherewith to make restitution. He is morally unable, when by making restitution he must needs want what is necessary for decently supporting himself according to his rank; or when he cannot make restitution without exposing his life or character. But observe, that many are grossly deceived in this point for want of adjusting what may be necessary for the support of their state and defense of their character; wherefore confessors should examine them very exactly in this point, and defer or deny them absolution, till they first put this matter to rights.

519. **If a person cannot make restitution in money or effects, is he bound to make it by serving the injured party in the state of a servant?**
He is, if he can so do without infamy or disgrace to himself or family.

520. **How ought we to make restitution, when we know not who is the right owner, nor where he is, or if he should happen to be in some very remote place?**
We ought to use all possible diligence to find out the right owner, or his heirs. If we know that the owner is a great way off, we should either wait for his return, or write him to dispose of his property. If we know the owner, but are ignorant of what part of the world he is in, we should wait for an opportunity of finding it out. But if after using all such diligence, the owner cannot be discovered, nor is there any probable hopes of his return, or the expenses of remitting the thing stolen are more than it is worth; then the thing stolen may be given to the poor; unless there be some particular law that appoints such things to be applied to other pious uses.

The Eighth Commandment Expounded in a Moral Sense

521. **What is prohibited by this commandment?**
All false testimony, judgment, suspicion, calumny, detraction, twitting or upbraiding others with their faults.

522. **How many sorts of detraction are there?**
Two. One is called calumny, which is a false charge of a crime, whereof the accused is wholly innocent. The other is called detraction or slander, which is the undervaluing or backbiting of our neighbor, by accusing him of crimes, which he has really committed; for though a person has committed faults, if he stands fair in the eyes of the world, he has a right to continue so, until his crimes betray themselves by becoming public and notorious.

523. Is detraction sometimes a venial sin?

It is in three cases. First, for want of a perfect advertency or deliberate consent. Secondly, when the evil told of our neighbor is of no great moment, nor detriment to him. Thirdly, when the crime told is public and notorious.

524. When is the subject of detraction of no great detriment to the person spoken of?

That must be regulated by the quality and circumstance of the person spoken of; for though it is commonly a mortal sin to divulge our neighbor's mortal crimes, and but a venial sin to publish his venial faults or natural imperfections; yet, in some circumstances, it may be a mortal sin to divulge venial faults; and a venial sin only, to publish mortal crimes. Thus, to say of an amorous spark, that he delights in criminal intrigues, or of a military man, that he is addicted to duels, is but a venial sin, (though the crimes told be mortal) because such people commonly glory in the like crimes. On the contrary, to say of a modest woman that she is a vast admirer of her own beauty, and of the company of libertines; or of a sober grave man that he lies upon all occasions, are in themselves subjects of a venial detraction only; though they may be mortal sins in some circumstances, when they give the hearers a bad opinion of, or do a notable hurt to the person spoken of.

525. When is a crime sufficiently public and notorious, so that the divulging of it to others ignorant thereof is not a mortal sin?

A crime may be notorious two ways. First, by the authority and public sentence of a judge. Secondly, by the notoriousness of the fact, because it is committed in a public place, or in such a public manner, that the criminal did not regard who might know it. If the crime be notorious by the public sentence of a judge, it is not a mortal sin to publish it in all parts of the world. If the crime be notorious by the notoriousness of the fact, that is: known to the majority of the inhabitants of the city, village, college, or convent, where the crime was committed; for example, if the crime be known to six out of ten, it is not a mortal sin to reveal it to the other four, who were ignorant thereof. But it is a mortal sin to publish the same crime in any other place, or to any other persons who do not reside in the place where it is notorious. But observe, that if a person be publicly defamed in the metropolis of a kingdom whither people flock from all parts of the same kingdom, his infamy is deemed to be notorious to the whole kingdom; nor is it required for the notoriousness of a crime committed in a very populous city, that it be known by the majority of the inhabitants; it is enough it be committed in such a public manner that it may easily come to the knowledge of the majority.

526. Is not a kind of defamation sometimes lawful?

It is in two cases, when fraternal correction precedes and has not the desired effect. First, when it is absolutely necessary for the amendment of the very delinquent. Secondly, when it is necessary for preventing a notable hurt to the state, ourselves, or our innocent neighbor.

527. Give me some examples of that.

First, when servants and children cannot be otherwise reclaimed, it is lawful to reveal their faults to their masters and parents. Secondly, it is lawful to discover the thief or murderer, when it is necessary for freeing the innocent from the imputation of theft or murder. Thirdly, if an ignorant person pretends to be an able artist, physician, or lawyer, in order to impose upon the public, it is lawful to reveal his incapacity, to prevent his doing mischief. Fourthly, when a worthless person is to be admitted into religion or holy orders, or to be promoted to a Church-benefice, it is lawful to reveal his hidden faults, to prevent his own spiritual ruin and a considerable detriment to the Church. Fifthly, it is very probable, that the defamed or injured person can lawfully tell a friend or two his grievance, in order to have it redressed, to ask their advice or unburthen his own mind of the affliction he is in.

528. Is it a mortal sin to hearken to or to connive at a grievous detraction?

To hearken or connive at it, so as to encourage the detractor, is a mortal sin against justice. To do it out of hatred or aversion to the defamed is a sin against charity, and a very heinous one in a superior to connive at the detractions of his subjects.

529. **What think you of private persons who neither delight in detraction, nor encourage detractors, but only out of fear, shame, or complaisance do not hinder detraction, when they can conveniently hinder it without any considerable detriment to themselves?**

I think it more probable, that they sin but venially, unless they know that some notable hurt will ensue to their neighbor from their not resisting the detractor. Wherefore a mortal obligation of resisting the detractor seldom binds equals, and very rarely a subject with regard to his superior. First, because he that hearkens to detraction seldom knows whether what the detractor tells be notorious or not; whereas several things may be sufficiently public and notorious without being known to him; and in case he should doubt whether the crime was sufficiently notorious, he should presume it was; because he should judge that he who now publishes it has a sufficient motive for so doing. Secondly, when the detractor has once begun, it is often more expedient to let him go on than to interrupt him; because by his being interrupted the hearers often form a worse notion (though but obscure) of the person defamed, than if they had heard his faults in particular. Thirdly, we can seldom resist the detractor without some great inconveniency to ourselves, and without offending the detractor, who commonly takes it very ill to be resisted or upbraided with his detractions.

530. **What is a lie, and when is it a mortal sin?**

A lie is an untruth spoken with an intent of deceiving the hearers. Wherefore when a person tells a falsity which he thinks to be a real truth, he does not properly lie; neither is he a liar, who relates falsities in such a jocose or ironical manner, that the hearers may easily perceive that he does not intend they should believe what he says. In the like manner, nurses and parents are not liars by telling children incredible things, to frighten or please them; because if the children believe such things, it is more owing to their weakness than to the falsity of the words. This being supposed, I say that a lie is a mortal sin when it does any great dishonor to God, or notable hurt to our neighbor; if it be merely officious or jocose, it is a venial sin.

531. What is a secret, when is it a mortal sin not to keep it, and when is it lawful to reveal it?

A secret is an affair not proper to be publicly known, and this may come to our knowledge three ways. First, by knowing our neighbor's faults casually, industriously, or by the relation of others, without promising to keep them secret. This is called a natural secret. Secondly, when the matter in itself does not bind to secrecy; neither is it communicated under any such obligation, but the hearer of his own accord obliges himself to keep it secret. This is called a promised, but not an enjoined secret. Thirdly, an affair is communicated to us as a secret, and we promise not to reveal it. This may happen two ways: First, when a matter is expressly communicated as a secret, and secrecy is expressly promised. Secondly, when by the circumstance of the matter and of the person to whom it is told, it appears that it is tacitly communicated as a secret and secrecy is tacitly promised. Thus, physicians, surgeons, midwives, and divines, who are consulted about cases of conscience, or prescribing remedies for disgraceful infirmities, are bound not to reveal what is communicated to them. This is called an enjoined and promised secret.

If the secret be a natural one in any matter of weight, it is a mortal sin to reveal it, unless the revealing of it be necessary for avoiding exquisite tortures. If the secret be promised but not enjoined, and no notable hurt follows from revealing it, the revealing of it is either a mortal or venial sin according to the intention of him who promised secrecy; for if, when he promised secrecy, he intended to bind himself thereto under mortal sin, he sins mortally by revealing it; but if he only intended to bind himself in courtesy and good manners, he sins but venially by revealing it. But observe that though he should bind himself under mortal sin, nay under oath, not to reveal this kind of secret; yet he is bound to declare it, when he is juridically examined. If the secret be promised and enjoined, the person to whom it was imparted is bound not to disclose it, though he should be juridically examined, for it is not in a judge's power to repeal the natural obligation, which this secret implies.

532. **But is it not sometimes lawful, or at most a venial sin only, to reveal a secret communicated under a promised secrecy?**

It is in three cases. First, when the matter is of no great moment. Secondly, when no infamy nor damage follows, it is but a venial sin to disclose it to one or two prudent men, who will keep it secret from others; unless these two be persons from whom he that entrusted the secret would have the matter concealed for certain motives, in which case it is a mortal sin to reveal it to such persons. Thirdly, when the keeping of a secret is contrary to justice or charity; wherefore it is lawful to disclose a secret promised to be kept even upon oath, when the disclosing of it is necessary for reclaiming the person who first disclosed it; for defending our own or innocent neighbor's life or fortune; for gaining a just lawsuit or the like. The secret of confession only binds at the loss of our lives, fortunes, and the common good of Church and state.

533. **Is it a mortal sin to pry into the secrets of others?**

It is, if the secret be an affair of moment; unless in case of necessity, such as: to confer a benefice; to elect a superior; to contract marriage, or the like, in which cases, these whom it may nearly concern, may pry into the private faults of those with whom they intend to be concerned. But observe that if they discover any secret faults, they are bound not to publish them without a lawful motive.

534. **What think you of a person who opens letters directed to others, or reads such as are found opened upon another man's table or desk?**

I think that he sins mortally in both cases; unless he has the express or tacit consent of either him who wrote the letters, or of him to whom they were directed. For example, if there be so great a familiarity between me and another, that I may reasonably presume he will not take it ill of me to open or read his letters, then I may lawfully do so. In the like manner I may lawfully intercept or open the letters of my enemy, when I presume they contain something, the knowledge whereof may prevent a considerable detriment to me or to the public. Wherefore generals may intercept the enemy's letters, and governors those of citizens, when they think it necessary for discovering the enemy's design, or conducive to the public good.

535. What is a rash judgment, and what is the difference between it and a rash suspicion or doubt?

A rash judgment is a certain and positive decision of an affair, grounded upon slight motives, or mere surmises. A rash suspicion is a jealousy or mistrust grounded upon insufficient motives. A doubt is a suspense and uncertainty of what to determine or resolve on. Wherefore the grounds that will suffice for forming a prudent doubt or suspicion, will not suffice for forming a prudent judgment.

536. How shall I know when I form a judgment, doubt, or suspicion?

If you be absolutely certain of what you determine in your mind, you form a judgment; if but mistrustful, though somewhat more inclined to think so, you form a suspicion; and if you know not which side of the question to take, you form a doubt.

537. When is a rash judgment a mortal sin?

For that, four conditions are required, any one of which being wanting, the sin is but venial. First, the judgment must be positive or certain, and of some particular known person; wherefore when I am only mistrustful of my neighbor's crimes, I sin but venially; unless I suspect him to be guilty of some uncommon or very heinous crime, such as: committing incest; or being a Jew in his heart, and a Christian exteriorly, in which or the like cases, it is probable, that I sin mortally. In the like manner, if I see an unacquainted person passing by, I do not sin mortally by judging him to be a rogue or a thief, because in supposition of his not being known to me, the injury done him is very insignificant.

Secondly, the judgment must be groundless; for if it be founded upon reasonable motives, it is not a rash, but rather a prudent judgment. For example, if I see a man scaling at night his neighbor's windows, it is not a rash judgment to think that he intends to rob or steal. In the like manner, if I see a man going to the public stews, or kissing a lady in the dark, it is not a rash judgment to think that his intentions are lewd and dishonest.

Thirdly, the evil which we judge of our neighbor must be of some moment, and very afflictive to him according to his rank and condition. But to know what is an important or insignificant matter of rash judgment with regard to the different ranks of people, see what I have already said in the present chapter about the matter and subject of detraction.

Fourthly, it is required that we perceive the motives of forming our judgment to be groundless, and yet persevere in our judgment; for though the motives may be unreasonable in themselves, they may seem very reasonable to us; wherefore for the ease of scrupulous persons, who are often perplexed about rash judgments, I shall observe to them one thing, viz: that they are seldom guilty of rash judgment, because though they be often tempted with sinister thoughts of their neighbors, yet they seldom give a positive and certain assent thereto, at least without thinking that the motives they have are reasonable and sufficient.

538. **If a person has sufficient grounds to doubt of his neighbor's honesty, how ought he to resolve the doubt?**

If he intends to proceed to a positive decision, he is bound to take that side of the question which is more favorable to his neighbor; if he only intends to continue in his doubt without determining it on one side or the other, he may suspend his judgment, for then he is not obliged to determine his doubt on the most favorable side to his neighbor.

539. **But is it not sometimes lawful to resolve and take the side of the doubt which is less favorable to our neighbor?**

It is both lawful and commendable to do so, when it is necessary for preventing a future evil, or applying a remedy against it; not that we can (even in these cases) positively judge it to be so, but we may imagine and suppose it to be so, and apply as efficacious a remedy against it, as if we had been positively certain thereof. Thus, if a master takes an unknown servant, he cannot positively judge him to be a thief, but he may make a false supposition of his being one, and be as cautious of him as if he had positively judged him to be a thief. The same I say of parents, husbands, and superiors; with regard to their children, wives, and subjects.

540. **What does a sin of rash judgment or suspicion oblige us to?**

To make restitution by forming a contrary judgment or suspicion of our neighbor.

541. **What does a sin of detraction oblige us to?**

To restore our injured neighbor his fame and reputation.

542. **But what if the detractor cannot do that without an evident risk of his own life or reputation?**

If he cannot make restitution without sustaining a considerably greater loss than the person defamed has suffered, then he may either defer it to another time, or retire to some remote place, whence he may make restitution without endangering his life or fortune.

543. **How shall I know, when the detractor sustains a greater loss by making restitution, than his injured neighbor has suffered by his detractions?**

If the loss be equal on both sides, then the detractor is bound to sustain it. For example, if the detractor has told a lie, which has been as prejudicial to his neighbor as the unsaying of it would be to himself, then he is bound to unsay it. But if by making restitution he must inevitably sustain a considerably greater loss than the person defamed suffers by his not making it, then the detractor is not bound to make it. For example, if he has told a lie somewhat prejudicial to his neighbor, and by unsaying it, he must unavoidably sustain the loss of his life or of all his substance, then he is exempted from the obligation of making restitution, which is deemed morally impossible in this or the like cases.

544. **If a calumniator has defamed his neighbor by publishing his secret, though real crimes, how ought he to make restitution?**

That is a point which requires a vast deal of prudence and circumspection;

for we often mistake the right method of making restitution, whereas by abruptly unsaying what we have said, we often furnish the hearers with a handle to think that we do so out of a remorse of conscience, and not because what we have said was false. Wherefore, two things should be duly weighed.

First, the prejudice that may follow to the injured party from his reputation not being immediately restored; as also, the damage that may follow to the calumniator from his unsaying what he has said; whether it be greater than that which the person defamed suffers, as I have already explained.

Secondly, the calumniator should wait for a seasonable opportunity of making restitution; for though he can justly say that he was mistaken, when he either belied his neighbor, or published his secret faults; whereas by revealing them he sinned, and every sin is a mistake. Yet when no considerable damage follows to the defamed from putting restitution off to another time, the calumniator should wait for a seasonable opportunity of praising and speaking well of the person defamed without giving the hearers to understand that he does so out of a remorse of conscience, or to comply with the duty of restitution; nay, if he prudently apprehends that by speaking of the person defamed or of his character, instead of giving the hearers a better opinion of him, he may do him a greater prejudice by renewing in their minds the ideas of past and perhaps forgotten faults; it is more expedient to say nothing at all about the affair, but rather bury it in oblivion.

The Ninth and Tenth Commandment Expounded in a Moral Sense

545. **What is prohibited by these commandments?**
The inordinate desire of lust and riches; as also, all voluntary delight or complacency in covetous and impure thoughts.

546. **Is not the desire of murder, perjury, and of all other things forbidden by the ten commandments, as much prohibited, as the unreasonable desire of lust and riches?**
It is.

547. **When then is the desire of lust and riches prohibited in a special manner by these two commandments? For that seems to have been forbidden by the sixth and seventh commandment.**

Though the sixth and seventh commandment, by expressly forbidding lust and theft, have implicitly prohibited all unreasonable desire thereof, yet God was pleased to prohibit expressly the desire of lust and riches, but not that of murder, perjury, etc., because those crimes which nature itself abhors are no ways pleasing nor delightful in themselves, but are committed merely to gratify some other passion of avarice, revenge, etc. But riches and venereal things are in themselves delightful objects, which play smoothly upon the external senses, and vehemently solicit the will to a desire of them. Wherefore it was proper to prohibit by different precepts not only all external facts, but also all unreasonable desire of lust and riches; in the curbing of which we find much more difficulty, than in checking other passions.

548. **How many kinds of deliberate desire are prohibited by this commandment?**

Two. The one is called efficacious, because it implies a will or design to perform the action itself. The other is a simple complacency or delight taken with full deliberation in evil thoughts without a consent to the execution or action. This is called in the school-language, a *morose delectation*, and it is a grievous and mortal sin, if it be perfectly willful, deliberate, and in a weighty manner, as all venereal objects are.

549. **How many kinds of consent are prohibited by this precept?**

Two. The one is called a formal consent, which is a willful consent of the mind and heart to a sinful delight, though not to the execution or action. The other is called a virtual consent, which is a negligence and carelessness in expelling evil thoughts.

550. **How shall I know when the will deliberately consents, either formally or virtually to evil thoughts?**

It is easy to know when there is a deliberate formal consent of the will; for the will consents formally when it expressly wills and consents to any sinful object. As to a virtual consent of the will, it is hard to know when that happens; for the vehemence of passion often blinds reason, so as to hinder it from reflecting upon the unlawfulness of the object. Wherefore, for a mortal virtual consent of the will, two things are required. First, that the person tempted should be perfectly in his senses, and have a perfect advertency of the unlawfulness of the object. Secondly, that he perceives the vehemence of passion to be gaining ground upon reason; and yet that he uses no proper diligence to curb his passion, but on the contrary, he is careless and negligent in expelling and resisting it.

551. **What diligence ought the tempted person to use to resist evil thoughts, so as not to consent to them?**

He should do two things. First, he ought to avoid all the immediate occasions and causes that excite and foment lustful thoughts, such as: lewd conversations; too much familiarity with libertines, or persons of a different sex; reading lewd books or pamphlets; beholding immodest pictures; an extraordinary excess in eating or drinking, when he finds that this excites lustful thoughts. Secondly, he should be very careful and vigilant to put away evil thoughts, when he perceives that they importune and solicit the will to consent; and also implore God's assistance, by considering him as an omniscient judge, to whom our most hidden thoughts are known. If he uses these or the like endeavors to repel evil thoughts, though they should not be immediately expelled, yet if he still endeavors to curb and abate the vehemence of them, though there may be some neglect in so doing, by not using all possible endeavors; in this case (I say) he does not sin mortally.

552. **What is the difference between a consent, a complacency, a morose delectation, and a curiosity, and when are they mortal sins, and when but venial?**

A consent is the yielding or agreeing of the will to what is proposed by the understanding. Complacency is the pleasure or delight which the will takes in what is proposed by the understanding.

A morose delectation is a willful delight and a continuance thereof in evil thoughts without a will or design to perform the action itself; it is called a continuance of the will upon evil thoughts, not on account of the time which the will spends in continuing thereon, but because after the tempted person knows the evil thoughts to be sinful, he still continues and willfully dwells thereon; for a temptation may continue a long time and be no sin, or at most a venial sin only, when the person tempted does not consent thereto, but rather endeavors to reject and suppress it, though he cannot speedily do it. On the contrary, temptations and evil suggestions may continue but a short time and be mortal sins, if the will fully consents to the sinful delight proposed by the understanding.

Curiosity is a desire to know and experience the sensual delight attending lust. This is a vice that often attacks young and unexperienced people, and as its malice is not easily perceived, it is often a nursery of impure thoughts, and leads them insensibly into a precipice before they are aware of the danger; wherefore they should be very careful to avoid all curiosity in this matter.

553. **If a person willfully delights in evil thoughts without a design of executing them, does he multiply the sin, or aggravate it according to the quality or circumstance of the object in which he delights?**

He does, and is bound to declare in confession the quality of the object; whether it was a relation and within what degree of affinity or consanguinity; whether a married, single, or religious person; or whether he delighted in sins against nature. See in Chapter 3, when the inordinate desire of another man's property is a mortal sin, and when but venial.

The First Commandment Expounded in a Controversial Manner

554. **What honor is due to God alone by this precept?**

A sovereign or divine honor, which cannot be given to any creature without a horrid sacrilege, much less to images or relics, which have neither virtue nor sense to do us any good.

555. **But do not Catholics worship the images of Christ and of his saints?**

That is a question about words; for if by the word *worship* is meant a sovereign and divine worship, Catholics worship God alone; but if by the word *worship* you understand a relative honor, or inferior respect, such as children show when they bow or kneel to receive their parent's blessing; subjects, to receive their prince's commands; and protestants, when they bow to the altar, or to the name of Jesus, without giving divine honor to any creature; in this sense, Catholics worship the images of Christ and of his saints, and also their relics, because they look upon their bodies to have been victims offered up to God either by martyrdom or by penance.

556. **Do Catholics pray to images?**

They do not, for they know very well that images can neither see, hear, nor help them; but Catholics pray before images, to keep them from distractions, and to excite in them a more lively remembrance of those they represent. Thus, a crucifix before us when we pray helps us to fix our wandering thoughts upon him whom it represents, bleeding and dying for us upon the cross; whence we are moved to testify our gratitude by some external signs, and by humbling ourselves before the image, we show what is our submission to our Savior; so that when Catholics honor the image of an apostle or martyr, "their intention is not so much to honor the image, as to honor the apostle or martyr in the presence of the image," as the *Roman Pontifical* observes. And the Council of Trent has expressly declared that the honor we render to images has such a reference to those whom they represent, that by the means of those images which we kiss and before which we kneel, we adore Jesus Christ and honor the saints whose types they are.[202]

557. **How could you thoroughly convince a protestant of Catholics being unjustly charged with giving divine honor to images?**

Laying aside the respect due to a crucifix upon account of the reference it has to Christ, whom it represents, I would break it in pieces, and throw it into the fire, and then show protestants the Council of Trent, Session

---

[202] Cf. Council of Trent, Session 25, "On the Invocation, Veneration, and Relics, of Saints, and on Sacred Images"

25, where it teaches, and forbids us expressly "to believe any divinity or virtue in images, for which they ought to be reverenced, to demand any favors of them, or to put any trust in them (as the gentiles did of old)…but because the honor that is exhibited to them is referred to the prototypes represented by them."[203]

558. **But how comes it, that protestants who are men of learning, and who can see our tenets explained in our catechisms, should be guilty of so black a calumny, as to accuse us of injuring the mediation of Christ by invoking saints, and adoring images in a manner which is peculiar and appropriated by scripture to God alone?**

If the words *adoration, invocation, mediator* were strictly kept to the sense in which they are used by the Catholic Church, then all their objections and accusations would lose their force; for one argument against a question misstated is better than twenty against the same fairly stated. So that it is more answerable to the uncharitable design of misrepresentation and calumny to misrepresent and misapply the said words, to render the Catholic doctrine more odious and contemptible to the vulgar and illiterate.

559. **Does the Catholic Church command us to worship images?**

She does not, but only recommends that practice as good and beneficial.[204] Wherefore her intention and motive for recommending the use of images is not because she places all her piety in the worship of images, or looks upon those external marks of humiliation as absolutely necessary for salvation; for she is sensible that the adoration due to God consists principally in adhering to him with all the powers of our soul, by faith, hope, and charity, and that this interior adoration which is rendered to God in spirit and truth, is exteriorly shown by our worship of images; because by humbling ourselves before an image, we show what is our submission to him whom it represents, and to whose remembrance and imitation we are excited by his image. So that when the Church recommends the use of images, her

---

[203] Council of Trent, Session 25, "On the Invocation, Veneration, and Relics, of Saints, and on Sacred Images"

[204] Cf. Ibid.

intention is only to condemn those who reject that practice out of error or disrespect; and this she is obliged to do, because it is her duty not to suffer any practice which is beneficial to salvation to be despised.

560. **For what end was the use of images brought into the Church, and why were so few used in the primitive times?**

To instruct the ignorant, and to give all that saw them good thoughts and affections towards the persons they represented. But it was not proper to observe this discipline till almost the memory of idolatry was banished out of the world; lest the enemies of Christianity might say that the Christian religion was only a change from one idolatry to another. Wherefore till idolatry was almost extirpated out of the Roman Empire, there were few images in places of public worship except that of Christ upon the chalice like a shepherd, mentioned by Tertullian.[205] For the Church never looked upon the use of images as absolutely necessary for devotion, but only recommended it as beneficial and conducive to excite in her children an affection towards the persons represented by them.

561. **But is there not some danger of idolatry in the frequent use of images?**

None at all; for it is not very possible that any rational man, (though but indifferently instructed in the principles of Christianity) should think a piece of wood or stone to be that God and man who was born of a virgin, died upon the cross, arose from the dead, and ascended into heaven; but if any such danger should happen out of ignorance or superstition, the abuse should be reformed and the institution not taken away, nor blamed.

562. **Why is God the Father painted like an old man, the Holy Ghost like a dove, and the angels with bodies?**

God the Father is so painted, because he appeared in that shape to the prophet Daniel.[206] The Holy Ghost is so painted, because he appeared in that shape at Christ's baptism.[207] The angels are so painted, because they

---

[205] Cf. Tertullian, *On Modesty*, Ch. 10
[206] Cf. Dn 7
[207] Cf. Mt 3:16

have appeared in bodies to men; so that those pictures are not images of them according to their being, but of the shapes in which they appeared to men.

563. **How do you prove it lawful to give a relative or inferior honor to the images of Christ and of his saints?**

First, out of Exodus 25, where God commanded "two cherubims to be made of beaten gold,"[208] and to be set on both sides of the ark, (before which the people were to pray) and promised that he would speak to them from the middle of the cherubims.[209] Secondly, out of John 3:14, where Christ approves the making of the brazen serpent[210] and owns it to have been an image or figure of himself exalted upon the cross.

564. **But is not all worship of images forbidden by these words of the first commandment: "Thou shalt not make to thyself any graven thing... Thou shalt not adore it"?[211] For I have heard some protestants positively say so, and that the said words, which make up the second commandment, are industriously omitted in our catechisms to authorize the use of images, and that the tenth commandment is divided into two to keep up the number of the commandments.**

The natural signification of the words quoted out of the first, or second commandment (as protestants will have it), is: not to make idols nor any graven thing to adore it as God or with divine worship; for these words: "Thou shalt not adore nor worship them"[212] equally regard the object of worship, as the forgoing words: "Thou shalt not have strange gods before me";[213] which is very different from worshiping the true God and his saints by images; whereas God, who cannot command and forbid the self-same

[208] Ex 25:18
[209] Cf. Ex 25:18-22
[210] Cf. Nm 21:9
[211] Ex 20:4, 5
[212] Ex 20:5
[213] Ex 20:3

thing, has commanded the ark and cherubims to be made with respect to his worship.[214]

The reason why the said words are not expressed at length in our common catechisms, is because they are sufficiently included in the preceding words: "Thou shalt not have strange gods before me."[215] For if we must have no other but the only true God, we must not have graven things to adore them with divine worship. Neither is the tenth commandment divided into two to put a trick upon the people, by hiding one commandment from them, and making them believe they had ten; but because St. Augustine divides the commandments[216] as we do, where he expressly maintains that what protestants call the second commandment is a fuller explanation of the first; for the scripture tells us only that there are ten commandments, but has nowhere determined nor specified whether the first or the tenth is to be divided into two.

565. **How do you prove it lawful to honor saints and angels with a relative or inferior honor?**

First, out of Josue 5, where, when the angel told Joshua that he was "the prince of the host of (our) Lord,"[217] Joshua fell flat upon the ground, and adoring, said, "What speaks my Lord to his servant?"[218] Secondly, out of Apocalypse 22, where St. John says: "And I fell down to adore before the feet of the angel who showed me these things,"[219] though the angel out of deference to his apostolical dignity had requested him not to do it.[220]

566. **Why is it lawful and laudable to honor the relics of saints with a relative or inferior honor?**

First, because a dead man was raised from death to life by touching the

---

[214] Cf. Ex 25:18
[215] Ex 20:3
[216] Cf. Augustine, *Quaestiones in Exodum*, q. 71
[217] Jo 5:14
[218] Jo 5:15
[219] Apoc 22:8
[220] Cf. Apoc 19:10

bones of the prophet Elisha.[221] Secondly, because a woman was healed of a bloody flux by touching the hem of our Savior's garment and believing it would cure her.[222] Thirdly, because the handkerchiefs and aprons, which touched the body of St. Paul, cast out devils and cured all diseases.[223] Fourthly, because "they brought the infirm into the streets, and laid them on beds and couches, that at least the shadow of Peter, as he came by, might overshadow any of them, and they might be healed of their infirmities."[224]

567. **But does not Christ reprehend the Scribes and Pharisees for building up the tombs of the prophets and adoring the monuments of the just?**[225]

He does not reprehend them for the action itself (says St. Chrysostom, *Homily 74*) but for the hypocrisy with which they did it; and for pretending thereby to be averse from the wicked dispositions of those who put the prophets to death, and thus obtain the favor of the people; when at the same time, they were contriving to do the like to their *Messias*, the Lord of all the prophets.

568. **Does not the practice of worshiping relics expose us to the danger of superstition, by honoring false relics?**

It does not, because if after all the care used by the pastors of the Church to prevent impostures, it should happen by the indiscreet zeal or wickedness of men, that we should be imposed upon, so as to honor a false relic for a true one, there would be no superstition in this case, but only an innocent mistake; as there is none, when a charitable Christian relieves an impostor, innocently believing him to be a real object of charity, because charity and all religious worship terminates in God alone.

569. **What do you mean by a relative honor of images?**

I mean an honor which is given to a thing, not for any intrinsic excellency

---

[221] Cf. 4 Kgs 13:21
[222] Cf. Mt 9:20-22
[223] Cf. Acts 19:12
[224] Acts 5:15
[225] Cf. Mt 23:29

in the thing itself, but only for the relation which it has to something else which it represents or brings to our remembrance; as when Christians bow to the crucifix, which is an image or remembrance of Christ to the eye, as the name of Jesus is to the ear.

570. **Does the Catholic Church bless inanimate things by way of imparting to them any intrinsic power or virtue?**

She does not, but only by way of devoting them to holy uses, and begging God's blessing for those that make use of them; that they may be serviceable to them, and that the devil may have no power to abuse them to their prejudice; so that whatever advantage may be supposed in the use of them after they are blessed more than before, is wholly to be attributed to the prayers of the Church.

571. **Has the Church any warrant in scripture for blessing inanimate things?**

She has: first, St. Peter's calling Mount Tabor a holy mountain, because Christ was transfigured upon it;[226] and St. Paul's saying, "Every creature of God is good, and nothing to be refused, if it be received with thanksgiving: for it is sanctified by the word of God and prayer";[227] and Christ sayeth that the Temple sanctifies the gold and the altar the gift.[228]

572. **Why is it pious and laudable to go on pilgrimages to holy places, such as Mount Tabor, or Calvary, the sepulchre of Christ, or to the shrines of the saints?**

First, because the Ethiopian eunuch's pilgrimage to Jerusalem was so pleasing to God, that in his return he was converted by St. Philip.[229] Secondly, because the bodies of the saints have been the living temples of God, in which he has in a particular manner inhabited, and which he has sanctified by his presence and grace; the remembrance and presence of which serve very much to encourage us to an imitation of their virtue, and to raise our

---

[226] Cf. 2 Pt 1:18
[227] 1 Tm 4:4-5
[228] Cf. Mt 23:17, 19
[229] Cf. Acts 8:38

souls from the love of things present and temporal to the love of things eternal. Thirdly, because God was pleased to work great cures and several miracles by the relics of saints; (which is what no one of the pretended reformed could ever do; wherefore they assert, that the power of working miracles has ceased in the Church) to confirm us in the truth of the doctrine which they preached, and to show that the persons to whom they are supposed to belong are his saints; as you may see in unquestionable historians, and in the holy fathers.[230] So that without denying all history, and accusing all those saints and famous lights of antiquity of forgery, error, superstition, and idolatry, the protestant doctrine of relics cannot subsist.

Of the Precepts of the Church

The Three First Precepts of the Church Expounded in a Moral Sense

573. **How many precepts of the Church are there?**
Six principal ones. The first is to hear Mass on all Sundays and holidays, as I have already explained above.

574. **What is the second precept of the Church?**
To confess our sins at least once a year.

575. **Is every Christian come to the use of reason, bound to confess once a year?**
He is, if he has sinned mortally; neither can he defer his confession to the following year, and in case he should, this precept still binds him.

576. **If a person has not committed any mortal sin during the whole year, is he obliged to confess his venial sins, or mortal ones already confessed?**
He is not; though to avoid scandal, he ought to let his pastor know his motive for not going to confession.

---

[230] Cf. Jerome, *Against Vigilantius*; Basil, *Homily on Psalm 115*; Gregory Nyssen, *Orat. de St. Theodoro*; Gregory Nazianzen, *Oration 3 Against Julian*; Chrysostom, *Orat. 42*; Ambrose, *Letter 22*; Augustine, *Epistle 212*; *Confessions*, Bk. 9, Ch. 7; *Sermon 317*; *City of God*, Bk. 22, Ch. 8; Theodoret, *Contra Graecos*, Bk. 8

577. **Is a person bound to confess about Easter, or can he comply with this precept at any time of the year?**

The Church has not determined any particular time of the year for complying with this precept; so it can be complied with at any time of the year. But as there is an obligation of communicating about Easter, and he that has committed any mortal sin, is bound to confess by way of a preparation for Communion; if he confesses and communicates about Easter, he complies with both precepts of annual confession and Communion.

578. **If a person has omitted his yearly confession for three or four years, is he bound to make three or four confessions?**

He is not, if he has culpably omitted it; for it is enough to declare in one confession all the sins he committed during that time, and his neglect in not having gone to confession; because thus, that one confession is equivalent to the three or four which he ought to have made.

579. **If a person has been for the most part of the year without committing any mortal sin, and sins mortally some few days before the end of the same year, is he bound to confess before the end of the year; or can he compute the time when he sinned, the beginning of the year with regard to himself?**

He is bound to confess before the end of the same year, which according to the most common opinion, begins about Easter, and ends at the same time of the year following.

580. **If a man has sinned mortally at the beginning of the year, and foresees that he may probably want an opportunity of a confessor at the end of the same year, is he bound to anticipate or make his yearly confession beforehand?**

He is, and also to confess a second time, if at the beginning of the year he confessed venial sins only, and afterwards sins mortally before the end of the same year.

581. **If a person makes a sacrilegious confession, does he comply with this precept?**

He does not; though it is very probable that if a person after having used proper diligence, forgets to confess some mortal sins, he is not bound to confess within the same year the sins he thus forgot.

582. **Are we obliged to confess once a year to our parish priest?**

We are not, for it is enough to confess to any confessor approved by the ordinary.

583. **If a person omits his yearly confession and Communion, is he excommunicated *ipso facto*?**

He is not, though he justly deserves to be excommunicated by the ordinary for those omissions.

584. **What is the third precept of the Church?**

To receive the Blessed Sacrament at Easter or thereabouts. I say thereabouts, because to comply with this precept it is enough to communicate at any time between Palm Sunday and Low Sunday; nay in some countries, at any time between the first day of Lent and the Third Sunday after Easter, and in some places even till Ascension.

585. **If a person has communicated at any other time of the year, is he bound to communicate at Easter?**

He is, and also to communicate in his parish church, unless he has leave from his parish priest to communicate elsewhere, or except he be upon a journey or voyage at Easter-time, in which case he may communicate in any church.

586. **At what age does this precept oblige us?**

Commonly about the age of ten, when we have sufficient discretion to know the devotion and preparation necessary for yearly Communion.

587. **If a person out of neglect or ignorance of the Christian doctrine does not communicate at Easter, does he transgress this precept?**

He does; and also those sin mortally whose duty it is to have instructed him in the mysteries of faith.

588. **If a person has not communicated at Easter-time, is he bound to communicate as soon as he has an opportunity?**

He is, if he has omitted so doing either culpably or inculpably. But observe, that if a person has communicated on the last day of Easter-time this year, which falls twenty days higher or lower in the season than next Easter, he is not obliged upon this account to communicate twenty days sooner at the next Easter-time; because the time limited for yearly Communion is the time of Easter, let it fall high or low in the season of the year.

589. **What think you of sick people who are not able to go to church?**

They are obliged to communicate at Easter, if the sacrament can be conveniently brought them to their houses.

590. **When is a person so dangerously sick as to be obliged to communicate by way of viaticum?**

It is not necessary that he be in the last extremity; it is enough he be in a probable danger of death; and physicians are obliged to let their patients know when they are in the said danger.

591. **If the same danger should continue for several days, can the sick person communicate a second time, or is he obliged to wait for his growing better, and afterwards relapsing?**

If the same danger continues for eight days, he may communicate every eighth day, though he should neither mend nor relapse.

592. **If a person has communicated out of devotion, and the very same day be seized with a dangerous fit of sickness, can he, or is he bound to communicate by way of viaticum?**

He is neither obliged to it, nor can he communicate twice on the same day according to the best divines.

593. **When the Eucharist is given to dying persons by way of viaticum, is it requisite that they receive it fasting?**

It is not; though sick persons who communicate out of devotion, or to comply with their yearly Communion, are obliged to receive the sacrament fasting, that is: without having taken the least bit of victuals, or drop of liquids (even by way of medicine) from the midnight before.

594. **If a person dangerously sick should be subject to vomiting, or seized with a frenzy, should the Eucharist be administered to him?**

It should not; neither is there any obligation of bringing the Eucharist to him to be adored, though not received by him.

595. **What think you of criminals sentenced to death?**

They are bound to communicate, and the judge is obliged to allow them time for so doing; wherefore the Eucharist is commonly given to them the day before they are executed.

The Other Three Precepts of the Church Expounded in a Moral Sense

596. **What is the fourth precept of the Church?**

To fast Lent, all vigils commanded, the Ember days, Fridays by custom in some countries, such as England and Ireland; as also to abstain from flesh on the Sundays in Lent, the Saturdays throughout the year, and in some countries on the three Rogation days, but observe that on those last, which are called days of abstinence only, we are obliged to abstain from flesh, but no ways confined to one meal.

597. Why does the Church prohibit flesh on days of fasting and abstinence?

That her children may better comply with the end of fasting, viz: mortification and penance, by abstaining from that kind of food which is most nourishing and commonly most agreeable; but the Church does not forbid flesh on those days because she looks upon any meats as unclean, and unlawful to be used at any time, as coming from an evil principle; as the Marcionites, Manicheans, and other heretics taught the use of meat to be forbid, whom St. Paul has condemned where he calls it a doctrine of devils[231] to command "to abstain from meats, which God hath created to be received with thanksgiving."[232] In which sense also Christ said: "That which goeth into the mouth doth not defile a man";[233] for it is not the uncleanness of the meat, or the eating of it without first washing the hands, (as the Pharisees imagined) which defiles the soul, but the disobedience to the Church; just as the uncleanness of blood or swine's flesh would not have defiled a Jew in the time of the old law, but only his disobedience to the Mosaic law; and the uncleanness of the forbidden fruit did not defile our first parents, but their disobedience to the law of God.

598. Why then does St. Paul say: "Eat of anything that is sold in the shambles, asking no questions for conscience sake"?[234]

The apostle speaks not of fasting days, as if any kind of meat might be eaten on those days, but he speaks of meats offered to idols; which some weak brethren were so much afraid of eating, that upon this account they would not eat the meat sold in the shambles, lest it might have been offered to idols. The apostle then prescribes them a rule, by which they were to govern themselves, as to the meats they met with: "Eat of anything sold in the shambles,"[235] or of anything you meet with at the table of infidels, when they invite you, "asking no questions for conscience sake,"[236] for all are

---

[231] Cf. 1 Tm 4:1
[232] 1 Tm 4:3
[233] Mt 15:11
[234] 1 Cor 10:25
[235] Ibid.
[236] 1 Cor 10:27

the Lord's creatures. "But if any man shall say: This is sacrificed to idols; eat not of it for his sake, and for conscience sake."[237] Because either he is an infidel that says it, and then, by saying so, he may mean that they who eat it ought to eat in honor of their gods. Or if a weak brother says so, he thereby signifies that his conscience judges it not lawful to be eaten; so that in one case, you seem to consent that things are to be taken in honor of idols; in the other, you give offence to your weak brother; the apostle then would have them to be without offence both to Jews and gentiles, and also not to judge meats sold in the shambles not lawful to be eaten, for fear of their having been offered to idols.

599. **What are the necessary conditions of the Church fast?**

The quality, quantity of food, and the proper time for taking it. As to the quality, the Church prohibits all flesh meat on fasting days, and in Lent, eggs, butter and cheese; of which hereafter. As to the quantity, the Church allows her children but one meal on fasting days, and a small collation at night, of which more hereafter; and the proper time for taking this meal, is midday an hour sooner or later according to custom; though if it should be deferred till evening, this precept is better complied with; but observe, that if a person takes no nourishment at all on a fasting day, he does not sin against this precept, though he may otherwise sin against the natural law of self-preservation.

600. **What persons are bound to fast and abstain, and who are excused by the Church from both or any of these two obligations?**

First, children under age, that is, before seven completed, are excused both from fasting and from abstinence; but at the age of seven completed they are obliged to abstain, though not to fast till one-and-twenty completed. Secondly, sick people and those who are mending or gathering strength after a dangerous fit of sickness are excused from fasting and abstinence, according as their sickness or weakness require an exemption from both

---

[237] 1 Cor 10:28

or either of these obligations; but if their necessity be not evident, they must consult a physician.

Thirdly, nurses and women with child are excused from fasting, but not from abstinence; unless they have some other indisposition besides nursing or being with child. Fourthly, superannuated people are excused from fasting, but not from abstinence; unless they have some other indisposition besides old age; but at what age they are excused from fasting is a subject as yet undecided by divines; for some imagine that old people are excused at the age of fifty; others, at the age of sixty; others again more probably judge that the proper age for enjoining the said exemption should be determined according to the strength or weakness of each particular; for some are stronger at the age of sixty than others at that of fifty.

Fifthly, common beggars are excused from the obligation of fasting, but not from that of abstinence (unless in case of sickness or extreme necessity) when they have not wherewith to make their meals at once, but only get a bit here and there; likewise those that upon fasting days are obliged to hard labor, such as: plough-men, carpenters, masons, smiths, weavers, shoemakers, cobblers; printers that work at the press, not those who only correct the press or compose; people that travel afoot, not those that travel on horseback or in a coach; cooks who work hard at dressing a great quantity of victuals; mariners that work for the most part of the day at rowing, weighing anchors, furling or unfurling the sails. Sixthly, those that upon fasting days are excused from abstinence, merely because fasting-food will not agree with their stomachs, are obliged to fast, and also not to eat fish and flesh at their one meal.

601. **What think you of tailors, barbers, periwig-makers, lawyers, painters, or solicitors?**

I think that their work is not laborious enough to excuse them either from fasting or abstinence, unless in case of some extraordinary labor, infirmity, or weakness.

602. **Does the Church not only prohibit all flesh meat on fasting days, but also milk, eggs, butter, and cheese even at the one meal?**

She does on the fast of Lent, but not on other fasting days, though in some countries, where there is a great scarcity of oil (such as England and Ireland) milk, butter, and cheese are allowed at one meal in Lent; as to the other fasting days, it is customary in some countries to take eggs, butter, and cheese at one meal; and in others, butter and cheese, but not eggs; so that the custom of each country, if it be not abuse, ought to be observed: but note, that where the bull of the crusade is in use, (as in Spain and Portugal) those that take it (though the intention alone of so doing will not suffice) are qualified to eat eggs, butter, and cheese at their one meal in Lent.

603. **Now that you have mentioned the bull of the crusade, pray explain the meaning and origin of it.**

It is called a "bull" (like all other letter of grace and favor granted by the pope) from the Greek word *bule*, which signifies deliberation; because it is granted by the head of the Church after a mature deliberation of the just motives for granting it. It was first granted by Urban II in 1166 (upon the occasion of recovering the Holy Land from the infidels) to the volunteers in that war, who wore a cross on their clothes as a badge and mark of distinction from infidels, whence it is called the *cruzade*. It is now a bull granting indulgences and an exemption from some Church precepts, to those in Spain or Portugal, that give the alms stipulated according to the condition of each, for ransoming Christian slaves, or for carrying on a war against infidels.

Neither is this practice any ways simoniacal, because the spiritual graces and favors granted thereby are not given for the temporal alms in themselves, but inasmuch as they are conducive and ordained for the spiritual good of propagating the Christian faith, and preventing Christians from forsaking their religion out of despair of their being never ransomed.

604. **Is a collation allowed on fasting days, and what is the proper food for it?**

It is, and the proper food for it is bread, fruits, salad, sweetmeats; but not butter, cheese, milk, or fish; unless it be a custom (as it is in Portugal) to collate upon a small quantity of fish fried in oil.

605. **What quantity of fasting-food is allowed at collation?**

A very small quantity; for custom has not introduced a collation to satiate hunger, but only to hinder what we drink from prejudicing our health; but to determine what quantity of food is necessary for this end is a very difficult point; for some divines think, that everyone may take at collation eight ounces of victuals; others again imagine that the quantity should be determined according to the stomach of each particular, so that the quantity allowed at collation is the fifth part of what a person takes at his meal.

606. **Does the Church prohibit any sorts of liquor on fasting days?**

She does not; wherefore we do not sin against this precept by being intoxicated with liquor on fasting days.

607. **What do you understand by liquors, or are all potable liquids deemed liquors?**

Liquids and liquors are different things; for liquors are potable things, that are drank merely to quench thirst, not to nourish the body; but liquids are things whose parts are fluid, and commonly taken by way of nourishment; so that chocolate, (though a liquid) as also apples, pears, and grapes are forbidden by this precept; but tea, coffee, cinnamon-water and the like are allowed by the Church on fasting days; because these things are taken by way of quenching thirst, or refreshing the body; for though some of the ingredients be solid things, yet by the composition they are so dissolved as to become fluids or liquors.

608. **If a vigil should fall upon a Sunday, when ought the fast to be kept?**

Upon the Saturday immediately before; the same should be observed when the feast of Corpus Christi falls upon a vigil.

609. **Is it lawful to transpose the usual hour of taking the one meal, so as to collate in the morning or at noon, and to sup at night?**

It is, if there by any necessity or reasonable motive for so doing, such as: some pressing business, traveling, or the like; nay, to transpose the usual hour of dinner or collation without any necessity at all, is but a venial sin.

610. **If Christmas day should fall upon a Friday or Saturday, are we excused from fasting and abstaining from flesh meat?**

We are; unless we have made a vow to fast on all Fridays and Saturdays of the year, in which case we are bound to fast and abstain on Christmas day, if it falls upon a Friday or Saturday.

611. **If a person does not fast upon a vigil that falls in Lent, or upon one of the Ember days; does he commit two mortal sins?**

He does not, but one only.

612. **If a person eats several times upon a fasting day, does he commit many sins?**

If he eats flesh meat, he sins mortally as often as he eats it; as also as often as he eats a considerable quantity of fasting-food, according to the best divines.

613. **What quantity of fasting-food is allowed at breakfast, so as not to sin mortally against this precept?**

About an ounce, a little more or less.

614. **Why do we fast and abstain on certain days?**

We fast in Lent, in imitation of Christ who fasted forty days and forty nights in the desert.[238] Upon vigils, to prepare ourselves for a devout keeping of the feasts that follow. On Ember days, because on these days the Church gives holy orders, and for this reason dedicates them to public prayer and fasting, in imitation of the apostles, who having fasted, prayed, and laid their hands upon Saul and Barnabas, dismissed them for the work to which the Holy Ghost had taken them.[239] We abstain on Fridays, in memory of Christ's passion; and on Saturdays, to prepare ourselves for a devout keeping of Sunday.

---

[238] Cf. Mt 4:2
[239] Cf. Acts 13:2-3

615. **But does not St. Paul reprehend the Galatians for observing "days, and months, and times, and years"?**[240]

St. Paul does not reprehend the Galatians for observing Christian fasts and feasts, but only for observing the Jewish fasts, feasts, and ceremonies, which some false teachers among the Galatians were for obliging all Christians to observe. This interpretation is agreeable to what goes before: "You are turning again to weak and poor elements, to which you are desirous to serve again."[241] And is also St. Jerome's,[242] where he tells us that some reformers in his time found the like occasion in St. Paul's words to blame the fasts and holy days kept by Catholics, that protestants now find. St. Jerome's answer was, that Catholics keep indeed diverse fasts and feasts, but that the days and motives of keeping them are different from those of the Jews. This same answer is to be given to what St. Paul says: "Let no one therefore judge you in meat, or drink, or in regard of a festival day."[243] That is, for abstaining from meats called unclean in the old law, for drinking out of a cup without a cover,[244] or for not keeping the Jewish fasts or festivals; for "these were a shadow of future things, but the body is Christ's,"[245] because he is the truth and substance signified by these shadows and types.

616. **What is the fifth precept of the Church?**

To pay tithes and the first fruits to our pastors, who feed us spiritually, and therefore should be corporally fed by us, according to that: "They who minister in the holy place, eat of the things of the holy place, and they who serve the altar, are partakers of the altar."[246]

617. **What tithes are due to our pastors?**

There are three sorts of tithes. The first are called pradial, which are such as are paid of those things that arise from or grow out of the ground only. The

---

[240] Gal 4:10
[241] Gal 4:9
[242] Cf. Jerome, Tom. 4, p. 271
[243] Col 2:16
[244] Cf. Nm 19:15
[245] Col 2:17
[246] 1 Cor 9:13

second are such as are paid of all sorts of cattle, either for labor or eating; as also of the emoluments that arise from them, such as: butter, cheese, wool, and the like. The third are such as are paid of those things that are acquired by any trade or calling. As to an obligation of paying these three sorts of tithes, the custom of each country or diocese should be observed; for in some places, it is not customary to pay the tithes of what is acquired by industry; in other places, it is a custom to pay the tenths of some kind of fruits, but not of all.

618. **What quantity are we obliged to offer by way of first fruits?**

Though that has been determined in the old law,[247] so that according to the tradition of the rabbis (as St. Jerome observes[248]) either the fortieth or sixtieth part of the first fruits (according to the devotion of the offerer) was offered by the Jews by way of an offering of obligation; yet as the canon law has not determined what quantity should be offered by Christians, and the offering of the first fruits has been a ceremonial part of the old law, which does not oblige Christians, unless it be renewed by the Church; for these reasons, the first fruits are commonly deemed among Christians offerings of devotion not of obligation, unless there be some particular law or custom to the contrary in some particular churches, in which case, the custom should be observed.

619. **What is the sixth precept of the Church?**

Not to celebrate marriages on times prohibited, that is: from the First Sunday of Advent till after Twelfth-day, and from Ash Wednesday till after Low Sunday; because the times of Advent and Lent are times of penance; Christmas and Easter are times of extraordinary devotion, and therefore not proper for feasting or carnal pleasures.

---

247 Cf. Ez 45:13
248 Cf. Jerome, *Commentary on Ezekiel*

Chapter 5

The Works of Mercy Expounded in a Moral Sense

620. How many are the works of mercy?

Fourteen; seven corporal, and seven spiritual. The corporal are: 1) To feed the hungry. 2) To give drink to the thirsty. 3) To clothe the naked. 4) To harbor the harborless. 5) To visit the sick. 6) To visit the imprisoned. 7) To bury the dead.

The seven spiritual are: 1) To give counsel to the doubtful. 2) To instruct the ignorant. 3) To admonish sinners. 4) To comfort the afflicted. 5) To forgive offences. 6) To bear patiently the troublesome. 7) To pray for the quick and the dead.

621. Are these works meritorious of an everlasting reward?

They are; because Christ has said: "Come you blessed of my Father, and possess the kingdom...For I was hungry, and you gave me to eat."[249] And also because, "They who instruct others in justice, shall shine as stars for all eternity."[250]

622. How shall I be able to know, when I sin mortally by omitting any of these works?

I shall endeavor to explain that at large with regard to the work of giving alms to the poor; that thus you may easily apply the same doctrine to the other works of mercy. First then, he that is to give alms must have something superfluous, or over and above what is necessary for the decent support of his person and rank. Secondly, he that is to receive alms must be either in a moral or extreme necessity. These two conditions are deduced from 1 John 5 where he says: "He that shall have the substance of this world, and shall see his brother in need, and shall shut his bowels

---

[249] Mt 25:34-35
[250] Dn 12:3

of compassion against him; how doth the charity of God abide in him?"[251] Which words denote three things. First, he must have the substance of this world. Secondly, he must see his neighbor in need. Thirdly, he must shut his bowels of compassion against him; so that these three conditions are required for a mortal sin in this matter, any one of which being wanting, the omission is not a mortal sin, but at most venial.

623. **How many sorts of necessities are there?**

Three, viz: an extreme, moral or grievous, and a common necessity. A person is deemed to be in extreme necessity, when he is in imminent danger of a grievous or mortal sickness, of losing his life or some of his limbs, for want of proper conveniences; if without any such danger he suffers great pains, afflictions, or penalties, he is in a moral or grievous necessity. Common necessity is that which common beggars labor under, whom we are bound to relieve by giving them alms (now and then) of such things as are not necessary for the support of our rank, though we are not bound (even under venial sin) to give charity to every beggar that asketh it.

624. **What do you mean by superfluities, or things over and above what is necessary for the support of a man's person and rank?**

Christ has explained that where he sayeth: "Of what remaineth, give alms";[252] in which text the words *what remaineth* do not signify quite needless and unnecessary things, so that no one would be obliged to give alms, unless he be so affluent of the substance of this world, that he cannot find means to spend it; for according to this interpretation no one would be bound to give alms, since every one can spend his substance in vain diversions and foolish extravagancies. The true meaning then of the said words is to give alms of such things as we can spare without any considerable detriment to ourselves or families, according to the state and rank of each of us; as also without any prejudice to our creditors; for charity begins at home, and the obligation of paying our debts is prior to that of giving alms.

---

[251] 1 Jn 3:17
[252] Lk 11:41

625. **Are we obliged to give alms of what remaineth, not only when our neighbor's extreme necessity, but also when his moral and common necessity requires it?**

We are, as it appears from James 2, where he sayeth: "If a brother or sister be naked, and want daily food: and any of you say to them: Go in peace, be warmed and filled; yet shall not give them things that are necessary for the body, what shall it avail them?"[253] Now it is evident, that the want of daily food is not an extreme, but only a moral or common necessity.

626. **When are we obliged to give alms of what is necessary for the support of our rank and condition?**

In two cases, viz: when our neighbor's extreme necessity or the public calamity of the state shall require it.

627. **If another supplies my neighbor in distress, do I sin mortally by not relieving him?**

You do not; because for a mortal sin against this precept, two things are required. First, that our neighbor be in want or distress. Secondly, he should remain or continue in his necessity. These two conditions are deduced from 1 John 3 where he sayeth: "He that shall see his brother in need, and shall shut his bowels of compassion against him."[254] So that though your brother be in need, if another opens his bowels of compassion for him, you may without committing a mortal sin, shut yours against him.

628. **How shall I apply the doctrine you have hitherto laid down to the other works of mercy in particular?**

The corporal necessities of our neighbor are very visible, and consequently our obligation of relieving them in those circumstances is easily perceived; but of all the corporal works of mercy, the most obligatory is that of visiting the sick, who cannot help themselves, and therefore should be visited not only in their dangerous or mortal infirmities, but also in their tedious and

[253] Jas 2:15-16
[254] 1 Jn 3:17

lingering disorders; not only provided with the conveniences and necessaries of life, but also comforted and consoled in their infirmities. Next to our obligation of visiting the sick, is that of visiting captives and the imprisoned, who upon account of their captivity and confinement want our relief and assistance. We are bound to do to the healthy any charitable office, when their extreme or grievous necessity shall require it.

As to the spiritual works of mercy, we are obliged to forgive offences[255] and to bear patiently the troublesome, so as not to desire or wish any evil, hurt, or detriment to them; as also, to comfort the afflicted, to instruct the ignorant, when their necessity or our office shall require it. We are also bound to correct sinners, when we have probable hopes that our corrections will reclaim, and not provoke, nor displease them. Finally, we are obliged to pray for the quick and the dead; but of this in the next section.

Prayer Expounded in a Moral Sense

629. **What is prayer?**

It is the lifting up of the mind to God.

630. **What is the difference between prayer and devotion?**

Though both of them be acts of religion; yet devotion is a propensity or liking to God, whence arises a pleasure and satisfaction in serving him, which pleasure is commonly called devotion, though it be more properly the effect of devotion rather than devotion itself. Prayer is an act of the understanding, whereby the mind is lifted up to God, whence arises a readiness in the will, which excites the mind to pray.

631. **How many parts hath prayer?**

Four, viz: oration, supplication, obsecration, and thanksgiving. Oration is the lifting up of the mind to God, and approaching him with our hearts and affections. Supplication is an earnest prayer, whereby we represent to God our wants, and either beg for good things, or to be freed from evils.

---

[255] Cf. Mt 6:15

Obsecration is a submissive entreaty, whereby we humbly propose to God the reasons and motives why he should grant our request, such as: his own infinite mercy and goodness; the passion and merits of Christ; the intercession of the Blessed Virgin and of other saints. Thanksgiving is a religious act, whereby we bless and praise God for the many favors which he has graciously conferred upon us.

632. **Why is not the love of God numbered among the parts of prayer?**
Because it is properly the effect of prayer; for the mind lifted up to God by prayer, excites and inflames our wills with the love of our omnipotent and beneficent Lord, who is both able and willing to relieve us in distress.

633. **What is required for oration or the first part of prayer?**
The royal prophet tells us that he has set the Lord before his eyes, because he is at his right hand, that he be not moved.[256] And St. Paul sayeth: "Whether you eat or drink, or do anything else, do all things to the glory of God."[257] So that for having God present to our minds, nothing is required, but that all our thoughts, words, and actions should be regulated by the law of God, and that we should abhor, detest, and avoid whatever is contrary to God's honor and glory; though if we desire to have God perfectly present to our minds, we should think often of him; for we think very often of what we earnestly desire; wherefore frequent and constant thoughts of God are strong indications of an excessive love for him.

634. **What are the best means for thinking frequently of God?**
Reading of spiritual books, meditation, and contemplation; wherefore St. Paul exhorted Timothy to apply himself to reading till he come,[258] for reading disposes the mind for meditation, and those that cannot read may either hear good sermons, exhortations, or get others to read for them; for it is often as beneficial to hear others reading, as if we ourselves should read. By meditation the mind reflects seriously upon the wonderful works

256 Cf. Ps 15:8
257 1 Cor 10:31
258 Cf. 1 Tm 4:13

of God, and thus excites the will to love him above all things, according to that: "The meditation of my heart shall be in thy sight always."[259] And, "My heart was hot within me: and in my meditation the fire shall burn."[260]

By contemplation the mind thoroughly considers the admirable works of God, and thereby excites the heart to be attached to them, and to find pleasure and satisfaction in the contemplation of them, according to that: "I shall fix my step upon a tower; and shall contemplate to see what may be said to me."[261] Nay, by contemplation the soul is transformed to be in some measure like unto God, whom we shall see and enjoy, when we pass from the less glory of grace and sanctification in this life, to the state of a more perfect glory and happiness in heaven, according to that: "But all we with face uncovered contemplating the glory of the Lord, are transformed into the same image from glory to glory, as by the Spirit of the Lord."[262]

635. **What kind of books do you esteem the best adapted to dispose the mind for meditation?**

The holy scriptures, according to what St. Paul says: the holy scriptures are able to instruct us to salvation by faith, and to teach us "to reprove, to correct, to instruct in justice, that the man of God may be perfect, and furnished unto every good work."[263] But because many texts of the holy scriptures are very abstruse and full of mysterious significations, which the unlearned wrest "to their own destruction":[264] for this reason, it is more profitable for the ignorant and illiterate to read spiritual books that explain the word of God, than to read the scriptures; wherefore St. Paul said to Timothy that he shall be a good minister of Christ, in proposing things to his brethren, when he is nourished by the words of faith and of the good doctrine, which he has attained to.[265]

---

[259] Ps 18:15
[260] Ps 38:4
[261] Hb 2:1
[262] 2 Cor 3:18
[263] 2 Tm 3:16-17
[264] 2 Pt 3:16
[265] Cf. 1 Tm 4:6

636. What is the best subject for meditation?

The law of God both day and night, according to that: the blessed man's will is in the way of our Lord, "and in his law he will meditate day and night."[266] Moreover, in the law of God we find two things, to which all subjects of religious meditation may be reduced.

The first regards God and his attributes, such as: his infinite goodness, beneficence, and mercy, in having created us from nothing, in having redeemed us with his precious blood, in having left us his body and blood present under the sacramental signs, in having preserved us in our being, and having delivered us from several evils, in having given us the light of faith, in having borne so patiently with our enormous offences, and in having graciously instituted the sacraments, as means of our reconcilement to him. This kind of meditation is called illumination, or the illuminative way of meditating; because it enlightens the mind, and gives it a clear prospect of divine and supernatural truths, whence arises in the will a lively confidence in God, and a firm adherency to him, on account of his amiable perfections, according to that: "It is good for me to adhere to God, to put my hope in my Lord God."[267]

The second kind of meditation is a serious consideration of our own insignificancy, misery, and dependence; of the number of sins which we have committed without having had the least regard for the greatness of God whom we have offended; for his love, whereby he has conferred several benefits upon us; for his patience, whereby he has patiently borne with our crimes; for his goodness, whereby he has often invited us to an amendment; nor for his presence and omniscience, whereby he sees and surveys all our thoughts, words, and actions. And yet we have made a god of our vanity, ambition, lust, or riches; wherefore we should look upon ourselves as a heap of filth, as poor indigent creatures made of nothing, subject to ignorance, temptations, passions, and evil inclinations; and as such, we should lift up our eyes to God, and implore his aid and assistance, by representing to him our indigency and insignificancy, and his mercy,

---

[266] Ps 1:2
[267] Ps 72:28

power, and beneficence, according to that: "I have lifted up my eyes into the mountains, from whence help shall come to me. My help is from (our) Lord who made heaven and earth."[268] This kind of meditation is called purgation, or of a purgative nature; because it cleanses the soul from the unlawful desire of all sorts of impurities or criminal enjoyments, which are commonly the greatest obstacle to its making a progress in devotion and meditation.

637. **Which of these two kinds of meditation, purgative or illuminative, must we first practice?**

Both together; for one is of very little benefit without the other; though each particular should practice more or less of either of them according to his different passions and evil inclinations. The proud and haughty should practice more of the purgative, because it is just they should be abased and humbled in their own conceit. The meek and humble may practice more of the illuminative.

But observe that such as have run on a long time in a continued course of debauchery, are often perplexed at the time of praying with the remembrance of their former crimes, particularly of sins of impurity; wherefore it is more convenient for these to practice more of the illuminative, than of the purgative meditation; that thus the mind may be more fixed in God, and the heart more affected towards divine and supernatural things; whence (as if it were from a great eminence) the sinner may behold his own meanness, and how far he has debased himself by forfeiting an everlasting satisfaction for a momentary pleasure. Thus, the sinner having his mind fixed upon God's perfections, is not carried away by the vehemence of passion, nor by the remembrance of past pleasures, according to that: "I have set my Lord before my eyes, (that is: I have meditated upon his perfections) because he is at my right hand, that I be not moved."[269] Wherefore many yield to temptations and distractions in their prayers, for want of meditating first upon God's presence and perfections.

---

[268] Ps 120:1-2
[269] Ps 15:8

638. **Which is the best way of contemplating God's perfections?**

Contemplation is the most perfect and most spiritual act of the understanding; for it is a thorough thinking of, and a strict considering upon every part and circumstance of the wonderful works and perfections of God. This contemplation is obtained two ways.

First, by infusion, which happens when the understanding is suddenly and unexpectedly enlightened with a superior light and knowledge of God's attributes and perfections, and the will is in the same manner inflamed with an excessive love for God, according to that: "His unction teacheth you concerning all things."[270] This kind of contemplation is the gift of wisdom, one of the seven gifts of the Holy Ghost, and consequently is perfectly known by him alone who infuses it, when and as he is pleased to do so; though it is seldom permanent in souls, which have not attained to an eminent degree of virtue. But though this gift be above the reach of human reason; yet we may in some measure know and distinguish the true and genuine spirit of contemplation from the false and counterfeit, by the effects which it produces in the soul. First then, we should observe whether it works not only upon the imagination, but also upon the heart, by enlightening our understandings with the knowledge of our duty, and by efficaciously exciting our wills to the practice and observance of it.

Secondly, we should mind, whether thereby we find in ourselves an increase of humility, faith, charity, patience, self-contempt, devotion, a firm resolution to undergo all penalties and persecutions for the love of God, whom we deem our chief support in all our tribulations and afflictions; for where the evil spirit enters, there he leaves his wicked inclinations and vicious habits, such as: tepidity, doubts, ignorance, impatience, pride, lust, and envy; and though he should dissemble for a little time, yet he soon discovers himself by those evil habits; wherefore when we see a person that pretends and appears to be devout, religious, or favored by God with extraordinary visions and revelations, and yet proud, envious, self-conceited, ignorant of his duty or tepid in the performance of it, we have reason to suspect him to be rather deluded by the spirit of hypocrisy

---

[270] 1 Jn 2:27

or enthusiasm than guided by a true spirit of devotion or contemplation. Contemplation is acquired, when by a repeated exercising of it often over, a readiness or perfection in the performance, or a satisfaction in, or a liking to contemplation is acquired.

639. Are there different degrees in contemplation?

There are, according as the mind is more or less alienated from the love of worldly things, and more or less attached to supernatural things; but the difficulty of quite alienating the mind from all temporal concerns is so great, that it is scarce attainable in this life; for though faith greatly disposes the mind for contemplation; yet as this virtue is essentially obscure, there are three different ways of contemplating God's perfections.

The first and most imperfect is that of contemplating the incarnation and humanity of Christ, his tender infancy, his death and passion, when thereby nothing is represented to the mind, but Christ's eminent virtue, sweet expressions, courteous behavior, tender compassion, and affable conduct. The consideration of these things gained so far upon the hearts of the apostles that St. Paul said: "I did not judge, I was to know anything among you, but Jesus Christ, and him crucified."[271] So that to enter upon a contemplative life by meditating upon Christ's incarnation and passion, is to tread in the footsteps of the apostles.

Secondly, the mind ascends to a higher degree of contemplation, when it contemplates the divinity and attributes of God, according to that: "If we have known Christ according to the flesh, but now we know him no more."[272] That is: if we have heretofore known and considered Christ as mortal and passible, now we neither know nor consider him as born a mortal man, but as he is risen glorious and immortal, and will bless us with an immortal and eternal glory.

The third and most perfect method of contemplating is when "all we with face uncovered beholding the glory of the Lord, are transformed from glory to glory into the same image."[273] That is: we are transformed in some

---

[271] 1 Cor 2:2
[272] 2 Cor 5:16
[273] 2 Cor 3:18

measure to be like unto God, by beholding his glory, and by passing from the contemplation of Christ's incarnation to that of his divinity, and from the contemplation of one attribute to that of another. Thus, our whole lives and actions are directed by the gift of wisdom to the honor of God, and the salvation of our souls.

640. **What think you of the clergy or religious, who spend little or no time in meditation and contemplation?**

I think no one justly deserves the name of a clergyman or religious who does not daily spend some time in meditation and contemplation, unless he be hindered from so doing by sickness or some other pressing business. But none of them can justly pretend to be so lawfully employed otherwise, as to be always excused from the exercise of meditation and contemplation. Nay, I am of opinion that all immorality and relaxation among religious, proceeds chiefly from their not meditating often upon and contemplating frequently the end of their profession; for as a learned ascetic divine observes,[274] the religious and clergy, who do not often seriously consider and contemplate the end of their profession, become tepid, avaricious, proud, turbulent, detractors, ambitious, lascivious, contemptible to the laity, and more obdurate than laymen; and unless God by an extraordinary grace reclaims them, they fall into dangerous precipices, whence they seldom rise.

641. **How can I know, when I reap benefit by prayer and make a progress in devotion and meditation?**

By the proneness, inclination, and affection which you find in yourself towards spiritual things.

642. **What think you of those who are distracted in their prayers?**

Distractions may proceed from two causes. First, from a loathing, weariness, or unwillingness of the mind for prayer; such as those have who omit their prayers under any frivolous pretext of business, and readily embrace every opportunity of diverting and recreating their bodies. These

[274] Cf. Avila 3. p. Epist.

distractions are strong indications of the little or no benefit which their souls reaped by prayer; for as the prophet Jeremiah observes, God in punishment of their loathing, permits a cloud or mist (that is: a number of vain and foolish thoughts) to be put before their eyes,[275] to distract and perplex them in their prayers.

Secondly, distractions may proceed not from any loathing of the will, but from a distrust of our want of true devotion, and of the acceptableness of our prayers to God; for though we be desirous to pray, and to be attentive thereto; yet the diffidence we have in our prayers, inasmuch as they are ours, makes us not to find any great pleasure or satisfaction in praying. This kind of distraction does not hinder the soul from benefiting by prayer; for the benefit obtained by prayer is not to be measured by the pleasure or satisfaction of the will, nor by the knowledge or comprehension of the understanding; but by the less or greater proneness and affection of the soul towards spiritual and supernatural things, according to that: "The soul that is sorrowful for the greatness of evil…and goeth crooked, and weak, and the eyes failing, and the hungry soul giveth glory and justice to thee their Lord."[276]

643. In regard to the second part of prayer called supplication, pray tell me, what ought we to beg of God?

First, and chiefly, all spiritual benefits, such as God's grace to comply with his commands, and final perseverance therein. Secondly, all temporal conveniences, inasmuch as they may be in some measure necessary for the support of this life, and conducive to the exercise of virtue.

644. In regard to the third part of prayer called obsecration, pray tell me, is it lawful and commendable to pray not only to God, but also to his holy saints and angels?

It is, as I have already explained and proved in Chapter 1.

---

[275] Cf. Jer 2:13
[276] Bar 2:18

645. **In regard to the fourth part of prayer called praise and thanksgiving, pray tell me, do we praise and thank God by either mental or vocal prayer?**

We do; for our words declare the inward affection and devotion of our hearts.

646. **What is vocal prayer?**

It is a prayer or request made to God by pronouncing the words that express and signify our request and desire.

647. **Do all Christians come to the use of reason, lie under an obligation of practicing both mental and vocal prayer?**

They do. First by a general precept, which obliges all sorts of people to earnestly beg God's pardon and assistance from him, to avoid sin, to resist temptations, and to offer up all their thoughts, words, and actions to the honor and glory of God. In this sense, St. Luke said it is necessary always to pray, and not to faint in it;[277] and St. Paul: "Pray without intermission."[278] Secondly, by a particular precept of the Church, which obliges all those who have received any of the three greater holy orders, or enjoy a Church-benefice, and the religious of both sexes deputed for choir; as also the laity who have made a vow of saying certain prayers. As to the Church-office, or form of prayer, which ought to be used by the clergy and religious, let them read casuists and moralists upon that subject, for this work is chiefly intended for the instruction of the laity.

648. **How do we comply with the general precept of praying without intermission?**[279]

First, by offering up all our thoughts, words, and actions to the honor and glory of God. Secondly, by saying the morning and evening prayers, which are commonly said by all good Christians. Thirdly, by begging the prayers of others; for the confidence we have in the prayers of others avails us, according to that: "Pray for one another, that you may be saved, for the

---

[277] Cf. Lk 18:1
[278] 1 Thes 5:17
[279] Cf. Ibid.

continual prayer of a just man availeth much."[280] Fourthly, every Christian is obliged by this precept to spend some time in prayer, according as his spiritual or temporal necessity shall require it.

649. **What are the essential conditions of vocal prayer?**
Attention and devotion.

650. **What attention is required?**
Either an actual or virtual one. An actual attention is that which a person has when he actually applies his mind to what he is saying. A virtual attention is a will and desire to be attentive, though the mind should be otherwise distracted on account of other things roving in the imagination; though there be some small neglect in expelling them, provided this neglect be not either designed or affected.

651. **How is an actual attention lost, and how both actual and virtual, so that a person does not comply with the precept of vocal prayer?**
An actual attention is lost three ways, and both actual and virtual, one way only. First, an actual attention is lost, not designedly, nor willfully, but merely out of human frailty, on account of the great difficulty of keeping the imagination fixed for a considerable time on any one subject; for this is a very slippery faculty, which cannot be depended upon, and which we can scarce curb or hinder from roving from one subject to another; and yet the person thus distracted does what he can to expel distractions, and to be attentive to his prayers. Secondly, an actual attention is lost, out of neglect or carelessness, when a person observes himself to be distracted in his prayers, and resolves to expel distractions and to renew his attention, but still is tedious and slow in executing his resolution. Thirdly, both actual and virtual attention are lost willfully and designedly, when a person is willfully distracted in his prayers, or is employed in any business that is incompatible with a due attention to prayer, such as: painting, writing, talking, or the like.

[280] Jas 5:16

If the attention be lost in the first manner only, a person complies with the precept of vocal prayer, so as not to sin either mortally or venially; if in the second manner, and the neglect be but small, he sins venially, but still complies with the precept; but if in the third manner, he transgresses the precept, and sins either mortally or venially, according to the quantity of prayer which he says in this manner. This doctrine may be easily applied to attention required for hearing Mass on Sundays and holidays.

652. **What quantity of prayer is deemed considerable, so that the omission of it, or a willful distraction in saying it, may be a mortal sin?**

That is a point hard to be determined on account of the great disagreement of divines concerning it. My humble opinion is that it ought to be regulated according to the quantity of the whole office or prayer; so that one psalm or *Pater Noster*, which may be deemed an insignificant part of eighteen or twenty, may be justly esteemed a weighty matter with regard to three or four.

653. **What think you of those who are willfully distracted in their prayers or in hearing Mass, not of obligation but of devotion only?**

I think they sin venially by so doing, on account of some small irreverence done to God, by speaking to him in a careless manner.

654. **To what things may a person be attentive when he is at prayer?**

To three things, (and by being attentive to any of them he complies with the precept of prayer) viz: to the words, that he should not err in reciting them; to the signification of the words; and to God, who is the Person spoken to and the end of all prayer. But observe, that he ought to be attentive to God, so as not to omit the words prescribed in the form of vocal prayer.

655. **If a person distracted in his prayers out of frailty or some small neglect, finds himself advanced and cannot remember whether he said the precedent part, is he obliged to say it over again?**

That is a difficulty that greatly perplexes scrupulous persons; the best rule I can find for quieting their minds and deposing their doubts, is that which

St. Thomas[281] prescribes for a priest, who finding himself advanced in that part of the Mass which follows the consecration, doubts whether or no he has said the words of consecration. In this case (I say) if his doubt be merely negative, that is, proceeding only from his not remembering whether or no he has said the words of consecration, he ought not to say them over again, but rather go on and depose his doubt; if the doubt be positive, that is, arising from probable motives to doubt whether or no he has said the said words, then he should do what seems more probable to him, that is: if he be more inclined to think that he has not said the said words, he ought to repeat them; but if he be more inclined to judge the contrary, he ought to depose his doubt, and proceed without repeating the said words, particularly if he be a scrupulous person who is often perplexed with the like doubts at the time of prayer.

656. **What kind of vocal prayer do you esteem best?**

I should recommend to the laity, first, the Lord's Prayer, the Angelical Salutation, the Apostles' Creed, the rosary of the Blessed Virgin, and the prayers before and after confession and Communion, which are in the common manuals. Secondly, I should recommend to the clergy and religious these same prayers, and the Church-office, which is divided into seven parts commonly called canonical hours, according to the different stages or stations of Christ's passion.

657. **What is the Lord's Prayer?**

It is a short prayer made by Christ;[282] which contains in seven petitions, all those chief things which we can ask of, or hope from God.

---

[281] Cf. *Summa Theologiae*, III, q. 83, a. 6, rep. 5
[282] Cf. Mt 6:9-13

658. **In regard to the third petition:** *Thy will be done on earth, as it is in heaven:* **pray tell me, are we obliged not only to obey God's commands but also to conform and resign ourselves to his will in all things?**
We are as to the motive of God's will, but not always as to the thing willed by him.

659. **Pray explain that a little more.**
The motive of God's will is the good which he intends to bring about by the dispositions of his providence; the thing willed is the event, which actually happens, as being either directly intended, or at least permitted by God. Now we are not obliged to rejoice at every event that actually happens; as for example: we are so far from being obliged, that on the contrary it is unlawful for us to will or to rejoice at the damnation of the soul of our neighbor, his temporal calamities or any other judgment which God executes against him; but the good which God proposes by punishments, to wit: either the amendment of sinners, showing of his own justice and glory, etc. is what we are obliged to will; because charity to our neighbor obliges us to will his amendment, and the love of God obliges us to desire his glory.

660. **In regard to the sixth petition:** *Lead us not into temptation:* **pray tell me, what do we ask in this petition?**
To be delivered from temptations, so as not to be overcome by them; for though God "tempts no man. But every one is tempted, being drawn away, and allured by his own concupiscence";[283] and though temptation be not properly a sin of itself; nay, it is morally impossible to be free in this life from all temptations; for the whole "life of man on earth is a warfare";[284] yet as a victory over temptations is impossible to corrupt nature and easy to grace, we should implore God's grace and assistance, not to yield or consent to them.

---

[283] Jas 1:13-14
[284] Jb 7:1

661. **Are there different degrees in temptations?**

There are three different ones. The first, by suggestion only. The second, by delectation. The third, by consent. For first the devil, or our own frail nature tempts us by a suggestion of evil thoughts in our imagination; to have such thoughts and imaginations may be no sin at all, though the objects represented be never so hideous, though they may continue never so long, and return never so often. (Though it seldom happens that these thoughts continue a very long time without a perfect advertency of the mind, and a deliberate consent of the will, particularly with regard to objects forbidden either by the first principles of reason, or by the immediate consequences from them.) The reason is because we often cannot hinder them; on the contrary, if our will remains displeased with them, and resists them, such a resistance is meritorious; for, "Happy is the man that endureth temptations; because when he shall be proved, he shall receive a crown of life, which God hath promised to them that love him."[285]

Secondly, these representations may be followed with a delectation in the senses or in the body only, and if this happens by an impression made against the will, to which we no ways consent, there is no sin at all. There may be also some neglect in the person tempted, by his not using sufficient endeavors to resist and repel those thoughts, and if this be only a small neglect, the sin is not mortal, but venial only; but if the person tempted has willfully taken delight in evil thoughts of any very sinful object; such a willful delight is a mortal sin, though he has not a will or design to put the action itself in execution. The reason is because he then consents in his mind and heart to a sinful delight, though not to the execution or action; for "when concupiscence hath conceived (that is: when man's free will has yielded to it) it bringeth forth sin."[286] And the sin may be mortal, though it be but for a short time; for temptation may continue a long time, and be no sin, and there may be a mortal sin in a short time; because we are to judge of sin by the dispositions and consent of the will, not by the length of time.

Thirdly, when the sinner yields to evil suggestions and temptations, so

[285] Jas 1:12
[286] Jas 1:15

that his will fully consents to what is proposed, and nothing is wanting, but an opportunity of putting his sinful desires in execution, he then has already committed the sin; because, "whosoever shall look on a woman to lust after her, hath already committed adultery with her in his heart."[287]

662. What is the Hail Mary or Angelical Salutation?

It is an honorable salutation of the Blessed Virgin Mary, and a prayer to her; which salutation has three parts. The first, viz: *Hail Mary full of grace our Lord is with thee*, was made by the Holy Ghost, and delivered by the angel Gabriel.[288] The second, viz: *Blessed art thou among women, and blessed is the fruit of thy womb*, was said by St. Elizabeth filled with the Holy Ghost.[289] The third part, viz: *Holy Mary*, etc. was made by the Catholic Church in the Council of Ephesus the year 451 against Nestorius, who denied our Blessed Lady to be the Mother of God.

663. What is the rosary?

It is a method of praying so as to meditate upon the chief mysteries of our redemption; wherefore it is divided into three parts; each part consisting of five mysteries to be contemplated, during the repeating of five decades, or one Our Father and ten Hail Maries upon the beads.

The first five are called the joyful mysteries, viz: the annunciation, when Christ was conceived in his Mother's womb; the visitation, when the Blessed Virgin visited her kinswoman St. Elizabeth; the nativity of Christ; his presentation in the Temple, together with the purification of the Blessed Virgin; and the finding of him in the Temple amidst the doctors. These mysteries are assigned for Mondays and Thursdays throughout the year, for the Sundays of Advent, and those after Epiphany till Lent.

The five next are the dolorous or sorrowful mysteries, as having an immediate relation to the passion of Christ, and are: his prayer, agony, and captivity in the garden; his being scourged at the pillar; his being crowned with thorns; his carrying of the cross to Mount Calvary; and his

[287] Mt 5:28
[288] Cf. Lk 1:28
[289] Cf. Lk 1:41-42

crucifixion, anguish, and death on the cross. These mysteries are assigned for Tuesdays and Fridays throughout the year, and Sundays in Lent.

The five glorious mysteries are: the resurrection of Christ from the dead; his ascension into heaven; the coming of the Holy Ghost to the disciples; the assumption of the Blessed Virgin into heaven; and her coronation in heaven. These mysteries are assigned for Wednesdays and Saturdays through the year, and for the Sundays after Easter till Advent.

664. **Why is the Hail Mary repeated in the rosary ten times oftener than the Lord's Prayer?**

The reason for so doing is not to signify that the Blessed Virgin is either more powerful or more merciful than her Son; nor that we have more confidence in her than in Christ. The true reason, then, is because the rosary is a devotion instituted to remind us of the mysteries of our redemption, the principal one whereof is that of the incarnation; and as the Hail Mary is a prayer that particularly relates to that great mystery; as also because in honoring the Mother we have principally in view the honor of her Son, and we think that her prayers are ten times better, and more acceptable to God, than ours. For these reasons we beg the Blessed Virgin ten times, to address her prayers to her Son, to remind us constantly of the mysteries of our redemption, particularly of that of the incarnation. For this same reason the devotion called *Angelus Domini* is used in all Catholic countries, and all good Christians perform that devotion when the bells toll every morning, noon, and night, three times with a short space between each time.

665. **But does not St. Paul say, "There is one God, one mediator of God and men, the man Christ Jesus"?[290] What room then is there for the mediation of the Blessed Virgin or of other saints?**

The meaning of St. Paul's words is, that Christ alone is our mediator of redemption; as it is visible from the immediately following words of the

---

[290] 1 Tm 2:5

text: "Who gave himself a ransom for all."[291] But as for mediators of intercession and prayer, as nothing hinders us from seeking the mediation of the faithful to pray for us, so nothing ought to hinder us from seeking the like from the Blessed Virgin and the other saints and holy angels; though neither the one nor the other can obtain anything for us any other way than through Jesus Christ; as I have already explained in Chapter 1. For Christ alone is the only mediator, who stands not in need of any other to recommend his petitions.

666. **Why has the Church prescribed seven canonical hours as a form of prayer for the clergy and religious of both sexes; and why has she ordained several ceremonies for the administration of the sacraments, particularly in the unbloody sacrifice called the Mass?**

Man being composed of soul and body, all the faculties of the soul depend in all their operations on the body; the mind then is more excited, moved, and affected towards spiritual things represented by sensible and material signs, than it is moved by them represented as in themselves. The Church then has instituted several ceremonies to stir up devotion in her children, and also to instruct the ignorant, and lead them gradually by visible means to a contemplation of the sublime mysteries represented by those external rites and ceremonies.

667. **Had the Church any authority from scripture for so doing?**

She had. First, the authority of God commanding in the book of Leviticus many stately ceremonies in things belonging to his service. Secondly, the example of Christ's sighing, looking up to heaven, putting his fingers into the ears of the dumb and deaf, spitting, and touching his tongue;[292] his having anointed with his spittle the eyes of the blind man, and having laid his hands upon him;[293] his having spit on the ground, having made clay of the spittle, and having spread the clay upon the eyes of the man blind from his

[291] 1 Tm 2:6
[292] Cf. Mk 7:33-34
[293] Cf. Mk 8:23

birth.[294] Christ also washed the feet of his disciples;[295] he prostrated himself at his prayer in the garden;[296] he groaned and lifted up his eyes when he raised Lazarus from the dead.[297] All which were ceremonies.

668. **Since the Church-office and the ceremonies of the Mass have been instituted by the Church to stir up devotion in us to the sacred mysteries represented by them, I would gladly know the meaning of them, particularly of those of the Mass; that thus instructed I may be able to accompany the priest through every part of the Mass, so as to accommodate my devotion to what he is then about, which (as I have been often told) is the best and most beneficial way of hearing Mass.**

That has been already so well done by three eminent pens, viz: D. Challoner in his *Catholick Christian Instructed*, Ch. 7, and Ch. 22;[298] D. Richardson in his *Manner of Hearing Mass*; and by the author of the *Doway Catechism*, Ch. 10-11[299] that it seems needless for me to undertake the same task; but lest you should not have the said authors at hand; I shall endeavor to extract out of them a brief explanation of the substance, ceremonies, and principal parts of the Mass, of the Church-office, and of the chief solemnities and feasts of the Catholic Church.

---

[294] Cf. Jn 9:6

[295] Cf. Jn 13:5

[296] Cf. Lk 22:41

[297] Cf. Jn 11:38, 41

[298] Editor's note: The catechism here mentioned by the author is included in Volume III of the Tradivox series.

[299] Editor's note: The catechism here mentioned by the author is included in Volume I of the Tradivox series.

Chapter 6

*The Substance and Ceremonies of the Mass, the Church-
Office, and the Principal Feasts and Solemnities of the Church,
Expounded; As Also the Ceremonies of Holy Week*

669. **What is the Mass?**

It is the only Christian sacrifice according to the new law, wherein the
same body and blood of Christ, which he once offered upon the cross in
a bloody manner, is here offered daily to God in an unbloody manner
under the outward signs of bread and wine, by Jesus Christ the victim and
the principal offerer, and by the ministry of priests lawfully consecrated
and empowered by Christ, in whose name and Person they officiate as his
vicegerents; and this oblation is accompanied with a real destruction of the
bread and wine; they being by virtue of the consecration really changed
into the body and blood of Christ, to acknowledge thereby the sovereign
power of God, with a real exhibiting of Christ our victim, who really died
upon the cross, and here only dies mystically, inasmuch as his death is
represented by consecrating separately the bread and wine, to denote the
shedding of Christ's blood from his body upon the cross.

670. **But does not St. Paul say that Christ does not offer himself often;[300] and
that Christ "by one offering hath perfected for ever them that are sanctified"?[301] What room then can there be for the daily Sacrifice of the Mass?**

It is true that we were perfected forever by the one offering of Christ upon
the cross, because we were all redeemed by it, and because all other means
of our sanctification have their force and efficacy from it; so that there is
no need of Christ's offering himself a second time in a bloody manner,
which was to be but once. Yet as that one offering is no ways injured by the

---

[300] Cf. Heb 9:25
[301] Heb 10:14

supplications which Christ as man makes for us to his Father in heaven, where: "He ever liveth to make intercession for us",[302] so neither is it any ways injured by daily representing the same offering in the Sacrifice of the Mass, as a perpetual memorial of the sacrifice of the cross; for though the price of our redemption was to be paid but once, yet the fruit of it was to be daily applied to us by the sacraments and Sacrifice of the Altar.

671. **How many parts hath the Mass?**

Five principal ones commonly called: preparation, oblation, consecration, Communion, and post-communion or thanksgiving. The preparation begins at the introit, and ends with the gospel or Creed, when it is said. The oblation begins at the first offertory, and ends with the secret prayers said before the preface, where the consecration begins, and ends with the prayer: *Nobis quoque peccatoribus.* The Communion begins at *per ipsum*, and ends when the priest communicates. And the whole Mass is terminated by post-communion or thanksgiving.

672. **Why is the Mass celebrated in Latin, rather than in the vulgar language?**

First, because Latin is the Church's ancient language used in all her liturgies even from the apostles' days, throughout all the western parts of the world. Secondly, for a greater uniformity in the public liturgy, that so a Christian in whatsoever country he happens to be, may still find the liturgy performed in the same language to which he is accustomed at home. Thirdly, to avoid changing her liturgy, according to the changes to which all vulgar languages are daily exposed, as we see by experience; for the English tongue as it was spoken a hundred years ago, is now scarce understood by an English man.

[302] Heb 7:25

673. But is it not a great prejudice to the faithful, that the Mass, which seems to be a common prayer for them, should be said in a language that the generality of them do not understand? Nay, St. Paul seems to condemn the use of unknown tongues in prayers, where he saith: "If I pray in a tongue, my spirit prayeth, but my mind is without fruit."[303] And, "If thou dost bless in the spirit, how shall he that supplieth the place of one without learning say Amen to thy blessing, because he knows not what thou sayest?"[304] How then can the clerk who understands not Latin, answer in the name of the people equally ignorant "Amen" to the prayers said in Latin by the priest, when he officiates?

Though the Mass be a common sacrifice that is offered for all, and in some manner by all who assist at it, yet as the faithful are not obliged to recite the prayers used by the priest at Mass for a devout and profitable assistance thereat; and to be able to say "Amen" to what the priest says, it is enough they be well instructed in the nature of the Mass, either by reading prayer books, wherein the mysteries contained in the Mass are interpreted, or by their pastors explaining to them what is contained in the Mass; as all pastors are commanded to do frequently, and especially on Sundays and holy days.[305]

Neither does St. Paul absolutely forbid the use of prayers in an unknown tongue, for "he that speaketh a tongue, speaks not to men, but to God: for no man understandeth him. But in Spirit he speaks mysteries."[306] Because in his spirit he is piously and devoutly affected; but his prayers are without fruit, profit, edification, or instruction to the ignorant, who have not had sufficient instructions concerning such prayers. Such were the infidels and new converted Christians who came to the Christian meetings of the Corinthians to be instructed by them, and who were no ways edified or instructed by the exhortations made to them in an unknown tongue by the Corinthians boasting of the gift of tongues; which abuse St. Paul

---

[303] 1 Cor 14:14

[304] 1 Cor 14:16

[305] Cf. Council of Trent, Session 22, "Doctrine on the Sacrifice of the Mass," Ch. 8; Session 24, "Decree on Reformation," Ch. 7

[306] 1 Cor 14:2

reprehends in the Corinthians, and lays them down rules, which they are to observe in their meetings: "One hath a psalm,"[307] the Spirit inspiring him with some spiritual canticle, whereby to praise God; "another hath doctrine,"[308] to instruct all there present; another the gift of tongues, which he will not have him to make use of, unless there be one to interpret, that "all things may be done"[309] in a most profitable manner, to the edification of the ignorant. But two to three at a meeting may speak tongues, if another interprets.[310] Which is exactly the practice of the Catholic Church, where all instructions, interpretations, (nay in some countries translations) of the Mass are made in the vulgar language; though it be the practice and discipline of all Christian churches both in the East and West, (the protestant only excepted) to stick to the words and languages of their ancient liturgies; the Grecians to the ancient Greek, which now the ignorant among them do not understand; as the Jews did to the ancient Hebrew, which the common people did not understand after their return from the Babylonian captivity. The like is to be said of the ancient Syriac, Arabic, Coptic, as Monsieur Simon observes in his critics.

To the reasons already offered in favor of this practice, we may add the constant changes to which all vulgar languages are liable and subject; whence arises a danger of changes as to the doctrine and belief of the faithful; especially when by another false principle of protestants, every private man has a right to expound the hard and obscure places of the holy scriptures, which make up the chief and greatest part of all public liturgies in all Christian churches. I might ask an English protestant whether the ignorant people among them, or the "idiots" (as St. Paul calls them[311]) can say "Amen" to the public protestant liturgy performed in French or Dutch, which they do not understand; or whether they can say, that all French and German protestants are mad at their meetings, because their liturgies are performed in languages not known by the idiots among English

---

[307] 1 Cor 14:26
[308] Ibid.
[309] Ibid.
[310] Cf. 1 Cor 14:27
[311] Cf. 1 Cor 14:16, 23, 24

protestants. If they answer in the negative, English protestants cannot join in public prayers with their foreign brethren, nor have their liturgy performed out of their own country. If they answer in the affirmative, why may not an ignorant Catholic accustomed to hear Mass in Latin at home, and well instructed in the mysteries of it, answer "Amen" to the prayers said by the priest in Latin, though he be ignorant of that tongue?

674. What is the meaning of the priest's vestments when he officiates?

The priest in saying Mass represents the Person of Christ the principal offerer, and the Mass represents Christ's passion; wherefore the priest puts on those vestments, to represent those with which Christ was ignominiously clothed at the time of his passion. Thus, the amice or linen veil represents the rag, wherewith the Jews muffled our Savior's face, when at every blow they bid him prophesy who it was that struck him.[312] The alb represents the white garment, which Herod put on Christ, to intimate that he was a fool. The girdle represents the cord that bound Christ in the garden. The maniple represents the cord that bound him at the pillar; and the stole, that by which he was led to be crucified. The chasuble or outward garment represents the outward garment with which Christ was clothed as a mock king in the house of Pilate. The priest's tonsure or crown represents the crown of thorns, which our Savior wore.

The altar signifies the cross upon which Christ offered himself. The chalice represents the sepulchre of Christ. The patin signifies the stone, which was rolled to the door of the sepulchre. The corporal, altar-cloths, and pall represent the linen in which the dead body of Christ was shrouded. The lighted candles represent Christ's shining divinity and the light of faith, which he brought into the world. The crucifix upon the altar is a sign of the Mass being said in remembrance of Christ's passion and death. The incense used in Solemn or High Masses is an emblem of prayer ascending to God from a heart inflamed with his love; as the smoke of the incense ascends on high from the fire of the censer, according to that: "Let my prayer

---

[312] Cf. Lk 22:64

(O Lord) be directed like incense in thy sight."[313] Lastly, the use of singing and of organs is to help to raise the heart to heaven, and to celebrate with greater solemnity the divine praises, according to that: "Sing unto the Lord a new song."[314] "Praise him with string instruments and organs."[315]

675. **Why is this sacrifice called the Mass?**

Some think this word is derived from the Hebrew word *missach*, which signifies a voluntary offering. Others are of opinion, that it is derived from the word *missa* or *missio*, that is, from the dismission of the catechumens and others, who were not permitted anciently to be present at this sacrifice; but be this as it will, the name is of very ancient use in the Church, as appears from St. Ambrose, Bk. 2, *Epistle 14 ad Sororem*; St. Leo, *Epistle 81 ad Dioscorum*; and St. Gregory, *Homily 6 in Evangelia*.

676. **Pray explain the ceremonies of the Mass and the order of them.**

First, the priest, before he begins, makes a low reverence, to signify the prostrating of Christ in the garden. Secondly, he bows at the *confiteor*, to move the people to humiliation, and to signify the cleanness of heart wherewith we should approach this sacrifice. Thirdly, coming to the altar he kisseth it in the middle, to signify the kiss of peace and unity which Christ gave to the Jews and gentiles. Fourthly, he reads the introit, or entrance of the Mass, which is generally taken out of the old testament, and twice repeated, to signify the frequent desires of the ancient fathers, longing for the coming of Christ. Fifthly, he says alternately with the clerk the *Kyrie eleison* or "Lord have mercy on us," which is repeated thrice in honor of God the Father, the *Christe eleison*, or "Christ have mercy on us" is repeated thrice in honor of God the Son, and *Kyrie eleison*, thrice again in honor of the Holy Ghost, to signify our great necessity and ardent desire to find mercy.

Sixthly, the priest recites the *Gloria in excelsis* or "Glory be to God on high," to signify that the mercy which we beg was brought us by the birth of Christ; but as this is a hymn of joy, sung by the angels at the birth of

313 Ps 140:2
314 Ps 149:1
315 Ps 150:4

Christ, it is omitted in Masses for the dead, and in the penitential times of Advent and Lent. After the *Gloria*, the priest turning about to the people says: *Dominus vobiscum*, or "The Lord be with you," to beg God's presence and assistance to the people in the performance of that work, to which the clerk answers in the name of the people, *Et cum spiritu tuo*, "And with thy spirit"; to signify that the people with one consent beg the like for him. Then the priest says: *Oremus* or "Let us pray," by which he invites the people to join with him both in his prayers and intention. Afterwards he reads the prayers or collects of the day, so called, because they collect and gather together the supplications of the multitude, which prayers are concluded with "Through our Lord Jesus Christ," to signify that we beg of God the Father no mercy, grace, or blessing, but through Jesus Christ.

Seventhly, after the collects, the priest reads the epistle, which is commonly out of the prophets or apostles, to signify their preaching; it is read before the gospel, to intimate that as the old law was not able to bring anything to perfection, it was necessary that the new should succeed it. The epistle is followed by the gradual or tract, which signifies the penance preached by the Baptist; to the tract is joined an *alleluia*, or a rejoicing word, which is omitted in the penitential times between Septuagesima and Easter, and often repeated in Easter-time to signify the joyful solemnity of Christ's resurrection. After the gradual, the book is removed to the other side of the altar, which removal represents the passing from the old law to the gospel; the priest before he reads the gospel, bows and prays to God to make him worthy to declare his gospel; then he says, *Dominus vobiscum*, to prepare the people, and beg of God to make them worthy hearers of his word. Afterwards the priest says: "The sequel of the holy gospel," to move the attention of the people, and signify to them what part of the gospel he then reads; the clerk answers in the name of the multitude, "Glory be to thee O Lord," to signify that the glory of the gospel is owing to the mercy of God, who made us partakers of it.

Eighthly, at the beginning of the gospel, the priest signs the book with the sign of the cross, to signify that the doctrine there delivered belongs to the cross and passion of Christ; after this both priest and people sign themselves with the cross in three places. First, upon their foreheads, to signify that they will not be ashamed of Christ's doctrine. Secondly, upon their mouths, to signify that they will confess it with their mouths. Thirdly, upon their breasts, to signify that they believe it and will keep it in their hearts. At the reading of the gospel, the people rise up, to signify their readiness to go and do whatsoever they shall be commanded by Christ in his gospel. At the end of the gospel, the clerk answers, "Praise be to thee O Christ," to give praise to Christ for his heavenly doctrine. The priest kisses the book in reverence to those sacred mysteries which he has read, and both priest and people bless themselves, that the devil may not steal the seed of God's word out of their hearts.

After the gospel on all Sundays and other solemnities, the priest says the Nicene Creed, which is a public profession of our faith, and both priest and people kneel down at these words, "And he was made man," in reverence to the mystery of the incarnation. After the Creed, the priest puts wine into the chalice and mixes it with a little water, to signify the blood and water flowing from the side of Christ. (But observe that this ceremony is performed by the Dominicans before they begin the Mass, that thus there may be more time for the water to be converted into wine before the consecration.) Then the priest makes the first offertory, which signifies the freedom wherewith Christ offered himself on the cross. After this he washes the tips of his fingers, to signify the purity of soul wherewith these mysteries are to be celebrated.

Ninthly, after saying the *secreta* or prayers of the day, the priest begins the preface in a loud voice, to signify Christ's triumphant entry into Jerusalem, after he lay hid a little time, as also to move the people to lift up their hearts to the approaching heavenly things, and say with the Hebrew children: "Blessed is he that cometh in the name of the Lord."[316] At which words, the priest signs himself with the sign of the cross, to signify that the entry of Christ into Jerusalem was not to a worldly kingdom, but to a death upon the cross. After the preface follows the Canon, or more sacred part of the Mass, which is read in a low voice, to signify the sadness and silence of Christ in his passion, and his hiding that time his glory and divinity. The

[316] Mt 21:9

Canon begins by invoking the Father of mercies, through Jesus Christ to accept this sacrifice for the peace, unity, and preservation of the Catholic Church, for the pope, bishop, for the king, and for all the professors of the Catholic faith throughout the whole world. Then follows the *memento*, or commemoration of the living, for whom in particular the priest intends to offer up that sacrifice, and of all there present, or who have been particularly recommended to his prayers. Then the priest makes a commemoration of the saints, to beg their prayers, and to signify our communion with them. After this, according to the *Roman Missal*, the priest spreads his hands over the offering, to signify that Christ bore all our iniquities; as also in imitation of the ceremony prescribed that priests or persons who offered sacrifice, should lay their hands upon the victim, and load it with their sins before it was immolated.[317] Before the consecration, he blesses the bread and wine five times with the sign of the cross, to signify the five days that passed between Christ's entry into Jerusalem, and his passion.

Then the priest proceeds to the consecration, first of the bread into the body of Christ, and then of the wine into his blood, which consecration is made by the words of Christ pronounced by the priest in his name, and as bearing his Person, and this is the chief action of the Mass, in which the very essence of the sacrifice consists; because by the separate consecration of the bread and wine, the body and blood of Christ are really presented to God, and mystically immolated.

Tenthly, after the consecration, the priest kneels and adores the host and chalice, to give sovereign honor to Christ veiled under these sacramental signs; then that the people may do the same, he elevates each, as also to signify Christ's elevation upon the cross for our sins. After the elevation, the priest signs the offerings five times with the sign of the cross, to signify the five wounds of Christ, which he presents to his eternal Father for us. After this follows the remembrance for the dead, then the priest raising his voice says: *Nobis quoque peccatoribus*, at which words he strikes his breast in token of repentance like the humble publican.[318] Then he signs the

---

[317] Cf. Lv 1:3-4
[318] Cf. Lk 18:13

offerings thrice with the sign of the cross, to signify that this sacrifice is available: for those in heaven, as an increase of their glory; for those in purgatory, to free them from their pains; and for those upon earth, to obtain an increase of grace, or a remission of their sins. After this, the priest uncovers the chalice, to signify that at the death of Christ, the veil of the Temple was rent asunder. Then he signs the chalice three times with the host. First, by making three crosses over the chalice, to signify the three hours during which Christ hung dead upon the cross. Secondly, by making two more, one at the brim, and another at the foot of the chalice, to signify the blood and water flowing from the side of Christ.

After this follows the *Pater Noster*, to signify by the seven petitions therein contained, the seven mystical words, which Christ spoke upon the cross with a loud voice. First: "Father forgive them, for they know not what they do."[319] Second: "Today thou shalt be with me in paradise."[320] Third: "Behold thy mother."[321] "Woman, behold thy son."[322] Fourth: "My God, my God, why hast thou forsaken me?"[323] Fifth: "I thirst."[324] Sixth: "Into thy hands I commend my spirit."[325] Seventh: "It is consummated."[326]

Before the *Pater Noster*, the priest lays down the host upon the corporal, to signify the taking down of Christ's body from the cross and his burial. The host is divided into three parts, to signify that Christ's body was divided upon the cross into three principal parts, viz: his hands, side, and feet. A particle of the host is put into the chalice by the priest saying, *Pax*, etc. or "The peace of our Lord be always with you," to signify the reuniting of the body, blood, and soul of Christ at his resurrection; and also the "Peace be unto you,"[327] which Christ spoke to his disciples when he first came to them after his resurrection. And the chalice is signed three times

---

[319] Lk 23:34
[320] Lk 23:43
[321] Jn 19:27
[322] Jn 19:26
[323] Mt 27:46
[324] Jn 19:28
[325] Lk 23:46
[326] Jn 19:30
[327] Jn 20:19

at the saying of these words, to signify the triple peace, which we have acquired by the cross, viz: external, internal, and eternal.

Eleventhly, the *Agnus Dei* or "Lamb of God" is said with a loud voice, to commemorate Christ's glorious ascension; and also to signify that he was slain like an innocent lamb to take away our sins. The *pax* or kiss of peace is given before the Communion, to signify that peace and mutual charity should be among the faithful who partake of this sacrifice. The Communion or consummation signifies the burial of Christ, and the consummation of his passion. The prayers called post-communion are collects of thanksgiving to God for having made us partakers of the Sacrifice of the Altar; after which the priest says: "Go, the Mass is done," to give the people leave to depart; and also to represent the angel dismissing the apostles, when they stood looking after Christ ascended into heaven.[328] Then the priest gives his blessing to all there present, to signify the blessing which Christ gave his apostles and disciples at his ascension into heaven. Finally, the Gospel of St. John signifies the apostles preaching the gospel to all nations, and at these words: *Verbum caro factum est*, "The Word was made flesh," both priest and people kneel in reverence to the mystery of Christ's incarnation.

677. **How many parts hath the divine office?**

Seven principal ones commonly called seven canonical hours, viz: *matins*, or the midnight office, to which are annexed *lauds* or the morning praises of God; *prime, tierce, sext, none, vespers*, and *compline*; according to that: "Seven times in the day I gave praise to thee."[329]

678. **Why is the office thus divided into seven hours?**

That so a memorial of Christ's passion, according to the different stations of it, should be daily performed by the clergy and religious of both sexes; for seven hours were spent in Christ's passion: three hours he hung dead, and the seventh was spent in taking down his body.

---

[328] Cf. Acts 1:11
[329] Ps 118:164

679. How does each of these hours represent some station of Christ's passion?

Thus: the *matins* and *lauds* represent his agony and binding in the garden; *prime*, his scoffs and false accusations; *tierce*, his being clothed with purple and crowned with thorns; *sext*, his condemnation and nailing to the cross; *none*, his yielding up the Ghost and the opening his side; *vespers*, his being taken down from the cross; and *compline*, his burial; according to the following verses:

> Hac sunt Septe'nis propter qua psallimus horis.
> Matutina ligant Christum, qui crimina solvit.
> Prima replet Sputis, Causam dat Tertia Mortis.
> Sexta Cruci nectit, Latus ejus Nona bipartit.
> Vespera deponit, Tumulo Completa reponit.

The nocturns of matins are so called, because they were commonly said in the night time. The gradual psalms are so called from a custom which the Jews had of singing these psalms, as they ascended fifteen steps or degrees towards Solomon's Temple, singing one psalm on every step.

680. What is the meaning of the Holy Week and of the ceremonies thereof?

The week before Easter is called the Holy Week, because it is a week of more than ordinary devotion in honor of Christ's passion. It begins with Palm Sunday so called from the palm branches which the people strewed before Christ at his entering into Jerusalem, making acclamations to him, as to their King and *Messias*.[330]

The Thursday in this week is called Maundy Thursday from the word *mandatum* or command, which Christ gave to his disciples to love one another.[331] Christ instituted the Blessed Sacrament upon this day, and began his passion by his bitter agony and sweat. From the *Gloria in excelsis* of the Mass of this day till Easter Eve, our bells are silent, because we are mourning for the passion of Christ; our altars are uncovered, because Christ our true altar hung naked upon the cross. On this day prelates wash the feet of their subjects, and princes, those of certain poor people, after the example of Christ.[332] On this day also, in order to meditate on the different stages of

---

[330] Cf. Mt 21:8-9
[331] Cf. Jn 13:34
[332] Cf. Jn 13

Christ's passion, the faithful visit the places where the Blessed Sacrament is reserved for the office of Good Friday, which places are commonly called sepulchres as representing by anticipation the burial of Christ.

The next day is Good Friday or the day on which Christ died for us upon the cross. On this day there is no consecration, because it is not proper to celebrate the mystical death of Christ in the Sacrifice of the Mass upon the day that the Church celebrates Christ's real death; wherefore if a holy day should fall upon this day, the faithful are not obliged to hear Mass, nor to assist at the ceremony performed in the Church, which is not properly a Mass, but only a consummation of the sacrifice offered the day before. On this day the faithful kneel to the cross of Christ and kiss it, to express by this exterior reverence their veneration for him who upon this day died for them on the cross.

Then comes Holy Saturday, on which the Church resumes in the Mass her *alleluia* of joy, which she has intermitted during the penitential time of Septuagesima and Lent. On this day also the baptismal fonts are blessed, and the paschal candle, as an emblem of Christ's light and glory; which burns at the High Mass during the whole time that Christ our light remained upon earth after his resurrection, that is, from Easter till Ascension.

During the *Tenebra Matins* of Thursday, Friday, and Saturday in Holy Week, there are fifteen lights set on a triangular figure. The three upper lights signify Jesus, Mary, and Joseph; the twelve lower, the twelve apostles. The triangular figure signifies that all light of grace and glory is from the Blessed Trinity. The lights are put out one by one after every psalm, (hence the *matins* are called *tenebra* or "of darkness") to signify the darkness which covered all the earth, whilst Christ hung upon the cross; and at the end of *matins* a noise is made, to represent the earthquake, the rending of the veil of the Temple, and the splitting of the rocks that happened at the time of Christ's death.

681. **What is the meaning of the festivals which the Catholic Church commands to be observed?**

Observe that there are immoveable and moveable feasts. The first are those which are observed on the same day of the month, but not always upon the same day of the week, but in different years, on different days of the week. The second are those that are observed on the same day of the week, but not always upon the same day of the month, but in different years, on different days, and sometimes on different months. The foundation and rule for all moveable feasts, is Easter, which is held on the Sunday following the first full moon after the 21ˢᵗ of March, that is: the Sunday following the first full moon after the vernal equinox. The most common moveable feast is Sunday, which is so called from the old Roman denomination of *Dies solis*, the day of the sun, to which it was sacred. It is kept holy by Christians in memory of Christ's resurrection, and of the descent of the Holy Ghost upon the apostles on a Sunday.

Now to begin with the year, observe that if there be any Sunday between New Year's day called also the Circumcision of Our Lord, and Twelfth-day called also Epiphany from the appearance of the star to the wise men,[333] such a Sunday has no name in particular assigned to it; but the Sundays following the Epiphany are called the First, Second, Third, etc. Sundays after Epiphany, which are sometimes more, and sometimes fewer, as Easter falls high or low, for they must give place to Septuagesima, which is always the tenth Sunday inclusively before Easter, and is called Septuagesima, as well as the two following Sundays are called Sexagesima and Quinquagesima, because they are the seventh, sixth, and fifth Sundays exclusively before Passion Sunday.

After Quinquagesima comes Lent, called also Quadragesima, from its being a fast of forty days in imitation of Christ's fasting in the desert forty days and forty nights.[334] The first day of Lent is called Ash Wednesday from the ceremony of blessing ashes on this day, and signing the people therewith on their foreheads, to prepare them for the fast of Lent by a due consideration of what they are made, and into what they must return. The Sundays following Ash Wednesday are called the First, Second, Third, and Fourth (this last is also called Mid-Lent Sunday) Sundays of Lent. The fifth is called Passion Sunday from the passion of Christ drawing nigh. On this day the crosses and images are covered, to signify that our sins, (for which we then do penance) interpose between God and us; as also to signify that the Church begins to mourn for the passion of Christ. The next is Palm Sunday and Holy Week, which I have already explained.

[333] Cf. Mt 2:2
[334] Cf. Mt 4:2

Then comes Easter celebrated in memory of our Savior's resurrection. After this follows a Quinquagesimal or space of fifty days between Easter and Whitsuntide, all which contain six Sundays; the first is called Low Sunday or *Dominica in Albis*, because the catechumens that were baptized at Easter, used to go in white garments all the week, which this day at night they left off. The four next Sundays are called Second, Third, Fourth, and Fifth after Easter; this last is also called Rogation Sunday, and the week Rogation week, because Christians then made their processions, said the litany, made their prayers and requests to God for the temperateness of the season of the year, and the fruitfulness of the earth; the Thursday in this week is called Ascension day, and kept in memory of Christ's ascension into heaven. The Sunday following is called the Sunday within the Octave of the Ascension.

Then succeeds the grand feast called Pentecost or Whitsuntide, because the catechumens used to appear in white clothes and be admitted on the eve of this feast to the sacrament of baptism; which, as it was observed by the Jews in memory of the promulgation of the law at Mount Sinai just fifty days after their Passover, so the Christians observe it the seventh Sunday after Easter, in commemoration of the Holy Ghost's being then sent down upon the apostles in the shape of tongues of fire, who were thereby endowed with the gift of tongues, prophecy, etc.[335] The first Sunday after Pentecost is called Trinity Sunday, because on that day we particularly commemorate the great mystery of three Persons in one God, and glorify the Blessed Trinity for the whole work of our redemption, which we have celebrated in the foregoing festivals. The Thursday in this week is called Corpus Christi day, because it was instituted by Urban IV about the year 1262 and has been ever since observed by the Church, to give God thanks for his goodness and mercy in having instituted the Blessed Sacrament; to this end during the octave, the Blessed Sacrament is exposed to be adored by the faithful, and solemn processions are made in honor of it.

The Sunday following is called the Second after Pentecost, and from thence the Sundays are reckoned in order, as Third, Fourth, etc. after Pentecost, to the First Sunday in Advent, which is the Sunday next to St. Andrew's day,

---

[335] Cf. Acts 2

either before or after, and is called Advent, because it is a time of preparation for the grand festival of Christmas kept in memory of Christ's nativity, and contains the four Sundays next before Christmas, which are the First, Second, etc. Sundays in Advent. The octave day of Christmas is called New Year's day, kept in memory of the circumcision of our Lord, which was performed on the eighth day from his nativity, according to the prescript of the old law,[336] as the Purification or Candlemas day is kept in memory of the presentation of Christ and of the purification of the Blessed Virgin in the Temple, the fortieth day after her happy childbirth, according to the law of Moses.[337] It is called Candlemas from the ceremony of blessing candles upon this day and making processions with them lighted, as an emblem of Christ, who at his presentation was proclaimed by Simeon to be the light of the gentiles.[338] The meaning of the other immoveable feasts is pretty obvious; if you desire to know more of them in particular, see Doctor Challoner's inimitable *Catholick Christian Instructed*, Ch. 23; and the *Doway Catechism*, Ch. 11.[339]

---

[336] Cf. Gn 17:12

[337] Cf. Lv 12:6

[338] Cf. Lk 2:32

[339] Editor's note: The catechisms here mentioned by the author are included in Volumes III and I of the Tradivox series, respectively.

Appendix

Practical Instructions for Confession, Deduced from the Method Laid Down by the Council of Trent for Disposing Ourselves for Justification[340]

He that would confess with due dispositions, would do well to begin his preparation by seriously considering the state which he is in; that he is guilty of crimes and offences against God, that he stands convicted of them before an offended God, whose eyes nothing can escape, whose power nothing can resist.

With these thoughts sinking deep into his heart, let him retire from the sight of men, and cast himself at the feet of his justly offended Lord, with few words and much interior confusion (in imitation of the royal prophet, who says: *Effundo in conspectu ejus orationem meam; et tribulationem meam ante ipsum pronuntio.*[341]) let him pour forth his soul before God in prayer, lay open in his presence his tribulation and affliction, represent to him that he is his creature, raised out of nothing by his omnipotent hand, and now sunk again into nothing by sin, as the same royal prophet says: *Et substantia mea tamquam nihilum ante te*: "My substance, (my being) is as nothing before thee."[342] With this humiliation and annihilation of himself it is that a sinner begins well his approach to God, and when he entirely abases himself, he may hope that God will quicken him, as David prays: *Humiliatus sum usquequaque...vivifica me secundum verbum tuum.*[343] And acknowledging himself nothing, may beg of God to create him anew, pure and clean in spirit, according to the words of the same prophet: *Cor mundum crea in me,*

---

[340] Cf. Council of Trent, Session 6, Ch. 6
[341] Ps 141:3
[342] Ps 38:6
[343] Ps 118:107

Deus:[344] "Create a new and clean heart in me, O Lord." Now, creation we know is out of nothing.

These and the like considerations, though expressed in few words, are not always for that reason less efficacious and hearty, as we scarce find any form of repentance in the gospel very long. It is said of Magdalen and St. Peter that they wept, but not that they spoke. The publican in the Temple only said: "O God be merciful to me a sinner."[345] He that owed a thousand talents fell prostrate on the ground and only said: Lord, have patience with me, and I will pay thee the whole debt.[346] Animated with these examples, howsoever great his sins may be, let the sinner, with a humble and contrite heart, though with few words, consider the great mercy of our Lord, who, though he justly might annihilate him or cast him into hell, still not only bears with him, but also offers him pardon; let him consider God as the fountain of mercy, of justification, of grace; let him cleave to him as such, let him take confusion on himself, abhor the sins, which have offended so great, so good a Lord; and with fear of his greatness and love of his goodness, let him detest and abominate the offence, which he has offered to his Lord.

Next let him begin to call to mind his sins, taking proper time for it, either continued or by intervals, as his necessary business will permit. For a long and perplexed confession, more time must be spent in the examination of conscience; for example, an hour a day for eight or ten days, if it be for a confession of a whole year, or less time, if the confession be of less time. Quickness of memory may shorten this task, as it may be also shorter in those whose consciences are not burthened with complicated guilt.

To make the examination of conscience more easy, let him consider his prevailing inclinations, the company he has kept, his conversation in it, his daily employ; and examine himself on the seven capital sins, and the ten commandments, to which are reduced most of what may burthen our consciences.

[344] Ps 50:12
[345] Lk 18:13
[346] Cf. Mt 18:26

To make this more easy, it is to be noted, that we sin against the first commandment by sinning against any of these four virtues: faith, hope, charity, and religion; as was observed in Chapter 1 and Chapter 4. The second commandment is transgressed by swearing falsely, by swearing without necessity, or by swearing against justice, by cursing ourselves or others; as it is explained in Chapter 4. We sin against the third commandment by not hearing Mass with attention and devotion; by working on Sundays or holidays of obligation; by omitting our yearly confession, or Easter Communion, or by omitting them at the supposed point of death; by not fasting on days commanded by the Church; by not paying tithes to our pastors; as is said in Chapter 2 and Chapter 4.

The fourth commandment is broken by children that do not honor their parents, or who disobey them; by subjects that do not obey their lawful superiors, priests or spiritual masters and directors; also fathers, princes, priests, and superiors sin against this precept, if they do not take care of their children and subjects; as explained in Chapter 4. The following sins are against the fifth commandment: anger, envy, hatred, or revenge against our neighbor, of which the greatest is murder; as explained in Chapters 3 and 4. The sixth commandment is transgressed by all immodest actions, by consent to them, and by delight in the thoughts of them, if out of matrimony; as explained in Chapter 4. We sin against the seventh commandment by taking away or desiring to take away our neighbor's goods, by doing damage to them, and also in not restoring what we have got unlawfully; for example, by usury, simony, or any other unlawful contract; as explained in Chapters 3 and 4. Lastly, we sin against the eighth by unjustly depriving our neighbor of his good name or his honor, by telling of him what is false or uncertain, by discovering any of his real though secret faults; as also by not restoring him his good name unjustly taken away, by not making up the losses or detriment which followed from our calumny or detractions. It is also a sin against this commandment to judge rashly of our neighbor, to reveal his secrets; as explained in Chapters 3 and 4. The ninth and tenth commandments are reduced to the sixth and seventh.

After this, the penitent must endeavor to reduce to a certain number his sins against each commandment, to reflect on the species of sin, the circumstances which change the species or only aggravate the sin; for which end, what was said (in Chapter 2) of the circumstances, which change the species or only aggravate, and of the way of determining the number of sins within the same species, may be of great service.

To make easier the knowledge of those circumstances, which change the species or kind of sin, and those, which only aggravate it; besides what has been said in Chapter 2, it is to be observed, that there are seven principal circumstances of sin to which the rest may be reduced, to wit: the circumstance of the person, of the object, of the place where we sin, of the means made use of to bring about our sinful designs, of the end or motive of sin, the manner or way in which we sin, and the time when we sin. These circumstances sometimes change the species, sometimes only aggravate; as I shall explain by the following examples.

The circumstance of the person changes the species of a sin of incontinence, if the person who commits it be married, or has made a vow of chastity. The circumstance of the person only aggravates the sin of perjury, if the person who commits it be particularly bound to give good example; for instance, if he be a priest, superior of a community, or a father of children, who are bound particularly to give good example to their subjects and children, and still commit such a sin in their presence.

In sins of incontinence, the circumstance of the object changes the species, as if the object of a criminal desire should be a married person, should be under the bond of a vow of chastity, should be a relation within those degrees of kindred by blood or marriage, in which matrimony is prohibited; so also in theft, the circumstance of the object or thing stolen changes the species, if it be itself sacred; that is: consecrated to divine worship, as a chalice for example. But the circumstance of the object sometimes aggravates only a sin of theft, as if we suppose it a mortal sin to steal a shilling, the circumstance of the greatness of the sum in a theft of five pounds considerably aggravates the sin, though it does not change the species.

The circumstance of place changes the species in theft, as if a person should steal in the church; but this circumstance aggravates only the sin of detraction, or unnecessary swearing in the church. The circumstance of means used to bring about criminal intentions, changes the species in a case wherein a man should employ three or four persons to carry on a criminal intrigue, to sin against chastity; but it aggravates only in him that uses the artifices of secret love-letters, of treats, or persuasions to bring about the same design.

The circumstance of the end or motive changes the species, if a person should steal to enable himself to carry on an intrigue against chastity, or if he should murder that he might afterwards rob; but it aggravates only if he sins through an ill-grounded confidence in the mercy of God. The circumstance of the manner changes the species of theft, when it is committed with violence done to the person robbed; but it only aggravates when only the desire of sinning is more vehement, or the action of longer duration, though not retracted, nor morally discontinued, as explained in Chapter 2.

The circumstance of time sometimes changes the species. Thus, if a person omits hearing Mass enjoined for a penance to be heard on a Sunday, or omits complying with any other good work enjoined for a penance, at a time when he was otherwise bound to do it under pain of mortal sin, he commits two distinct sins. The circumstance of time aggravates only in him who should sin on a Good Friday, or on another day on which he had received some signal favor from God.

If by these means the penitent can reduce his sins to a certain number, he must express it in confession; if not, let him recollect how long he continued in a custom of such a sin, and how often he might sin every day, every week, or every month of that time. If he cannot do even this, let him declare how long he might have been in his bad habit, and the frequency of his sins; as also if he was constantly in a readiness to commit those sins. After this let him again lay before God his heart with all its abominations and miseries, casting all at the feet of our Lord, begging that through the merits of his precious blood shed for so many sins, he would be pleased to show mercy to a soul for which he died.

Let him choose a confessor of knowledge and abilities according to the difficulties of conscience which he has to resolve, or sins he has to seek remedies against; one of patience to hear him without roughness or surprise, to ask him questions and clear up his doubts, to hear him at length, that may instruct him to prefer his soul and his eternal salvation (which is here the point in question) before life, before worldly ease and comfort, and before all temporal advantages and pleasures.

Kneeling before his confessor (if he be not disabled) let him again consider himself as a criminal convicted of capital crimes, of crimes punishable with eternal death; let him conceive, that in the person of the priest, God himself is sitting in his judgment seat to judge his cause, and that the sentence there pronounced passes in heaven itself for a legal determination of the cause. With these thoughts, full of submission and humility, let him bless himself saying: "In the name," etc. then say the general confession to these words: "Through my exceeding great fault." And if his confessor does not know him, let him declare before confession: what is his state; how long it is since he has confessed, if he be under an excommunication; if he be in an immediate occasion of sin, or in a habit of sin; for if he be so, by these means no time will be lost. Only his confessor will tell him what he must do to make himself worthy of absolution, of which he is at present incapable. Let him declare besides, if he has complied with his last penance, what time he has taken to examine his conscience, that his confessor may judge if it be sufficient.

Let him then declare his sins in the best order he can, beginning by the first commandment, and not proceed to the second till he has declared all that regards the first; and so of the rest. For this end, two things are specially to be noted. First, that he should not use many words nor round about ways of expressing himself, not relate his sins like a story, nor divert himself with explaining those causes and occasions of his falling into sin, which do not regard the knowledge of the sin itself; nor should he speak of himself with superfluous severity and exaggeration, but merely express the species, number, and necessary circumstances of his sins without farther enlargement. Secondly, that he should not discover any third person so as to discredit him, nor even name him, or any other way signify who he is. If his confessor asks anything regarding his conscience for the better information of the state of it, let him answer clearly and humbly. If his confessor reproves him, or speaks more harshly to him, let him not take it amiss; let him consider that it is Christ who reproves him, who says that he reproves and chastises those whom he loves. Let him reflect that hell is open for the chastisement of his faults, and how much worse it would be to be reproved and chastised there; though indeed confessors should not speak harshly, nor reprove their penitents, till they have finished their confession.

When he has confessed his sins, and can remember no more, let him finish the general confession: "Therefore I beseech," etc. Let him humbly ask pardon, wait for the sentence, bear patiently his confessor's reprehension without replying or excusing himself; for that is only a place to accuse himself; unless it be necessary to say something to explain his sins, if he has not yet been sufficiently understood. Let him receive the advice given him with a good will. Let him always understand that the penance enjoined is small in regard to his sins; let him not bargain with his confessor, nor endeavor to obtain an abatement of it; for we merit more by satisfactions enjoined in this sacrament, than by voluntary ones; and it is a sign of want of due submission of heart not to yield to the penalties inflicted by the judge. If anything be enjoined which he cannot comply with, let him modestly tell his confessor so, and desire him to change it.

After absolution, go immediately to give thanks to God for so great a benefit, as he has done you to permit you to receive the sacrament of penance, and to grant you pardon of your sins, which he has denied to innumerable souls, which are now in the eternal flames of hell. Offer him your heart now cleansed from sin, and worthy of the eyes of our Lord, newly washed with his blood, shining with his light, and robed in his grace. Beg of God with great earnestness not to permit you again to defile yourself, to make void the merits of Christ's blood, or to stain so bright a robe as that of his grace. Kiss the feet of our Lord, where sinners always find mercy. Return thanks to our Blessed Lady, that she has again received you for her son by the means of the Spirit of God the Son, who by her means has come to dwell in your heart. Recommend yourself to your angel guardian, and to the saints your patrons. In a word, as a man renewed in spirit, just escaped from imminent danger, ponder well the words of Christ to another whom he healed: "Behold thou art cured: sin no more, lest something worse befall thee."[347]

<hr />

[347] Jn 5:14

ABOUT THIS SERIES

Tradivox was first conceived as an international research endeavor to recover lost and otherwise little-known Catholic catechetical texts. As the research progressed over several years, the vision began to grow, along with the number of project contributors and a general desire to share these works with a broader audience.

Legally incorporated in 2019, Tradivox has begun the work of carefully remastering and republishing dozens of these catechisms which were once in common and official use in the Church around the world. That effort is embodied in this *Tradivox Catholic Catechism Index*, a multi-volume series restoring artifacts of traditional faith and praxis for a contemporary readership. More about this series and the work of Tradivox can be learned at www.Tradivox.com.

SOPHIA INSTITUTE

Sophia Institute is a nonprofit institution that seeks to nurture the spiritual, moral, and cultural life of souls and to spread the Gospel of Christ in conformity with the authentic teachings of the Roman Catholic Church.

Sophia Institute Press fulfills this mission by offering translations, reprints, and new publications that afford readers a rich source of the enduring wisdom of mankind.

Sophia Institute also operates the popular online resource Catholic Exchange.com. *Catholic Exchange* provides world news from a Catholic perspective as well as daily devotionals and articles that will help readers to grow in holiness and live a life consistent with the teachings of the Church.

In 2013, Sophia Institute launched Sophia Institute for Teachers to renew and rebuild Catholic culture through service to Catholic education. With the goal of nurturing the spiritual, moral, and cultural life of souls, and an abiding respect for the role and work of teachers, we strive to provide materials and programs that are at once enlightening to the mind and ennobling to the heart; faithful and complete, as well as useful and practical.

Sophia Institute gratefully recognizes the Solidarity Association for preserving and encouraging the growth of our apostolate over the course of many years. Without their generous and timely support, this book would not be in your hands.

www.SophiaInstitute.com
www.CatholicExchange.com
www.SophiaInstituteforTeachers.org

Sophia Institute Press® is a registered trademark of Sophia Institute. Sophia Institute is a tax-exempt institution as defined by the Internal Revenue Code, Section 501(c)(3). Tax ID 22-2548708.